CW00616370

13. 00
03

Teach Yourself®
PCs

Teach Yourself®
PCs

Barry Press and Marcia Press

IDG Books Worldwide, Inc.
An International Data Group Company

Foster City, CA • Chicago, IL • Indianapolis, IN • New York, NY

Teach Yourself® PCs

Published by
IDG Books Worldwide, Inc.
An International Data Group Company
919 E. Hillsdale Blvd., Suite 400
Foster City, CA 94404
www.idgbooks.com (IDG Books Worldwide Web site)

Library of Congress Catalog Card Number: 98-88723

ISBN: 0-7645-7510-4

Printed in the United States of America

10 9 8 7 6 5 4 3 2 1

1B/QR/RS/ZY/IN

Distributed in the United States by IDG Books Worldwide, Inc.

Distributed by Macmillan Canada for Canada; by Transworld Publishers Limited in the United Kingdom; by IDG Norge Books for Norway; by IDG Sweden Books for Sweden; by Woodslane Pty. Ltd. for Australia; by Woodslane (NZ) Ltd. for New Zealand; by Addison Wesley Longman Singapore Pte Ltd. for Singapore, Malaysia, Thailand, Indonesia, and Korea; by Norma Comunicaciones S.A. for Colombia; by Intersoft for South Africa; by International Thomson Publishing for Germany, Austria, and Switzerland; by Toppan Company Ltd. for Japan; by Distribuidora Cuspide for Argentina; by Livraria Cultura for Brazil; by Ediciencia S.A. for Ecuador; by Ediciones ZETA S.C.R. Ltda. for Peru; by WS Computer Publishing Corporation, Inc., for the Philippines; by Unalis Corporation for Taiwan; by Contemporanea de Ediciones for Venezuela; by Computer Book & Magazine Store for Puerto Rico; by Express Computer Distributors for the Caribbean and West Indies. Authorized Sales Agent: Anthony Rudkin Associates for the Middle East and North Africa.

For general information on IDG Books Worldwide's books in the U.S., please call our Consumer Customer Service department at 800-762-2974. For reseller information, including discounts and premium sales, please call our Reseller Customer Service department at 800-434-3422.

For information on where to purchase IDG Books Worldwide's books outside the U.S., please contact our International Sales department at 317-596-5530 or fax 317-596-5692.

For consumer information on foreign language translations, please contact our Customer Service department at 800-434-3422, fax 317-596-5692, or e-mail rights@idgbooks.com.

For information on licensing foreign or domestic rights, please phone +1-650-655-3109.

For sales inquiries and special prices for bulk quantities, please contact our Sales department at 650-655-3200 or write to the address above.

For information on using IDG Books Worldwide's books in the classroom or for ordering examination copies, please contact our Educational Sales department at 800-434-2086 or fax 317-596-5499.

For press review copies, author interviews, or other publicity information, please contact our Public Relations department at 650-655-3000 or fax 650-655-3299.

For authorization to photocopy items for corporate, personal, or educational use, please contact Copyright Clearance Center, 222 Rosewood Drive, Danvers, MA 01923, or fax 978-750-4470.

is a trademark under exclusive license to IDG Books Worldwide, Inc., from International Data Group, Inc.

ABOUT IDG BOOKS WORLDWIDE

Welcome to the world of IDG Books Worldwide.

IDG Books Worldwide, Inc., is a subsidiary of International Data Group, the world's largest publisher of computer-related information and the leading global provider of information services on information technology. IDG was founded more than 30 years ago by Patrick J. McGovern and now employs more than 9,000 people worldwide. IDG publishes more than 290 computer publications in over 75 countries. More than 90 million people read one or more IDG publications each month.

Launched in 1990, IDG Books Worldwide is today the #1 publisher of best-selling computer books in the United States. We are proud to have received eight awards from the Computer Press Association in recognition of editorial excellence and three from Computer Currents' First Annual Readers' Choice Awards. Our best-selling ...For Dummies® series has more than 50 million copies in print with translations in 31 languages. IDG Books Worldwide, through a joint venture with IDG's Hi-Tech Beijing, became the first U.S. publisher to publish a computer book in the People's Republic of China. In record time, IDG Books Worldwide has become the first choice for millions of readers around the world who want to learn how to better manage their businesses.

Our mission is simple: Every one of our books is designed to bring extra value and skill-building instructions to the reader. Our books are written by experts who understand and care about our readers. The knowledge base of our editorial staff comes from years of experience in publishing, education, and journalism — experience we use to produce books to carry us into the new millennium. In short, we care about books, so we attract the best people. We devote special attention to details such as audience, interior design, use of icons, and illustrations. And because we use an efficient process of authoring, editing, and desktop publishing our books electronically, we can spend more time ensuring superior content and less time on the technicalities of making books.

You can count on our commitment to deliver high-quality books at competitive prices on topics you want to read about. At IDG Books Worldwide, we continue in the IDG tradition of delivering quality for more than 30 years. You'll find no better book on a subject than one from IDG Books Worldwide.

John Kilcullen
Chairman and CEO
IDG Books Worldwide, Inc.

Steven Berkowitz
President and Publisher
IDG Books Worldwide, Inc.

WINNER

*Eighth Annual
Computer Press
Awards ≥1992*

WINNER

*Ninth Annual
Computer Press
Awards ≥1993*

WINNER

*Tenth Annual
Computer Press
Awards ≥1994*

WINNER

*Eleventh Annual
Computer Press
Awards ≥1995*

IDG is the world's leading IT media, research and exposition company. Founded, in 1964, IDG had 1997 revenues of $2.05 billion and has more than 9,000 employees worldwide. IDG offers the widest range of media options that reach IT buyers in 75 countries representing 95% of worldwide IT spending. IDG's diverse product and services portfolio spans six key areas including print publishing, online publishing, expositions and conferences, market research, education and training, and global marketing services. More than 90 million people read one or more of IDG's 290 magazines and newspapers, including IDG's leading global brands — Computerworld, PC World, Network World, Macworld and the Channel World family of publications. IDG Books Worldwide is one of the fastest-growing computer book publishers in the world, with more than 700 titles in 36 languages. The "...For Dummies®" series alone has more than 50 million copies in print. IDG offers online users the largest network of technology-specific Web sites around the world through IDG.net (http://www.idg.net), which comprises more than 225 targeted Web sites in 55 countries worldwide. International Data Corporation (IDC) is the world's largest provider of information technology data, analysis and consulting, with research centers in over 41 countries and more than 400 research analysts worldwide. IDG World Expo is a leading producer of more than 168 globally branded conferences and expositions in 35 countries including E3 (Electronic Entertainment Expo), Macworld Expo, ComNet, Windows World Expo, ICE (Internet Commerce Expo), Agenda, DEMO, and Spotlight. IDG's training subsidiary, ExecuTrain, is the world's largest computer training company, with more than 230 locations worldwide and 785 training courses. IDG Marketing Services helps industry-leading IT companies build international brand recognition by developing global integrated marketing programs via IDG's print, online and exposition products worldwide. Further information about the company can be found at www.idg.com.

10/8/98

Credits

Acquisitions Editor
Martine Edwards

Development Editors
Kathleen McFadden, Chip Wescott

Technical Editor
Bill Karow

Copy Editors
Timothy J. Borek, Corey Cohen,
Michael D. Welch

Project Coordinator
Karen York

Book Designers
Daniel Ziegler Design, Cátálin Dulfu,
Kurt Krames

Illustrator
Anthony Stuart

Layout and Graphics
Lou Boudreau, J. Tyler Connor,
Maridee Ennis, Angela F. Hunckler,
Shelley Lea, Brent Savage,
Kathie Schutte, Janet Seib, Kate Snell

Proofreaders
Christine Berman, Kelli Botta,
Rachel Garvey, Rebecca Senninger,
Robert Springer, Ethel M. Winslow,
Janet M. Withers

Indexer
York Publishing Services

About the Authors

Barry Press is the author of the blockbuster *PC Upgrade and Repair Bible, Professional Edition* from IDG Books Worldwide. He has designed leading-edge computer hardware, software, and networks for more than 25 years, including a unique cable television modem, campus-wide ATM networks, a desktop computer capable of analyzing adverse drug interactions, and an artificial intelligence planning system. He has programmed Windows since version 1.0 and has taught as an adjunct professor of computer science at the University of Southern California.

Marcia Press worked in public accounting as a tax CPA for what was then one of the Big Eight, moving later to her own practice. She handles the administrative part of the work for the Press's computer books — the tracking, calls, followups, and research — and does the sanity checks on the initial drafts. She's a fan of good wine, gardening, reading, and shopping, and is a serious gourmet cook.

To Jen and Kate

Welcome to
Teach Yourself

Welcome to Teach Yourself, a series read and trusted by millions for nearly a decade. Although you may have seen the Teach Yourself name on other books, ours is the original. In addition, no Teach Yourself series has ever delivered more on the promise of its name than this series. That's because IDG Books Worldwide recently transformed Teach Yourself into a new cutting-edge format that gives you all the information you need to learn quickly and easily.

Readers told us that they want to learn by doing and that they want to learn as much as they can in as short a time as possible. We listened to you and believe that our new task-by-task format and suite of learning tools deliver the book you need to successfully teach yourself any technology topic. Features such as our Personal Workbook, which lets you practice and reinforce the skills you've just learned, help ensure that you get full value out of the time you invest in your learning. Handy cross-references to related topics and online sites broaden your knowledge and give you control over the kind of information you want, when you want it.

More Answers . . .

In designing the latest incarnation of this series, we started with the premise that people like you, who are beginning to intermediate computer users, want to take control of their own learning. To do this, you need the proper tools to find answers to questions so you can solve problems now.

In designing a series of books that provides such tools, we created a unique and concise visual format. The added bonus: Teach Yourself books actually pack more information into their pages than other books written on the same subjects. Skill for skill, you typically get much more information in a Teach Yourself book. In fact, Teach Yourself books, on average, cover twice the skills covered by other computer books — as many as 125 skills per book — so they're more likely to address your specific needs.

WELCOME TO TEACH YOURSELF

...In Less Time

We know you don't want to spend twice the time to get all this great information, so we provide lots of time-saving features:

▶ A modular task-by-task organization of information: Any task you want to perform is easy to find and includes simple-to-follow steps.

▶ A larger size than standard makes the book easy to read and convenient to use at a computer workstation. The large format also enables us to include many more illustrations — 500 screen shots show you how to get everything done!

▶ A Personal Workbook at the end of each chapter reinforces learning with extra practice, real-world applications for your learning, and questions and answers to test your knowledge.

▶ Cross-references appearing at the bottom of each task page refer you to related information, providing a path through the book for learning particular aspects of the software thoroughly.

▶ A Find It Online feature offers valuable ideas on where to go on the Internet to get more information or to download useful files.

▶ Take Note sidebars provide added-value information from our expert authors for more in-depth learning.

▶ An attractive, consistent organization of information helps you quickly find and learn the skills you need.

These Teach Yourself features are designed to help you learn the essential skills about a technology in the least amount of time, with the most benefit. We've placed these features consistently throughout the book, so you quickly learn where to go to find just the information you need — whether you work through the book from cover to cover or use it later to solve a new problem.

You will find a Teach Yourself book on almost any technology subject — from the Internet to Windows to Microsoft Office. Take control of your learning today, with IDG Books Worldwide's Teach Yourself series.

Teach Yourself
More Answers in Less Time

Search through the task headings to find the topic you want right away. To learn a new skill, search the contents, chapter opener, or the extensive index to find what you need. Then find — at a glance — the clear Task Heading that matches it.

Go to this area if you want special tips, cautions, and notes that provide added insight into the current task.

Learn the concepts behind the task at hand and why the task is important in the real world. Time-saving suggestions and advice show you how to make the most of each skill.

After you learn the task at hand, you may have more questions, or you may want to read about other tasks related to that topic. Use the cross-references to find different information to make your learning more efficient.

Use the Find It Online element to locate Internet resources that provide more background, take you on interesting side trips, and offer additional tools for mastering and using the skills you need. (Occasionally you'll find a handy shortcut here.)

Backing Up Your System

It won't take long for you to be convinced that computers are not perfectly reliable. The computer might break or you might do something you didn't intend, but the chances are that every so often you're going to have a problem. What to do? Hardware can be fixed, so the risk is to your files. There's really only one option to make sure you can recover from a crash or mistake — have copies of your files somewhere besides your computer.

In practice, that means you need to copy the files to another computer, if you have a network, or to a removable storage device. You have a range of choices for removable storage, including floppy disk (up to 120MB), removable disk (up to several gigabytes), and tape (4 to 8 gigabytes at reasonable prices). Of these, floppies are impractical for all but limited data backups and removable disks are expensive. Tape is your best alternative — you can get tape drives to install inside your machine for a few hundred dollars and tapes for $10 to $20. Compare that to the cost of losing all your work.

It can take longer than you'd like to back up everything on your computer to tape, so you use several types of backup. A full backup copies everything on the machine to tape, including a critical Windows data store called the *registry*. A differential backup copies everything since the last full backup. An incremental backup copies everything since the last full or

incremental backup. Because differential and incremental backups only copy new or changed files, they do less work and take less time.

Setting up the backup or restore operations can be confusing, so Windows Backup provides wizards, sequences of dialog boxes that help you do the job. You simply start the wizard and answer the questions.

TAKE NOTE

▶ **BE READY TO RECOVER YOUR SYSTEM**

If you lose your entire system, recovery could be hard. You need Windows running before you can run Windows Backup to reload your tapes. Windows 98 provides System Recovery to solve this problem. All you need is your full system backup, your startup disk, and the Windows 98 CD-ROM. Find all the directions in the file \tools\sysrec\recover.txt on the CD-ROM.

▶ **PING PONG YOUR TAPES**

If you really understand that computers can foul up at the worst times, you realize that one of the worst times to have a problem is when you're writing a backup tape. If it's your only backup, a worst-case disaster would take out not only your computer, but also your tape. Don't let that happen — have at least two sets of tapes and use them in rotation.

CROSS-REFERENCE
Install Windows Backup using the "Adding and Removing Windows 98 Components" lesson in Chapter 9.

142

FIND IT ONLINE
The heavy-duty version of Windows 98 Backup is from Seagate. See http://www.seagatesoftware.com/bedesktop98

WELCOME TO TEACH YOURSELF

The current chapter name and number always appear in the top right-hand corner of every task page spread, so you always know exactly where you are in the book.

RUNNING THE WINDOWS 98 APPLICATIONS

Backing Up Your System

CHAPTER
10

① Backup (Start   Programs
Accessories   System Tools
Backup) copies files to tape,
floppy disk, or other storage.

② Backup wizards work to make
operation simple.

③ A backup job copies to
storage.

④ Restore brings files back from
storage to your computer.

⑤ Questions from Backup
Wizard let it create what you
need. Here, tell it the storage
destination.

⑥ Backup knows floppies (A:)
are removable and uses as
many as it needs.

⑦ Tape drives show up here as
another option.

⑧ The main window shows the
files selected for backup or
restore.

⑨ Drives and folders show up in
the left pane, folders and files
in the right.

⑩ A gray check says some files
are selected.

⑪ A blue check says all files are
selected.

⑫ This dialog shows progress as
the backup runs.

⑬ The values in these areas
show the total backup
(Estimated) and the progress
so far (Processed).

⑭ This dialog shows backup has
filled the current floppy and is
waiting for the next.

143

Ultimately, people learn by doing. Follow the clear, illustrated steps on the right-hand page of every task to complete a procedure. The detailed callouts for each step show you exactly where to go and what to do to complete the task.

Who This Book Is For

This book is written for you, a beginning to intermediate PC user who isn't afraid to take charge of his or her own learning experience. You don't want a lot of technical jargon; you *do* want to learn as much about PC technology as you can in a limited amount of time. You need a book that is straightforward, easy to follow, and logically organized, so you can find answers to your questions easily. And you appreciate simple-to-use tools such as handy cross-references and visual step-by-step procedures that help you make the most of your learning. We have created the unique Teach Yourself format specifically to meet your needs.

Personal Workbook

It's a well-known fact that much of what we learn is lost soon after we learn it if we don't reinforce our newly acquired skills with practice and repetition. That's why each Teach Yourself chapter ends with your own Personal Workbook. Here's where you can get extra practice, test your knowledge, and discover ideas for using what you've learned in the real world. There's even a Visual Quiz to help you remember your way around the topic's software environment.

Feedback

Please let us know what you think about this book, and whether you have any suggestions for improvements. You can send questions and comments to the Teach Yourself team on the IDG Books Worldwide Web site at **www.idgbooks.com**.

Personal Workbook

Q&A

❶ What can you do if you don't find WordPad or Paint on your system?

❷ What is *TrueType*?

❸ How do you install new fonts?

❹ When should you avoid using tab stops?

❺ Why might fonts in documents look funny on another machine?

❻ What file types can Paint handle?

❼ What can go on a CD-ROM?

❽ What track holds the information in a mixed data/video CD-ROM?

ANSWERS: PAGE 339

144

After working through the tasks in each chapter, you can test your progress and reinforce your learning by answering the questions in the Q&A section. Then check your answers in the Personal Workbook Answers appendix at the back of the book.

WELCOME TO TEACH YOURSELF

Another practical way to reinforce your skills is to do additional exercises on the same skills you just learned without the benefit of the chapter's visual steps. If you struggle with any of these exercises, it's a good idea to refer to the chapter's tasks to be sure you've mastered them.

RUNNING THE WINDOWS 98 APPLICATONS

Personal Workbook

CHAPTER
10

Read the list of Real-World Applications to get ideas on how you can use the skills you've just learned in your everyday work. Understanding a process can be simple; knowing how to use that process to make you more productive is the key to successful learning.

EXTRA PRACTICE

1. After you ve played a few audio CDs, look in the file C:\Windows\cdplayer.ini.

2. Start Paint and maximize the window. Let a young child scribble with the mouse.

3. Type a letter into WordPad and format it with the different fonts you find on your system.

4. Run the command Insert Object Wave Sound in WordPad. When Sound Recorder starts, insert a file from C:\Windows\Media or record your own.

5. Double-click the icon you created in practice step 5. What happens?

REAL-WORLD APPLICATIONS

Your computer is stolen when thieves break into your apartment, and they take all your data with them. You restore from the backup tapes you made the previous night.

A power failure shuts down your computer unexpectedly, and when the power comes back on you find the computer won t start. You boot the startup disk and run the SCANDISK program. After it repairs problems in your file system, your computer starts and runs normally.

In a dream, you see yourself loading CDs into your computer at work while you explore entertainment Web sites. The Internet Faerie appears in your dream, noting you re violating your company s Internet use policy. Chastened, you leave the CDs at home.

Visual Quiz

What is this dialog box? How do you get to it?

145

Take the Visual Quiz to see how well you're learning your way around the technology. Learning about computers is often as much about how to find a button or menu as it is about memorizing definitions. Our Visual Quiz helps you find your way.

Acknowledgments

Marcia and Barry gratefully acknowledge the assistance of the following people and companies in the development of this book: 3Com Corporation, Altec Lansing Technologies, Inc., American Megatrends Incorporated, American Power Conversion Corporation, America Online, Inc., Ask Jeeves, Inc., ATI Technologies Incorporated, Martha Badigian, The Benjamin Group Incorporated, Block Financial Corporation, Brodeur & Partners, Sonya Chan, Andy Cummings, Debbie DeFreece, Dogpile, EarthLink, Inc., Eastman Kodak Company, Martine Edwards, Electronic Arts Inc., ESC Technologies, Excite Inc., Dan Francisco, Craig Garbiner, Marci Pedrazzi-Gottleib, g. o. d. Inc., Dan Greenblat, Layne Heiny, Brian Hentschel, Hewlett-Packard Company, Tyson Heyn, Chuck Hollenbeck, Mark Huffman, Imation, Intel Corporation, Heather Jardim, Bill "Spongeman" Karow, Kensington Technology Group, Kingston Technology Company, Labtec Enterprises Incorporated, Vicki Langel, Logitech, Nico Mak, Kathleen McFadden, Microsoft Corporation, Netscape Communications Corporation, Nico Mak Computing Incorporated, Kelly Odle, Rick Perry, James Peters, Jen Press, Kate Press, Tara Poole, Joe Runde, Billy Rudock, Seagate Technology, S C & T International, Spacetec IMC Corporation, Staccato Systems, Symantec Corporation, Real Networks Company, Toshiba America Information Systems Incorporated, Manny Vara, Matt Wagner, Seth Walker, Brooke Wallace, Weber Group, Michael Welch, Chip Wescott, Glenn Wilk, Mike Wilson, Yahoo!, and Yamaha Systems Technology Incorporated.

Special thanks to Eastman Kodak Company for use of the DC210 digital camera used to take the photographs in this book.

Entries for the Glossary were contributed by 3Com Corporation, Seagate Technology, and Kingston Technology Company.

Thanks to all of you.

Contents

CONTENTS

CONTENTS

CONTENTS

CONTENTS

Teach Yourself®
PCs

My Computer
Recycle Bin
My Briefcase
DE Phone List
Device Manager
Iomega Tools

PART I

Starting Up

We're believers in the idea that you don't really understand something until you've done it yourself, so the first lessons in this book focus on doing the very first things you need to do with a computer — unpack it, set it up, and turn it on. You learn what the different parts of your computer are and what you're looking at when the computer first starts up. Once you have your computer running, you want to get some work done (and we want you to build some confidence), so the next lessons show you how to write a letter.

Traditional letters need to be on paper and put in the mail, so after your letter's done you progress to setting up your printer and printing the letter. You're building skills one by one, so it's a later part of the book when you learn how to send letters electronically across the Internet.

The fourth chapter in this part gives you the lessons to build deeper knowledge, starting to build the foundation you need to get the most out of your computer. You learn what disks and files are and how to use Windows to organize what's on your disk. By the time you're done with this part, you'll be able to walk up to any Windows computer, figure out what's on it, and start working with it.

CHAPTER 1

MASTER THESE SKILLS

▶ Identifying the Pieces

▶ Setting Up and Plugging In

▶ Turning On the Power

▶ Understanding the Windows Desktop

Unpacking and Booting Your PC

It's exciting to get a new computer — whether you're a novice or expert. Your first computer is the gateway to a world of information and new experiences. A replacement for an old one will likely be faster than the one you had, with better capabilities and new features. Computer manufacturers call unpacking and setup the "out of box experience," ignoring the wonderfully cosmic parallels to "out of body experience."

This chapter is your guide to a smooth, painless setup. As with everything else relating to computers, the key to success is a patient methodical approach combined with careful observation. You're going to have to resist the impulse to rip and shred the packing, jam all the cables in place, and whack the power switch, because if that's what you do, you're going to skip past some learning and thinking that can help you avoid problems later. The time to start thinking and planning is before you buy the machine.

The standard buying decisions are choosing your computer's manufacturer, monitor size, disk size, memory size, processor speed, and expansion options. Monitor size determines how big text and images will be in front of you. Disk size determines how many programs you can install for later use and how much data you will be able to save, while memory size determines how many programs you can run at once before the machine slows down. Processor speed determines how fast everything will run, and expansion options ultimately determine how long you will own the machine.

Of all your choices, choose the manufacturer most carefully. Because you're going to need tech support and want to upgrade during the life of your computer, choosing a quality manufacturer committed to customer satisfaction is crucial. You can save hundreds of dollars buying a bargain machine at the local swap meet, but unless you really know what you're doing, you could be in trouble from the beginning.

We've focused on a Toshiba Equium 7000S computer in this book. The machine we worked with came with a 266 MHz Pentium II processor, 64MB (megabytes, or millions of bytes) of memory, a 4GB (gigabytes, or billions of bytes) hard disk, 24X CD-ROM, network card, and Windows 95.

Identifying the Pieces

Your computer typically consists of six pieces: a system unit, a monitor, a keyboard, a mouse, and two speakers. The system unit contains most of the electronics, including the processor, memory, and disk. The monitor displays pictures the system unit generates, much like a TV displays pictures a video game console generates. The keyboard lets you type characters, and the mouse lets you point at and choose things on the screen. Speakers let the computer prompt you with sounds and play music.

Computers come in a variety of sizes and shapes, from small pizza box shapes around a foot and a half square by a few inches high to servers several feet high, two feet wide, and three feet deep. Monitors can be as small as flat panels a foot or so square and inches deep or as large as several feet wide, several feet deep, and a foot and a half high. The largest monitors can weigh nearly 100 pounds.

The first thing to do when your computer arrives is to check the boxes. There should be no holes or pushed-in corners that might indicate rough handling or concealed damage. Read the carrier's form you sign. If signing the form confirms that the shipment was received in good condition and waives claims for hidden damages, you'll want to do some inspection before signing. Verify that the entire shipment arrived by checking against the count on the packing slip. If you buy the computer at a store, complete an inventory before you leave.

TAKE NOTE

MEASURE YOUR WORKSPACE BEFORE YOU ORDER

You don't want to have to live with a computer or monitor that's too big for the place where you work or play, so be sure to measure how much space you really have. Don't forget that the keyboard and mouse can use as much as a foot and a half of depth and two and a half feet of width on your desk in front of the monitor.

GET THE RIGHT VIDEO OPTIONS

The amount of *video memory* you get (memory in the computer used to produce the images you see) determines the *number of colors* and *resolution* you can see. You want a 17-inch or larger monitor for easy readability and lots of room to work onscreen, and you want to run the Windows High Color mode (the lesser alternative is 256 colors, which creates problems for some software). A 17-inch monitor should be capable of resolution of 1280×1024 dots horizontally and vertically, but inexpensive computers that come with only 2MB of video memory limit you in High Color to an onscreen resolution of 1024×768. If you're going to get a 17-inch or larger monitor, get at least 4MB of video memory.

CROSS-REFERENCE

Part 5 covers maintenance and upgrades, including troubleshooting.

FIND IT ONLINE

Toshiba (http://www.csd.toshiba.com), Micron (http://www.micronpc.com), Compaq (http://www.compaq.com), and Dell (http://www.dell.com) make top-quality computers you can

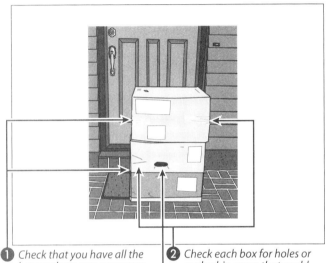

1 Check that you have all the boxes when your computer arrives.

2 Check each box for holes or pushed-in areas that could indicate concealed damage.

3 Lift the boxes carefully using handles if they're provided.

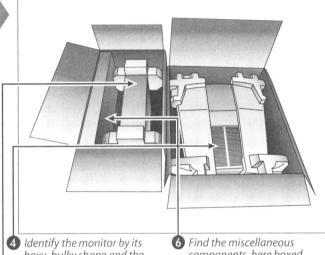

4 Identify the monitor by its boxy, bulky shape and the heat vents on top.

5 Identify the system unit as the largest component besides the monitor.

6 Find the miscellaneous components, here boxed together next to the system unit.

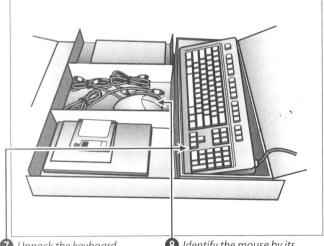

7 Unpack the keyboard, identified by the individual keys on its face.

8 Identify the mouse by its general shape and the two or three buttons at one end.

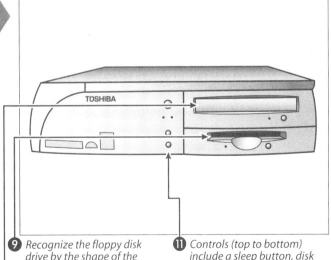

9 Recognize the floppy disk drive by the shape of the opening and the eject button.

10 The CD-ROM or DVD has a distinctive carrier that slides out of the computer.

11 Controls (top to bottom) include a sleep button, disk activity light, power on light, reset button, and power button.

Setting Up and Plugging In

Methodical setup begins when the machine arrives. Plan on doing some rearrangement and cleanup on the desk where the computer will go. You need room to work and a chair that provides good support and a relaxed position at the keyboard. Your computer needs space for the monitor, system unit, keyboard, and mouse. Your computer needs stable power and airflow for good ventilation. Your computer *must* have good airflow to stay cool — take a look at "Cleaning the Computer" in Chapter 19 for the reasons why.

You're likely to need a lot of outlets — system unit, monitor, and speakers are commonly the minimum — so plan on using a power strip. Using a power strip reduces the number of wall outlets you need to just one and provides a convenient single point (the switch on the power strip) to turn the system on and off. Get a power strip with a surge protector. Plugging everything into the power strip, including the printer, helps protect your equipment from power surges and lightning. See the sidebar "Cheap Insurance" later in this chapter for more information on how to pick a surge protector.

Unpack boxes one at a time. If you open them all first, but leave the contents in the box, you can see what's in which box. Once you know what's where, you can decide the order in which you want to take the equipment out of the box. The system unit is the box-shaped cabinet, often about two feet by one foot by less than a foot. The monitor is the TV-like unit. If you plan to put the monitor on top of the system unit, take the system unit out of the box first and place it so you can then set the monitor down on it.

Physical setup of your computer mostly consists of connecting the cables to the right places. Many computers now come with clear drawings showing how to connect the cables. Some (such as the Toshiba Equium 7000) come with color-coded connectors — match the colors and you can't go wrong. Because PCs follow industry standards for cables and connectors, though, it's hard to get it wrong. Compare the connectors on the ends of the different cables, looking at the number of connections (typically 9, 15, or 25 for data connections; sound connections have one thick prong) and their gender (pins are termed male, sockets female). As long as you plug compatible connectors together, you're likely to get the setup right. Connections that might be confused (such as those for the keyboard and mouse and for speakers and microphones) are usually labeled on the back panel of the computer right next to the connector.

Continued

CROSS-REFERENCE

Chapter 3's lessons, "Unpacking and Cabling the Printer to the Computer," cover setting up your printer.

FIND IT ONLINE

Don't overlook ergonomics when you choose computer furniture. Look at **http://www.ahandyguide.com/cat1/e/e401.htm**, **http://www.computercomforts.com/default.htm**.

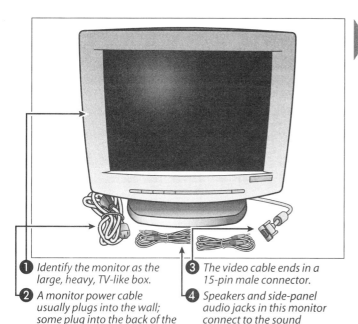

❶ Identify the monitor as the large, heavy, TV-like box.

❷ A monitor power cable usually plugs into the wall; some plug into the back of the system unit.

❸ The video cable ends in a 15-pin male connector.

❹ Speakers and side-panel audio jacks in this monitor connect to the sound connectors on the system unit.

❺ This monitor power connector accepts a standard modular power cord.

❻ Normally the video cable is permanently attached to the back of the monitor.

❼ These connectors, only found on monitors with embedded audio, accept the audio patch cables for speaker and microphone connections.

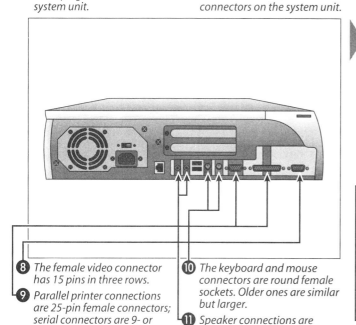

❽ The female video connector has 15 pins in three rows.

❾ Parallel printer connections are 25-pin female connectors; serial connectors are 9- or 25-pin male.

❿ The keyboard and mouse connectors are round female sockets. Older ones are similar but larger.

⓫ Speaker connections are small mini-connectors.

⓬ The fan on the power supply is the primary source of cooling for the computer. Keep it clean.

⓭ Here's where the power cord for the computer connects.

⓮ Many computers have a switch like this that lets you choose 115- or 240-volt operation. Keep the switch set for the wall power you have.

Setting Up and Plugging In
Continued

The many kinds of connectors on the back of your computer reflect the different kinds of interfaces for devices plugging into the computer. It matters that you plug things in only where they belong, so computer manufacturers have standardized different connectors for different purposes to help simplify setup and upgrades. With the exception of the connections for speakers and microphones, and for mice and keyboards on recent computers, all the connectors you're likely to find look different when their purposes are different. The audio connections are similar because computers use the same cables as are common on personal stereo equipment. The keyboard and mouse connections are similar because they both use a European-standard connector to reduce size on the back panel.

It's never too soon to avoid a rat's nest of cables behind and around your computer. The many cords between the system unit and the monitor, keyboard, mouse, speakers, network, joystick, and power strip — each with some extra length so one size fits all — can easily get so tangled that your only hope to straighten it out is to disconnect everything, move to a new city, and start over. Instead, wind up the excess and bind the cords with cable ties, Velcro, or even wire ties.

TAKE NOTE

▶ LET YOUR MOUSE HITCH A RIDE ON YOUR KEYBOARD

If your computer is at the side of your desk or below the desktop, the mouse cable is going to keep sliding off the desk and you're going to be constantly pulling it back so you can easily move the mouse to where you want it. You can tie the mouse cord to the keyboard cable with a cable tie (or even a rubber band), binding the two so there's just a little spare mouse cord on the desk. Because the keyboard keeps its cable from sliding off the desk, the attached mouse cord stays where you want it. Use the same idea for other mobile devices on your desktop, including joysticks and microphones.

▶ DON'T FORGET TO DUST

Computers accumulate a lot of dust, even in reasonably clean places. The fan in the system unit moves more air than you might expect, and dust in the air settles out in the nooks and crannies of the case. Although you don't want to be opening the case and cleaning all the time, it's a good idea to clean the outside of the computer periodically, including vacuuming the air inlets and the fans. Keep cleaning and maintenance in mind when you first set up your computer. If the parts you need to clean are hard to get to, you're likely to ignore doing it.

CROSS-REFERENCE

Part V covers maintenance in Chapter 19 and upgrades in Chapter 20. Lay out your work area when you first set it up to simplify such tasks.

FIND IT ONLINE

You can find cable organizers, clips, and ties at **http://www.smarthome.com/cableorg.html**.

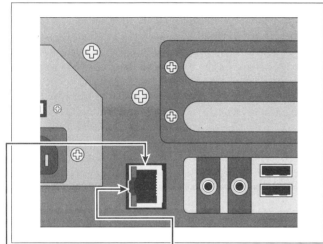

15 Looking like an overgrown phone jack, this is an Ethernet connection for connection to a computer network.

16 Like modular phone jacks, the Ethernet connection has a prong on one side to make sure you insert the plug the right way.

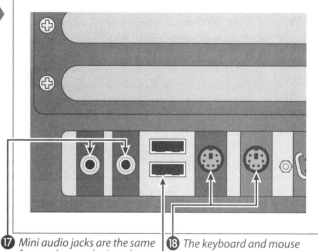

17 Mini audio jacks are the same for speakers and microphone, so check the pictures or labels carefully.

18 The keyboard and mouse connections can be interchanged too, so check drawings and color codes.

19 These connectors are for the Universal Serial Bus.

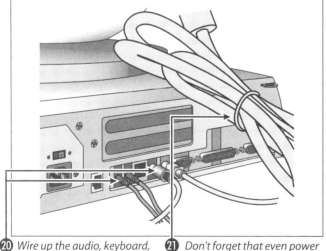

20 Wire up the audio, keyboard, and mouse cables to the right ports, and then tie the excess.

21 Don't forget that even power cords and the monitor cable can be tied.

22 Here's a complete view of the finished wiring. Note how many cables even a small system requires.

23 Remember to leave just enough cable length for the mouse and keyboard to reach their positions on your desk.

Turning On the Power

You could smack all the power cords into outlets, flip the power switches, and let the software take over at this point, but there's a lot to learn about how your computer starts if you continue the methodical approach instead.

Windows doesn't run first when the computer powers up, because at that point it's still on the disk. The first software to run is something called the Basic Input/Output System, or BIOS, that is kept in special memory that remembers things when the power's off. (That's why Windows is still on the disk — the disk remembers things, but the memory that the programs run in does not.) The job of the BIOS is to do a simple check of the parts of the hardware and load the operating system (Windows). Watch and listen to your computer as it starts; knowing the normal behavior can help you know if something's goes wrong.

The BIOS startup may be hidden during boot — try pushing the Escape key (marked Esc) if you get a picture at first. The first thing the BIOS does is to display its version. Common BIOS manufacturers are AMI, Phoenix, and Award, so if you see a message with one of these names, or of your computer manufacturer, you've probably found the version sign-on. The BIOS then counts the memory, checking to see how much memory seems to be installed and working, and goes looking for disk drives. Once the BIOS

finishes inventorying drives, it starts loading Windows.

If you push the F8 key near the end of BIOS startup, you get a menu from Windows that includes some options you'll want during troubleshooting and that gives you one way to get to DOS without Windows. You can look for the message "Starting Windows 95" and push F8 immediately or, for Windows 98, just push F8 as the BIOS is identifying disk drives. (There's usually a single beep as Windows starts loading that you may key on too.)

TAKE NOTE

▶ COMPUTERS ARE PATHOLOGICAL LIARS

The BIOS testing is pretty minimal — don't believe everything's fine because the BIOS comes up and starts to load Windows. Even the BIOS memory tests can lie. The BIOS may not check all the memory you have and isn't likely to find all but the grossest failures.

▶ DOS IS STILL THERE IF YOU NEED IT

The extended set of capabilities in Windows 95 and 98 means that a lot of things get loaded and have to be working correctly for Windows to run. Sometimes, you need plain DOS without the trimmings. If you do, you can shut down Windows to use just MS-DOS or use the Windows startup menu to go directly to a command prompt.

CROSS-REFERENCE

See Chapter 23 to learn better ways to troubleshoot than believing what the BIOS has to say.

FIND IT ONLINE

American Power Conversion at **http://www.apcc. com/go/lit/surguide** has information on protecting against power loss and surges.

Cheap Insurance

It's no surprise that you don't ever want your computer to have a close encounter with a lightning strike. A good surge protector can help it ride out almost anything but a direct hit on your local power lines. Lightning and wind from storms can shut power down too, though, and no surge protector keeps your computer alive through a power failure. Lose power and you lose all the work since your last save.

To protect against loss of power, use a device called an Uninterruptible Power Supply (UPS). Even a low-cost UPS (under $100) can keep your computer and monitor up long enough to save your files and shut the system down.

It's hard to tell if the surge protector or UPS sold in the local hardware store is well made — you can't tell the difference visually, and the packaging rarely provides specifications you can examine. Your best choice is to buy from a reputable company, such as American Power Conversion, or to check specifications from a catalog or on the Internet before you buy. Look for compliance with safety agency specifications such as UL 1449 TVSS (Transient Voltage Surge Suppressors), and UL 1363 (Safety for Relocatable Power Taps), along with UL 1283 for devices acting as noise filters.

```
PhoenixBIOS 4.0 Release 6.0.6
Copyright 1985-1997 Phoenix Technologies Ltd.

Copyright 1998 by Toshiba, Inc.
KX615 Release 00.01.05
CPU = Pentium II 266 MHz
00000640K System RAM Passed
00064512K Extended RAM Passed
0512K Cache SRAM Passed
System BIOS shadowed
Video BIOS shadowed
UMB upper limit segment address: F0E7
Mouse initialized
Fixed Disk 0: WDC AC24300L
ATAPI CD-ROM: TOSHIBA CD_ROM XM-6102B




Press <F2> to enter SETUP
```

In Touch with Tomorrow
TOSHIBA

1 Power up for the Toshiba 7000S starts with the BIOS sign-on, giving manufacturer and version.

2 This BIOS identifies the processor as a Pentium II.

3 Total memory is system RAM plus extended RAM.

4 The BIOS finds the mouse, disk drive, and CD-ROM, and then starts Windows.

```
Microsoft Windows 95 Startup Menu
==================================

    1. Normal
    2. Logged (\BOOTLOG.TXT)
    3. Safe mode
    4. Safe mode with network support
    5. Step-by-step confirmation
    6. Command prompt only
    7. Safe mode command prompt only

Enter a choice: 1








F5=Safe mode  Shift+F5=Command prompt  Shift+F8=Step-by-step confirmation [N]
```

5 This is the startup menu you see if you push F8 immediately as the BIOS starts to load Windows.

6 Safe mode lets you start Windows if a problem keeps the computer from starting normally.

7 The command prompt gets you to DOS, without Windows.

Understanding the Windows Desktop

At the most basic level, what computers do is run programs. The BIOS is a program, as is Windows. Everything your computer can do, it does under the direction of a program. This means that the key thing you need to be able to do is start a program.

In the paper world, a file is a collection of information about a single topic — a file of bills, of pictures, or whatever. Computers use the same idea — a computer file is a set of data that collectively is some single thing. Programs are files, as are the documents you write with a word processor or images you create with a drawing program. To run a program, you need to tell Windows to locate and load its file, and to execute the instructions it carries.

Windows offers *shortcuts*, packages containing all the information Windows needs to start a program, to make running programs easier. You see shortcuts as little pictures, or *icons* — the picture usually reminds you of the function of the program. You can place icons on the Windows desktop (what you see onscreen when Windows starts), where they sit lined up waiting for you, usually on the left side. You *select* an icon by putting the mouse cursor (the small arrow on the screen that moves when you move the mouse) over it and pushing the left button once (*clicking the icon*). You *activate* it by putting the mouse over it and pushing the left button twice rapidly (*double-clicking the icon*).

TAKE NOTE

▶ **FIND HIDDEN POWER IN THE RIGHT-HAND MOUSE BUTTON**

Windows 95 was the first version of Windows to get some value out of the right button on the mouse, popping up menus of useful commands when you pushed the button. If you push the right mouse button in an empty area of the Windows desktop, for instance, you get a small pop-up menu that includes commands for rearranging the icons on the desktop and for lining them up in a regularly spaced grid.

▶ **MAKE THE DESKTOP LOOK THE WAY YOU WANT**

You can use the Line up Icons command (in the desktop right mouse button menu) to help arrange the icons on your Windows desktop anywhere you want. You can move an icon by putting the mouse cursor over it, holding down the left button, and dragging the icon to any position on the desktop. Release the left button when the icon is where you want it. Repeat the process for the rest of the icons you want to move, and then use the Line up Icons command to snap them into regular positions. Try moving the icons to the right edge of the screen for practice.

CROSS-REFERENCE

You can learn lots about files and folders in Windows, which we cover in Chapter 4, starting with "Opening the Windows Explorer."

FIND IT ONLINE

Customize your desktop with Tweak UI at http://www.microsoft.com/windows/downloads/contents/PowerToys/W95TweakUI.

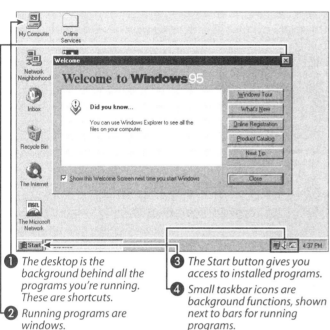

1 *The desktop is the background behind all the programs you're running. These are shortcuts.*

2 *Running programs are windows.*

3 *The Start button gives you access to installed programs.*

4 *Small taskbar icons are background functions, shown next to bars for running programs.*

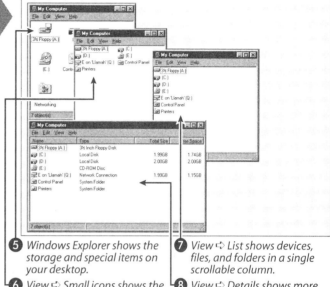

5 *Windows Explorer shows the storage and special items on your desktop.*

6 *View ⇨ Small icons shows the desktop items in compact form.*

7 *View ⇨ List shows devices, files, and folders in a single scrollable column.*

8 *View ⇨ Details shows more information about each item.*

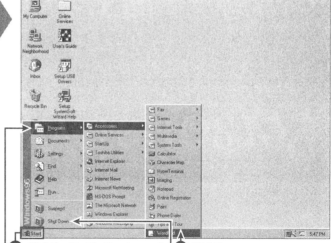

9 *Right-click My Computer ⇨ Explore for more information.*

10 *Choose View ⇨ Toolbar, View ⇨ Status Bar, and View ⇨ Details for this two-pane version of Explorer.*

11 *The left pane shows the disks in your computer and the folders they hold.*

12 *The right pane shows you what's in the item you selected on the left.*

13 *Click the Start button to reach your installed programs.*

14 *Hold the mouse on a menu item to cause the menu's next level to appear.*

15 *Click the program you want (WordPad in this figure) to start it running.*

16 *Find the commands to shut down or restart the computer here under Shut Down.*

15

Personal Workbook

Q&A

1 What's the difference between CD-ROM and DVD?

_____

_____

2 Describe the use for each of these connectors: video, monitor power, speakers, microphone, keyboard, and mouse.

_____

_____

_____

3 What is a BIOS, and what does it do?

_____

_____

_____

4 What can a surge protector do for you? What about a UPS?

_____

_____

_____

5 How much video memory do you need to run High Color mode on a display with a 1,280 × 1,024 resolution?

_____

_____

_____

6 What happens when you hit the F8 key at the end of the BIOS initialization?

_____

_____

7 How do you access pop-up menus to gather information or execute a command in Windows?

_____

_____

_____

8 What happens if the cooling airflow to your computer gets blocked by dust?

_____

_____

_____

ANSWERS: PAGE 333

UNPACKING AND BOOTING YOUR PC

Personal Workbook

CHAPTER 1

EXTRA PRACTICE

1 Open the Windows Explorer in the two-pane mode and right-click with the mouse in different places. What happens?

2 Left-click with the mouse on the + symbols in the Windows Explorer left pane. What happens?

3 Watch the messages from the BIOS of your computer as the machine boots. Press the Pause key on the keyboard as the BIOS executes. What happens? Press the spacebar while the machine is paused. What happens?

4 Read the User's Guide for your computer. How much power do the monitor and system unit draw? Compare the two to a light bulb. Does the computer use much power?

REAL-WORLD APPLICATIONS

✔ You move to a new office location in your company, but the people scheduled to set up your computer are too busy to do the work the day you move. You call them on the phone to find out what precautions you need to take, and do the setup yourself.

✔ You take a job in Fillmore, Utah, moving your entire household. You take apart your computer and pack it securely in the shipping cartons you remembered to save. When the move is done, you unpack the computer and set it back up.

✔ Your monitor goes up in smoke when you turn it on one morning. You turn it off, and then disconnect it at the video cable and the power cord. When the replacement arrives, you know to hook up the video cable and power cord, turn on the power, and check the picture on the screen.

Visual Quiz

Describe the number of pins and gender of this connector. What signals will go through the connector? Will you find it on the system unit or on a cable?

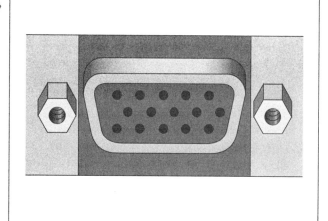

17

CHAPTER 2

MASTER
THESE
SKILLS

▶ **Starting and Stopping WordPad**

▶ **Using the Parts of the Window to Type a Letter**

▶ **Saving Your Work to a File**

▶ **Getting Help**

Writing Your First Letter

Completing Chapter 1 left you with a running computer, so now it's time to make it do something. You start with something very simple (but useful), and then use Windows' built-in word processor to write a letter. In the process, you learn the basics of how Windows works — ways to start and stop a program, what's common in how programs look onscreen, what commands most programs have, and how to run commands in programs.

It's not accidental that you can learn the essentials of one program and apply that knowledge to most Windows programs — indeed, it's one of the triumphs of modern computers that software written for Windows or the Macintosh makes this possible. The reason it works is that Windows programs are built on a few common concepts, which include a standard top-level window layout and standard commands. The standard window layout starts with a title bar on the top, with icons on the left and right. The icons on the right include ones to minimize the window (take it offscreen), maximize the window (make it fill the screen), and close the program. The icon on the left of the title bar contains a menu with commands equivalent to the right-hand icons, plus ones to move and resize the window. You can move the window by holding the left mouse button down and dragging the title bar. The edges and corners of the window are handles you can use to resize it.

Below the title bar is the menu bar, containing words such as File, Edit, View, and Help. Each of these words names a menu of commands that appears if you click the mouse on the keyword. The commands in the menus are similarly standardized, so if you know what a command does in one program, you are likely to know what it does in the next. The details vary somewhat, but the essential purpose is the same. Menu commands are written to reflect the sequence of choices you make — for example, the Save command under the File menu is written File ➪ Save.

Some programs have a bar of small icons below the menu bar. Each icon represents a commonly used command, represented by standardized images. Commands unique to a program are likely to have unique icons.

Starting and Stopping WordPad

You're going to write a letter with WordPad to explore and understand the basics of how Windows works. Before getting to WordPad, though, start a simpler program — Windows' built-in calculator — and play around with it. You can trace through the Start button (Start ⇨ Programs ⇨ Accessories ⇨ Calculator) to get the program running, or if you know the name of the program's file, you can use Start ⇨ Run and type the name. The name of the program for the Windows calculator is *calc*. The two methods are equivalent, because Windows already knows where the calc program is. What both methods do is tell Windows to load and run the program.

Calc is a typical calculator with memory. The title bar (that says Calculator) has a window's usual left and right icons. The menu bar has the words Edit, View, and Help. The white area just below the menu bar is where numbers you type and results you calculate show up. The extruded-looking buttons below the white area are buttons you can click with the mouse. You can also type numbers and operators. For example, divide 11,111,111 by 9 by typing the number 1 eight times, then the forward slash (/), followed by 9. Then press Enter. Don't type the commas.

Now that you've practiced with calc, the figures and steps on the next page show how to start WordPad, how to stop it, the key features in the window, and some of the key commands. Not only are WordPad's capabilities enough for you to do useful work, they're the beginning of your understanding of every Windows program.

CROSS-REFERENCE

Read more about application software in Part III. Chapter 11 covers Microsoft Word, the heavy-duty

FIND IT ONLINE

You can find info on alternative word processors at http://www.corel.com/products/wordperfect/ and http://www.lotus.com/home.nsf/tabs/wordpro.

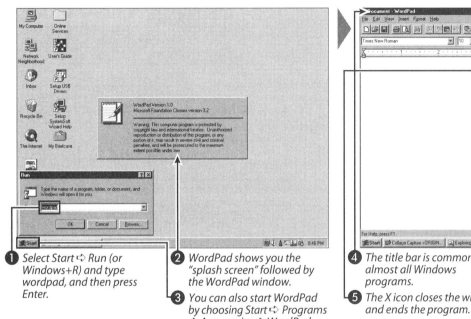

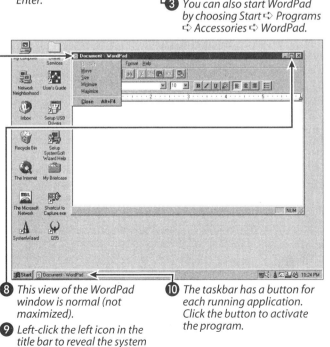

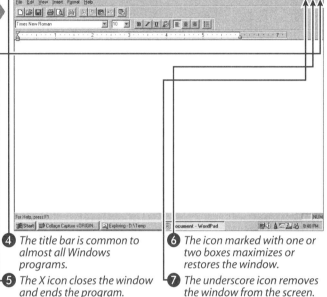

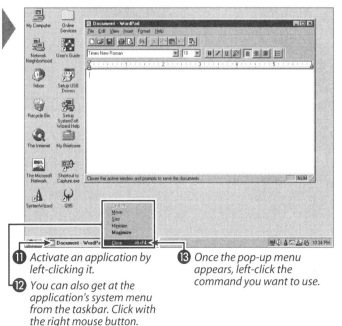

1 Select Start ➪ Run (or Windows+R) and type wordpad, and then press Enter.

2 WordPad shows you the "splash screen" followed by the WordPad window.

3 You can also start WordPad by choosing Start ➪ Programs ➪ Accessories ➪ WordPad.

4 The title bar is common to almost all Windows programs.

5 The X icon closes the window and ends the program.

6 The icon marked with one or two boxes maximizes or restores the window.

7 The underscore icon removes the window from the screen.

8 This view of the WordPad window is normal (not maximized).

9 Left-click the left icon in the title bar to reveal the system menu.

10 The taskbar has a button for each running application. Click the button to activate the program.

11 Activate an application by left-clicking it.

12 You can also get at the application's system menu from the taskbar. Click with the right mouse button.

13 Once the pop-up menu appears, left-click the command you want to use.

Using the Parts of the Window to Type a Letter

Look at the WordPad window more closely. Right under the title bar and menu bar are the toolbars, the ruler, the area where Word-Pad displays your text, and the status bar. The first figure on the next page identifies each of these parts.

It's time to do some work. Start WordPad and type the following text. Type the individual paragraphs without stopping and use the Enter key to end paragraphs, not lines. WordPad wraps text to the next line for you. Don't worry about errors as you type.

> Dear Dan's Lawn Service:
> I'm writing to express my displeasure with the gopher removal billed in the latest statement you sent.
> It's hard to understand how it is that you describe the effort by your technician as gopher removal. You might have had a case if you'd termed it entertainment, but not gopher removal. In a contest of wits between your tech and the gopher, the gopher won. Only relative size prevented it from performing a technician removal. Seeing as how your tech was not only unsuccessful at removing the subject gopher, but also left behind many large holes which were quickly occupied by its friends and relatives, I can't see why I'd be billed for the service. Please adjust the statement, including removal of the technician's psychiatric expenses, and send me the corrected version.
> Sincerely,

You can correct typing errors and revise the text several ways. Small corrections are easy by using a left mouse click between characters to position the cursor, backspacing, and typing the corrected text. The third figure shows how to correct larger errors — drag the mouse cursor over the entire block you're interested in, press Delete to remove the text, and type the new text.

The fourth figure shows how to insert text at the front of the letter, and how to use scroll bars to see hidden parts of the document when it gets too long to see all at once in the window.

TAKE NOTE

▶ USE THE TOOLBAR

The lower toolbar in WordPad gives you the common formatting commands. From left to right, the toolbar lets you change font; change type size; make the text bold, italic, and underlined; choose text color; align paragraphs left, center, and right; and create bulleted paragraphs.

▶ USE THE KEYBOARD

You can move the cursor and select text with the keyboard. The arrow keys move the cursor. If you hold down Shift and use the arrow keys, you get a selection block starting at the cursor position when you pressed Shift. If you hold down the Ctrl key, the cursor moves greater distances when you press an arrow key. You can use Shift and Ctrl in combination.

CROSS-REFERENCE
You need to print your letter to mail it. Read Chapter 3 to find out how to install and set up a printer and to print your letter.

FIND IT ONLINE
Find a guide to writing business letters at **http://www.qesn.meq.gouv.qc.ca/ssn/letter/guidebk.htm**

WRITING YOUR FIRST LETTER

Using the Parts of the Window to Type a Letter

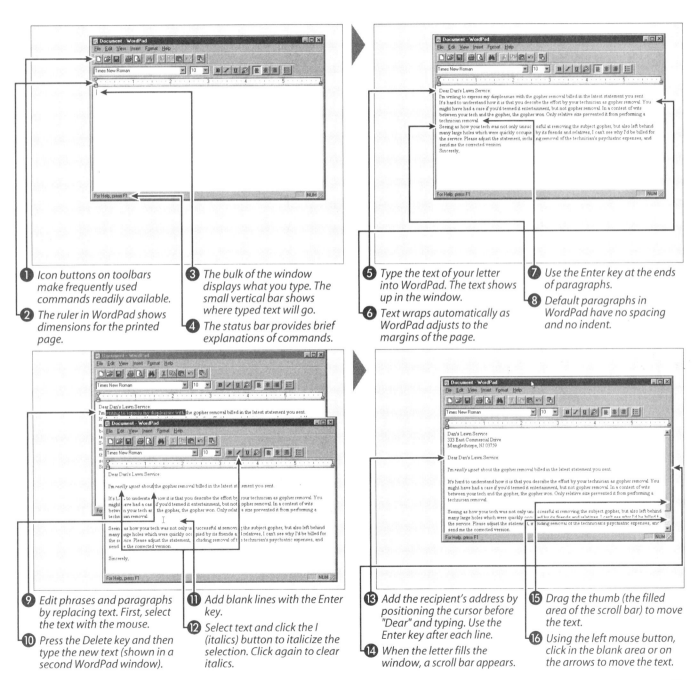

1 Icon buttons on toolbars make frequently used commands readily available.

2 The ruler in WordPad shows dimensions for the printed page.

3 The bulk of the window displays what you type. The small vertical bar shows where typed text will go.

4 The status bar provides brief explanations of commands.

5 Type the text of your letter into WordPad. The text shows up in the window.

6 Text wraps automatically as WordPad adjusts to the margins of the page.

7 Use the Enter key at the ends of paragraphs.

8 Default paragraphs in WordPad have no spacing and no indent.

9 Edit phrases and paragraphs by replacing text. First, select the text with the mouse.

10 Press the Delete key and then type the new text (shown in a second WordPad window).

11 Add blank lines with the Enter key.

12 Select text and click the I (italics) button to italicize the selection. Click again to clear italics.

13 Add the recipient's address by positioning the cursor before "Dear" and typing. Use the Enter key after each line.

14 When the letter fills the window, a scroll bar appears.

15 Drag the thumb (the filled area of the scroll bar) to move the text.

16 Using the left mouse button, click in the blank area or on the arrows to move the text.

Saving Your Work to a File

Sooner or later, you'll want to turn off your computer — or it may crash, forcing you to restart it. When you turn the computer off or have to restart, you lose everything in memory that you haven't saved to disk. Power failures and crashes are simply a fact of life with personal computers. Everyone would be happier if they didn't happen, but they do. Get used to it.

It's time to learn how to save your work. When you shut down the computer, what you save to disk stays there and can survive most crashes.

You learned in Chapter 1 that a file is a collection of information about a single thing. When you save the letter you wrote, WordPad stores all the information in a file on the disk — the text, formatting, and everything else it needs. Files have names so you can retrieve them later. Filenames in Windows 95 and 98 can be fairly long so they're descriptive of the contents, and they can contain spaces so they're easier to read. You can put almost any characters in a filename, including both upper- and lowercase letters, numbers, and many punctuation characters. You have to avoid these symbols: \ / : * ? " < > |. Windows uses these symbols for specific purposes, so they're reserved.

You tell WordPad to save your file with the Save command under the File option in the menu bar.

CROSS-REFERENCE

Lessons on how to navigate in the file system appear in Chapter 4. Look particularly at the task called "Understanding Folders."

FIND IT ONLINE

Lost files may be recoverable, even after hardware failures. Take a look at Ontrack Data International: **http://www.ontrack.com**.

Saving to a Floppy Disk

You're not restricted to saving files to your C drive. If you want, you can save to other disks inside your computer (D if you have it, for example) and to floppy disks. The disks inside your computer are much faster than a floppy, but you can hand a floppy to someone else to work with. If the work you're doing will take any time, or if you will need the document later, save to the internal disks until everything is done, and then save the final version a second time to the floppy. An easy way to redirect the save to floppy is, using the File ⇨ Save As command, prefix the filename with A:\ so that yourfile.doc becomes A:\yourfile.doc. Using this approach, you get the speed of the internal disk while you work and avoid the problem that floppy disks aren't reliable enough to be the only storage medium for important work.

The more general way to save to other drives is to use the Save In drop-down control in the Save As dialog box. If you click on the down arrow on the right side of the control, you'll see all the disks — floppy and fixed — on your computer. If you select one of them, the larger window within the dialog box will change to show the files and top-level folders on that drive. As with Windows Explorer, you can double-click on any of the folders shown to move down into the folder. Once you've positioned the dialog box to the drive and folder you want, check the filename, then click on Save to store the file.

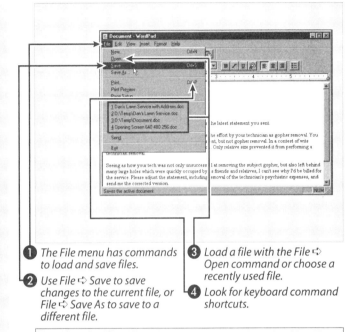

❶ The File menu has commands to load and save files.

❷ Use File ⇨ Save to save changes to the current file, or File ⇨ Save As to save to a different file.

❸ Load a file with the File ⇨ Open command or choose a recently used file.

❹ Look for keyboard command shortcuts.

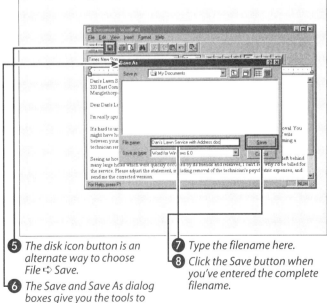

❺ The disk icon button is an alternate way to choose File ⇨ Save.

❻ The Save and Save As dialog boxes give you the tools to save files to disk.

❼ Type the filename here.

❽ Click the Save button when you've entered the complete filename.

Getting Help

Windows software of any complexity, including Windows itself, comes with the capability of giving you help on the program's operation. Most programs use the help program built into Windows to display their help information, so learning how to get help applies to all Windows programs.

The Windows help program displays help files as a reference book. You can access pages in the book through a dialog box that provides a table of contents, index, and text search. You get the dialog box in one of two ways in WordPad: by accessing the Help ⇨ Help Topics command, or by pressing the F1 key. At the top or your keyboard is a row of keys labeled F1, F2, and so on up to F12. The F1 key might also say Help on it. Those twelve keys are called the function keys because Windows and many programs assign commands to the keys and execute the command when you press the key. If you position the mouse on the empty Windows screen and press F1, you get help for Windows itself.

The dialog box you get when you press F1 has tabs along the top, making it a little different from the one for saving files. If you left-click once (also called a left mouse) on a tab, the controls in the dialog box change to reflect the function that the tab names. The Help dialog box shows tabs for Contents, Index, and Find, which let you look through the table of contents, search the index, and do a text search through the help pages. Each tab lists subjects you can look at. In the Contents, you open a closed *chapter* by double-clicking it with the left mouse button or by left mousing it and pressing the Enter key on the keyboard. When you get to individual objects, you can similarly double-click one to see the page, or select one and press Enter.

TAKE NOTE

▶ SELECT ITEMS WITH THE MOUSE AND KEYBOARD

Selecting items onscreen is a common operation in Windows. You select items with the mouse, using a single left click, and with the keyboard, using the tab key to move between parts of the dialog box. You can also use arrow keys to move from one item to the next within a part of the dialog box, and the spacebar to select or deselect the item.

▶ OPEN ITEMS WITH THE MOUSE AND KEYBOARD

You can open selected items with the mouse and keyboard too. Left double-clicks with the mouse open the item under the mouse. The Enter key opens whatever's selected, but because you don't point at something onscreen with the Enter key, be sure to select what you're interested in first.

CROSS-REFERENCE

Chapter 5 teaches you how to customize the mouse to your preference, including setting mouse speed, right- or left-handedness, and double-click speed.

FIND IT ONLINE

Vendor sites may have *knowledge bases,* such as Microsoft's at **http://www.microsoft.com/support/**.

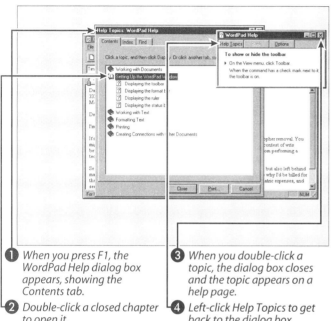

1 When you press F1, the WordPad Help dialog box appears, showing the Contents tab.

2 Double-click a closed chapter to open it.

3 When you double-click a topic, the dialog box closes and the topic appears on a help page.

4 Left-click Help Topics to get back to the dialog box.

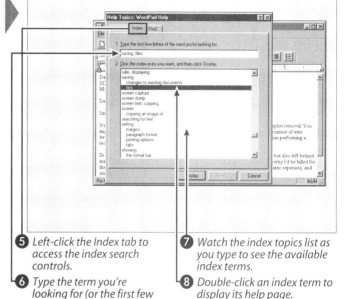

5 Left-click the Index tab to access the index search controls.

6 Type the term you're looking for (or the first few letters) here.

7 Watch the index topics list as you type to see the available index terms.

8 Double-click an index term to display its help page.

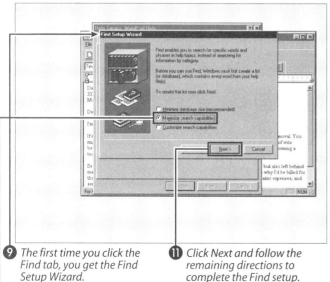

9 The first time you click the Find tab, you get the Find Setup Wizard.

10 Unless you're short on disk space, choose to maximize search capabilities.

11 Click Next and follow the remaining directions to complete the Find setup.

12 Once you get the Find dialog box, type a word. You can add more words to refine the search.

13 Topics matching your search show up in the dialog box.

14 Double-click the topic or select it and click Display to get to the help page.

Personal Workbook

Q&A

1 Name components of the WordPad window that you're likely to find in other Windows programs and state what they do.

_____

_____

_____

_____

2 Identify the toolbar icons for File ⇨ New and File ⇨ Open.

_____

_____

_____

3 Notepad is a simpler text editing program than WordPad. Where is Notepad in the Start button menu?

_____

_____

_____

4 What window elements are common in both WordPad and Notepad?

_____

_____

_____

5 Notepad has a Search menu on the menu bar. What and where are the equivalent commands in WordPad?

_____

_____

_____

6 What are the WordPad keyboard shortcuts for File ⇨ Save, File ⇨ Open, and Edit ⇨ Find?

_____

_____

_____

7 Is the Edit ⇨ Find keyboard shortcut in WordPad the same as Search ⇨ Find in Notepad?

_____

_____

_____

ANSWERS: PAGE 334

EXTRA PRACTICE

① Click with the right mouse button on the title bar of an application. What happens? How else can you get to this menu?

② Click with the right mouse button on a blank area of the taskbar. What happens? Try the different commands you find and see what they do.

③ Try the different commands in WordPad's View menu. What is the format bar? The ruler? The status bar? How does the menu indicate if the different window elements are turned on?

④ Click with the left mouse button once on the desktop and press F1 to get Windows help. Press the Esc key to close it. Use the menus through the Start button to find another path to Windows help. How do you get there?

REAL-WORLD APPLICATIONS

✔ You're a gourmet cook and want to file your recipes on your computer so you can print or search them later. You write each one to a different file, naming the file with the recipe's title.

✔ You have credit card accounts with many companies, and worry that if your cards are stolen you won't have the information you need to notify the companies. You put all the card numbers, with company contact information, into a file on your computer.

✔ You need simple signs to organize an event at your office. You type the text into WordPad, and then apply font faces and sizes until the signs look the way you want.

Visual Quiz

This is a shot of a page in WordPad Help under Windows 98. Find the equivalent page on your system, either in Windows 95 or 98.

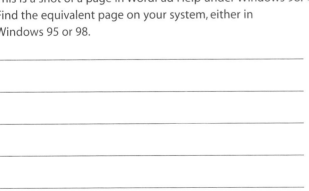

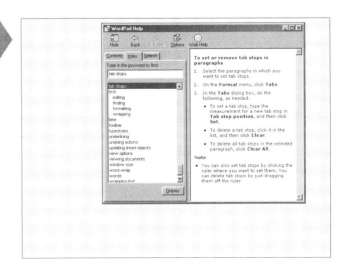

CHAPTER 3

Setting Up Your Printer

Far from eliminating paper and printing, computers have increased the volume of printing. They've changed the balance of what goes on paper, relegating many letters and mundane interoffice memos to electronic form only, but making it easier to develop, distribute, and print other material.

Twenty years ago, printers capable only of text output were large, expensive mechanical contraptions. Today, printers that give you high-resolution color graphics are commonly available for a few hundred dollars. Combined with the processing power in your computer and the relative simplicity of configuration and setup with Windows, printing has come a long way.

Most printers use one of two basic technologies. Printers based on the same technology as copiers use lasers to write images on a drum, rolling the drum against the paper to deposit dry ink called toner. Less expensive printers use microscopic squirts of ink on the paper, dispensed from a head that flies across the paper. Laser printers are more expensive to buy, but less expensive to operate, than ink-jet printers.

Color laser printers are still quite expensive, while essentially all ink-jet printers are color.

Both printing technologies work well with paper intended for copiers, which is inexpensive and widely available. Paper is available with a harder surface designed to improve image sharpness on ink-jet printers, but isn't all that effective. More expensive papers for very high-resolution ink-jet printers are worthwhile when you need them — those papers and a high-quality printer (still well under $1,000) can produce photographic-quality results.

Printers connect to a computer through something called a *port*. The port is the path through which data and control signals pass information from computer to printer and signal the computer when the printer is out of paper or otherwise needs attention. Software you install into Windows, called a printer driver, communicates between your programs and the printer.

Printer cables — running from computer to printer — shouldn't be more than 10 to 15 feet long. This length limits how far away the printer can be, which affects how you lay out your work area. Printers make a fair amount of noise, too, so take that into account when you plan.

Unpacking Your Printer

The biggest issue in unpacking a printer (unless it's one of the very large, heavy, high-capacity laser units) is making sure you find all the bits and pieces, and making sure you carefully follow the manufacturer's directions to remove all the blocks and tape used to protect the unit during shipment.

Don't take our caution about removing the blocks and tape lightly. In some cases, printers put dots on the page at 1,440,000 dots per square inch, requiring the dots to be positioned with an accuracy of eight ten-thousandths of an inch vertically and horizontally. A 1,200 dot-per-inch printer has to maintain that accuracy across the entire width and length of the page. That a mechanism costing a few hundred dollars (including the electronics) can do this reliably is nothing short of amazing. You shouldn't be surprised that the packaging is important in protecting and preserving that accuracy while the printer gets bounced around in ships, airplanes, and trucks. Manufacturers package printers to keep the panels from flying open and to keep the printing mechanism tightly aligned in a rest position. You have to free all those restraints or the printer will try to break them when you power it up.

Get a cable when you buy the printer; it's not likely to be included. Check when you buy the printer to see if it includes ink or toner cartridges; few things are more frustrating than getting back to the office or home and finding you have to make a trip back to the store for ink cartridges. You might want to keep a spare on hand, too.

TAKE NOTE

▶ LOWER PRINT COSTS WITH FOUR COLORS

The best ink-jet printers include a black ink cartridge as well as one with three colors of ink. That's important because it cuts your cost of printing. The color cartridge is useless when any one color empties, yet each color has only one third the amount of ink in a black cartridge. Overall, you get one-third to one-half of the ink in the cartridge and then have to throw it out.

▶ EXTEND TONER CARTRIDGE LIFE

The toner in a laser printer cartridge is a dry, dusty powder, not a liquid, so it can pack down on one side or in the end of the cartridge. If it does, parts of the image print with streaks or gaps — looking like you're out of toner — while other parts print well. When you start seeing streaks or gaps, take out the cartridge and rotate it briskly forward and back to redistribute the toner. You'll be sure to get the most life out of your cartridge.

CROSS-REFERENCE

Check out Chapter 19 for the lesson on "Maintaining Your Printer" to learn how to detect when you need to change printer cartridges.

FIND IT ONLINE

Hewlett-Packard recycles both ink-jet cartridges and laser printer cartridges. Visit http://www.hp.com/support/recycle.

Recycling Laser Cartridges Is Smart and Easy

Laser printer cartridges are large and almost universally recyclable. Many companies include a shipping label for used cartridges with the new one. Some companies then refill them; others recycle. Some printer manufacturers actively discourage using refilled cartridges, and we use new cartridges instead of refills to be sure we get the best print quality. No matter what happens to your used cartridge after it's empty, though, don't just throw it out — recycle it.

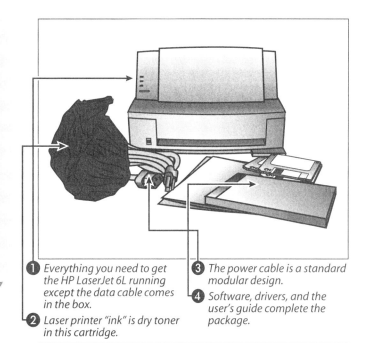

❶ Everything you need to get the HP LaserJet 6L running except the data cable comes in the box.

❷ Laser printer "ink" is dry toner in this cartridge.

❸ The power cable is a standard modular design.

❹ Software, drivers, and the user's guide complete the package.

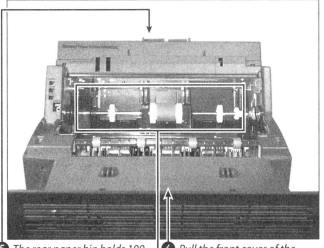

❺ The rear paper bin holds 100 sheets and provides a manual feeder for envelopes and letterhead.

❻ Pull the front cover of the printer gently toward you to reveal the mechanism.

❼ The toner cartridge fits in and covers these paper-handling rollers.

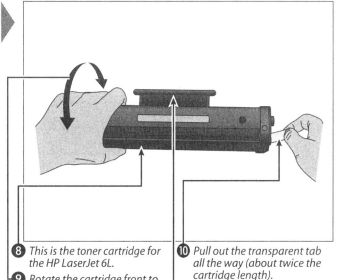

❽ This is the toner cartridge for the HP LaserJet 6L.

❾ Rotate the cartridge front to back several times to evenly distribute the toner.

❿ Pull out the transparent tab all the way (about twice the cartridge length).

⓫ Hold this handle and install the cartridge gently into the printer.

Cabling the Printer to the Computer

Connecting your computer to the printer is similar to what you did to hook up your monitor, but with a few wrinkles. The first difference is that printers have many kinds of connections, each with unique cables and connectors. The four most common connections are a *parallel* cable, a *serial* cable, a *network* cable, and an *infrared* light beam. Of those four, the parallel cable is the one you're most likely to see.

Characters stored in your computer consist of eight *bits*, each of which is a zero or a one. A parallel cable presents all eight bits to the printer at the same time, while a serial cable presents them in sequence. (Network and infrared connections send characters serially too, but require capabilities beyond those of a basic computer.)

The photos on the right show the connectors on a parallel printer cable. Printers using a serial connection use a 25- or 9-pin connector at both ends of the cable. The Centronics connector on the printer end of a parallel cable (named after the company that started using it on printers around 15 or 20 years ago) is different than the connectors anywhere else on most systems, distinguished by the shape of the connector and the clips that secure it to the printer.

CROSS-REFERENCE

See Chapter 23's "Making Simple Fixes for Printers" section for a lesson on troubleshooting printer problems.

There's a Limit to Printer Cable Lengths

You can't run a printer cable from one end of the building to the next. A parallel cable should typically be limited to about 10 to 15 feet. Some sources will tell you that well-shielded cable will extend this limit to 50 feet, but we don't recommend trying. The problem with longer cables is similar to what happens when you try to push water through a hose that's too long, which is that the extra length of the hose reduces the water pressure. If you're watering pansies, you can just stand there longer; if you're running a printer, it will start working erratically. If your printer malfunctions with a longer cable, try a cable of only 10 to 12 feet.

When you buy printer cables, get ones meeting the IEEE 1284 standard. In older printers, the signals in the printer cable going from printer to computer merely indicated if the printer was out of paper, or if it was not yet ready to accept more data. Today, using the additional signals carried in IEEE 1284–compatible cables, printers tell the computer if the heads aren't aligned, if the ink cartridge needs to be replaced, and a wealth of other status information.

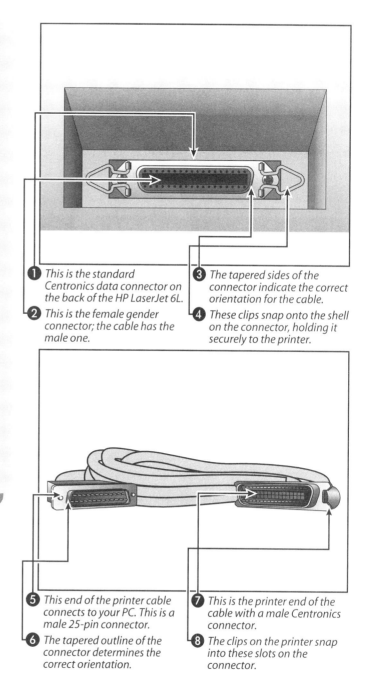

1 *This is the standard Centronics data connector on the back of the HP LaserJet 6L.*

2 *This is the female gender connector; the cable has the male one.*

3 *The tapered sides of the connector indicate the correct orientation for the cable.*

4 *These clips snap onto the shell on the connector, holding it securely to the printer.*

5 *This end of the printer cable connects to your PC. This is a male 25-pin connector.*

6 *The tapered outline of the connector determines the correct orientation.*

7 *This is the printer end of the cable with a male Centronics connector.*

8 *The clips on the printer snap into these slots on the connector.*

Installing the Printer Software

You need a special piece of software, called a *driver*, to translate the text and images in your programs to the language your printer understands. This software shows up on your computer one of two ways. First, Windows 95 and 98 are fairly good at detecting that you've installed a new printer when you power on the computer. If a driver for your printer is in the library, Windows goes ahead and installs it. Second, you should receive drivers and other software with the printer that you can install by following the manufacturer's instructions. The driver from the manufacturer often has features and capabilities not found in the driver shipped with Windows.

Even if Windows installs a driver automatically, you can choose to install the manufacturer-supplied driver. Check the instructions in the manual to see if you have to remove the Windows-supplied driver first. There's also likely to be a file called *readme* (or some variation of that) on the disk with the driver that has later information than could be printed in the manual.

Installing the manufacturer's driver is often simply a matter of finding a file called *setup.exe* on the supplied disk and running it. If the driver comes on CD-ROM, when you first insert the disk, a program is likely to start that offers you the option of installing the driver. If not, just find the setup program with Windows Explorer and run it. You have to make some choices about the install; unless you have some specific option you want to choose, the defaults offered by setup are probably fine.

TAKE NOTE

▶ FIND DRIVER UPDATES ON THE WEB

Good or bad, few things on this Earth change as fast as software. The drivers you get with Windows or with your printer are likely to be out of date by the time you get them. Newer versions bring new features, bug fixes, and (perhaps) new bugs. Don't despair that your software is old, though — go look at the manufacturer's Web site for updates. If you're running Windows 98, let Windows Update check out your system periodically, too. See Chapter 19's lesson on "Checking for Software Updates" for more details.

▶ SETUP JUST WANTS TO BE ALONE

Installing software, whether drivers or applications, can be a tricky business. A Windows program often includes many files, not just one, with some of those files shared with other programs. If a shared file or program file is in use, Windows won't let the installer replace the file (the other program using it would likely crash). Your best bet, to help installations complete successfully, is to close all programs before starting the install.

CROSS-REFERENCE

The next lesson shows you how to configure your printer's options using the driver you've installed.

FIND IT ONLINE

Look for drivers at **http://www.hp.com/cposupport/ eschome.html** and **http://www.epson.com/connects/**

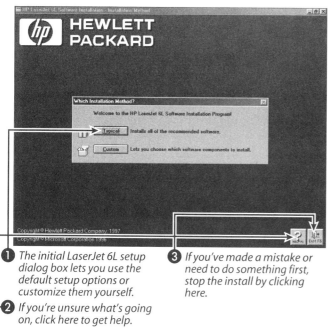

❶ The initial LaserJet 6L setup dialog box lets you use the default setup options or customize them yourself.

❷ If you're unsure what's going on, click here to get help.

❸ If you've made a mistake or need to do something first, stop the install by clicking here.

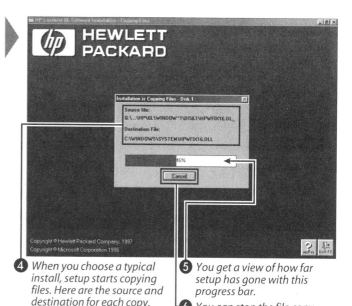

❹ When you choose a typical install, setup starts copying files. Here are the source and destination for each copy.

❺ You get a view of how far setup has gone with this progress bar.

❻ You can stop the file copy operation by clicking Cancel.

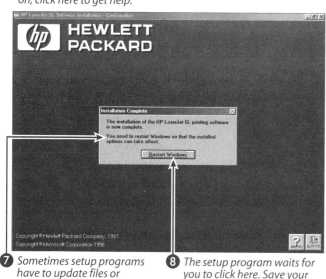

❼ Sometimes setup programs have to update files or settings belonging to Windows.

❽ The setup program waits for you to click here. Save your work first if you have programs open.

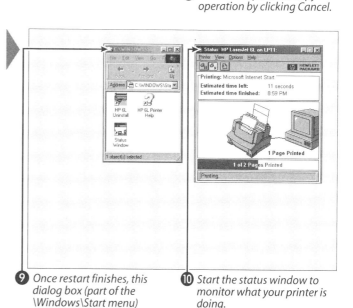

❾ Once restart finishes, this dialog box (part of the \Windows\Start menu) appears onscreen.

❿ Start the status window to monitor what your printer is doing.

Printing Your Letter

Once you've made it this far, printing itself is almost anticlimactic: open your letter in WordPad and select File ➪ Print. You can be a little more methodical, though, and step through getting the printed copy just the way you want it.

Windows lets programs output print faster than the printer itself can work. Each document you print becomes a *print job* for Windows listed in a *print queue*. You can see all the printers installed in your computer by executing Start ➪ Settings ➪ Printers. If you double-click the printer you're interested in, you open a window displaying the print queue for that printer.

Printers include setup functions that control how they operate. You get to the setup functions from the print queue window by choosing Printer ➪ Properties. You typically see tabs in the resulting dialog box, including ones that let you set the default paper size and orientation and how graphics are rendered for the printer. You get higher quality images if you choose finer graphics rendering, but on a slow or limited-memory computer, you might wait a long time for prints to happen.

Page setup options (choose File ➪ Page Setup) include which way the paper is turned — *portrait* means the long edge is vertical, while *landscape* means the long edge is horizontal. Other options include controls that let you choose the paper size (if your printer supports it) and margins. Most printers have an *unprintable area* where the print mechanism can't reach, which means you won't be able to print all the way to the edge of the paper. It's common for the minimum margin settings that keep text out of the unprintable area to be at least a quarter of an inch.

TAKE NOTE

▶ FEED LETTERHEAD PAPER AUTOMATICALLY

Printers equipped with a manual feeder have an option to select manual feed in the page setup dialog box. You probably don't need it to print the first page of a letter on your company's letterhead. Instead, just put the sheet in the manual feeder and print as usual. Many printers take the sheet from the manual feeder first and then revert to the main bin.

▶ ORIENT PAPER IN THE PRINTER

It can be confusing to remember which way to put letterhead paper in the printer. Should it go in facing up or down? Should the top go in first or last? Put the sheet in top first. Your first check for printed side up or down is to look on the printer near the feeder for a drawing; if you can't find one, take a blank sheet of paper, mark one side, and print it through the manual feeder. Check the results to see which side should be up.

CROSS-REFERENCE

If you need more control over your pages, look at "Using What You Know From WordPad" in Chapter 11.

FIND IT ONLINE

Avery Dennison Corporation makes a living from specialized papers and labels for your ink-jet and laser printer. Find them at http://www.avery.com.

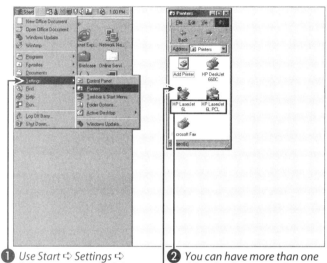

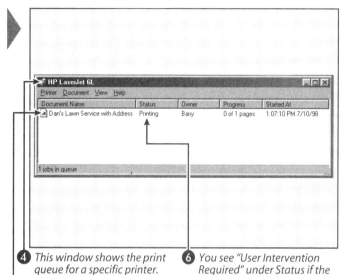

❶ Use Start ➪ Settings ➪ Printers to open the Printers folder and show the printers installed on your computer.

❷ You can have more than one driver for the same printer offering different features.

❸ In Windows 98, the black-circled check indicates your default printer.

❹ This window shows the print queue for a specific printer.

❺ WordPad (and many other programs) use the filename for the document name.

❻ You see "User Intervention Required" under Status if the printer needs help.

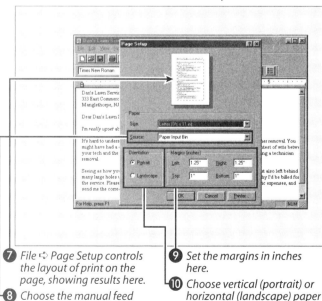

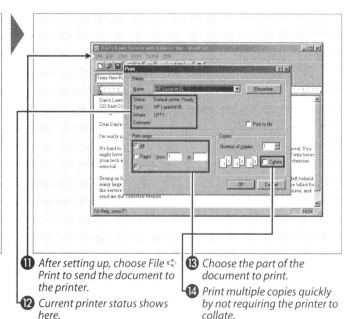

❼ File ➪ Page Setup controls the layout of print on the page, showing results here.

❽ Choose the manual feed option here.

❾ Set the margins in inches here.

❿ Choose vertical (portrait) or horizontal (landscape) paper orientation.

⓫ After setting up, choose File ➪ Print to send the document to the printer.

⓬ Current printer status shows here.

⓭ Choose the part of the document to print.

⓮ Print multiple copies quickly by not requiring the printer to collate.

Personal Workbook

Q&A

1 Name the two most common printer technologies in use today.

_____

_____

_____

2 Name the common printer connection types.

_____

_____

_____

3 How long should a parallel printer cable be?

_____

_____

4 Why are four-color ink jet printers superior to ones using only three?

_____

_____

_____

5 What should you do when a laser printer toner cartridge starts streaking or missing print?

_____

_____

_____

6 How can you recycle printer cartridges?

_____

_____

_____

7 How many pins are on a printer parallel connector (the computer end)? And on a serial connector?

_____

_____

8 What can happen if you disconnect a parallel printer with the power on?

_____

_____

_____

ANSWERS: PAGE 334

EXTRA PRACTICE

1. Search the Web for printers capable of printing large banner signs. What kinds of printers do you find?

2. Compare the manufacturer's rated speeds for ink jet and low-end laser printers. Which do you expect to be faster?

3. Measure the actual speed of your printer. Does it change based on what you print?

4. Compare the cost of printer supplies at your local stores and on the Internet.

5. Set the margins on a page to zero and try to print. What happens?

6. Print a picture using the different rendering quality options in your printer and compare results.

REAL-WORLD APPLICATIONS

✔ You research background material on the Web for a term paper you're writing, printing and filing the relevant articles to ensure you have them for later reference.

✔ You write the great American novel, print it in multiple copies, and submit it to publishers. You're surprised when they question if your name is really Tom Clancy.

✔ You write a detailed technical proposal, using the color capabilities of your printer to emphasize important points and strengthen product highlights.

✔ You order Photo CD copies of your grandchildren's photographs, printing copies on photo-quality paper.

Visual Quiz

What happened here? Where would you look if trouble occurs?

_____

_____

_____

_____

_____

_____

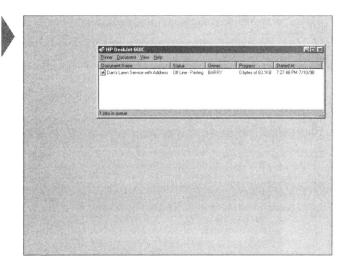

CHAPTER 4

A First Look at Disk Drives

Disk drives are where your computer stores your files, your programs, and Windows itself. Although that sounds like a simple thing, it gets complicated because the sizes and numbers involved can be large. We looked at one of the machines we've been using for a few years and found that its drive is storing over 2 billion characters (2 gigabytes, also written as 2GB) of data in nearly 30,000 files! Suppose your computer displayed its inventory of files as a single list. Even if the list were alphabetized, you'd be hard pressed to find what you want in a list of 30,000 files. At 100 names per page (two columns), you'd still be searching through 300 pages.

Fortunately, you don't really care about most of the files on your computer because they're simply part of Windows or the programs you run. On the same computer, for example, we counted 5,100 files that were part of Windows, occupying nearly half a billion bytes.

What all this means is that you need to organize your disk to separate files for one purpose from files for another, and you need powerful tools to help you see and work with what's on your disk. The lessons in this chapter give you these skills, showing you the tools Windows provides for looking at and organizing disks, and covering the concepts you need for keeping your disk orderly.

The organization necessary for storing files on disk in ways you can remember is much like organizing files in folders in a file cabinet. Some folders have to be a certain way so others will find what they expect. Of the ones that are exclusively yours, some you organize by type (all the newspaper clippings go *here*), while others you organize by subject (all the letters and invoices for Dan's Lawn Service go *there*). In your computer, some folders have to be a certain way (the folders that hold Windows, for instance). Some folders you organize by type of file (all the photos you've scanned into your computer go *here*), while others you organize by subject (all the documents and spreadsheets you've done concerning Dan's Lawn Service go *there*).

The primary tool for looking at and working with your disk is the Windows Explorer program, while the primary tools for keeping your disk organized are your own discipline and good sense.

Opening Windows Explorer

The upper-left corner of the standard Windows desktop has an icon labeled My Computer, gateway to the Windows Explorer. Double-click the icon and you see a window reminiscent of Apple Macintosh displays, a view with large icons representing accessible computer elements. Each icon for a disk drive has a letter assigned, starting with A for your floppy (and B if you have two floppies) and continuing with C and on for your hard drives. If you have more than one hard drive, or if your hard drive is organized into two or more parts, you have drives assigned D and on.

The main disk in your computer is called a hard drive to distinguish it from the floppy drive. In contrast to a floppy, a hard drive contains a rigid, nonremovable disk for recording your data.

Your computer likely has a CD-ROM, which is assigned the next letter after your last hard drive. On many computers, the one hard drive is C and the CD-ROM is D. If you double-click one of the icons, the window displays what's in the drive. You don't see 30,000 files, though, because the drive is organized with folders.

You see both folders and files in this view. Although filenames have *extensions*, they're often suppressed in Explorer unless you choose otherwise. We suggest you force filename extensions to display, as explained here, so you always know what you're dealing with. Extensions help define what kind of file you're looking at. (For instance, extensions of BAT, COM, and EXE are programs; DOC is a WordPad or Word document.) If you follow the pictures to do that, and follow the sequence below to make the two-pane version of Explorer the default, you can always have the most powerful navigation tools Windows offers right at hand.

CROSS-REFERENCE

Fix your frustration about how little you can see in Explorer at the default 640 × 480 resolution with Chapter 7's lesson "Getting More on the Screen."

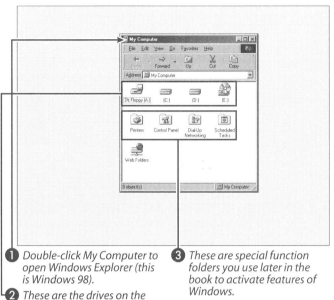

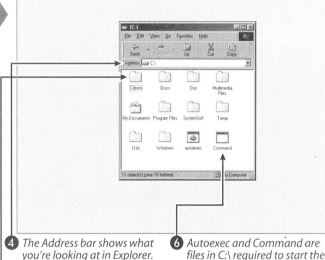

1 Double-click My Computer to open Windows Explorer (this is Windows 98).

2 These are the drives on the computer, each with a drive letter assigned.

3 These are special function folders you use later in the book to activate features of Windows.

4 The Address bar shows what you're looking at in Explorer.

5 These are folders found in C:\ on the Toshiba Equium 7000S as initially delivered.

6 Autoexec and Command are files in C:\ required to start the computer.

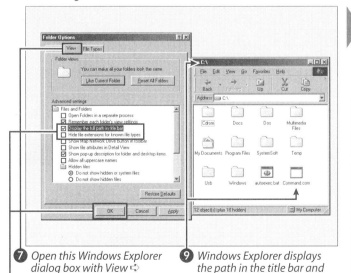

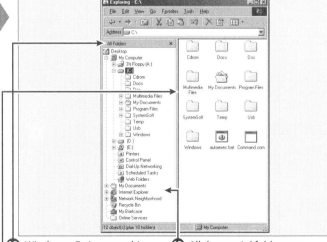

7 Open this Windows Explorer dialog box with View ⇨ Folder Options, and then select the View tab.

8 Click Display the full path in title bar.

9 Windows Explorer displays the path in the title bar and extensions in the filenames.

10 Windows+E gives you this two-pane view in Explorer.

11 When you click the C drive icon in the left pane, the right pane shows the contents of that drive.

12 All the special folders are shown in the left pane.

Getting the Details about Disks

Like any other storage space, disks require housekeeping, and to do that housekeeping you need to know what you have to work with. Windows gives you tools to get that information.

Your first tool is Windows Explorer itself in Details view (View ⇨ Details). Using the two-pane view (consider that view the default for the rest of this book, along with having the window sized so you can see the columns in Details view), if you select My Computer in the left pane, you get a summary of your disks in the right pane, including the total size of each hard disk and the remaining free space. If you select a disk or folder in the left pane, you get information on each file or folder it contains, including name, size, type, and the date it was last modified.

There's more power hidden in Explorer. In Windows 98, if you right-click a folder and choose Properties, Windows gives you a dialog box with more information about the folder. Included are the number of files (including ones in subfolders underneath this one) and the total space the files use. If you right-click on a file and choose Properties, you (at least) get a dialog box showing the filename; size; creation, modification, and last access dates; and file attributes including whether the file can be written to or is read-only. Depending on what software you've installed, some file types (documents, for instance) might include other tabs in the dialog box that show

you more detailed information about the contents of the file, such as its title, subject, author, number of pages, and more.

TAKE NOTE

► ### USE EXPLORER TO MONITOR FREE DISK SPACE

If you open the single-pane version of Explorer and set it to details view, you can collapse the column widths to just the minimum required (try a mouse double-click on the line between column headings). If you then turn off the toolbar and the status bar, you can resize the window to the minimum required to display the disk information and have a compact window that monitors remaining disk space.

► ### UNDERSTAND DISK SPACE OVERHEAD IN WINDOWS

Although the actual size of files stored on your disk can vary by as little as one character, Windows allocates file space in one or more fixed-size chunks. The extra space, beyond what your file needs to the end of the last chunk, is not used. You can see how much space that's costing you by comparing the total file size in a folder to the total size used.

CROSS-REFERENCE

In Chapter 19 you learn how to minimize the wasted space on your disks.

FIND IT ONLINE

Get powerful tools for working with disks, with Power Quest's PartitionMagic (**http://www. powerquest.com**).

A First Look at Disk Drives
Getting the Details about Disks

CHAPTER 4

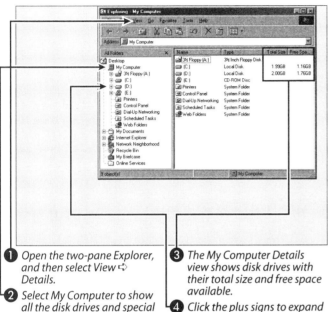

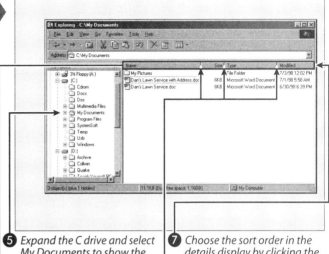

1 Open the two-pane Explorer, and then select View ⇨ Details.

2 Select My Computer to show all the disk drives and special folders.

3 The My Computer Details view shows disk drives with their total size and free space available.

4 Click the plus signs to expand the display.

5 Expand the C drive and select My Documents to show the files there.

6 For each file, Explorer displays its size, type, and date of last modification.

7 Choose the sort order in the details display by clicking the column headers.

8 Set the column widths by dragging the divider lines.

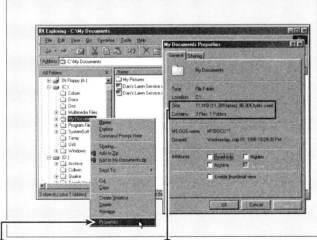

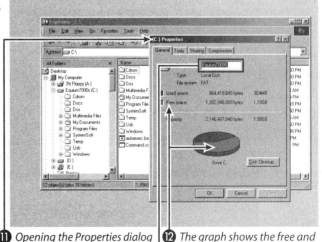

9 Right-click My Documents and then choose Properties.

10 This dialog box pops up showing the number of files and the space used by the folder and its contents.

11 Opening the Properties dialog box for a disk drive gives you this graphical display.

12 The graph shows the free and used space on the drive.

13 The label field shows the name of the disk and lets you change it.

47

Understanding Folders

Windows and your programs create folders on your disk. You need to understand the structure of the folders so you can work with them and avoid damaging structures required for programs to run correctly. Most computers have Windows installed on the C drive in a folder named *Windows*. You must not delete, rename, or move the Windows folder — doing so will likely damage Windows so badly that the computer will not start. You should be careful doing things to anything inside the Windows folder too. (Another important folder to leave alone is *Program Files.*)

Two folders exist inside Windows, however, that you should explore and work with (carefully). One is *SendTo*, and the other is *Start Menu*. If you look at those folders using Explorer as we showed you how to configure it, you see a complete *path* to those folders that looks like C:\Windows\SendTo and C:\Windows\Start Menu, respectively.

Both folders are places to put shortcuts (see "Understanding the Windows Desktop" in Chapter 1), and both are connected to features on the desktop and in Explorer. Putting shortcuts in the SendTo folder adds options to the SendTo menu you see when you right-click a file. Shortcuts in and underneath the Start Menu folder appear in corresponding places under the Start button.

You can create your own folders. The easiest way is in Explorer: right-click with the mouse inside the folder (or disk drive) that is to contain your new folder, and then choose New ⇨ Folder. Windows initially names the new folder *New Folder*; type the name you want and press Enter. But don't keep many files at the top level of the drive (C:\) — Windows can hold only so many files there, and you're likely to hit that limit well before the disk fills.

TAKE NOTE

▶ MOVING FILES AND FOLDERS

You can choose where files and folders belong after you create them. Select a file or folder, and then drag it to a new destination. If its new home is on the same drive, Windows moves it. If the new home is on another drive, Windows copies it. If you drag with the right mouse button instead of the left, Windows displays a menu of commands when you drop the file or folder.

▶ DELETING AND RECYCLING FILES

When you want to delete a file, select it in Explorer and press the Delete key. Windows asks if you want to move the file to the Recycle Bin; select Yes. Windows won't really delete the file; you can open the Recycle Bin and drag files back to the disk. Don't wait too long, because eventually files are squeezed out of the Recycle Bin by new deletions and are lost.

CROSS-REFERENCE

See Chapter 15 for how to use Internet Explorer, which alters the contents of the Favorites folder under Windows.

FIND IT ONLINE

A program called AddLink, found at **http://users.aol.com/felhasan/AddLink.zip**, makes it simple to add links to the Start Menu.

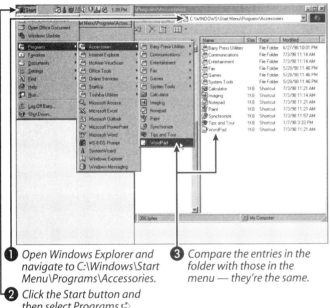

1 Open Windows Explorer and navigate to C:\Windows\Start Menu\Programs\Accessories.

2 Click the Start button and then select Programs ➪ Accessories.

3 Compare the entries in the folder with those in the menu — they're the same.

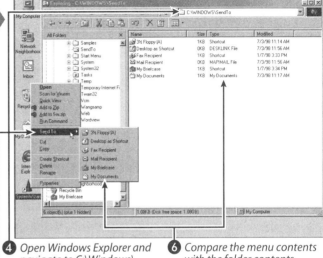

4 Open Windows Explorer and navigate to C:\Windows\ SendTo.

5 Right-click a file (here, a shortcut on the desktop) and move the mouse to SendTo.

6 Compare the menu contents with the folder contents — they're the same.

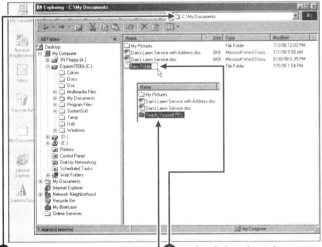

7 Navigate in Windows Explorer to C:\My Documents or C:\Windows\Temp (your choice).

8 Right-click in the right pane; choose New ➪ Folder, resulting in the new folder being shown in Explorer.

9 Type the folder name and press Enter (this is an inset).

10 Create a file in My Documents with WordPad if you haven't yet.

11 Right-click the file and drag it to another folder (here, C:\Temp).

12 Choose Cancel to abort the operation.

Organizing Your Disk for the Way You Work

In the lesson after this one, you're going to see that you can choose not only the name of a file when you save it, but also the folder you save it in. This means you need to think through how you want to organize your work.

You need a plan for creating sets of folders that let you sort files apart from each other so you can quickly find the ones you want. If you organize by type of file, you might choose to have one folder for all your documents (files created with WordPad or Microsoft Word, for instance), another for all your spreadsheets (files created with Microsoft Excel), and another for all your sound clips (files you record with the sound recorder or perhaps download from the Internet). This organization works well when files are independent of each other, because it gives you a way to discriminate among otherwise unrelated files. You could subdivide file types, making subfolders for letters, reports, and notes.

Some work you do, though, requires combining information in several files. These files might be the same or different types, and might arrive all at once or separately. If you collect all the related files into a common folder for the project, you've separated them from everything else on your computer. Within this project folder you could mix files of different types, or (if you have a lot of files in the project) create subfolders. The subfolders themselves could divide files by type or by subproject.

TAKE NOTE

▶ CONSIDER HOW YOU'LL PROTECT YOUR FILES

Don't ever forget that computers can fail and take your work with them. *Backing up* is what you do to make a copy of your work that you can reload if your computer dies and loses the contents of the disk. Backup is something you want to do regularly, but if you always back up both programs and data it's likely to take hours and hours and hours. Solve that problem by *carefully* keeping data folders separate from program folders so you can easily choose what needs to be backed up.

▶ FIX FILE LOCATIONS BY SETTING THE WORKING FOLDER

Programs that don't remember or let you tell them where to keep files usually store files in the same folder as where the program started, often the folder the program is in. Edit the properties of the shortcut you use to start the program to change the starting folder. Right-click the shortcut (probably underneath the Start Menu folder), choose Properties, and then the Shortcut tab. Edit the folder shown for *Start in*.

CROSS-REFERENCE

Look at the lesson on "Backing Up Your System" in Chapter 10 to find out how to make reloadable copies of your work.

FIND IT ONLINE

WinAmp, the program mentioned in the lower right of the next page, plays compressed music files. Find it at http://www.winamp.com.

Housekeeping After the Fact

You don't have to get your disk organization perfect from the start, nor do you have to figure out an organization that will serve you forever. Remember that you can always move things around, dragging and dropping files and folders using Windows Explorer. If a by-type folder becomes unwieldy, you can subdivide it or convert it to by-project. If new projects come in, you can create new folders for them. Your disk layout can change to meet your needs.

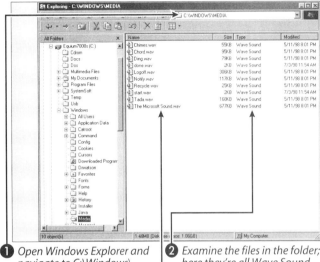

① Open Windows Explorer and navigate to C:\Windows\Media.

② Examine the files in the folder; here they're all Wave Sound files. This folder is organized by file type.

③ Double-click a file to hear the sound.

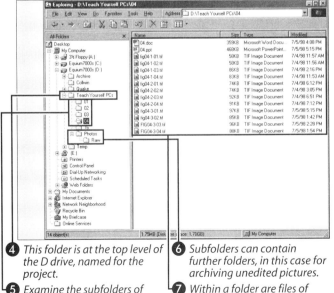

④ This folder is at the top level of the D drive, named for the project.

⑤ Examine the subfolders of D:\Teach Yourself PCs — we create one per chapter.

⑥ Subfolders can contain further folders, in this case for archiving unedited pictures.

⑦ Within a folder are files of several types specific to the chapter the folder holds.

⑧ Drag the icon for a program (here, WINAMP.EXE) to C:\Windows\Start Menu to create a shortcut under the Start button.

⑨ Type the path to a folder in the Start in field so the program uses that folder as the default.

Saving a File Where You Want It

Now that you know how to organize folders for your files so you can find things, you want to be able to save files in those folders. The File ⇨ Save and File ⇨ Save As menu commands control writing files to disk. File ⇨ Save updates the existing copy of your document on the disk, or (if you've never saved the document) switches over to File ⇨ Save As. The File ⇨ Save As command lets you give an initial name to a file or save a copy of the current version with a new name and/or somewhere other than where the file has been.

The Save As dialog box is the tool you use for both simple and complex operations saving files. Small as it seems, it has much of the power of the complete Windows Explorer in its one-pane view. Using this dialog box, you can navigate through the disk, list files in a folder matching a name pattern you choose, create folders, rename files and folders, delete files and folders, and choose the type of file you want to save.

The buttons and fields arrayed about the main area that lists folders and files give you a lot of power. Buttons on the top let you move to the folder above the one you're looking at, create a folder in the current one, and choose between icon and details view. A control on the bottom lets you pick among supported file formats. (The dialog box is common to most Windows programs; the program determines supported file formats.)

The main area in the dialog box supports many of the Explorer operations. You can drag and drop files and folders and use all the usual commands you see by clicking the right mouse button on a file or folder. These commands include opening, printing, renaming, and deleting items, plus opening the Properties dialog box.

TAKE NOTE

▶ SORT THE FILE VIEW THE WAY YOU WANT

Switching the Save As dialog box to details view adds columns in the main dialog box area for the filename, size, type, and last modification date. If you click one of the column headings, the list of files and folders gets sorted by that heading. Click again and it sorts in the reverse order.

▶ SPECIFY WHAT YOU WANT TO SEE WITH WILD CARDS

You can limit the files you see to simplify finding things in a folder full of files. Type a filename in the File name control using an asterisk (*) for any number of arbitrary characters and a question mark (?) for a single arbitrary character; then click Save. The items shown are filtered as you specify. You can have multiple wild-card file specifications separated by semicolons.

CROSS-REFERENCE

Load enough programs and save enough files, and you run out of disk space. Chapter 20's lesson "Adding a Disk" shows you what to do then.

FIND IT ONLINE

Compression programs such as WinZip (http://www.winzip.com) let you store files at reduced size yet get the full file back when you need it.

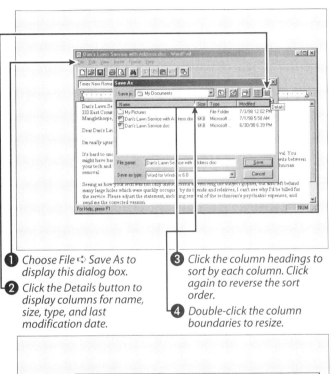

1 Choose File ➪ Save As to display this dialog box.

2 Click the Details button to display columns for name, size, type, and last modification date.

3 Click the column headings to sort by each column. Click again to reverse the sort order.

4 Double-click the column boundaries to resize.

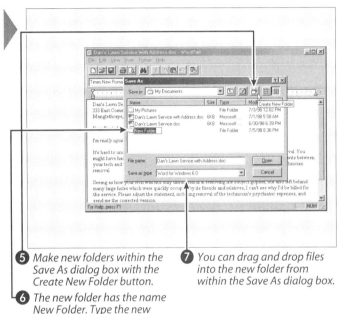

5 Make new folders within the Save As dialog box with the Create New Folder button.

6 The new folder has the name New Folder. Type the new name and press Enter.

7 You can drag and drop files into the new folder from within the Save As dialog box.

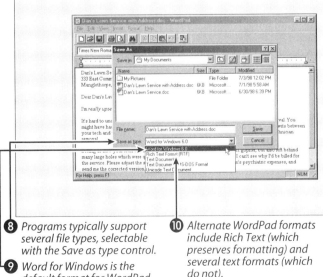

8 Programs typically support several file types, selectable with the Save as type control.

9 Word for Windows is the default format for WordPad.

10 Alternate WordPad formats include Rich Text (which preserves formatting) and several text formats (which do not).

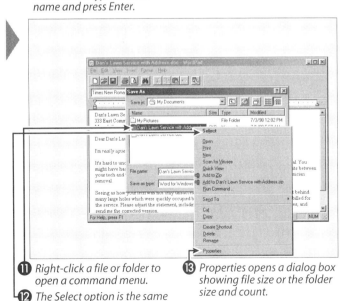

11 Right-click a file or folder to open a command menu.

12 The Select option is the same as left-clicking the file or folder directly.

13 Properties opens a dialog box showing file size or the folder size and count.

Personal Workbook

Q&A

1 What are the differences between hard and floppy disks?

_____

_____

_____

2 What kind of file should you expect to have a .doc extension?

_____

_____

_____

3 Suppose the one-pane Windows Explorer is the default when you double-click My Computer. Name two ways to start the two-pane Explorer.

_____

_____

4 How big is your Windows folder (including subfolders)?

_____

_____

_____

5 How big is the file GENERAL.TXT in the Windows folder? How much space does it really occupy?

_____

_____

_____

6 How big is the disk in your computer? Do you have more than one?

_____

_____

7 A vertical bar appears to the left of the menu bar and other bars in Windows 98. What happens if you drag the bar?

_____

_____

8 Turn off the display of file extensions in Windows Explorer (View ⇨ Folder Options ⇨ View) and look at the files in C:\Windows. How can you tell what kinds of files you're looking at?

_____

_____

ANSWERS: PAGE 335

A First Look at Disk Drives

Personal Workbook

CHAPTER

4

EXTRA PRACTICE

1. Find files with WAV or MID extensions on your computer. Double-click them. What do they contain?

2. Put a shortcut to a program into C:\Windows\Start Menu\Programs\Startup and restart your computer (Start ⇨ Shut Down ⇨ Restart). What happens? Delete the shortcut when you're done.

3. Start Windows Explorer and press F3 (or choose Tools ⇨ Find ⇨ Files or Folders). What happens?

4. Use the Find Files dialog box to find all the text files (*.txt) on the C drive. How many do you find?

5. Read the text files you just found on your C drive (double-click each one in the Find Files dialog box).

REAL-WORLD APPLICATIONS

✔ You take on a new project, requiring that you write reports, do calculations, and draw pictures as part of your work. Recognizing that you'll have several different file types in the project, you create a folder on your disk to hold the project files.

✔ You need to transfer all the data files on one computer to another. You've kept your data in folders separate from Windows and from your programs, so all you have to do is back up the data directories on one machine and restore them on the other. (And install your programs on the other computer too.)

✔ You write a series of articles for a newsletter, and need to keep the old ones around for reference. You create a subfolder for each one under a Newsletter folder, making it easy to identify the complete set of files for each article.

Visual Quiz

Find the file ARIAL.TTF on your computer. Do you get this window when you double-click the file?

_____

_____

_____

_____

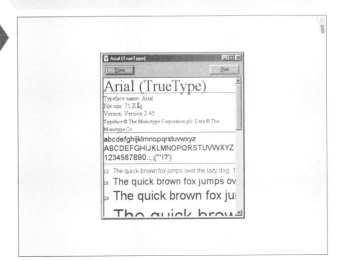

55

PART

II

Hardware the Way You Want It

Too many people focus on the *computer* part of personal computer, forgetting the *personal* even though Windows gives you the tools to customize how your computer works. The lessons in this part take you through most of these customizations, starting with setting up your mouse, joystick, and keyboard to work just the way you want.

You then move on to learning how to personalize your display, choosing colors, backgrounds, and behavior when you're not using the computer. You learn how to set the display hardware to put more on the screen and to improve the color resolution you see.

In the final chapter of this part, you learn how to hook up speakers, how to tie specific sounds to events within Windows, and how to control sound volume. You learn the different ways your computer handles music and sounds, and how to get the best sound from your hardware. By the time you're done, you'll definitely be sitting in front of *your* computer.

CHAPTER 5

MASTER
THESE
SKILLS

▶ Opening the Windows Control Panel

▶ Mouse Basics — Buttons, Wheels, and Movement

▶ Using the Right Mouse Button with Windows 98

▶ Setting Mouse Speed, Handedness, and Double-
Click Speed

▶ Choosing Your Joystick

▶ Setting Up and Calibrating Your Joystick

Mouse and Joystick

The mouse on your computer is a pointing device — a tool you use to point at things on the screen. (Few computers can detect your finger.) There are other pointing devices, including trackballs and joysticks, but all have in common the ability to move a *cursor* on the screen and to signal the computer (such as by a button push). Mice are almost universal on desktop computers and broadly applicable to most graphics-based software. Devices like joysticks move in different ways and work better for different purposes than mice, which require room to move and tend to fall off airplane tray tables.

The two most common mouse replacements are trackballs and tablets. A trackball is something like a mouse turned upside-down, so you turn the roller ball directly with your fingers. Tablets sense pressure either from your finger or a stylus. Both trackballs and tablets communicate the results to your computer much as a mouse does, and the onscreen result is the same. Both have the advantage that they stay put, not having to move around as a mouse does. Some people find it hard to be accurate with them, though, so try using them before you buy.

Joysticks are the most common game controllers besides mice, but look in stores and magazines for ones specialized for the games you play. Joysticks work very well for driving and flying games, but if you're really intense, you can get steering wheels and pedals for driving games and flight yokes for flying. The best action-game players seem to use the mouse and keyboard in combination.

You're going to have something of a problem if you're left-handed (big surprise, right?). Many of the mice, trackballs, joysticks, and other pointing devices you find are fitted for people's right hands. Most of the time, you end up using devices that are neither right- nor left-hand specific (this is particularly true for joysticks). A source of left-handed devices is The Left Hand; computer products are at **http://www. thelefthand.com/comp.htm**.

The electrical connection to your computer works one of two ways — mice connect through serial or *PS/2* ports, while joysticks connect through a *gameport*, a 15-pin female connector.

Opening the Windows Control Panel

The key to configuring most of what's in Windows itself is the Control Panel, a collection of small programs (*applets*) that each address setup of one aspect of Windows. Bring up the Control Panel via Start ⇨ Settings ⇨ Control Panel or by opening the two-pane Windows Explorer and selecting Control Panel in the left pane.

There are a lot of applets in the Control Panel, some of which have clear names and some of which do not. You can turn on the Details view to get a short description of each one (admittedly, though, it's hard to see how "Maintains 32-bit ODBC data sources and drivers" can help someone who doesn't already know what the ODBC applet is for). Three good general rules are (1) it's safe to open a Control Panel applet and look to see what's there, (2) you can do a lot of damage with some of the applets if you don't know what you're doing, and (3) it's safe to click Cancel to exit the applet.

The applets you're most likely to use are Add/Remove Programs, Date/Time, Desktop Themes, Display, Game Controllers, Internet, Keyboard, and Mouse. Of those, you need to be careful with Add/Remove Programs and Display (and possibly Internet), but you can be pretty cavalier with the rest.

Some applets deserve special caution. Being careless with Add New Hardware, Display, Network, or System can render your system inoperable, as in unable to start or to be used and possibly requiring professional help to recover. All four of them do things you may care about, so approach them with the patient, methodical care we've been recommending throughout this book.

TAKE NOTE

▶ TAKE THE FAST LANE TO THE CONTROL PANEL

Microsoft documented a trick for Windows 95 that's no longer mentioned in Windows 98 (but works). Use Explorer to create a new folder under \Windows\Start Menu and name it **Control Panel.{21EC2020-3AEA-1069-A2DD-08002B 30309D}**. If you get the name exactly right, Control Panel shows up under your Start button with all the applications visible on a foldout menu. Click one to start it.

▶ GET WINDOWS 95 PLUS! PACK FEATURES IN WINDOWS 98

The Desktop Themes control panel applet, a convenient way to set your background, icons, sounds, and other desktop characteristics, originated in Microsoft's Windows 95 Plus! Pack but is free with Windows 98. The Internet has hundreds of theme packs you can download — you're not restricted to the ones Microsoft ships. Better yet, if you create a combination you really like (or think others would like), organize all the files into a single folder and use the Save As button in the Desktop Themes applet to save the theme definition file.

CROSS-REFERENCE

Chapter 23, and particularly the lesson "Figuring Out Whom to Call for Help," is where to turn if your computer is out of commission.

FIND IT ONLINE

The mother lode for desktop themes would appear to be at **http://www.rad.kumc.edu/win95/themes.htm**.

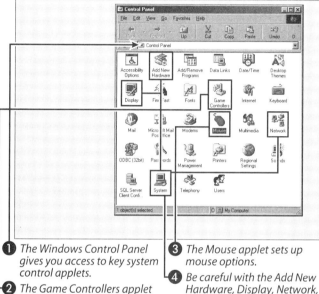

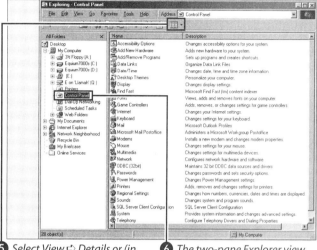

① *The Windows Control Panel gives you access to key system control applets.*

② *The Game Controllers applet installs, calibrates, and tests joysticks.*

③ *The Mouse applet sets up mouse options.*

④ *Be careful with the Add New Hardware, Display, Network, and System applets.*

⑤ *Select View ⇨ Details or (in Windows 98) use this icon to get more information on the applets.*

⑥ *The two-pane Explorer view lets you access special folders like Control Panel and Printers directly.*

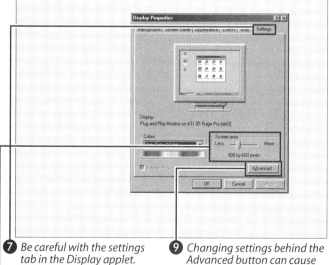

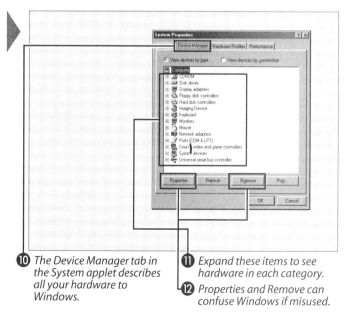

⑦ *Be careful with the settings tab in the Display applet.*

⑧ *Using too high a resolution can exceed the capabilities of your monitor, making the screen unreadable.*

⑨ *Changing settings behind the Advanced button can cause Windows to load the wrong hardware drivers.*

⑩ *The Device Manager tab in the System applet describes all your hardware to Windows.*

⑪ *Expand these items to see hardware in each category.*

⑫ *Properties and Remove can confuse Windows if misused.*

Mouse Basics — Buttons, Wheels, and Movement

A computer mouse fits in your hand much like a bar of soap, with the body of the mouse filling your palm and supporting your three middle fingers. Your thumb and little finger rest on the desk on each side of the mouse. The wire on the mouse goes out the top (away from you), placing the buttons on the mouse under the ends of your fingers. The body may be straight and symmetrical, making the mouse suitable for left- or right-handed operation, or it may be curved.

The bottom of a mouse has smooth plastic pads or strips that let it slide smoothly on a desk or mouse pad. A ball sticks out of the bottom and rotates against the desk when you move the mouse. Smooth, accurate mouse operation requires that the mouse track the surface it's on without slipping, and that no dirt inside the mouse interferes with free rotation. Most people use a mouse pad to provide a good surface and improve operation. Pretty photographs or drawings notwithstanding, the mouse pad we like best by far is the 3M Precision Mousing Surface. We get better mouse control and (for some reason) less dirt in the mouse. A rubber surface on the back of the mouse pad helps keep it in one place on the desk, too.

Recent generations of mice include a wheel, which Microsoft programmed into Office 97 and Windows 98 to support scrolling. The wheeled Microsoft mouse has two buttons alongside the wheel. Other manufacturers' mice have two or three buttons plus (maybe) the wheel. Unless you've reversed buttons for left-handed use, the left button is the primary one, while the right accesses auxiliary functions. The wheel can be used on some mice as a third button.

TAKE NOTE

CHAIN ADAPTERS TO MAKE THE MOUSE CONNECTION

Most computers now being made use the small six-pin PS/2 mouse connector, so most mice do too. If you happen to need a mouse for an older computer, or for a newer one using a serial port, you need adapters from one connector type to the other. If you need to convert from PS/2 to 25-pin serial, you probably need two adapters strung together — one from PS/2 to 9-pin serial, and one from 9-pin serial to 25-pin.

BEWARE OF MOUSE-COMPATIBILITY ISSUES

PS/2 mice work fine with adapters to connect to standard serial ports, but you can't count on things working the other way. Small differences between the messages a PS/2 mouse sends over its wire and what a serial mouse sends mean that a serial mouse adapted to a PS/2 mouse port might not work.

CROSS-REFERENCE

Now and then, mouse manufacturers update their software to add new competitive features. See the "Checking for Software Updates" lesson in Chapter 19.

FIND IT ONLINE

One of the most useful Web sources we've found for cables and adapters is Cables N Mor at **http://www. cablesnmor.com**.

Keep a Clean Mouse

No matter how careful you are, dirt is going to accumulate inside the mouse as the roller picks up dust rolling along. When dirt sticks to the ball or builds up on the internal rollers, the onscreen cursor moves erratically. Common effects include jumping along or refusing to move further in one direction. If that happens, open the cover panel, take out the ball, and blow everything clean. If that's not enough, wipe the rollers and ball to remove tougher problems.

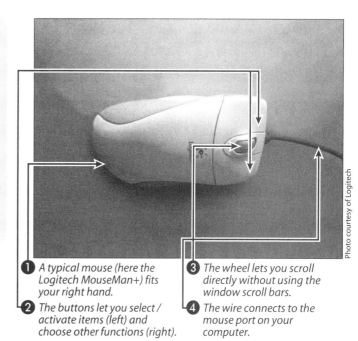

Photo courtesy of Logitech

❶ *A typical mouse (here the Logitech MouseMan+) fits your right hand.*

❷ *The buttons let you select / activate items (left) and choose other functions (right).*

❸ *The wheel lets you scroll directly without using the window scroll bars.*

❹ *The wire connects to the mouse port on your computer.*

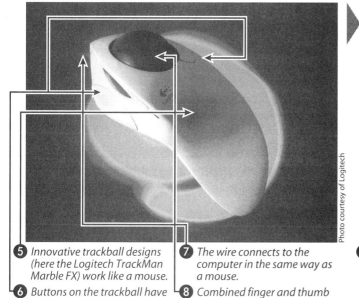

Photo courtesy of Logitech

❺ *Innovative trackball designs (here the Logitech TrackMan Marble FX) work like a mouse.*

❻ *Buttons on the trackball have the same function as on a mouse.*

❼ *The wire connects to the computer in the same way as a mouse.*

❽ *Combined finger and thumb control of the ball improves accuracy.*

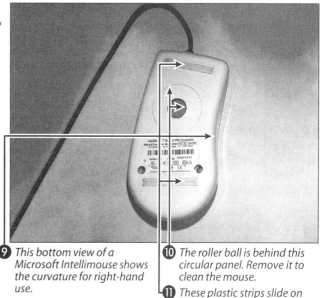

❾ *This bottom view of a Microsoft Intellimouse shows the curvature for right-hand use.*

❿ *The roller ball is behind this circular panel. Remove it to clean the mouse.*

⓫ *These plastic strips slide on your desk, but can gather dirt.*

Setting Mouse Speed, Handedness, and Double-Click Speed

The mouse control panel applet gives you a lot of control over the operation of the mouse. It's the central point for mouse configuration, including how fast the mouse cursor moves, which hand you hold it in (and therefore which button has which function), how quickly you execute double-click pushes on the button, and more.

Start the mouse control panel applet from the open Control Panel, or with Start ⇨ Control Panel ⇨ Mouse if you followed the instructions in the last lesson to add Control Panel to your Start Menu folder.

You're likely to have more functions in the mouse control panel than shown in this lesson if you've installed an upgraded mouse. Added capabilities in the Logitech mouse software include the ability to assign functions such as double-click, close program, or key presses to each button, to report the functions assigned to each button, and to orient how you hold the mouse. The mouse orientation is really intended for portable trackballs used with laptop computers, but you could use it to switch the mouse around so the cord points down and not up.

The ability to leave mouse trails is valuable on laptop computers, where the cursor can be hard to see, but can be used on any computer. Turning it on causes the last several positions of the mouse cursor to remain visible while you're moving the mouse, leaving more points on the screen for a longer period of time. Collectively, the images in the trail are far easier to see and speed recognition.

TAKE NOTE

▶ USE EXTRA MOUSE BUTTONS FOR COMMON OPERATIONS

A third or fourth mouse button (excluding the wheel) is essentially never used by Windows programs, although Windows does let the program know when the button is pushed. Most manufacturers of three- and four-button mice therefore allow you to assign special functions to the button. It's common, for instance, to set the middle button to execute a left button double-click.

▶ ROLL THE MOUSE WHEEL AS WELL AS DRAG IT

More than 20 years after the invention of the mouse (by Douglas Englebart at the Stanford Research Institute), the mouse wheel appeared. Most people use a wheel as a third button, panning windows by dragging the button. It's a little awkward to roll the button but not to press it; if you do, you can scroll up or down, and in some cases you can hold the Shift or Control key and zoom in and out by rolling the wheel. Try Ctrl+wheel in WordPad — it zooms in and out on the text.

CROSS-REFERENCE

See the "Starting and Stopping WordPad" and "Using the Parts of the Window to Type a Letter" lessons in Chapter

FIND IT ONLINE

Microsoft's Tweak UI at **http://www.microsoft.com/windows/downloads/contents/PowerToys/W95TweakUI**

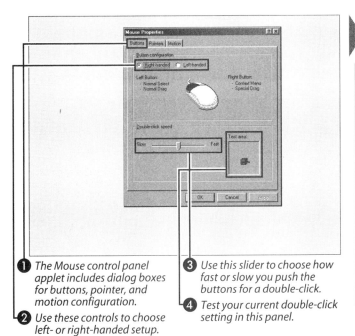

1 *The Mouse control panel applet includes dialog boxes for buttons, pointer, and motion configuration.*

2 *Use these controls to choose left- or right-handed setup.*

3 *Use this slider to choose how fast or slow you push the buttons for a double-click.*

4 *Test your current double-click setting in this panel.*

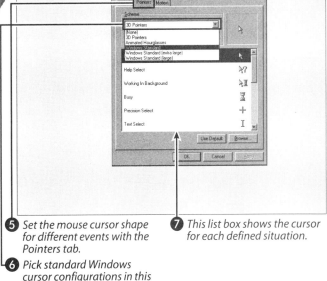

5 *Set the mouse cursor shape for different events with the Pointers tab.*

6 *Pick standard Windows cursor configurations in this control.*

7 *This list box shows the cursor for each defined situation.*

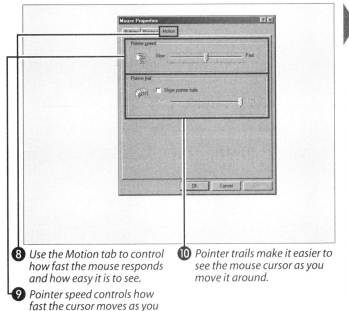

8 *Use the Motion tab to control how fast the mouse responds and how easy it is to see.*

9 *Pointer speed controls how fast the cursor moves as you move the mouse on your desk.*

10 *Pointer trails make it easier to see the mouse cursor as you move it around.*

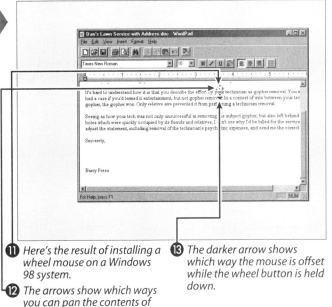

11 *Here's the result of installing a wheel mouse on a Windows 98 system.*

12 *The arrows show which ways you can pan the contents of the Window.*

13 *The darker arrow shows which way the mouse is offset while the wheel button is held down.*

Using the Right Mouse Button with Windows 98

Pre–Windows 95 versions of Windows essentially ignored the right mouse button, but Windows 95 introduced new functions for the right button, attaching small, but useful, pop-up menus to many items on the desktop. Windows 98 carries this convention further, as do current versions of application software that follow the Windows pattern.

The pop-up menu displayed by a right-click depends on what the mouse cursor is pointing to. On the Windows desktop, for instance, you get a different popup if you point at the background area than if you point at one of the icons. Special Windows icons give different results. For instance, the choices for My Computer, Network Neighborhood, and Recycle Bin are similar to each other, but different than the ones for shortcuts to programs you might find on the desktop. Each program determines what its right-mouse menus look like. For instance, the Internet Explorer icon on the desktop has a different list than the other icons do.

The menu choices available on the desktop operate similarly in Windows Explorer.

You can add items to the right-mouse menu and change the default (double-click) action. You did this in Chapter 4 when you changed the Windows Explorer default on My Computer to the two-pane view. The actions in the right-mouse menu are tied to the file type (that is, the DOC, EXE, and other extensions at the end of the filename). Select View ➪ Folder Options in Windows Explorer and choose the File Types tab to start looking at what's there. Be careful about changing existing settings.

TAKE NOTE

▶ ADDING "COMMAND PROMPT HERE" TO THE RIGHT-MOUSE MENU

If you're a computer user more comfortable with DOS than Windows, you might want a quick way to open a DOS window active in a specific folder. In Windows Explorer, go to View ➪ Folder Options ➪ File Types, select Folder in the list box, and click Edit. Click New, type **Command Prompt Here** for the action, and **COMMAND.COM** for the application. (Some systems require **C:\COMMAND.COM**.) Click OK, Close, Close, and then right-click a folder to use your new command.

▶ CLICK EVERYWHERE

You find surprising things by double-clicking the left mouse button or single-clicking the right mouse button in different places. A right mouse click in most any place you can type text (WordPad, for instance) gives you a menu with the choices Cut, Copy, Paste, Font, Bullet Style, Paragraph, and others. Right-click in Notepad gives you a menu with Undo, Cut, Copy, Paste, Delete, and Select All.

CROSS-REFERENCE

Microsoft Word 97 is particularly rich in right-mouse functionality. See Chapter 11 for more details.

FIND IT ONLINE

RightOn, at **http://www.halcyon.com/sjm/ righton.html**, lets you set up your right or middle

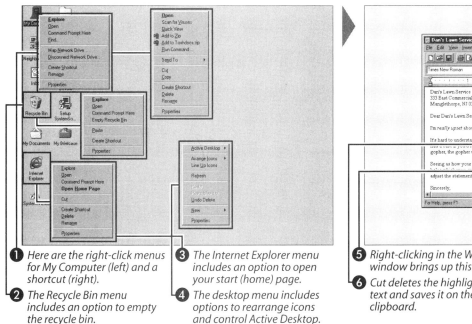

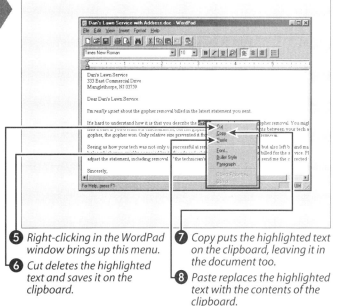

1 *Here are the right-click menus for My Computer (left) and a shortcut (right).*

2 *The Recycle Bin menu includes an option to empty the recycle bin.*

3 *The Internet Explorer menu includes an option to open your start (home) page.*

4 *The desktop menu includes options to rearrange icons and control Active Desktop.*

5 *Right-clicking in the WordPad window brings up this menu.*

6 *Cut deletes the highlighted text and saves it on the clipboard.*

7 *Copy puts the highlighted text on the clipboard, leaving it in the document too.*

8 *Paste replaces the highlighted text with the contents of the clipboard.*

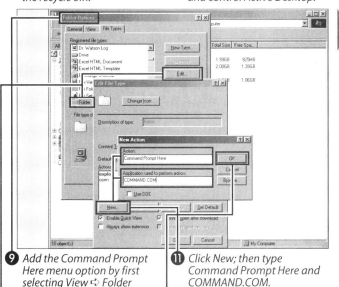

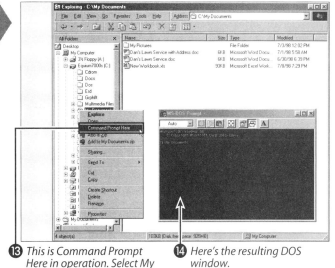

9 *Add the Command Prompt Here menu option by first selecting View ⇨ Folder Options in Windows Explorer.*

10 *Choose Folder; then click Edit.*

11 *Click New; then type Command Prompt Here and COMMAND.COM.*

12 *Click OK, Close, and Close and you're done.*

13 *This is Command Prompt Here in operation. Select My Documents and then right-click with the mouse.*

14 *Here's the resulting DOS window.*

Choosing Your Joystick

A fast PC is a wonderful games platform, equal to or better than the best dedicated game consoles in many ways (not the least of which is the amount of memory and disk storage a PC has). If you're the least bit serious about playing games on your PC, you'll eventually decide that the keyboard or mouse may not be the ideal controllers for many games.

Games that play in real time are the ones that benefit from specialized controllers because they give you finer, faster control. Real-time games include ones where you are flying, driving, shooting, and fighting. Not surprisingly, controllers are specially designed for each of these game types. Joysticks are best for flying, wheels (and pedals) for driving, and game pads for fighting. Top players use a variety of controls for action/shooter games. Many of the best use the mouse and keyboard in combination; others use controls that let them maneuver and turn easily.

Recent joysticks include force feedback that uses motors in the base of the joystick to move against your hand and simulate resistance or response from the game. The first wave of force-feedback products has been actual joysticks, but because most specialized controllers look like joysticks to the computer, the technology has begun migrating to wheels. There may eventually be force-feedback game pads as well.

Games commonly require sequences of commands, done as control inputs, to execute advanced moves. Examples include rocket jumping in Quake (a shooter) and more powerful attacks in Mortal Kombat (a fighting game). Controllers that let you attach commands to specific buttons, to carry out the sequence automatically, can make game play easier and more enjoyable.

TAKE NOTE

▶ WHEN IN DOUBT, GO DIGITAL

The newest joysticks use digital technology instead of the older analog system to communicate from stick to computer. A digital interface is not only more accurate, it's faster, so play should be smoother and more responsive. The digital interface also makes more buttons possible on the stick, giving you options like throttles.

▶ STICK WITH YOUR STICK

Don't make the mistake of thinking your scores will go up immediately when you plug in a new game controller. Good scores in fast games rely on reflex and muscle memory, which take time to develop. A controller well suited to a game can make those moves more intuitive and easier to learn, but learn them you must. Until you become adept, your scores could actually be worse. Give the controller enough time before you decide how you like it. For example, people have been known to play Quake with the Spacetec Spaceorb 360 for weeks before deciding it really did improve their game.

CROSS-REFERENCE
See Chapter 21, "Setting Up a Network," to learn how to build a network for local multiplayer gaming.

FIND IT ONLINE
Use the keywords *game hardware* on Pricewatch (**http://www.pricewatec.com**) for a list of most game controller products.

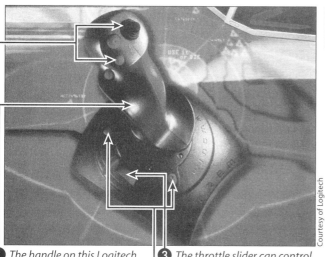

Courtesy of Logitech

1 The handle on this Logitech Wingman Extreme Digital joystick fits your right hand.

2 In addition to fire buttons on the stick, the hat switch gives you point-of-view control

3 The throttle slider can control car or plane engines.

4 You can never have enough buttons, so here are two more.

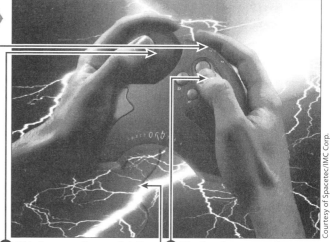

Courtesy of Spacetec/IMC Corp.

5 This Spacetec Spaceorb 360 has a moving ball that both rotates and slides in three directions.

6 Two buttons on top are your primary and secondary fire

7 The four buttons under your thumb let you command auxiliary functions.

8 This cable runs to a serial port on your computer.

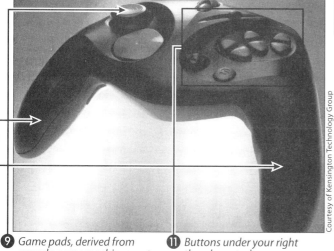

Courtesy of Kensington Technology Group

9 Game pads, derived from console game machines, put a directional control under your left thumb.

10 Hold the game pad with these handles.

11 Buttons under your right thumb control game functions.

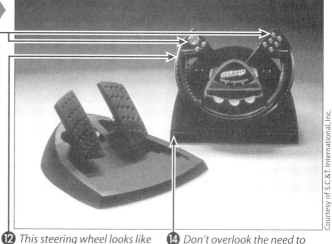

Courtesy of S.C.&T. International, Inc.

12 This steering wheel looks like a joystick to your computer.

13 Buttons and sliders on the wheel keep your hands in place while you accelerate, brake, and shift.

14 Don't overlook the need to clamp the wheel to your desk.

Setting Up and Calibrating Your Joystick

Joysticks connected to the gameport don't support Windows Plug and Play (ones on the serial port might), so you usually have to manually install the software. Windows 95 has a Joystick control panel applet, and Windows 98 recognizes the wide variety of products available in the market by providing much improved support in the Game Controllers applet.

You use the Game Controllers applet to add the controller, pointing it at the manufacturer's disk if necessary. Once the controller shows up in the list, the Properties button takes you to a dialog box that lets you calibrate and test the unit. Calibration is required for analog joysticks because it's not possible to make all of them exactly the same at a reasonable cost. Some digital sticks retain the calibration process (such as the Logitech Wingman Extreme Digital), while others do not (such as the Microsoft SideWinder 3D Pro).

You're only half done when you've completed the Windows setup for your joystick — each game has its own functions you can attach to buttons and sliders. You set up those *mappings* in the game. The more complex the game, the more important it is to set up the buttons carefully. Activision's MechWarrior 2 has 31 functions you can choose from. If you're really industrious, you might create different mappings for different parts of the game, saving each as a different custom configuration. This can be a difficult process when you're new to the game because you won't know which commands are the most important for how you play. Check the joystick or game manufacturers' Web sites (and the help file!) for suggestions.

TAKE NOTE

▶ **THERE CAN BE ONLY ONE**

Don't be misled by the fact that Windows lets you install support for many joysticks, or by the fact that you can buy Y-cables that let you connect two joysticks to the same port. Only the very simplest joysticks (one- or two-button analog units) work with a Y-cable. You can only use the multiple configurations in Windows if you have several gameports or if you unplug one stick and plug in another.

▶ **USING A HEAVYWEIGHT JOYSTICK**

You'll quickly realize when you calibrate a joystick that it's really important for the stick to be heavy — not just solid, but heavy with a good surface on the base that keeps it from sliding around. Anything less and you need your other hand to hold the stick in place. That puts you at a distinct disadvantage, because you can't use that hand with the keyboard, and can't use all those keys on the keyboard for operations in the game.

CROSS-REFERENCE

See "Figuring Out Whom to Call for Help" in Chapter 23 if you have trouble making your joystick work.

FIND IT ONLINE

Find joystick troubleshooting hints from Microsoft at **http://search.microsoft.com/default.asp**; search for *joystick troubleshooter* using *All Words* as the criteria.

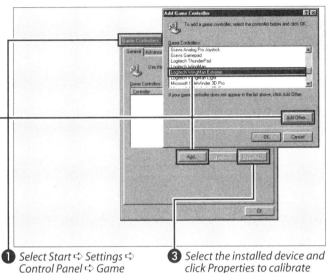

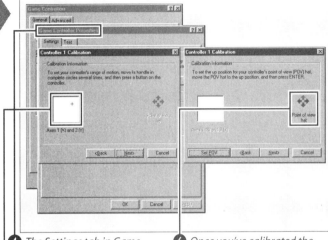

❶ *Select Start ⇨ Settings ⇨ Control Panel ⇨ Game Controllers to begin installing a new controller.*

❷ *Click Add; then choose your controller from the list.*

❸ *Select the installed device and click Properties to calibrate and test.*

❹ *The Settings tab in Game Controller Properties lets you calibrate the stick.*

❺ *You move the stick through its full range of motion in this dialog box.*

❻ *Once you've calibrated the stick, this dialog box lets you set the directions for the hat on top of the stick.*

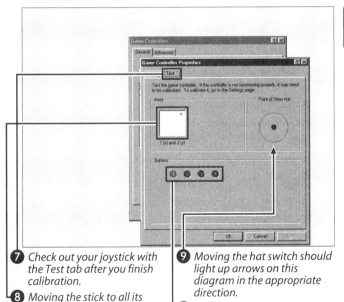

❼ *Check out your joystick with the Test tab after you finish calibration.*

❽ *Moving the stick to all its extremes should move the cross to the corners.*

❾ *Moving the hat switch should light up arrows on this diagram in the appropriate direction.*

❿ *Pushing each button should light up these dots.*

⓫ *Options ⇨ Control Configurations gets you this setup screen in MechWarrior 2.*

⓬ *Select the joystick for configuration.*

⓭ *Select the game function to map to the joystick.*

⓮ *Select the joystick element to control the game function.*

Personal Workbook

Q&A

1 Name two ports that are used to connect mice to your computer.

_____

_____

_____

2 Name the potentially dangerous Control Panel applets.

_____

_____

3 What's the most common mouse connector style in computers now being made?

_____

_____

4 Under Windows 98, Internet Explorer and WordPad are different in how they respond to the mouse-wheel scrolling operation. What's the difference, and how can you tell?

_____

_____

_____

5 There's a key on a Windows keyboard that looks like a menu with a mouse cursor on it. What happens when you push it? What's it equivalent to?

_____

_____

_____

6 What's the most common use for the mouse wheel?

_____

_____

_____

7 What commonly happens when you push Ctrl or Shift and roll the mouse wheel?

_____

_____

8 What are the common problems caused by dirt in the mouse?

_____

_____

_____

ANSWERS: PAGE 336

EXTRA PRACTICE

1. The distance you move the mouse from the initial point after you hold down the mouse wheel determines how fast the window scrolls. Experiment to see how sensitive it is.

2. Open the cover on the bottom of your mouse and look inside. Clean it if it's dirty.

3. Turn on mouse trails and move the mouse around.

4. Experiment with different surfaces under your mouse. Which ones slip on the desk? Which ones work the best?

5. Visit a nearby computer store and compare weight and features of different game controllers. Which would work well for what types of games?

REAL-WORLD APPLICATIONS

✔ Perhaps you decide that the no-frills mouse that came with your computer lacks the features you want, and you buy a replacement mouse as an upgrade. You check the connectors on your system first to be sure you get the right version.

✔ You might be exploring for mouse-sensitive places in Windows, and happen to leave the mouse sitting over a toolbar button. You notice that a small text window pops up describing the function of the button.

✔ You regularly play NASCAR Racing in a competitive league. It might help to invest in a steering wheel game controller and discover your performance goes up tremendously.

Visual Quiz

How can you use the mouse to select multiple items on the desktop, as shown here?

_____

_____

_____

_____

_____

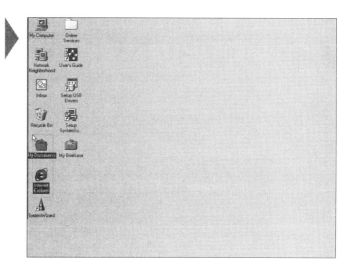

CHAPTER 6

MASTER
THESE
SKILLS

▶ Setting Repeat Delay and Rate

▶ Coordinating the Keyboard with the Mouse

▶ Using the Windows Keys

▶ Choosing Languages and the Dvorak Keyboard
Layout

▶ Enabling Accessibility

Keyboard

Today's computer keyboards are the direct descendents of those on electric typewriters and owe much of their layout to manual typewriters. The standard manual typewriter keyboard had the Sholes (QWERTY) layout, preserved in hundreds of millions of computer keyboards today. Electric typewriters introduced automatic repeat keys, a feature now present on all keys on your computer keyboard.

We're not saying keyboard design has been stagnant. Computer keyboard designers have added function keys that trigger specific program operations, a keypad like that on a ten-key adding machine, cursor control keys, additional Shift keys, and more. In response to increasing keyboard usage and concerns about repetitive stress injuries, designers split the two halves of the keyboard and angled the surface to help keep wrists straight. Considering the amount of use (and abuse) keyboards get, they're remarkably reliable. Switches absorb continuous impact, and the housing resists dust and spills.

Designers have created a seemingly unlimited range of improvements to keyboards. You can get big keyboards designed for children or keyboards with speakers, calculators, scanners, and mouse touchpads built in. You can get wireless keyboards and ones designed for people with impaired mobility. You can get keyboards with a soft feel and ones with a tight, clicky feel.

Windows includes options to customize your keyboard setup and increase your productivity. You can control the repeat action, set up support for several languages, and choose alternate keyboard layouts (including the Dvorak layout). Enhancements included with keyboards such as the Microsoft Natural Keyboard let you access Windows functions with a few keystrokes. Other keyboard software tools let you reprogram troublesome keys, such as disabling the Windows keys in DOS applications or converting the Caps Lock key to a simple caps Shift key.

Windows controls can also help provide computer access to people who cannot work with keyboards in conventional ways, offering options to remember Shift keys while you press characters, to filter out short accidental key presses, and to disable repeat keys. Windows can also simulate mouse movement with the keypad.

Setting Repeat Delay and Rate

The most basic changes you might make to your keyboard configuration are setting the repeat delay and rate. *Repeat delay* adjusts how long you have to hold a key down before the character starts to repeat. *Repeat rate* adjusts how fast repeated characters occur once the first one comes. Your preferences depend a lot on how you use repeat. If you never use it except to add line breaks as repeated underscores, you want a reasonably long delay (because you infrequently need repeats) and fast repeat rate (so you can get tens of underscores quickly). If you use repeat with the arrow keys to move the text insertion point around in a word processor or the selected cell in a spreadsheet, you want a short delay and relatively slow repeat rate.

As with the mouse in the prior chapter, the Windows Control Panel is the key to customizing your keyboard. Use the command sequence Start ⇨ Settings ⇨ Control Panel ⇨ Keyboard.

Exactly what you get in the keyboard applet depends on what you've installed in your computer. The standard Windows 98 keyboard applet lets you control repeat delay and rate, insertion point cursor blink rate, and installed language. The tools included with the Microsoft IntelliType software (with the Microsoft Natural Keyboard) add the capabilities discussed later in the chapter to coordinate with the mouse, add sounds, and provide other features.

The controls on the Speed tab are primarily sliders you can drag with your mouse or select and move with the keyboard. Move the slider to the left to lengthen the delay or slow the repeat; move it to the right to shorten delay or hasten the repeat.

TAKE NOTE

▶ USE THE CONFIGURATION YOU LIKE

Don't fall into the trap of thinking that advanced computer users have to work as fast as possible. Being skilled with a computer — a *power user* — is a matter of knowing what needs to be done and an effective way to do it, not of flipping through commands at high speed. For example, no one we know sets all the keyboard settings as fast as possible. Ours are at the shortest repeat delay, but at a middle repeat rate and two-thirds to the right on the cursor blink rate.

▶ TRY BEFORE YOU BUY

The repeat delay and rate dialog box lets you test the behavior of settings you make without having to exit from the dialog box. Use the test area in the middle of the dialog box to see if you've adjusted the keyboard in a way you like. Don't just hold down a repeat key; do a mix of repeat and nonrepeat typing. It's okay to fill the control — the text just slides to the left.

CROSS-REFERENCE

"Setting Mouse Speed, Handedness, and Double-Click Speed" in Chapter 5 shows you corresponding options

FIND IT ONLINE

Search the Microsoft Web site (http://www.microsoft.com/windows/downloads) for the Kernel Toys Keyboard

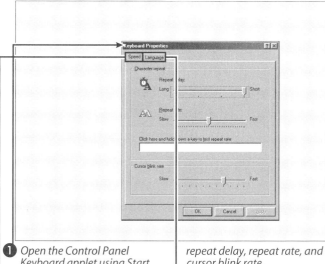

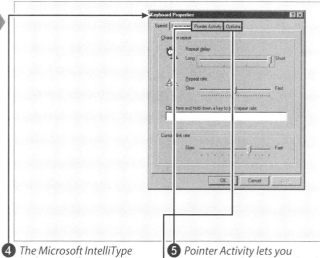

1 Open the Control Panel Keyboard applet using Start ➪ Settings ➪ Control Panel ➪ Keyboard.

2 Use the Speed tab on the dialog box to adjust keyboard

repeat delay, repeat rate, and cursor blink rate.

3 The Language tab lets you configure for other languages and layouts.

4 The Microsoft IntelliType keyboard software adds options to the Control Panel Keyboard applet.

5 Pointer Activity lets you coordinate the keyboard with the mouse.

6 The Options tab lets you control how the keyboard starts when you boot.

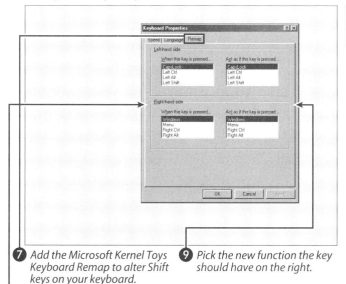

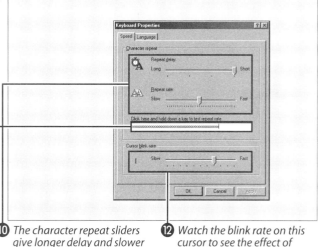

7 Add the Microsoft Kernel Toys Keyboard Remap to alter Shift keys on your keyboard.

8 Select the key you'll press on the left of the dialog box.

9 Pick the new function the key should have on the right.

10 The character repeat sliders give longer delay and slower rate toward the left.

11 Test key repeat by typing into this area, mixing normal and repeat typing.

12 Watch the blink rate on this cursor to see the effect of moving the blink rate slider.

Coordinating the Keyboard with the Mouse

It's surprising how many people use the keyboard or the mouse, but not the two at the same time. It might be that the coordination is unusual, or it might be that people just don't think of the two at the same time. Whatever the reason, people who don't coordinate the mouse and keyboard don't get all the power Windows has to offer.

The Control Panel is once again a focus for some of this coordination. Install the IntelliType software Microsoft ships with the Natural Keyboard (or the equivalent from other keyboard vendors) and you get additions to the standard Windows Control Panel Keyboard applet. The Pointer Activity tab lets you enable new options: one helps you find the mouse cursor onscreen; another takes the insertion point off the screen while you're typing in case you find it distracting. Another keyboard/mouse coordination option controls how drag and drop works with the mouse in Windows Explorer. If you're dragging a file or folder to a new place on the same disk drive, the default action is to move what you drag. You can change that to a copy by holding the Ctrl key down. Dragging from one drive to a different one (including a floppy) is a copy by default; change that to move by holding down the Shift key. Menus change in some programs when you hold down the Shift key. In Microsoft Word, for instance (see Chapter 11), the usual File menu includes Save. Hold the Shift key down and mouse on File, though, and you get Save All. The Shift key converts the Word toolbar icon for Save to Save All too.

CROSS-REFERENCE

There's a lot more information on Microsoft Word in Chapter 11. Look at the lesson named "Importing from Other Applications."

FIND IT ONLINE

Drag and View (http://www.canyonsw.com/dnv.htm) lets you look at a variety of files by simply dragging them around on your desktop.

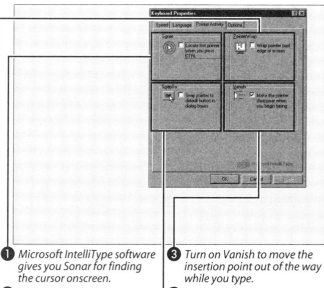

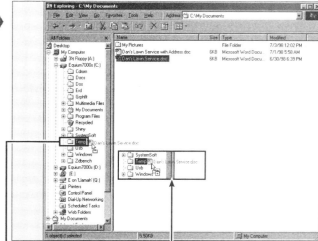

① *Microsoft IntelliType software gives you Sonar for finding the cursor onscreen.*

② *Turn on PointerWrap and the mouse doesn't stop at the edge; it flips to the other side.*

③ *Turn on Vanish to move the insertion point out of the way while you type.*

④ *Use SnapTo to put the cursor on the OK button in most dialog boxes.*

⑤ *You can use the keyboard to control file and folder drags. The default on the same drive is move.*

⑥ *Use the Ctrl key to force the drag to be copy (shown in the inset).*

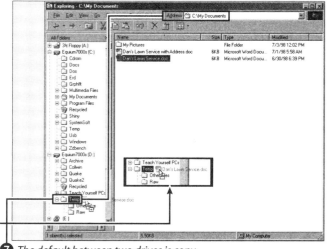

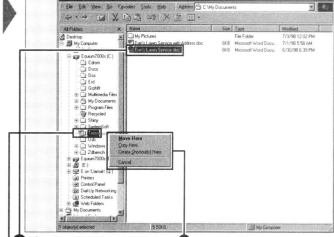

⑦ *The default between two drives is copy.*

⑧ *Use the Shift key to force the drag to be move (shown in the inset).*

⑨ *If it's hard to remember the rules, drag the file or folder with the right mouse button.*

⑩ *When you release the mouse button at the destination, you get a pop-up menu.*

⑪ *The default action is highlighted in bold.*

Using the Windows Keys

In the same way that applications use the function keys (F1 through F12) for specific commands, the Windows key on current-generation keyboards gives you access to common Windows functions. Microsoft defined ten; manufacturers can define their own functions tied to the keys as Windows+*number*.

Few of the standard Windows keys have functions important enough to be worth remembering. After you've used Windows for a while and become used to having open windows all over your screen, you begin to notice that desktop icons for starting programs aren't as useful as they seem because you can't easily get to them. The Windows keys help solve that problem because they put functions you're likely to need right at hand.

For example, we find it very common to have to switch out of a program to Windows Explorer to find a data file. With the mouse you could do that by closing enough windows to expose the icon on the desktop or by using the sequence Start ⇨ Programs ⇨ Windows Explorer. Using the Windows key, though, you only have to key in Windows+E and the program opens.

The other Windows key we use the most is Windows+R, which gives you the Start ⇨ Run dialog box. Not only can you type the name of Windows programs (calc, notepad, or wordpad, for instance) or the path to any program, you can type in Web addresses. This means that if you want to see a specific Web site, you don't have to fish around to open a browser and then type in the address. You can simply type Windows+R, the Web address, and press Enter. Your default Web browser opens and navigates to the site.

This Web trick not only works with addresses prefixed with `http://`, it assumes the prefix for any address you type that starts with *www*. Press Windows+R, type **www.idgbooks.com**, press Enter, and you're at the IDG Books Worldwide Web site.

TAKE NOTE

▶ KEEP PRIVATE THINGS TO YOURSELF

At times you may be working on something that's not for everyone to see, and sometimes reaching for the mouse to minimize or close a program takes more time than you want. Press Windows+M instead; it minimizes every open window on your screen, leaving you with a clean, empty desktop. Windows+Shift+M reverses the change, bringing windows back to their initial state.

▶ STAY IN THE GAME

Useful as it is, the Windows key is the bane of DOS gamers playing under Windows because it switches most games away to the Start menu — not exactly a good idea when you're in a heated competition across the Internet. If the game doesn't lock up, you're likely to get creamed. See "Find It Online" below for a remedy.

CROSS-REFERENCE

Learn the basics of Web browsing in Chapter 15, starting with "Visiting Your First Home Page."

FIND IT ONLINE

Another of the Windows Kernel Toys, Logo Key Control at **http://www.microsoft.com/windows/downloads**, lets you suppress the Windows key in DOS programs.

Use All the Windows Key Has to Offer

Here's the list of what's built into Windows itself (Microsoft's IntelliType software adds others):

Keystroke	Function
Windows	Display Start menu
Windows+Break	Display Device Manager
Windows+E	Open Windows Explorer
Windows+F	Find files or folders
Windows+Ctrl+F	Find computers (on a network)
Windows+F1	Run Windows Help
Windows+M	Minimize all open windows
Windows+Shift+M	Undo minimize all
Windows+R	Display Run dialog box
Windows+Tab	Cycle through task buttons on taskbar

Of these commands, Windows+R and Windows+E are easily the most useful. Not only can you type a command line ("wordpad") into the Run dialog box Windows+R displays, but you can also type Internet Web addresses. Even though your Web browser (see Chapter 15) might not be running, you can type an address such as Adrenaline Vault's (http://www. avault.com). When you do, your Web browser opens and displays the page you called for, all in one step. You don't need to dredge through the Start button menus — just type the address.

Similarly, Windows+E gives you fast access to Windows Explorer without leaving spaces on your desktop uncovered or using the Start menu. You simply push the keys and Windows Explorer opens in the two-pane view, giving you access to all the drives and special folders on your machine.

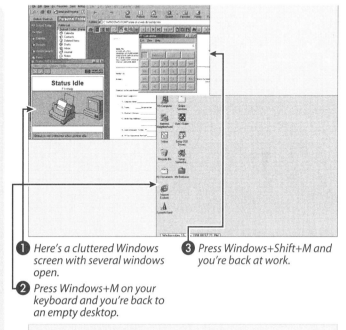

① *Here's a cluttered Windows screen with several windows open.*

② *Press Windows+M on your keyboard and you're back to an empty desktop.*

③ *Press Windows+Shift+M and you're back at work.*

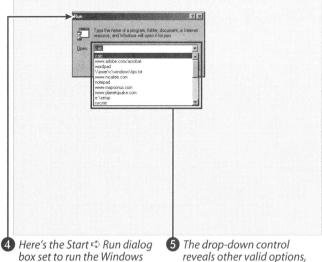

④ *Here's the Start ⇨ Run dialog box set to run the Windows calculator.*

⑤ *The drop-down control reveals other valid options, including Web pages.*

Choosing Languages and the Dvorak Keyboard Layout

The standard QWERTY keyboard layout was created by Christopher Sholes early in the history of manual typewriters. The legend that Sholes designed the keyboard to slow down fast typists isn't quite true. The point of the QWERTY layout was to keep common pairs of keys away from each other to reduce jamming during fast typing, helping to make early typewriters a success. (In fact, some tests suggest that it's possible to type as fast on the Sholes keyboard as on other layouts.) Most keyboards retain the Sholes layout. Next most popular is the Dvorak layout, created in 1936 by August Dvorak and William Dealey. The two layouts look like this (ignoring numbers and punctuation), where the split is at the break in the now-common split keyboards:

Sholes		Dvorak	
QWERT	YUIOP	PY	FGCRL
ASDFG	HJKL	AOEUI	DHTNS
ZXCVB	NM	QJKX	BMWVZ

Windows lets you remap your keyboard from the Sholes to the Dvorak layout. The same Windows tools let you install support for languages other than English and to pick what language you want supported as you work. The tools you use for layout and language configuration appear in the Control Panel Keyboard applet.

Standard Windows language support in the Keyboard applet (U.S. version of Windows 98) includes support for around 70 different languages and variants. Windows lets you choose your default keyboard setup and offers you an indicator in the taskbar showing the currently active language. When you type into a program with national language support (NLS), text appears in the characters of the language you've selected. (WordPad and Word have NLS support.)

The taskbar indicator does more than report your current language setting. Left-click the indicator and a popup menu lets you choose any of your other installed languages. For some real confusion, switch this way between the Sholes and Dvorak keyboards!

TAKE NOTE

► KNOWING THE LANGUAGE YOURSELF

Windows isn't smart enough to translate text in one language to another. The fact that you can type in Greek characters doesn't make Greek language out of what you type. Programs exist that attempt language translation, but don't expect a reliable, polished, idiomatic translation. You can experiment with translation with AltaVista at **http://babelfish.altavista.digital.com/cgi-bin/translate?**.

CROSS-REFERENCE
Chapter 1 showed you how to connect a keyboard in "Setting Up and Plugging In." Use the same lesson to install an upgraded keyboard.

FIND IT ONLINE
The main source for Dvorak keyboard information is Dvorak International at **http://www.dvorakint.org**.

KEYBOARD

Choosing Languages and the Dvorak Keyboard

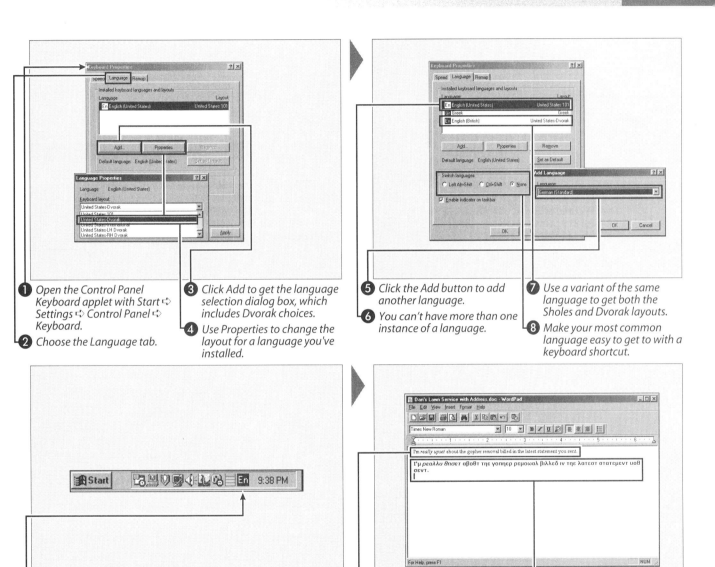

1 Open the Control Panel Keyboard applet with Start ➪ Settings ➪ Control Panel ➪ Keyboard.

2 Choose the Language tab.

3 Click Add to get the language selection dialog box, which includes Dvorak choices.

4 Use Properties to change the layout for a language you've installed.

5 Click the Add button to add another language.

6 You can't have more than one instance of a language.

7 Use a variant of the same language to get both the Sholes and Dvorak layouts.

8 Make your most common language easy to get to with a keyboard shortcut.

9 The language indicator fits neatly in the taskbar.

10 Choose a different language to type characters in that language.

11 Here's the text in English.

12 Here are the same keystrokes in Greek. We're sure it's gibberish.

Enabling Accessibility

If you can't type with both hands, or you can't hear, see, or coordinate to control the mouse, the basic Windows setup fails you miserably.

But Windows offers configuration options to help, options Microsoft has improved steadily in each version. If you install the accessibility components, you can alter the behavior of the keyboard, sound, display, and mouse to make them more easily controllable. If you didn't install Accessibility, go to Start ⇨ Control Panel ⇨ Add/Remove Programs ⇨ Windows Setup ⇨ Accessibility; make sure it's checked and that both components — Accessibility Options and Accessibility Tools — are selected. Close the dialog box with OK and supply the Windows CD-ROM if requested. You will probably have to reboot when you're done.

You can configure options to have keys "stick" down, to ignore accidental or repeated keystrokes, to use sound to indicate you've pressed a Shift key, to use screen flashes instead of sound to request attention, to set the display to very high-contrast colors, and to use the keypad on the keyboard to control the mouse. Settings buttons for each configuration item give you finer control over how the feature works.

Windows 98 includes help for people with limited vision: Microsoft Magnifier. This program displays — in a strip at the top of the screen — a magnified version of the image near the mouse or around where you're typing. Find the magnifier at Start ⇨ Programs ⇨ Accessories ⇨ Accessibility ⇨ Magnifier.

You can control the degree of magnification and how the program decides what part of the screen to show in expanded view.

TAKE NOTE

▶ GETTING NEW TECHNOLOGY FOR VOICE COMMANDS

The arrival on the market of Dragon Naturally Speaking and IBM's ViaVoice Gold is some of the best news ever for people who need alternative ways to access computers. These products are among the first to perform continuous speech recognition and text-to-speech output. Modules in the programs connect speech to commands and operations in the computer, making hands-off work possible. Neither is completely accurate; both should improve.

▶ GETTING HELP SETTING AN ACCESSIBILITY CONFIGURATION

Windows 98 includes Microsoft's Accessibility Wizard, a program that steps you through configuring Windows 98's accessibility options. It starts by helping make sure text on the screen is readable, and then proceeds to the other options shown (in the Control Panel version) on the facing page. If other people use the same computer and don't want the modified settings, use the desktop properties (Start ⇨ Settings ⇨ Control Panel ⇨ Display ⇨ Appearance) to save and reload window appearance setups.

CROSS-REFERENCE

See the "Adding and Removing Windows 98 Components" section in Chapter 9 for help with using Add/Remove Programs to set up Windows

FIND IT ONLINE

Find the Screen Magnifiers Home Page at http://www.plex.nl/~pverhoe/main2.html.

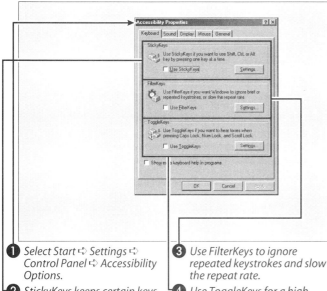

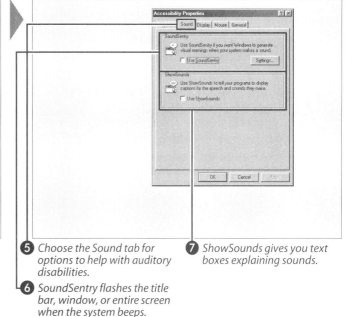

① Select Start ⇨ Settings ⇨ Control Panel ⇨ Accessibility Options.

② StickyKeys keeps certain keys pressed until you type a regular key or click the mouse.

③ Use FilterKeys to ignore repeated keystrokes and slow the repeat rate.

④ Use ToggleKeys for a high beep when you press certain keys.

⑤ Choose the Sound tab for options to help with auditory disabilities.

⑥ SoundSentry flashes the title bar, window, or entire screen when the system beeps.

⑦ ShowSounds gives you text boxes explaining sounds.

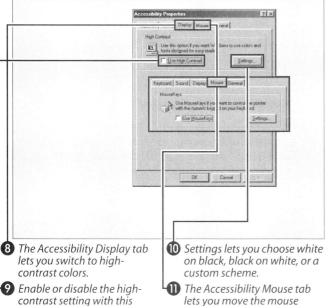

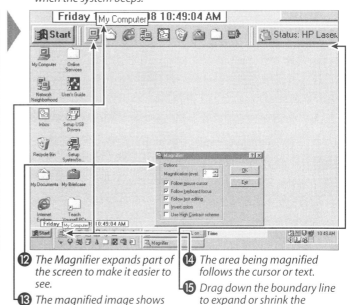

⑧ The Accessibility Display tab lets you switch to high-contrast colors.

⑨ Enable or disable the high-contrast setting with this checkbox.

⑩ Settings lets you choose white on black, black on white, or a custom scheme.

⑪ The Accessibility Mouse tab lets you move the mouse cursor using the keyboard.

⑫ The Magnifier expands part of the screen to make it easier to see.

⑬ The magnified image shows up at the top of the screen.

⑭ The area being magnified follows the cursor or text.

⑮ Drag down the boundary line to expand or shrink the magnified area.

Personal Workbook

Q&A

1 What's the layout on your keyboard? What's an alternative?

_____

_____

_____

2 What are function keys and what are they used for?

_____

_____

3 What's the default drag action for files and folders within one drive? From one drive to another?

_____

_____

_____

4 What's the Start button sequence to open Windows Explorer? The Windows key?

_____

_____

_____

5 What's the Windows key to open the Run dialog box?

_____

_____

_____

6 What does Windows+M do?

_____

_____

_____

7 How do you reverse Windows+M?

_____

_____

_____

8 In Windows 98, how can you help people with low vision see what's onscreen?

_____

_____

_____

ANSWERS: PAGE 337

EXTRA PRACTICE

1. Select some text in WordPad and drag it to the desktop. What happens?

2. Adjust the keyboard repeat rate. Do you prefer higher or lower settings?

3. Try the Crtl and Shift keys as you drag icons on the desktop. What happens?

4. There's a key next to the right Windows key marked with a menu and mouse cursor. Open Windows Explorer and press the key. What does it do?

5. In the same location described in question 4, press Shift+F10. What happens?

6. In the same location described in questions 4 and 5, click the right mouse button. What happens?

REAL-WORLD APPLICATIONS

✔ One of your neighbors wants to look for cheesecake recipes on the Internet, but has very limited vision. You set up the magnifier and spend the afternoon consuming virtual calories.

✔ One of your children comes home from preschool with an art project assignment to make a picture out of Xs and Os. You reprogram the repeat rate on the keyboard to make the assignment less tedious.

✔ Being multilingual, you receive an assignment to translate a proposal into the customer's native language. You install language support into Windows, and then open two copies of WordPad. You read from one while you write in the other.

Visual Quiz

How do you get to this dialog box?

_____

_____

_____

_____

_____

_____

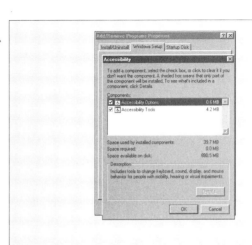

CHAPTER 7

Display

Windows makes using a PC intensely visual and gives you enormous control over how things look onscreen. You can choose colors, sizes, backgrounds, icons, fonts, and mouse cursors. You can open many programs and work with all of them at once. That's a more productive way to work because you don't fumble around closing one program and launching the next. Better yet, by having several programs open, you can move data between them easily, adding more power to the tools.

Unfortunately, each program displays one or more windows, so space on your screen is at a premium. The answer to fitting more onscreen is a large monitor and a display card that can generate more dots onscreen (*pixels*) to fill it. The default Windows screen resolution is 640 × 480 pixels. If you invest in a 21-inch monitor and a board capable of 1,600 × 1,200 resolution, you get over twice the monitor area (compared to a 14-inch monitor) and over six times the pixels onscreen. This means you can show more windows without overlapping, and you can show finer detail per square inch of monitor.

We're fanatics about big monitors. Most of the computers we work with have 17-inch monitors; the one we use for writing has a 21-inch Hitachi screen. No matter what writing task we need to carry out, the program we need is immediately available. Without question, better display hardware helps you get your work done faster and more easily.

Display boards that can give you the display power of 1,600 × 1,200 resolution cost little more than ones limited to 1,280 × 1,024 (which is the practical limit for a 17-inch monitor). Your existing card might do it already or do it with nothing more than a video memory upgrade.

Bigger monitors, though, cost significantly more than smaller ones. For comparison, a 14-inch monitor made by ViewSonics sold for as little as U.S. $140 in July 1998, while you'd have paid U.S. $300 for a 17-inch monitor from the same vendor. The lowest price for a 21-inch monitor (still ViewSonics) was around $800.

Choosing the Background and Appearance

Start putting the personal in *personal computer* by setting your computer's background, window colors, and display fonts. You can get to the Display applet through your trusty friend the Control Panel or simply by right-clicking the desktop background (what you see when no windows are open) and choosing Properties. Under Windows 98, the resulting dialog box has six tabs: Background, Screen Saver, Appearance, Effects, Web, and Settings. They're enough to completely revamp what you see onscreen.

You can put a solid color or an image on your desktop. You control desktop images with the Appearance tab, choosing from patterns built into Windows or images (*wallpaper*). Both patterns and images smaller than your desktop can be *tiled* (repeated across and down the desktop) or centered. A centered pattern isn't very interesting, because it's too small to notice. You have a third option for small images: you can choose the Stretch option, or you can use an image processing program such as LView Pro to resize the image to fit your desktop.

The Appearance tab controls several settings, but it's not complex to use. Click the part of the sample window shown in the dialog box, and its name and characteristics show up in the bottom half of the dialog box. Change the characteristics you're interested in; options that don't make sense for a given window element are grayed out and inactive.

Don't overlook the Effects tab — it hides some interesting options. You can change the icons for My Computer and other standard desktop items, make large fonts look better, and make windows visible while you're moving them around. Use the Apply button to experiment with the effects without closing the dialog box. The option to show window contents while dragging is particularly useful because it not only lets you see where windows end up after you move them, it lets you see the effects of resizing a window as you change it. This lets you know when you've reached exactly the right point.

On the next two pages, you learn the options for how the Windows desktop works. These options are very different from what's on these pages. What you learn there is how to make your desktop work like a Web browser; what you're learning here is how Windows has traditionally worked. These two are not exclusive choices. You do choose to have the Web page desktop turned on or not, but all the conventional desktop items (including background and icons) are available with the Web desktop. (An option on the Effects tab lets you eliminate the desktop icons when you're using the Web page version. Turn on the desktop toolbar in the taskbar to make them readily accessible again.)

Continued

CROSS-REFERENCE

See the Chapter 15 lesson "Linking and Navigating" to learn how to work with Web pages on your desktop.

FIND IT ONLINE

Get LView Pro at http://www.lview.com.

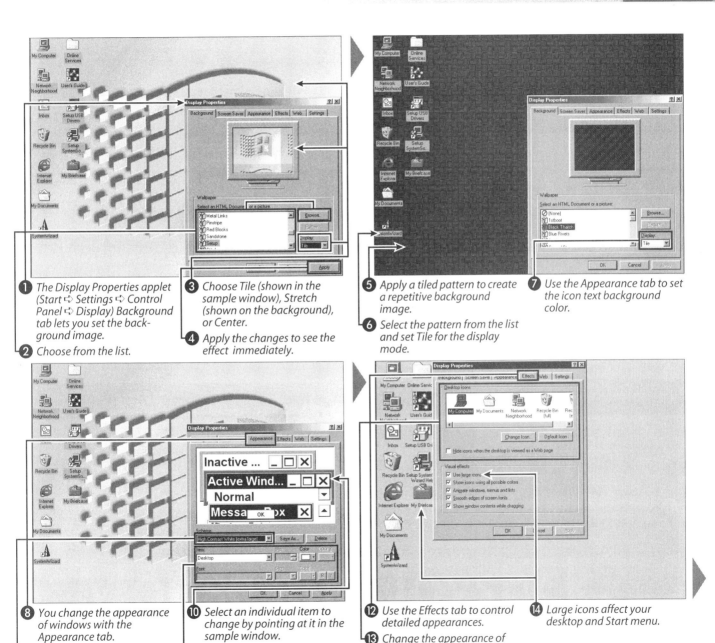

① The Display Properties applet (Start ➪ Settings ➪ Control Panel ➪ Display) Background tab lets you set the background image.

② Choose from the list.

③ Choose Tile (shown in the sample window), Stretch (shown on the background), or Center.

④ Apply the changes to see the effect immediately.

⑤ Apply a tiled pattern to create a repetitive background image.

⑥ Select the pattern from the list and set Tile for the display mode.

⑦ Use the Appearance tab to set the icon text background color.

⑧ You change the appearance of windows with the Appearance tab.

⑨ Choose a complete scheme from the scheme list.

⑩ Select an individual item to change by pointing at it in the sample window.

⑪ Change item size, color, and font with these controls.

⑫ Use the Effects tab to control detailed appearances.

⑬ Change the appearance of My Computer and other standard desktop icons with these controls.

⑭ Large icons affect your desktop and Start menu.

Lots of services and information are available on the Internet. If your computer is always connected to the Internet, as is true in many businesses and some homes or home offices, the Internet is a resource beyond comparison because of its breadth and immediacy. Some of what's on the Internet is worth keeping close at hand as a tool or news source, or simply because you use it frequently.

Keeping the Web sites you use close at hand is awkward unless you have a *really* large monitor and desktop. You can keep a browser open, but as you navigate to other pages, the places you want won't be handy. You can keep multiple browsers open, but that consumes screen space. Microsoft's Active Desktop is another attempt to solve the problem. Active Desktop lets you set Web pages and services as part of your desktop. All those items remain behind your open windows, but of course the Windows+M and Windows+Shift+M keystrokes get you to the desktop immediately.

How you can exploit Active Desktop is bound to evolve. Already you can get rolling news headlines, weather, Internet searches, clocks, and more.

You control Active Desktop from the Web tab in Display Properties. The New button takes you to the Internet Explorer Active Desktop Gallery (you need a Web connection); the list box shows what you have installed, letting you turn individual items on and off on the desktop. Once on your desktop, items work

something like windows, with an abbreviated title bar that appears as the mouse moves up the window towards the top. You can move windows by dragging their title bar and resize them by dragging their edges. It can be a little touchy to move and resize the windows — it's not quite the same as doing those operations on conventional windows.

TAKE NOTE

▶ TELL ME AGAIN HOW I DID THAT

It's frustrating to have someone else (or a program) change the appearance you so carefully set up. Instead of losing it, use the Save As button on the Appearance tab's dialog box to save all the settings with a name you choose. The name gets added to the drop-down list to the left of the Save As button, letting you get your settings back.

▶ EXPLORE THIS, ICON THAT

Sometimes you'd like to change appearances that aren't offered in the sample window or the Item drop-down list. This doesn't mean they can't be changed, just that it's probably some other setting. For instance, try changing the font and font size for the Icon item, and then open Windows Explorer. You discover that the Icon font setting is what's used for text in the Explorer window.

CROSS-REFERENCE
One of Chapter 15's lessons, "Searching the Web," shows you how to search the Active Desktop.

FIND IT ONLINE
The Internet Explorer Active Desktop Gallery is at http://www.microsoft.com/ie/ie40/gallery.

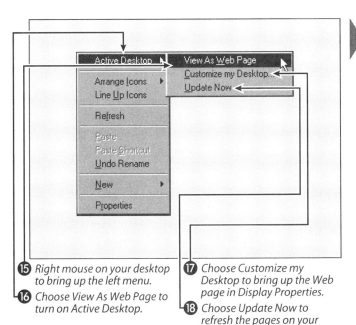

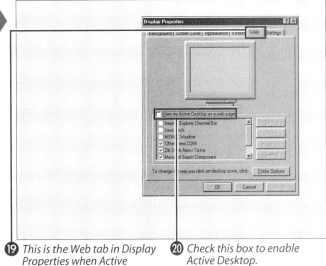

🕛 *Right mouse on your desktop to bring up the left menu.*

🕗 *Choose View As Web Page to turn on Active Desktop.*

🕗 *Choose Customize my Desktop to bring up the Web page in Display Properties.*

🕗 *Choose Update Now to refresh the pages on your Active Desktop from the Web.*

🕗 *This is the Web tab in Display Properties when Active Desktop is inactive.*

🕗 *Check this box to enable Active Desktop.*

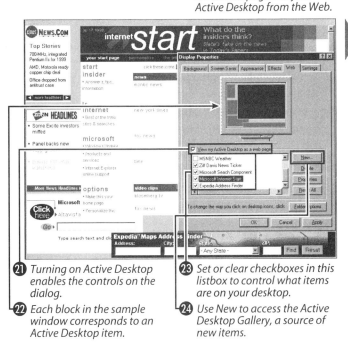

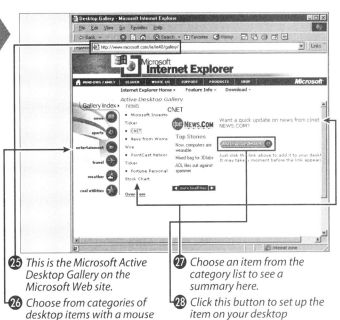

🕗 *Turning on Active Desktop enables the controls on the dialog.*

🕗 *Each block in the sample window corresponds to an Active Desktop item.*

🕗 *Set or clear checkboxes in this listbox to control what items are on your desktop.*

🕗 *Use New to access the Active Desktop Gallery, a source of new items.*

🕗 *This is the Microsoft Active Desktop Gallery on the Microsoft Web site.*

🕗 *Choose from categories of desktop items with a mouse click.*

🕗 *Choose an item from the category list to see a summary here.*

🕗 *Click this button to set up the item on your desktop inventory.*

Choosing a Theme

Using the Desktop Properties Appearance dialog box from the previous lesson, you can set and recall colors and fonts, but not the screen saver, not the background, not the sounds (see the next chapter), not the mouse cursors, and not the icons. That larger group of settings completely defines what your system looks and sounds like.

You can set every one of the elements in the preceding list with standard capabilities supplied with Windows. Display Properties handles the background, screen saver, appearance, and icons; the Sounds applet ties sound files to events; and the Mouse applet controls mouse pointers. All you need is a way to save and restore all those elements as a coherent group.

Microsoft calls this collection of information a desktop theme. The Desktop Themes control panel applet handles this chore, both loading themes you have and letting you create files that define new theme files. Desktop Themes first appeared in the Windows 95 Plus! Pack, a collection of additions Microsoft developed for Windows 95. Desktop Themes (and much of the Display Properties Effects tab) migrated from the Plus! Pack into Windows 98, so if your computer came with Windows 98 (or you upgraded) you have the tools you need to load and save themes.

The figures on the opposite page show the Desktop Themes applet in operation. You save the current Windows settings using the Save As button. The drop-down list lets you pick a different theme for loading. The figure on the top right and the two across the bottom show the effect of selectively choosing the theme elements that the applet loads.

You have two options for what to do with theme files you download from the Web. Normally, you download a compressed archive that contains the entire file set for the theme. The most straightforward approach is to download to a temporary place, decompress to the Themes folder (see Chapter 18's "Running WinZip" lesson for details on how to decompress these files), and then delete the compressed file. Alternatively, if you have lots of disk space, you might create a folder that contains all your Internet downloads sorted by type, and not delete the compressed file. Finally, if you're really disciplined, you could keep a file in Notepad, WordPad, or some other editor that contains the Web links you used for downloads. Either of the last two approaches lets you recover the original download if you ever need it.

Some theme authors use sound formats that require added software not included with Windows itself. Check the download Web page and any readme file in the compressed archive for instructions if things don't work. The additional software you need is usually a free download from somewhere else on the Internet.

Continued

CROSS-REFERENCE

Chapter 18's "Downloading from the Web" lesson shows you how to bring new themes into your computer.

FIND IT ONLINE

The Winfiles site has many themes at http://www.winfiles.com/apps/98/themes.html.

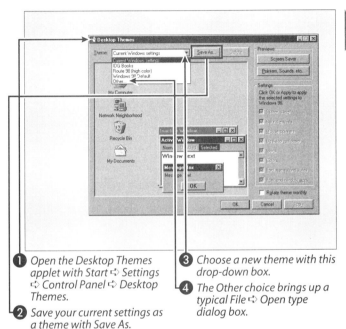

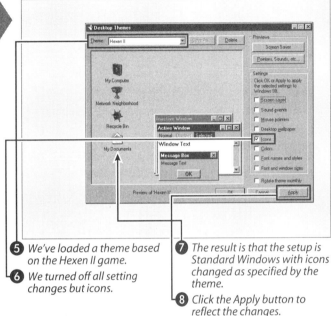

❶ Open the Desktop Themes applet with Start ➪ Settings ➪ Control Panel ➪ Desktop Themes.

❷ Save your current settings as a theme with Save As.

❸ Choose a new theme with this drop-down box.

❹ The Other choice brings up a typical File ➪ Open type dialog box.

❺ We've loaded a theme based on the Hexen II game.

❻ We turned off all setting changes but icons.

❼ The result is that the setup is Standard Windows with icons changed as specified by the theme.

❽ Click the Apply button to reflect the changes.

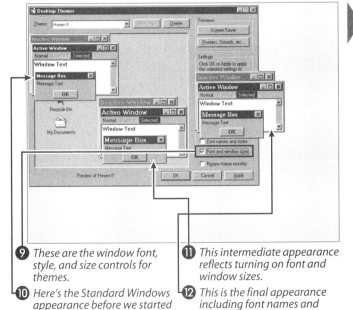

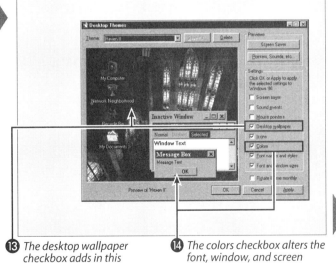

❾ These are the window font, style, and size controls for themes.

❿ Here's the Standard Windows appearance before we started applying theme elements.

⓫ This intermediate appearance reflects turning on font and window sizes.

⓬ This is the final appearance including font names and styles too.

⓭ The desktop wallpaper checkbox adds in this background.

⓮ The colors checkbox alters the font, window, and screen background colors.

Choosing a Theme

Continued

Whether the Windows 95 Plus! Pack or Windows 98 provides the Desktop Themes applet, there's a standard folder structure it expects to use. Your computer has a folder — C:\Program Files\Plus!\Themes — in which Windows expects to find themes. Plus! stored all the files for a theme (plus its definition file) directly in that folder. If you create your own themes, make a subfolder for each one. Put all the related files there — icons, sounds, cursors, and backgrounds. This way, it's easy to package the entire theme and send it to a friend.

If you decide to build your own theme, you have to collect the elements.

▶ **Find or create a background.** Scanners are very useful for making files of printed images. You want the file in the Windows bitmap (BMP) or Joint Photographic Experts Group (JPEG or JPG) format. Install the background with Desktop Properties Background.

▶ **Find or create the icons.** Icon files have file type ICO. You need two icons for the Recycle Bin, one for full and one for empty. Install the icons with Desktop Properties Effects. Set the window appearance (with the Appearance tab) and the screen saver (with the Screen Saver tab) while you're there.

▶ **Find or create the sounds.** Sound files have the file type WAV. You can record sounds with your sound card and the Sound Recorder program (choose Start ⮑ Programs ⮑ Accessories ⮑ Entertainment ⮑ Sound Recorder). Install them with the Sounds control panel applet.

▶ **Find or create the mouse cursors,** which are files of type CUR or ANI (the latter are animated cursors). Install them with the Pointers tab in the Mouse control panel applet.

Once you've gathered all the elements, start the Desktop Themes applet and click Save As. Name the theme and save the file in the same folder as the theme files themselves.

CROSS-REFERENCE

See Chapter 8's "Setting the Windows Sounds" lesson for more on associating sounds with events in Windows.

FIND IT ONLINE

A great tool for making your own icons and cursors is Microangelo, at **http://www.impactsoft.com/ muangelo/muangelo.html**

Copyrights

Think some about copyrights when you decide to create a desktop theme. Think about where the content you're using comes from and what you plan to do with the theme once it's done.

Looking at the desktop themes available on the Internet, it's quickly obvious that most people create themes based on movies, bands, people, and other popular topics. Many of the graphics and sounds you're likely to find, including all the ones from movies, are copyrighted. That means you can't necessarily copy them into your themes without permission, and almost certainly can't give or sell those themes to others without permission.

How do you tell what's okay? The first thing to look for, of course, is a copyright notice. Copyright means that the material's owner has the right to say which uses are permitted and which are not. The situation is more complicated than that, though, because copyright law allows for what's called *fair use*. The law says (in part) that a copy "for purposes such as criticism, comment, news reporting, teaching (including multiple copies for classroom use), scholarship, or research, is not an infringement of copyright." It goes on to give four tests regarding fair use. Deciding what's fair use can be complex, more so than we can explain in this book. You can find more information on Ivan Hoffman's Web site in his article on fair use (**http://home.earthlink.net/~ivanlove/fair.html**). As he says in his article, the safest thing to do is to request and obtain permission.

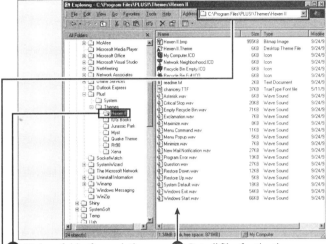

⑮ *Make a folder for each theme you create.*

⑯ *Theme folders should go under the Plus! Pack Theme folder.*

⑰ *Put all files for the theme there — wallpaper, icons, sounds, cursors, and the theme file itself.*

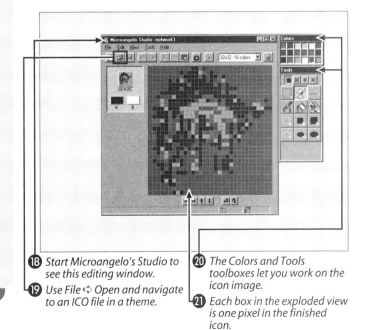

⑱ *Start Microangelo's Studio to see this editing window.*

⑲ *Use File ➪ Open and navigate to an ICO file in a theme.*

⑳ *The Colors and Tools toolboxes let you work on the icon image.*

㉑ *Each box in the exploded view is one pixel in the finished icon.*

Setting Up the Screen Saver and Power Down

In the early days of personal computers, unchanging images left onscreen would burn themselves into the face of the monitor. Programmers developed screen savers to combat this problem — programs that kick in after your computer has been idle for a set amount of time to clear the screen or put a changing image on it. Over time, monitors have improved to the point that burning in an image is much less of a problem, but at the same time screen savers have gained value so that they still survive. A screen saver can hide your work from prying eyes, give you background information (such as the time), check your disks for latent problems, and simply be entertaining.

You choose a screen saver in Windows from the Screen Saver tab in the Control Panel Display applet. The dialog box has a sample window, showing you what to expect when the screen saver kicks in. Below this is a drop-down list that lets you choose the screen saver you want. A Settings button configures options for the selected screen saver, while a Preview button lets you see the program in operation.

When you stop using the keyboard or mouse, Windows waits for the time interval specified in the Screen Saver dialog box and then starts the screen saver. Moving the mouse or pushing a key on the keyboard stops the screen saver. (Some screen savers only respond to specific keystrokes.)

A mild form of security is built into Windows screen savers. You can set up a password that's required to clear an active screen saver and return Windows to normal operation. When you move the mouse or press a key, Windows displays a dialog box over the screen saver requesting the password. If you enter the right one, the screen saver shuts down; otherwise, it keeps running.

Windows comes with a small selection of screen savers, including ones that display moving curves, a starfield, and a variety of 3D scenes including pipes, a maze, and text. Some companies started selling screen savers (millions of copies at $10 or $20 is still a lot of money), but today your best source for additional screen savers is the Internet. They're reasonably small and quick to write for a good programmer, so thousands of them are available. For some reason, screen savers that make your monitor look like a tropical fish tank are always favorites, as are ones that display a slide show of different outdoor panoramas.

Screen savers continue to grow in function. The latest idea is to download content from the Web, showing you news or content updates as they run.

Continued

CROSS-REFERENCE

Chapter 18 includes the lesson "Downloading from the Web" to show you how to pull in new files such as

FIND IT ONLINE

Find over 2,000 screen savers at **http://www. bonanzas.com/ssavers/windows95S.html** and

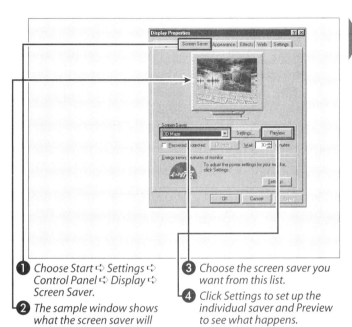

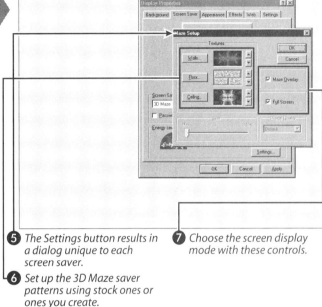

① Choose Start ➪ Settings ➪ Control Panel ➪ Display ➪ Screen Saver.

② The sample window shows what the screen saver will look like in operation.

③ Choose the screen saver you want from this list.

④ Click Settings to set up the individual saver and Preview to see what happens.

⑤ The Settings button results in a dialog unique to each screen saver.

⑥ Set up the 3D Maze saver patterns using stock ones or ones you create.

⑦ Choose the screen display mode with these controls.

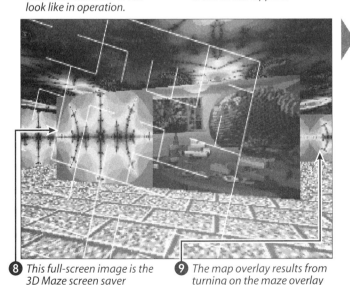

⑧ This full-screen image is the 3D Maze screen saver running.

⑨ The map overlay results from turning on the maze overlay in the setup dialog box.

⑩ Click the Password protected checkbox to enable screen saver security.

⑪ Type your password twice, once in each box.

99

Setting Up the Screen Saver and Power Down *Continued*

PCs sit idle a lot while people do other work, wasting the power they consume while they wait. There are literally hundreds of millions of PCs in the world. If each one uses 100 watts (a bright light bulb), 200 million PCs consume over 1 percent of total U.S. power generation. That's a lot of power and a lot of resources to waste while computers are idle, so it's not surprising that manufacturers have extended the technologies originally developed to lengthen laptop computer battery life to reduce the power that desktop PCs waste.

The monitor on your desk consumes a large percentage of the total power your PC uses, so shutting it down when you're busy elsewhere is a good start on reducing power consumption. You don't have to keep switching the monitor on and off, though — essentially all monitors and PC s made in the last several years can do the job for you. Software in Windows 95 and Windows 98 makes your monitor shut down after an interval you specify.

Monitor power control has several stages, typically called *on*, *standby*, *suspend*, and *off*, which correspond to successively lower power consumption. United States Environmental Protection Agency guidelines require monitors to consume less than 30 watts in standby/suspend, and less than 15 watts in the off mode.

Windows 95 put controls for monitor shutdown on the Screen Saver tab. Windows 98 moved those controls into the Control Panel Power Management applet. You can get to Power Management through the Control Panel or from the Settings button near the bottom of the Screen Saver tab. Windows gives you several power management profiles, including Home/Office Desk, Portable/Laptop, and Always On. Depending on your computer, you have options to turn off the monitor and your disks while you're not using your computer.

TAKE NOTE

▶ RECOVER FROM A LOST SCREEN SAVER PASSWORD

You can hurt yourself in lots of ways. One of the electronic ways is to forget a password, such as one you've used to secure your machine with a screen saver. If you forget your screen saver password, turn off the machine and restart it. Once Windows comes up, find the file with extension PWL in the C:\Windows folder, and delete it. That removes the screen saver password altogether. Not too secure, is it?

▶ CHOOSING SCREEN SAVER AND POWER OFF INTERVALS

There are no widely accepted times for when to kick in a screen saver or to turn off a monitor because it depends on you. You want a screen saver to hold off long enough that it doesn't irritate you. Set the monitor shutdown time somewhat longer — you shorten a monitor's life by making it cycle on and off all the time.

CROSS-REFERENCE

See Chapter 23's "Deciding When Something's Wrong with Your Computer" lesson if you don't have Power

FIND IT ONLINE

You can't save power if you have none. See American Power Conversion at **http://www.apcc.com** for

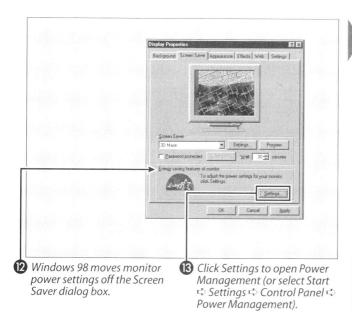

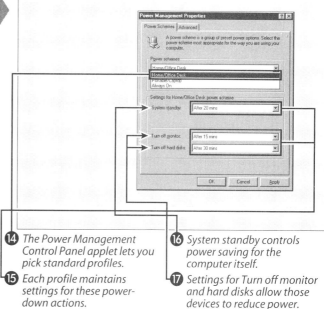

⑫ *Windows 98 moves monitor power settings off the Screen Saver dialog box.*

⑬ *Click Settings to open Power Management (or select Start ➪ Settings ➪ Control Panel ➪ Power Management).*

⑭ *The Power Management Control Panel applet lets you pick standard profiles.*

⑮ *Each profile maintains settings for these power-down actions.*

⑯ *System standby controls power saving for the computer itself.*

⑰ *Settings for Turn off monitor and hard disks allow those devices to reduce power.*

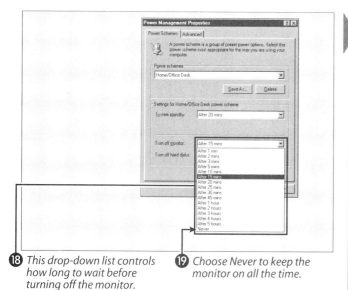

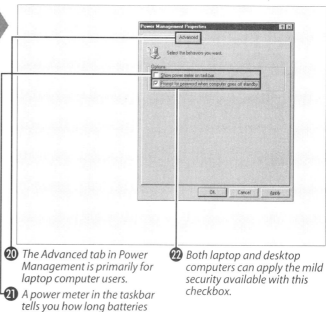

⑱ *This drop-down list controls how long to wait before turning off the monitor.*

⑲ *Choose Never to keep the monitor on all the time.*

⑳ *The Advanced tab in Power Management is primarily for laptop computer users.*

㉑ *A power meter in the taskbar tells you how long batteries will last.*

㉒ *Both laptop and desktop computers can apply the mild security available with this checkbox.*

Getting More on the Screen

We firmly believe that a key way to be more productive with Windows is to have several programs open at once. In the office, this might be electronic mail, a word processor, and some desk accessories (such as a calendar). In the home, this might be electronic mail and a Web browser, plus the tools you're using on your current project.

One way to get more on the screen is to use less of it when it's not required. You can set properties for the taskbar (right-click the taskbar and choose Properties) to make it disappear unless touched by the mouse. Slide the mouse to where the taskbar was and it appears. Slide it off (or click another program) and the taskbar goes away. You can move the taskbar to any of the edges of the screen (click the clock and drag it around). Combine that with the setting in taskbar properties to keep the taskbar on top of all other windows when it's visible, and you've saved as much screen space as it used to use.

Nor do you have to leave the icons on the desktop uncovered to reach them — all that desktop space is recoverable too. You can activate a Windows 98 toolbar on the taskbar that displays all the desktop icons, making them accessible just by sliding out the taskbar. Do this by clicking the right mouse button on the taskbar, slide out the Toolbars submenu, and turn on Desktop.

Even with these tricks, resolutions of 640×480 and 800×600 can seem very small when you have a lot to work with. Large Web pages, page view layouts in word processors, and fine details in images can be awkward to deal with when you only get a thimbleful on screen. Even if your monitor is as small as 14 inches (diagonal measurement), you should try the $1,024 \times 768$ resolution, switching over to large fonts (see the next page in this lesson). If you have a 17-inch monitor, the $1,280 \times 1,024$ resolution (at large or small fonts depending on your preferences) should be good. Make these changes by using the Settings tab in the Control Panel Display applet. You're not likely to need to worry about getting in trouble in the Settings tab until you go into the Advanced button (next page), so experiment with different numbers of colors and screen area.

What you're doing by changing the number of colors is controlling the maximum number of different colors Windows can put onscreen at once. What Windows calls High Color (16-bit) is a good general-purpose choice — you avoid the color flickering that happens with only 256 colors and avoid the performance slowdown at 24- or 32-bit True Color.

Continued

CROSS-REFERENCE

See the next page in this lesson for more on screen resolution.

FIND IT ONLINE

Learn more about monitors at
http://www.monitorbuyersguide.com.

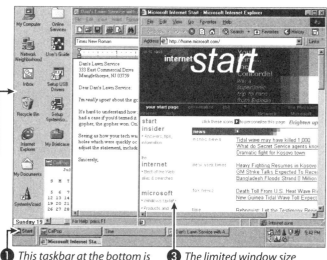

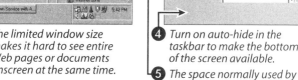

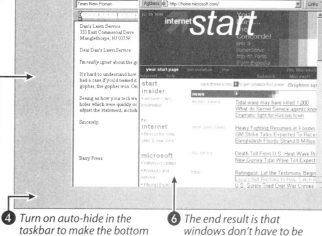

❶ *This taskbar at the bottom is two units high.*

❷ *We left the background clear of windows on the left to make sure the icons were accessible.*

❸ *The limited window size makes it hard to see entire Web pages or documents onscreen at the same time.*

❹ *Turn on auto-hide in the taskbar to make the bottom of the screen available.*

❺ *The space normally used by icons becomes available using a taskbar option.*

❻ *The end result is that windows don't have to be squeezed into as small a space.*

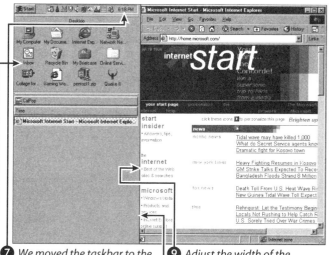

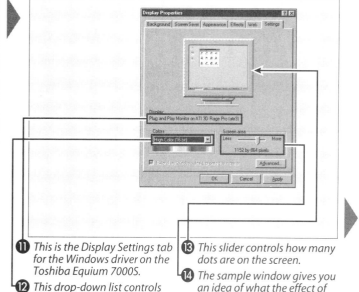

❼ *We moved the taskbar to the left by dragging the clock.*

❽ *Turn on the desktop toolbar with the right mouse ⇨ Toolbars menu on the taskbar.*

❾ *Adjust the width of the taskbar by dragging the edge of the window.*

❿ *You can use a wide toolbar if you choose because it slides out of sight.*

⓫ *This is the Display Settings tab for the Windows driver on the Toshiba Equium 7000S.*

⓬ *This drop-down list controls the number of colors displayed.*

⓭ *This slider controls how many dots are on the screen.*

⓮ *The sample window gives you an idea of what the effect of the chosen resolution is.*

Increasing screen resolution lets you display finer detail because more dots appear on the screen. Text and images onscreen are made from different colored dots, with the text being drawn from a rectangle of dots much like in the stylized electronic-looking displays you see. If you increase the number of dots, text gets smaller because the rectangle making up each character takes less space on the screen.

If you've been running your screen at 640 × 480 resolution, Windows has been using what it calls small fonts (that's the only choice at that resolution). If you change to a higher resolution, Windows offers you the choice of small fonts or large fonts, which look much the same but are built with larger rectangles of dots. The large fonts option makes characters look bigger onscreen, and improves the detail for each character. For a 14-inch monitor, try 800 × 600 with small fonts or 1,024 × 768 with large fonts. For a 17-inch monitor, try 1,280 × 1,024 with either large or small fonts. For a 21-inch monitor, the way to go is 1,600 × 1,200 with large fonts (small if you can read it).

If you enable the settings icon in the taskbar, Windows gives you the ability to change screen resolution and color depth (but not font size) on the fly, without having to restart your computer. That's useful when some of the programs you want to run only support fixed resolutions. Children's games are infamous for this — some of them simply refuse to run

at anything but 640 × 480. Others refuse to run at other than 256 colors. If you want to adjust your monitor, you need test patterns to see if edges are straight. You might find simple ones built into the display driver. If not, look at Display Mate at **http://www.displaymate.com**.

TAKE NOTE

► ELIMINATE FLASHING COLORS ON THE SCREEN

If you set your screen to 256 colors, you're likely to see the colors in the windows change when you switch from one program to the next. While 256 colors are often enough for a single program, the choice of *which* 256 colors are used is likely to be different from one program to the next. Get rid of the flashing by switching to High Color (16-bit).

► DON'T ASSUME VIDEO PROBLEMS ARE YOUR FAULT

Funny video effects are a common Windows problem. For example, we had a children's game program that ran fine except that all the movie sequences were upside down. The source of these problems is likely in either the program itself or in the video drivers. Don't hesitate to call the software publisher and the computer manufacturer for help.

CROSS-REFERENCE
Chapter 19 shows you how to find driver updates in "Checking for Software Updates."

FIND IT ONLINE
Check the top-ten Display Mate tips at **http://www.displaymate.com/tips.html**.

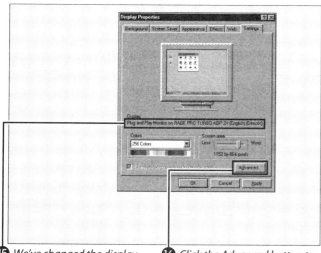

⑮ *We've changed the display driver to an upgraded one from ATI.*

⑯ *Click the Advanced button to access fine-tuning features of the driver.*

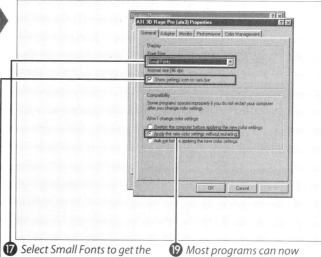

⑰ *Select Small Fonts to get the most onscreen, Large Fonts to make text more readable.*

⑱ *Turn on the settings icon to be able to change resolution from the taskbar.*

⑲ *Most programs can now accommodate changes in colors and resolution automatically.*

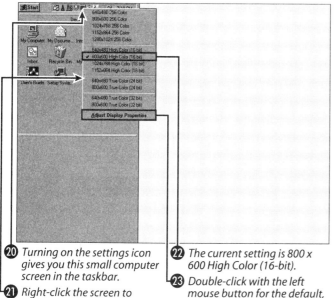

⑳ *Turning on the settings icon gives you this small computer screen in the taskbar.*

㉑ *Right-click the screen to immediately choose number of colors and resolution.*

㉒ *The current setting is 800 x 600 High Color (16-bit).*

㉓ *Double-click with the left mouse button for the default, the Display Properties applet.*

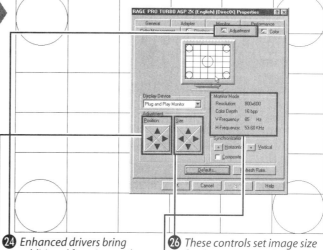

㉔ *Enhanced drivers bring additional functions — here, the ATI dialog to adjust image size and position.*

㉕ *Click these controls to adjust position.*

㉖ *These controls set image size for the current resolution.*

㉗ *Click in the sample window to see test patterns for adjusting your monitor.*

Personal Workbook

Q&A

1 What is the default Windows screen resolution?

_____

_____

_____

2 What can you control from the Control Panel Display applet's Appearance tab?

_____

_____

_____

3 What can you control from the Display applet's Effects tab?

_____

_____

4 How do you control Active Desktop, making your desktop look like a Web page?

_____

_____

_____

5 How can you save your desktop appearance, sound scheme, icons, screen saver, and mouse pointers?

_____

_____

_____

6 How do you set mouse pointers? Screen savers?

_____

_____

7 How can you avoid switching your monitor on and off to reduce power consumption?

_____

_____

_____

8 How can you recover from the loss of your screen saver password?

_____

_____

_____

ANSWERS: PAGE 337

EXTRA PRACTICE

1. Set up a screen saver for your computer.

2. Set up your monitor to power off after an interval and then wait that long. How can you tell it's powered down?

3. Get the specifications for your computer. How big is the monitor? What's the maximum resolution it supports? What's the maximum resolution the computer supports?

4. Experiment with the Display Backgrounds tab to look at the different wallpapers using different center/tile/stretch settings.

5. Reset your screen resolution and font size to find what works best for you.

6. Combine several desktop themes into a new, different theme. Save that theme.

REAL-WORLD APPLICATIONS

✔ You make a desktop theme of your kids to send to your mother, using a group photo for the desktop and individual portraits for each icon.

✔ You connect a microphone to the sound card and have the kids record short clips for the Windows sounds.

✔ You set up Active Desktop during the NBA playoffs to keep track of scores while you work. You lament that the Jazz lost again.

✔ You use one of the high-contrast appearance schemes on your laptop computer to make the screen more readable in poor light. You finish your work in the airport and sleep soundly on the plane.

Visual Quiz

What were we doing here? What went wrong?

_____

_____

_____

_____

_____

_____

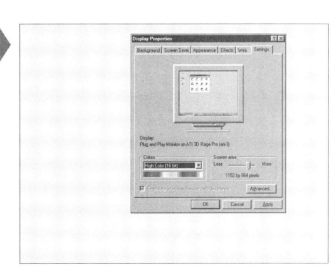

CHAPTER **8**

MASTER
THESE
SKILLS

▶ **Cabling Your Speakers**

▶ **Setting the Windows Sounds**

▶ **Using the Sound Mixer**

▶ **Setting Up MIDI**

Sound

Until relatively recently, sound has been the unloved stepchild of the computer industry. Early personal computers had little or no support for sound, but inventive programmers first programmed the electronics driving the speaker to produce semi-musical tones, and later found ways to make the primitive speaker electronics reproduce recorded sounds.

In a way, the evolution of sound hardware for PCs reflects the most wonderful aspect of the PC industry—you can have what you want if enough people want it. The first dedicated sound cards for PCs could only generate a range of notes, with limited control over timbre and other effects. Later cards added the ability to handle digitized recorded sounds, and then stereo, quality instrument note playback, and 3D positional sound. New technology enables programs to generate high-quality sounds with precise details. Games developers exploit these developments to make game sounds accurate—soft or loud footfalls, sharp or muffled impacts, wooden or metal doors.

Your PC is also growing in capability because manufacturers believe you want computer functions tied to your TV and will sometimes want to see TV-like video on your computer. You can buy add-ons for your TV today that let it do some of the work of a PC's Web browser. You can add DVD hardware to your computer that lets you watch full-length movies on your computer screen with full home-theater sound.

For all of that, sound on a PC has its complications. You can have several sound sources, each of which does a different thing well, but can only do one thing at once. What's called *wave audio*, most often in WAV files, is a digital sound recording. *MIDI audio*, in MID files, is recorded musical notes. Your computer can play audio CDs too, plus take in sound from a microphone or stereo system. That's five kinds of inputs, and all five can be going on at once. What you can't do is have two wave audio tracks, two MIDI tracks, or two CDs, microphones, or stereos.

The most important of these restrictions is that you can't have more than one wave audio track. So if two programs want to play a digital sound, only one will be able to. The other one will be silent. Keep that straight and these lessons should be a breeze.

Cabling Your Speakers

Hooking up speakers to your computer is a job that starts when you pick a set of speakers. If the speakers came with your computer and the sounds your computer makes will be more than beeps and bonks telling you the computer wants your attention, you probably ought to go buy a good set of computer speakers. Many of the ones shipped packaged with computers are — to say this politely — not very good. Computer speakers are different than most stereo speakers because the amplifiers are built in, but as with stereo speakers, there's only one good way to buy them: listen. You can narrow down the field looking at specifications, but only your ears can tell you which ones you like.

The best speakers have a *subwoofer*, a third speaker that handles the bass frequencies. Avoid speakers built into monitors and keyboards — they aren't large or powerful enough to give you good sound.

You can cable speakers to your computer one of two ways — with audio cables like the ones for personal stereos or with a new digital cable called *Universal Serial Bus*, or *USB*. USB is good for hooking many kinds of devices to your computer, including digital cameras and scanners as well as speakers. It's very common for one speaker to cable to the computer, and then chain from there to the other one. You also have to cable the power supply for the speakers to drive the internal amplifier (don't rely on batteries unless you have to).

TAKE NOTE

▶ TAKE YOUR PERSONAL CD PLAYER TO TEST SPEAKERS

Computers aren't the best medium for testing speakers, and most computer stores aren't well equipped for testing. You can plug computer speakers into a handheld CD player, though, which means you can use your favorite music to test and compare. That's a great test, because almost any kind of music is more sustained than what you get from computer software. Plus, you know what the music should sound like.

▶ KEEP SPEAKERS AWAY FROM MONITORS

It matters a lot where you put your speakers. The magnets in speakers can distort the beam on its way to the face of your monitor, creating discolorations over time. (This is one reason speakers in monitors are awful.) Keep paired speakers at the very back of the monitor if you can. Speaker sets including a subwoofer might be okay to put alongside the monitor because they need smaller magnets for the higher frequencies they handle. Put the subwoofer on the floor. If you see distortion or waviness in the image on the monitor, try moving the speakers away. (Remember that there's a left and right speaker. Switch them if they're wrong.)

CROSS-REFERENCE

We covered the basics of placement and cabling in Chapter 1's "Setting Up and Plugging In" lesson.

FIND IT ONLINE

Find lots of USB products at **http://www.usbstuff.com**.

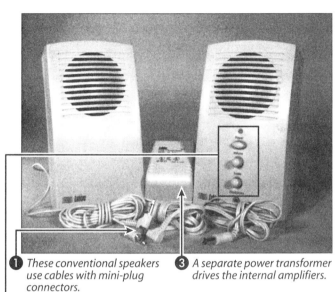

1 These conventional speakers use cables with mini-plug connectors.

2 Typical controls include power, volume, and treble.

3 A separate power transformer drives the internal amplifiers.

4 Computer speakers have different left and right units to form a pair.

5 The left speaker gets its signal from the right unit.

6 The right unit (top to bottom) inputs signal from the computer, outputs signal to the left unit, and receives power.

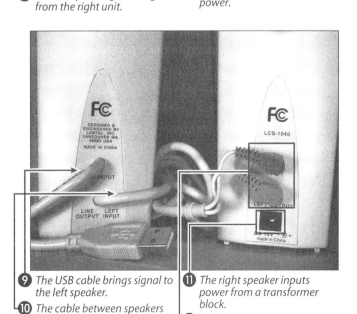

7 These Universal Serial Bus speakers have the same controls as more conventional units.

8 Besides the label, the computer connection cable distinguishes the speakers.

9 The USB cable brings signal to the left speaker.

10 The cable between speakers carries signal from left to right and power from right to left.

11 The right speaker inputs power from a transformer block.

12 Mini-plug connections transfer signal and power on the right speaker.

Setting the Windows Sounds

Computers can work independently on your behalf; they can post reminders of appointments or receive electronic mail, for example. But computers take time to accomplish tasks, and you lose interest after a few seconds of waiting. These factors lead to situations where it's useful for your computer to be able to get your attention. For example, you might press the End key to send the cursor in your word processor to the end of the line when it's already there. You might have entered information about a meeting but need a reminder so you don't forget to attend. You might have started a proposal printing and want to know when it has all been sent to the printer.

Programs under early versions of Windows either ran silently or alerted you to events with a simple beep. At some point, Microsoft gave Windows the ability to play different wave audio files for events instead of simple beeps and tapped into the desire people have to personalize their PCs. Although the default sound announcing the Windows startup is the fairly lame "The Microsoft Sound," and the default Windows sounds are short innocuous beeps and dings, people customize the sounds on their PCs to deliver a little attitude. Your Windows startup sound might be a clip from a favorite TV show, and more than a few PCs shut down with Lieutenant Worf exclaiming, "It is a good day to die."

There's a certain consistency to how you configure Windows — you run the applet in the Control Panel that sets up what you're interested in. The applet to set up the sounds your computer makes is — with good clarity, but poor originality — named Sounds. Opening the applet reveals a dialog box that shows you what events can have sounds tied to them, lets you attach new or different sounds to each event, lets you preview sounds, and lets you save the overall set of sound/event associations as a sound scheme.

TAKE NOTE

► MAKE IT SHORT AND TO THE POINT

There's a limit to how long you want sound clips tied to your Windows events to be. The ideal sound clip both reminds you of the event it denotes (crashing cars for a critical program error, for instance) and is short. Putting a ten-second clip on common events (Asterisk, Exclamation) brings new meaning to the word *annoying*. Short, quiet sounds work well for the Menu popup and Menu command events.

► RESIST TEMPTATION

Don't think that you have to put a sound on every Windows event. Open Program and Close Program are two to avoid. Windows opens and closes programs on its own at times for housekeeping purposes, and the constant or unexpected noise is irritating.

CROSS-REFERENCE

The Internet is the best source of new clips. Learn to download in Chapter 18's "Downloading From the Web."

FIND IT ONLINE

A good tool to edit and modify sound clips is GoldWave at **http://www.goldwave.com**.

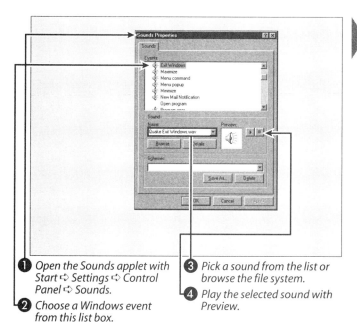

1 *Open the Sounds applet with Start ➪ Settings ➪ Control Panel ➪ Sounds.*

2 *Choose a Windows event from this list box.*

3 *Pick a sound from the list or browse the file system.*

4 *Play the selected sound with Preview.*

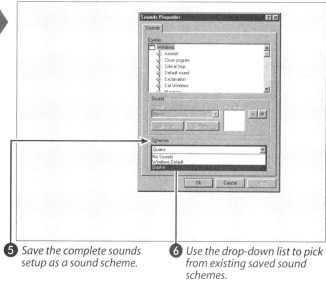

5 *Save the complete sounds setup as a sound scheme.*

6 *Use the drop-down list to pick from existing saved sound schemes.*

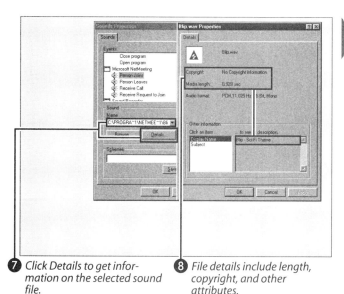

7 *Click Details to get information on the selected sound file.*

8 *File details include length, copyright, and other attributes.*

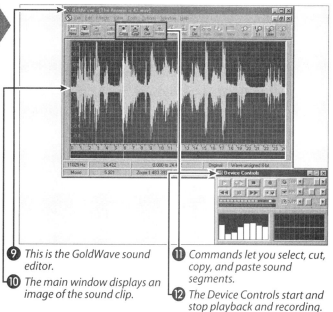

9 *This is the GoldWave sound editor.*

10 *The main window displays an image of the sound clip.*

11 *Commands let you select, cut, copy, and paste sound segments.*

12 *The Device Controls start and stop playback and recording.*

Using the Sound Mixer

You've probably noticed that the volume levels change from one channel to the next on your television and between the CD player and FM tuner on your stereo. Your computer is no different — you have multiple input and output channels, all of which can operate at different volumes. To compensate, each of these channels also has independent volume controls. The collection of volume controls is in an applet called the sound mixer.

Unlike other configuration applets, you don't get to the sound mixer directly from the Control Panel. Instead, you do one of two things: double-click the speaker icon in the taskbar, or click one of the volume slider icons in the Control Panel Multimedia applet. If you single-click the taskbar speaker icon, you get a master volume control for all outputs. Double-clicking the taskbar icon gives you the playback mixer — the one for output devices.

The mixer controls each have a left–right stereo balance on top and a high–low volume slider at the bottom. The control at the far left is the master volume control. The wave audio and master record volume controls add a vertical bar graph to show output level; keep the volume down at least far enough on the slider so the graph stays out of the red area at the top. Otherwise, you're likely to get distorted sound.

You can switch to the recording mixer from the playback mixer by selecting Options ⇨ Properties, followed by choosing the mixer you want.

The Options ⇨ Properties command lets you choose what devices are shown in each mixer, too. Use the list box at the bottom of the dialog box, checking the items you want to see and unchecking the rest. Typically you only show the controls for devices you have and use. It's a good idea to mute the rest before you take them out of the display so you don't hear low-level noise picked up by the open inputs.

TAKE NOTE

▶ SHADDAP!

There's a checkbox in the master volume control that lets you quickly turn off all sound from your system — it's useful when you're playing music and the phone rings. Click once on the speaker in the taskbar, and then check the box. Muting takes effect immediately. Uncheck it to get your sounds back.

▶ SHADDAP! (TAKE TWO)

Fumbling with the mouse isn't for everyone. Another answer if you need to turn off the sound right away is to turn off your speakers. On some systems, this kills all sound; on others, the speakers get enough power from the computer itself to play at reduced volume. Try yours before it matters to see what happens.

CROSS-REFERENCE
Review "Understanding the Windows Desktop" in Chapter 1 if you're unclear on what the taskbar and its icons are.

FIND IT ONLINE
Yamaha's XG MIDI synthesizer at **http://www.yamaha-xg.com/english/xg/s-synth/s-synth.html** gives you better MIDI sound.

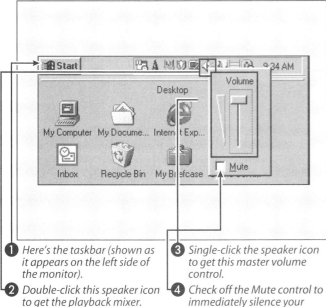

❶ Here's the taskbar (shown as it appears on the left side of the monitor).

❷ Double-click this speaker icon to get the playback mixer.

❸ Single-click the speaker icon to get this master volume control.

❹ Check off the Mute control to immediately silence your computer.

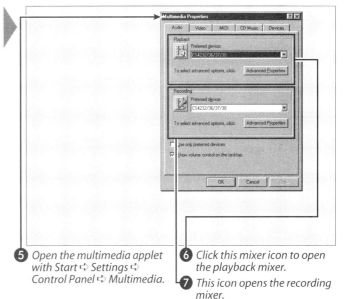

❺ Open the multimedia applet with Start ➪ Settings ➪ Control Panel ➪ Multimedia.

❻ Click this mixer icon to open the playback mixer.

❼ This icon opens the recording mixer.

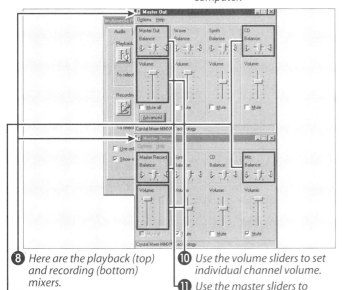

❽ Here are the playback (top) and recording (bottom) mixers.

❾ Use the balance sliders to control left-right stereo balance.

❿ Use the volume sliders to set individual channel volume.

⓫ Use the master sliders to control all channels at the same time.

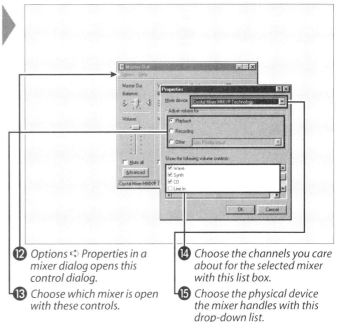

⓬ Options ➪ Properties in a mixer dialog opens this control dialog.

⓭ Choose which mixer is open with these controls.

⓮ Choose the channels you care about for the selected mixer with this list box.

⓯ Choose the physical device the mixer handles with this drop-down list.

Setting Up MIDI

We mentioned in the introduction to this chapter that your PC handles several kinds of sound, including wave audio and MIDI (Musical Instrument Digital Interface). What we didn't mention is that the storage required for files in either format is vastly different. We have a beautiful MIDI file of the *Sorcerer's Apprentice* that requires only 54 thousand bytes (54 kilobytes, or KB); converting this file to CD-quality wave audio produces a WAV file of 20 million bytes (20 megabytes, or MB). The two sound precisely the same although one is nearly 400 times larger.

What's the difference? WAV files contain all the information needed to reproduce any sound, while MIDI files contain only sequences of notes for chosen instruments. MIDI files can't reproduce any sound, just instrumental music. At that, although professional musicians use MIDI and computers extensively, MIDI wasn't even good quality sound on most computers until recently. A technology called *wavetable audio* improved MIDI quality immensely; most recently, complete MIDI sound synthesizers as programs on your computer improved wavetable MIDI even further.

Early versions of MIDI were sort of like whistling a tune — the song might be recognizable, but it's a caricature of real music. The problem was that although fancy electronics could shape signals to sound something like a flute, piano, or other instrument, it was always clear that it was a fake. What wavetable audio does is replace the fake with the real thing — when the MIDI file wants to play middle C on a clarinet, that's what it gets: middle C played on a clarinet and kept as a small wave audio clip stored in the sound card.

TAKE NOTE

▶ DON'T PULL THIS OCEAN LINER WITH A PICKUP TRUCK

The Yamaha XG synthesizers produce wonderful, clear, clean sound from XG-extended MIDI files. Don't run a synthesizer on an underpowered computer, though — not only will the sound be terrible, the computer's likely to become slow and unresponsive. Yamaha's S-YG20 synthesizer requires a Pentium processor at 75 MHz or faster; the S-YXG50 requires a Pentium MMX (an extension Intel added to later Pentium and Pentium II chips) at no less than 166 MHz.

▶ FINISH THE JOB FOR BEST RESULTS

For whatever reason, many systems that ship with wavetable audio sound cards or XG synthesizers don't have them turned on. Follow the steps on the next page to select them with the Multimedia applet and get the best MIDI sound your system can deliver.

CROSS-REFERENCE

Good sound is useless if it gets distorted. Go back to "Cabling Your Speakers" in this chapter to learn how to pick good computer speakers.

FIND IT ONLINE

Get all the MIDI you want at http://www.webthumper.com/midi.

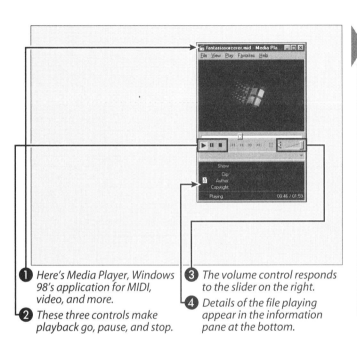

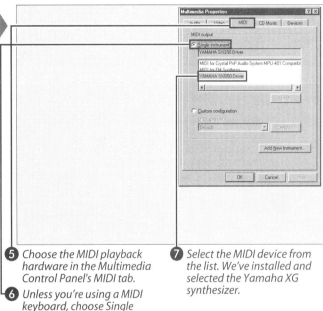

❶ Here's Media Player, Windows 98's application for MIDI, video, and more.

❷ These three controls make playback go, pause, and stop.

❸ The volume control responds to the slider on the right.

❹ Details of the file playing appear in the information pane at the bottom.

❺ Choose the MIDI playback hardware in the Multimedia Control Panel's MIDI tab.

❻ Unless you're using a MIDI keyboard, choose Single instrument.

❼ Select the MIDI device from the list. We've installed and selected the Yamaha XG synthesizer.

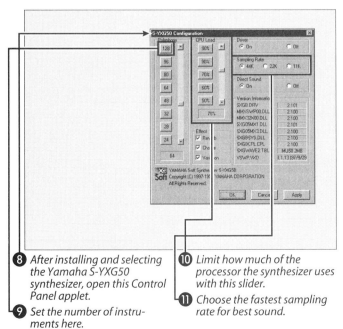

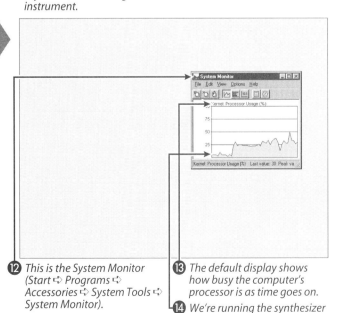

❽ After installing and selecting the Yamaha S-YXG50 synthesizer, open this Control Panel applet.

❾ Set the number of instruments here.

❿ Limit how much of the processor the synthesizer uses with this slider.

⓫ Choose the fastest sampling rate for best sound.

⓬ This is the System Monitor (Start ▷ Programs ▷ Accessories ▷ System Tools ▷ System Monitor).

⓭ The default display shows how busy the computer's processor is as time goes on.

⓮ We're running the synthesizer on a Pentium II 266 MHz, resulting in a moderate load.

Personal Workbook

Q&A

1 Name the types of sound your computer can handle.

_____

_____

_____

2 Name two types of speaker connections.

_____

_____

_____

_____

3 Why does speaker location matter?

_____

_____

_____

4 What characterizes a good sound clip for use with a Windows event?

_____

_____

_____

5 What Windows events should you avoid giving sounds?

_____

_____

_____

6 How do you open the sound mixer applet?

_____

_____

_____

7 How can you quickly mute sounds on your computer?

_____

_____

_____

_____

8 What's the difference between *wave audio* and *MIDI*?

_____

_____

_____

_____

ANSWERS: PAGE 338

EXTRA PRACTICE

1 Play a MIDI file in Windows and use the volume slider. Which volume control on the mixer will move? Open the mixer to confirm your answer.

2 Download WinAmp from **http://www.winamp.com** and some MP3 files from **http://www.mp3.com**. Compare the sound from WinAmp to other sources.

3 Compare the per-minute size of MP3 files to MIDI and wave audio.

4 Install and configure the Yamaha XG synthesizer. Compare the different hardware and MIDI synthesizers on your machine.

5 Download XG MIDI files and compare them to normal MIDI using the Yamaha synthesizer.

REAL-WORLD APPLICATIONS

✔ You record words and messages from your children, adding the sound clips to the desktop theme you built for their grandparents in Chapter 7.

✔ You replace the tiny speakers that came with your computer with a great set including a subwoofer, discovering that the games you play have much better sound effects and cues than you knew.

✔ You add a sound event to make sure you hear it when new electronic mail arrives, enabling you to work across the room from your computer without missing urgent messages from remote offices.

Visual Quiz

What did we do to get this message?

_____

_____

_____

_____

_____

_____

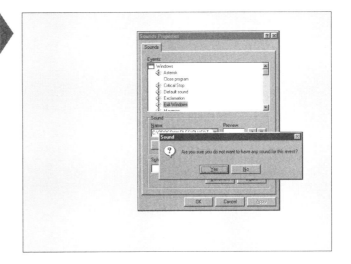

PART

III

Contents of 'Desktop'

Name

My Computer

Network Neigh

Internet Explor

Microsoft Outloo

Recycle Bin

My Briefcase

3252-9

3259-6

3261-8

3262-6

3281-2

3286-3

DE Phone List

Device Manager

In

Iomega Tools

Application Software

You can do a lot with the programs that are part of Windows itself, but to really get the most out of your computer you'll want to add other programs too. In Part III, you learn how to install programs and how to remove installed programs you don't want any longer. You discover that Windows has optional components that you can tune exactly to your needs. You then learn the basics of running a handful of key programs that are built into Windows.

The built-in Windows applications run out of gas easily, though, so eventually you're likely to want more capable software. The last three chapters in this part get you started running the leading word processing, spreadsheet, and fax software — Microsoft Word, Microsoft Excel, and Symantec WinFax. The lessons are specific to these programs, but the skills and concepts you'll learn transfer directly to the major competing applications.

CHAPTER **9**

MASTER
THESE
SKILLS

▶ **Installing a New Program**

▶ **Uninstalling a Program**

▶ **Choosing Installation Options**

▶ **Adding and Removing Windows 98 Components**

Install and Uninstall

A computer is a lot like a garage. There's always something new to go in it, and there's always trash to be taken out. To take this metaphor a little further, every time you clean out your computer, you find leftovers that don't seem to belong to anything, but you're really worried about dumping.

This correspondence is strongest when you think about installing or removing programs from your computer. Adding and removing programs was completely out of control prior to the release of Windows 95. Software developers — often with the best intentions — wrote installation programs that followed no particular guidelines. Most programs offered no built-in way to remove themselves from your system. (This was seen as reasonable — who could possibly live without instant access to Frobishmark's Turbo Smacker Deluxe Gold, Pentium Edition?)

With the cooperation of software developers selling tools to build installers, Microsoft went to great lengths to solve the install/uninstall problem with the release of Windows 95. Their effort was successful to the point that what was starting to become a battle cry in PC magazines has now become a nonissue. Most of what Microsoft did was to draft and coordinate a set of guidelines for installer/uninstaller software — little was required technically in Windows itself. Software written prior to those guidelines has all the old problems, but less and less of that old code survives as time goes on.

It's now routine for programs to include tools to remove the software from your computer, meaning that you can delete programs and be reasonably confident you got all the pieces. The messy part of both install and uninstall is what's called *Dynamic Link Libraries* (DLLs), which are files containing code and data that can be shared among several programs. Most install and uninstall problems are the result of conflicts between different versions of DLLs, or of Windows not knowing which programs want which DLLs. Windows tries to track that information, but it's error prone. There are ways to deal with the problem, though, and we cover them in this chapter.

More than anything, this is the part of owning and maintaining a computer that demands some thought and judgment on your part. If you can do the job you want to effectively with software you already have, it may not pay to install a different program to do the same thing.

Installing a New Program

Installing new software is often no more complicated than popping a CD-ROM into the drive, answering a few questions, and sitting back to watch. Before you do that, though, ask where that software came from. Do you have an original or a copy? If it's a copy, do you have a legitimate license to install the software? Do you know it's free of viruses? If you downloaded the software from the Internet, did it come from a long-term, reputable source, or from someone not involved in the software or in Internet software distribution? Buying software is like buying anything else — watch what you're doing, and know the people with whom you're dealing.

The majority of CD-ROMs automatically start a program to help you install and use the software when you put the disk in the drive. If that doesn't happen, look for a program named SETUP.EXE or INSTALL. EXE on the CD-ROM and run that. A simple way to start the install is Start ⇨ Settings ⇨ Control Panel ⇨ Add/Remove Programs ⇨ Install. (Before you run SETUP or INSTALL, you might want to look for a readme file on the CD-ROM with current information.)

The typical install program collects information from you, such as who you are, what components you want to install, where you want to put the program on your disk, and where you want the program's icons under the Start button.

Once you tell the installer what you want, it should copy files and create icons. During the copy, if the installer detects a shared file — a DLL — that is older than what's on your computer, it's likely to ask for help. Keeping the newer version you already have is usually best unless you know the one being installed is the right one. (For instance, right at the release of Windows 98, it was a safe bet that any DLL Windows wanted to install was the latest and best version.) If the program malfunctions later, you can reinstall the software and let the installer go ahead and replace the file it questioned.

TAKE NOTE

▶ GET YOUR SOFTWARE ON CD-ROM, NOT FLOPPY

Software has migrated almost exclusively to distribution on CD-ROM, which is cheaper, less prone to unreadable or corrupted files, and simpler to install than software on floppies. If you have a choice, always take the CD-ROM option.

▶ THINK ABOUT REGISTERING YOUR SOFTWARE

Many installers request that you register your software after installing. The manufacturers state that registering lets them provide you support, information on updates, and special offers; some actually deliver on this promise, but many do not. You need to decide if you want to provide the information they request or if you'd rather maintain silence and keep your privacy.

CROSS-REFERENCE

See "Installing Antivirus Software" in Chapter 22 to help protect your computer from malicious software.

FIND IT ONLINE

When you run out of disk space, go to **http://www. seagate.com** to figure out what to buy.

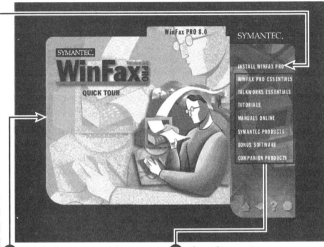

❶ This is the program the WinFax CD-ROM starts when you put it in a CD-ROM drive.

❷ The first option is to install the software. Click it to select it and run the installer.

❸ The other options are tutorials, manuals, and promotions.

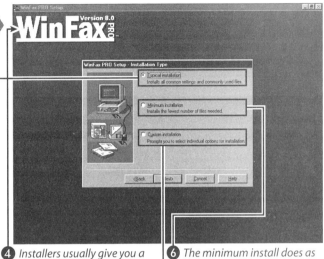

❹ Installers usually give you a choice of how much of the program to install.

❺ The typical install chooses what the manufacturer thinks most people need.

❻ The minimum install does as little as possible, sometimes running from the CD-ROM.

❼ The custom install lets you pick exactly what you want.

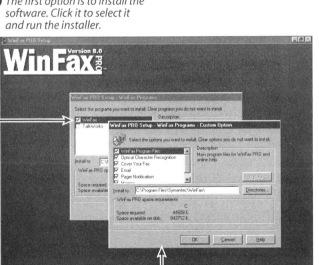

❽ Here's the top-level WinFax dialog box to choose custom options.

❾ A details button leads to this more specific set of choices (see the lesson "Choosing Installation Options").

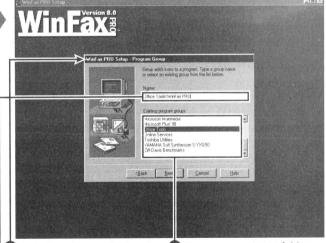

❿ Installers always ask where to put icons under the Start menu.

⓫ Some installers allow you to put one icon folder under another this way.

⓬ You can see existing folders under Start ⇨ Programs in this list.

125

Uninstalling a Program

You uninstall programs with the Add/Remove Programs Control Panel applet (Start ⇨ Settings ⇨ Control Panel ⇨ Add/Remove Programs). Select the entry for your program from the list and then click the Add/Remove button. (The button is named Add/Remove because for some programs it lets you change or add installed options, not just remove options or the entire program.) Don't just delete the program folder — uninstall won't work if you do.

It would be nice if uninstall were as straightforward as install, but it's not. Nor is it that programmers are by nature stupid or slothful — they're not. The problem is that it's difficult to predict everything that might be on your computer or might happen between when you install the program and when you start the uninstall. The fact that the uninstallation software programmer can't know all those things means that some assumptions are going to have to be in play. Sometimes they are right and sometimes they are wrong.

Programmers can't assume all files in the program's install folders are fair game. You might have put data files in there (a generally bad idea), and if the program wipes out your files you're going to be in a real snit by the time tech support answers. Rightly so. The programmer can assume that any DLLs in the install directory are fair game, but ones installed to C:\Windows or C:\Windows\System may not be, and there's no reliable way to know. Some programs don't

try to delete them, some ask permission, and some just do it as long as Windows thinks the files aren't otherwise useful. All three approaches have problems — leaving unnecessary shared DLLs on the disk consumes space that may be recoverable, asking assumes the user would know the answer (not likely), and wiping them out could break other programs. Given the choice, leave the files on the disk. Some disk space is a small price to pay for improving your chances of keeping a running system.

TAKE NOTE

► **CLEANING UP INSTALLED FOLDERS**

Once the uninstall routine finishes, look at the disk to see if the folder containing the program is gone. If it's not, you have some detective work to do. The most common reason programs leave folders behind is that there are files in the folders the uninstaller doesn't recognize or thinks you've modified. If you decide everything's expendable, go ahead and delete the folder.

► **DON'T EXPECT A WELL-ORDERED LIST**

Companies aren't consistent about the names they use in the Add/Remove Programs list of programs you can uninstall. Some programs include the company name (Frobishmark Turbo Smacker Deluxe Gold), but others don't (Turbo Smacker Deluxe Gold). Look through the list before you decide the program didn't have an uninstaller.

CROSS-REFERENCE

The process for installing and uninstalling Windows components is a little different. See "Adding and Removing Windows 98 Components" in this chapter.

FIND IT ONLINE

Find some other disk space saving hints at http://www.pcworld.com/pcwtoday/article/0,1510,5 300,00.html.

Forget What the Software Says: Reboot Early and Often

It's a good idea to reboot right before you install new programs — that way, you start with fewer programs running. Close all the ones you can, and then do the install. Programs that are running cause Windows to mark the program files as busy, and when that happens, an installer can't put in new versions. By making sure no earlier version of the program you're installing is running, you help make sure the installer can do its work.

It's not enough to make sure no earlier version of the program you're installing is running. Files common to two or more programs, called shared files, can also make software installation and removal tricky, because a shared file in use by a running program can't be modified or replaced by another program. That's why nearly all setup programs recommend you close *all* running programs — if a shared file doesn't get installed, the new program might not work. (Yes, there's a problem of what version of the file is installed. You usually want the latest one.)

Programs that deal with shared files correctly use a mechanism Microsoft built into Windows that writes the file to disk with a temporary name, and then moves it to the right place and name when you reboot. That's much of what's happening when you see the message "Windows is updating your configuration files. Please wait." at boot time.

That update process only happens when you reboot, and setup programs don't always properly tell you when you need to reboot. You can solve that problem by always rebooting after an install — it's a good idea to reboot after any installation.

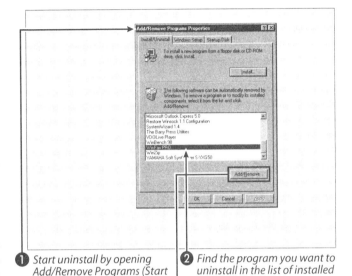

① Start uninstall by opening Add/Remove Programs (Start ⇨ Settings ⇨ Control Panel ⇨ Add/Remove Programs).

② Find the program you want to uninstall in the list of installed programs.

③ Click Add/Remove to start the uninstaller.

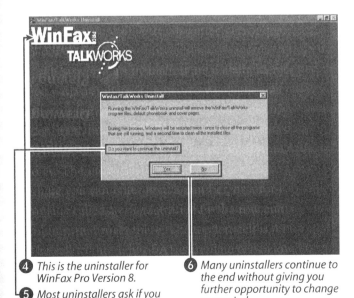

④ This is the uninstaller for WinFax Pro Version 8.

⑤ Most uninstallers ask if you want to do the uninstall as the first step.

⑥ Many uninstallers continue to the end without giving you further opportunity to change your mind.

Choosing Installation Options

At one time, when personal computers were smaller and less capable, software had fewer features. Increases in PC resources — disk, memory, processing, and graphics, for instance — combined with increasing demands by users for functionality have resulted in enormous application suites with tens or hundreds of options. A product like Microsoft Office isn't one size fits all, it's one size covers all. The chances you'd use every function and feature in the program are nearly zero.

It's unreasonable for software developers to expect their customers to install everything in the package when the installation will consume hundreds of megabytes of disk space, especially if a significant part of the space is to hold features they won't use. Developers solved this problem, in part, by writing their installation programs to let you choose what options you want and which ones you don't. You make those choices at several levels: a top level that offers packaged install options (typical or custom; and small, medium, or large are common top-level options), and more detailed levels that let you fine-tune each part of the whole.

A typical install choice automatically selects what the manufacturer thinks are the most common options, while a custom install gives you control over what happens. The examples on the facing page are from Microsoft Office 97 Setup, which offers some of the most extensive setup customization capabilities we've seen. The hierarchy of choices in Office's custom setup may seem tedious by the time you get to the end, but all those functions are in the software.

Almost all installation programs ask you where you want to put the programs. The default folder for many programs is underneath the C:\Program Files (one of Microsoft's Windows software installer guidelines). That's typically a good choice, because programs end up in a place you can remember that's somewhat out of the way.

CROSS-REFERENCE

"Installing a New Program" in this chapter gives you an overview of how the installation process works.

FIND IT ONLINE

A frequent critic of software bloat is John Dvorak. See one column at **http://search.zdnet.com/pcmag/insites/inside_track/it971104.htm.**

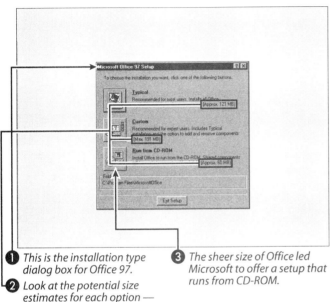

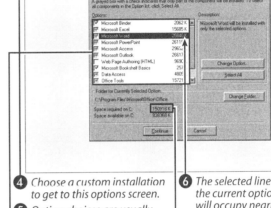

1 This is the installation type dialog box for Office 97.

2 Look at the potential size estimates for each option — they're big.

3 The sheer size of Office led Microsoft to offer a setup that runs from CD-ROM.

4 Choose a custom installation to get to this options screen.

5 Option choices are usually in a hierarchy. For Office, individual applications are on top.

6 The selected line shows that the current options for Word will occupy nearly 26MB on disk.

7 The overall install options presently need nearly 151MB.

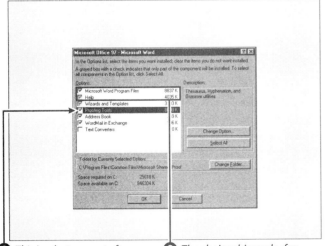

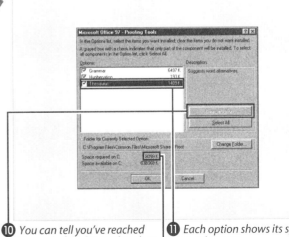

8 This is what you get after clicking Change Option in the previous figure with Word selected.

9 The choices hierarchy for Word includes the program and help files, plus options expanding what the program does.

10 You can tell you've reached the end of the hierarchy when the Change Option button grays out.

11 Each option shows its space requirement.

12 The total space for the displayed set of options is maintained in each dialog box.

Adding and Removing Windows 98 Components

Windows 95 installation and upgrades ask a ton of questions about what you want to install if you chose a custom install. If you had a job where you did a lot of installs, it could be a colossal pain.

Windows 98 is much quieter during install — especially for upgrades. It gets a little information and then simply copies files. Once installation is done and Windows 98 is up and running, you can fine-tune what's installed with the Add/Remove applet's Windows Setup tab. The organization of what's in the applet is similar to the hierarchical choices you see in Office 97 in the previous lesson, "Choosing Installation Options." The items in the list correspond to the functional groups of capabilities in Windows. Click Details to get the individual list of components in the group.

The check marks you see in the figure in the upper left are representative of what you see in most programs for choosing components. No check mark means that the item will not be installed, a gray check mark means that some of the components in the item will be installed, and a black-and-white check mark means that all components will be installed.

The Startup Disk tab in Add/Remove Programs is particularly important. If you don't have a startup disk, make one now — it's what you need to have any chance of recovering your system if something goes wrong and it won't start. (For instance, if your computer crashes or loses power without an orderly shutdown, it's possible to create problems on the disk. The startup disk can find those. It's enough to reinstall Windows over itself, too, which can fix many seemingly severe problems.)

TAKE NOTE

HOOK A CD-ROM INTO THE STARTUP DISK

Windows 95 had a critical weakness in the startup disks it created — they didn't include the drivers you needed to read CD-ROMs. If you didn't modify the startup disk yourself to add CD-ROM drivers, you were likely to be severely out of luck if you ever had to use the disk. Microsoft addressed this problem with Windows 98. The CD-ROMs in most computers are handled by drivers provided on the standard startup disk.

FIND GOLD IN WINDOWS SETUP

You can install a lot of Windows components through Windows Setup. Some components are little known and incredibly useful. Many of them are in System Tools in Windows 98. Two of the most interesting are System Monitor, which looks at performance counters in Windows, and System Resource Meter, which tracks how much of key parts of your system the programs you run are using. If the System Resource Meter gets below 25 percent or so, your system is likely to start having problems — close some programs or reboot.

CROSS-REFERENCE

One of the valuable Windows applications is Backup. See how to use it in the Chapter 10 lesson, "Backing Up Your System."

FIND IT ONLINE

Restore a missing startup disk file after reading http://www.pcworld.com/pcwtoday/article/0,1510,6 786,00.html

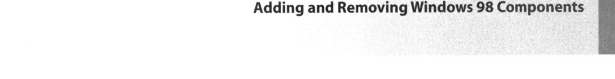

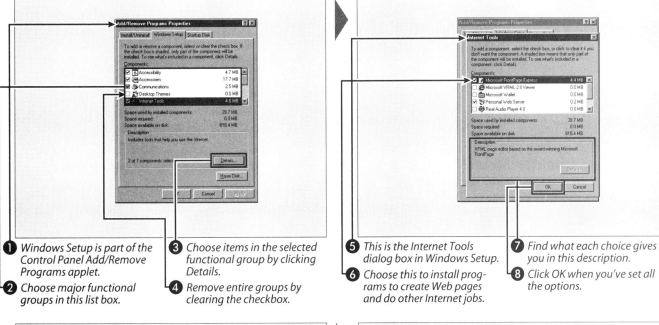

① *Windows Setup is part of the Control Panel Add/Remove Programs applet.*

② *Choose major functional groups in this list box.*

③ *Choose items in the selected functional group by clicking Details.*

④ *Remove entire groups by clearing the checkbox.*

⑤ *This is the Internet Tools dialog box in Windows Setup.*

⑥ *Choose this to install programs to create Web pages and do other Internet jobs.*

⑦ *Find what each choice gives you in this description.*

⑧ *Click OK when you've set all the options.*

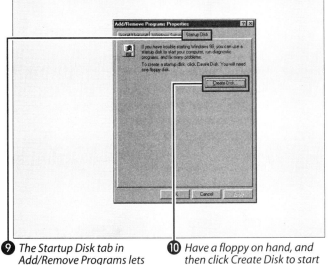
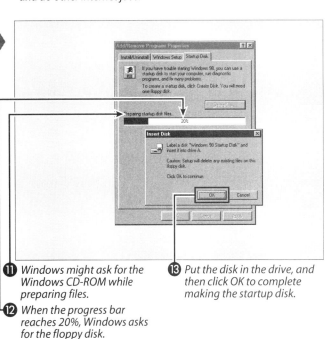

⑨ *The Startup Disk tab in Add/Remove Programs lets you make a floppy that could save your system.*

⑩ *Have a floppy on hand, and then click Create Disk to start the process.*

⑪ *Windows might ask for the Windows CD-ROM while preparing files.*

⑫ *When the progress bar reaches 20%, Windows asks for the floppy disk.*

⑬ *Put the disk in the drive, and then click OK to complete making the startup disk.*

Personal Workbook

Q&A

1 What's a *Dynamic Link Library*?

_____

_____

_____

2 What's a common source of install and uninstall problems?

_____

_____

_____

3 What important step should you take before installing or uninstalling programs?

_____

_____

_____

4 What's the first thing you should do before installing a program?

_____

_____

_____

5 How are the installed components chosen for a typical installation type?

_____

_____

_____

6 How are the installed components chosen for a custom installation type?

_____

_____

_____

7 What's the most common top-level folder for program installation?

_____

_____

_____

8 What's a *startup disk*?

_____

_____

_____

ANSWERS: PAGE 338

EXTRA PRACTICE

1. Make a Windows startup disk.

2. Boot your computer from the Windows startup disk. What programs are on drive A?

3. If you're running Windows 98, look for a new drive D or E after you start the startup disk. What's there?

4. Read the README.TXT file on your Windows CD-ROM and some of the other files it refers you to.

5. Look at the folders under C:\Program Files. Try to associate each one with the program it contains.

6. For one of your installed programs, right-click its folder in Windows Explorer and choose Properties. How big is the total size? What percentage of your disk is that? If your disk cost $200, how much does it cost to store that program?

REAL-WORLD APPLICATIONS

✔ After installing a particularly buggy piece of software, you discover your system becomes unstable every time you run it. You uninstall the software and return it to the place you bought it.

✔ You discover that an advertised feature you'd expected to find in your word processor isn't available on your system. You check the installed components using Add/Remove Programs and find that feature wasn't installed. You add it to your system and return to your work.

✔ A new game for your children doesn't automatically install when you insert the CD-ROM. You find the SETUP.EXE program on the disk and start the installer.

Visual Quiz

What's happening here? How did we get this dialog box?

_____

_____

_____

_____

_____

_____

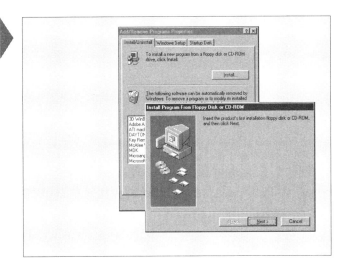

CHAPTER **10**

MASTER THESE SKILLS

▶ Formatting in WordPad

▶ Drawing in Paint

▶ Playing Music with CD Player

▶ Backing Up Your System

Running Windows 98 Applications

If you've been reading this book from front to back, you've seen the basics of Windows and should be comfortable with starting your computer, configuring Windows, installing and uninstalling programs, and starting programs. Now it's time to dive into some of the applications that come packaged with Windows 98 to learn more about what they can do and how to make them do it.

The Windows applications are typically lightweight when compared to fully featured programs. WordPad gives you some of the power of Microsoft Word, Paint gives you a small amount of the power of Adobe Photoshop, and Backup gives you a little of what Seagate Backup Exec can do. If these bundled programs do everything you need, they're a great value. The ideas and techniques you learn in this chapter are useful whether you use the Windows programs or similar heavy-duty products.

The reason so much learning carries over from one program to another is that, from the early days of windowed computer systems, companies have realized the value of consistency and published guides for developers. Xerox knew it for the Star, Apple for the Macintosh, and Microsoft for Windows. What that means for

you is that as you learn what Windows applications can do and what the different file formats for those applications are, you find that other programs use the same ideas.

This is a more powerful idea than you may at first realize. Think about what you've learned. You know that programs are going to appear onscreen as windows, that you can launch programs from icons found under the Start button, and that programs have commands that you access through the menu and the toolbar. You've also learned that most Windows elements can be configured through applets in the Control Panel, that the information programs manipulate is stored in files, that files are stored in folders, and more. Every bit of that is the way it is because it helps you remember how to use Windows.

Consider the alternative — programs with so-called *improved* user interfaces. One in particular was supposed to simplify Windows for kids; you accessed everything there was to do through spots onscreen that were sensitive to the mouse, but there were no cues that you were near one of those spots. Even when you did find a sensitive spot, nothing onscreen really suggested what happened when you clicked the mouse there. We literally threw the program away — it was that bad.

Formatting in WordPad

What you write has to stand on its own, but presentation, layout, and formatting can help readers understand what you have to say. Remember the letter to Dan's Lawn Service in Chapter 2? Assume that the complaints department needs a little help getting the idea. Almost everything you do in this lesson is in the top-level Format menu, including commands to set the font, change the paragraph to bulleted items, and set tabs. Those are basic tools compared to fully featured word processors, but with a little patience, you can do a lot.

WordPad is like an old IBM Selectric typewriter — the ones with the golf ball-style heads — that let you set margins, tabs, and (by changing the ball) fonts. Anything you could do with one of those typewriters you can do with WordPad. The equivalent of the golf balls is the font files stored in the C:\Windows\Fonts folder. Windows fonts use TrueType technology, so each font is stored in a file with a TTF extension. Although older versions of Windows needed separate files for different type sizes, TrueType synthesizes all required sizes from the one file. Windows includes the key workhorse fonts — Arial, Times New Roman, and Courier New.

While it didn't matter what combination of spaces and tabs you used to move the head over with a typewriter, using lots of tabs and spaces with a word processor is a bad idea. The right way to use tabs is to put them exactly where you want them and use one keystroke — the tab — to get there. You can use the default half-inch tab settings and lots of tabs and spaces, but if you want to reformat your spacing, you have a mess on your hands.

TAKE NOTE

▶ ADD FONTS TO WINDOWS

You're not limited to the fonts included in Windows — the Internet is a rich source of new fonts of all sorts, many of which you can download and use for free. New fonts are simple to add to Windows — just drag and drop the TTF file into the C:\Windows\Fonts folder. Windows 95 handles all the work to make the font available to programs behind the scenes.

▶ FONTS ARE IN WINDOWS, NOT THE DOCUMENT

Some people go wild with fonts, using so many fonts in a document that looking at it is painful. It's common for those masterworks to have all the fancy fonts vanish on another machine. The problem is that only the font settings are in the document; the fonts themselves are stored by Windows. If the fonts a document needs aren't on the system, Windows substitutes something else.

CROSS-REFERENCE

A key skill for enhancing your system is downloading files from the Internet. See Chapter 18's "Downloading From the Web."

FIND IT ONLINE

Find new fonts at SoftSeek, **http://www.softseek.com/ Graphics_and_Drawing/Fonts**.

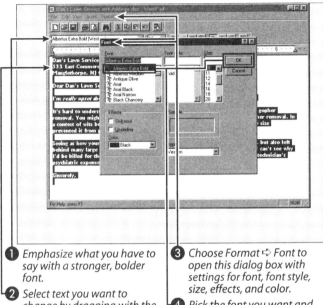

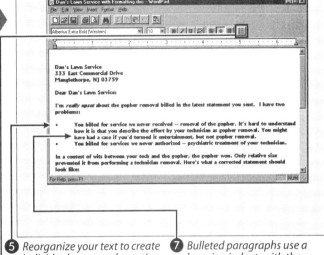

① *Emphasize what you have to say with a stronger, bolder font.*

② *Select text you want to change by dragging with the left mouse button.*

③ *Choose Format ⇨ Font to open this dialog box with settings for font, font style, size, effects, and color.*

④ *Pick the font you want and click OK.*

⑤ *Reorganize your text to create individual paragraphs stating points you want to highlight.*

⑥ *Make the paragraphs stand out by using the bulleted paragraph button.*

⑦ *Bulleted paragraphs use a hanging indent, with the second and subsequent lines indented from the first.*

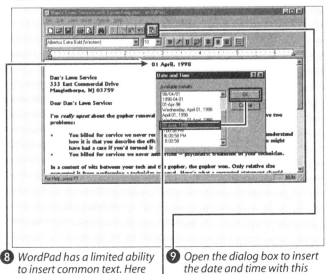

⑧ *WordPad has a limited ability to insert common text. Here we've inserted the date.*

⑨ *Open the dialog box to insert the date and time with this toolbar button or use the command Insert ⇨ Date and Time.*

⑩ *Select the format you want.*

⑪ *Create a table with tab stops in the table paragraphs.*

⑫ *Set the tab stops with the Format ⇨ Tabs command.*

⑬ *Set each tab by entering its position, and then clicking Set.*

⑭ *Use the Tab key to sequence to the next column in your table.*

Drawing in Paint

Paint (Start ⇨ Programs ⇨ Accessories ⇨ Paint) is one of the oldest programs in Windows. Few of the character-based PCs before Windows had drawing tools, so Paint was a real advance.

Not for long. Paint's advantage is that it's simple to learn and use, but that simplicity carries a price: It's very limited in what it can do. Paint manipulates a limited set of file types, including bitmaps (BMP) and two types commonly found on the Internet (GIF and JPEG). Its biggest limitation is that (with the exception of text) once you draw something, it's part of the image and can't be handled separately, making changes difficult.

More sophisticated drawing programs know more file types, keep track of the individual things you do, and let you modify them later. You want to understand, though, the kinds of drawing work you do to pick a program. For example, Adobe Photoshop excels at working with bitmap images like photographs, while Adobe Illustrator excels at drawings of the sort you might do with pencil, pastels, or ink. Microsoft PowerPoint is simpler in some ways than Illustrator, because it's focused on creating and delivering visual presentations.

The basic operations in all programs like Paint are to draw and erase with tools in a toolbar. You get a variety of tools that are mostly related to physical tools, including a pen, eraser, pencil, brush, airbrush, and paint bucket. Some tools are computer versions of physical tools, including template-like tools that draw shapes or text. Tools also have attributes. For example, you can set the color and line width of a pen. Some tools are computer-only tools, such as an eraser that only erases the color you choose.

TAKE NOTE

▶ YOU DON'T HAVE TO DRAW WITH THE MOUSE

A mouse is one of the clumsiest drawing tools around — exceeded only by the keyboard — so it's reasonable to expect you could find a better way to draw with a PC. You can — the device you want is called a *drawing tablet*. Most have a stylus that works like a pencil; the best ones are both pressure and slant sensitive. You need a drawing program such as MetaCreations Art Dabbler, Adobe Photoshop, or Adobe Illustrator that knows how to work with the tablet. Paint doesn't.

▶ TABLETS ARE FOR YOUNG ARTISTS TOO

A drawing tablet can be the key to unlock your computer for a kid too young to write. WACOM Technology (makers of tablets) describes drawing with a mouse as "like trying to draw with a bar of soap." Some tablets come bundled with software that works with the tablet, so your preschooler could be up and running on your computer with no more of an investment than the tablet itself.

CROSS-REFERENCE

Make sure you've installed Paint. See "Adding and Removing Windows 98 Components" in Chapter 9 for help.

FIND IT ONLINE

WACOM Technology Corporation makes excellent tablets. Find them at **http://www.wacom.com**.

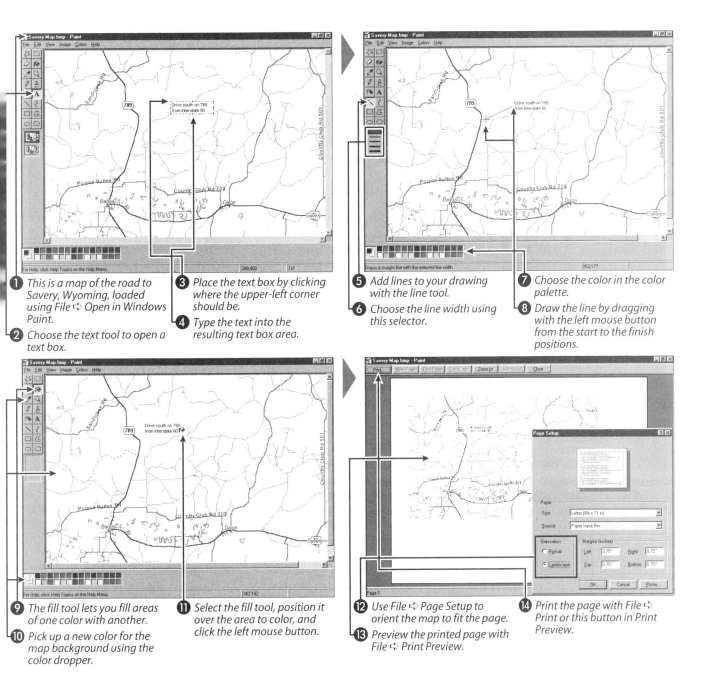

① This is a map of the road to Savery, Wyoming, loaded using File ➪ Open in Windows Paint.

② Choose the text tool to open a text box.

③ Place the text box by clicking where the upper-left corner should be.

④ Type the text into the resulting text box area.

⑤ Add lines to your drawing with the line tool.

⑥ Choose the line width using this selector.

⑦ Choose the color in the color palette.

⑧ Draw the line by dragging with the left mouse button from the start to the finish positions.

⑨ The fill tool lets you fill areas of one color with another.

⑩ Pick up a new color for the map background using the color dropper.

⑪ Select the fill tool, position it over the area to color, and click the left mouse button.

⑫ Use File ➪ Page Setup to orient the map to fit the page.

⑬ Preview the printed page with File ➪ Print Preview.

⑭ Print the page with File ➪ Print or this button in Print Preview.

139

Playing Music with CD Player

There's been an interesting evolution in the application of computers, from the belief that only a handful would ever be needed, to their use to run companies and businesses, to their use by individual workers in companies, to their use in the home and for games. All these changes have been driven by the radical increases in power and reductions in price for which the computer industry is famous.

The history of CD-ROM drives follows this pattern in miniature. Early CD-ROM drives were expensive and few discs were available because the cost to make discs was high, so few machines had them. Prices for drives and titles came down to the point where it became cheaper to distribute software on CD-ROM than on floppy. At that point, essentially every computer started to have a built-in CD-ROM drive. The CD-ROM is idle in many of those machines most of the time, though, so it was inevitable that (because they can play audio CDs) the drives would be put to work playing music. Doing that requires software for control, of course, leading to the usual gentle competition among programmers as to who could pack in the most features. The Internet was, as with other accessory programs, the best place to look for players.

The CD player in the Microsoft Plus! Pack for Windows 98 (Deluxe CD Player of all things) is a contender for the feature prize. Beyond the usual CD player controls, it has a feature that makes it worth the entire price of the Plus! Pack — it can download disc and track titles from the Internet. You simply put the disc in and let the player loose on the Net. It downloads from Tunes.com or Music Boulevard, sets the playlist, and shows you the results onscreen. Use the Options ⇨ Playlist command to edit the tracks for the disc to just the ones you want to hear.

TAKE NOTE

▶ GET MORE THAN YOU MIGHT EXPECT

Game CD-ROMs often contain sound tracks starting at track 2 (the programs are track 1). Not only can your computer play those audio tracks, for some games, the Plus! Pack Deluxe CD Player can download titles. (id Software's Quake disc displays as being by Nine Inch Nails; Quake II disc shows up as by Sonic Mayhem. The first Quake II audio track is named "Operation Overlord.")

▶ TARGET YOUR WEB SEARCHES

Don't overlook the commands on the Plus! Pack CD player's Internet button when you're looking for information about music groups and albums. You can use those commands to search Internet music sites for more information on the artist that recorded the CD you're playing, the album itself, and other albums of the same type.

CROSS-REFERENCE
Install the Plus! Pack with the assistance of the lesson "Installing a New Program" in Chapter 9.

FIND IT ONLINE
Tunes.com is at (big surprise here) **http://www.tunes.com.**

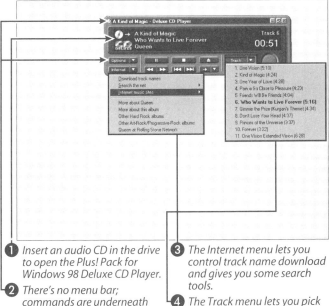

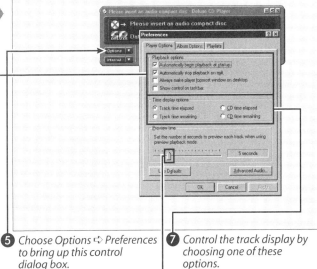

1 Insert an audio CD in the drive to open the Plus! Pack for Windows 98 Deluxe CD Player.

2 There's no menu bar; commands are underneath the buttons in the window.

3 The Internet menu lets you control track name download and gives you some search tools.

4 The Track menu lets you pick tracks by name.

5 Choose Options ⇨ Preferences to bring up this control dialog box.

6 Control how the player runs and appears on the desktop with these controls.

7 Control the track display by choosing one of these options.

8 Lengthen or shorten the preview time with this slider.

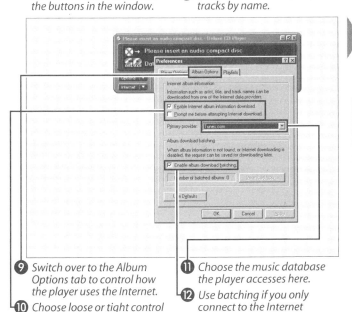

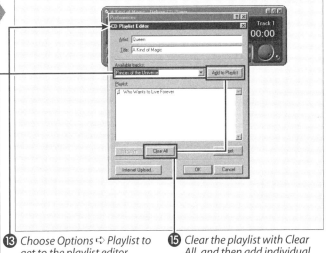

9 Switch over to the Album Options tab to control how the player uses the Internet.

10 Choose loose or tight control over Internet access with these checkboxes.

11 Choose the music database the player accesses here.

12 Use batching if you only connect to the Internet occasionally.

13 Choose Options ⇨ Playlist to get to the playlist editor.

14 All the known tracks show up in this drop-down box.

15 Clear the playlist with Clear All, and then add individual tracks with Add to Playlist.

Backing Up Your System

It won't take long for you to be convinced that computers are not perfectly reliable. The computer might break or you might do something you didn't intend, but the chances are that every so often you're going to have a problem. What to do? Hardware can be fixed, so the risk is to your files. There's really only one option to make sure you can recover from a crash or mistake — have copies of your files somewhere besides your computer.

In practice, that means you need to copy the files to another computer, if you have a network, or to a removable storage device. You have a range of choices for removable storage, including floppy disk (up to 120MB), removable disk (up to several gigabytes), and tape (4 to 8 gigabytes at reasonable prices). Of these, floppies are impractical for all but limited data backups and removable disks are expensive. Tape is your best alternative — you can get tape drives to install inside your machine for a few hundred dollars and tapes for $10 to $20. Compare that to the cost of losing all your work.

It can take longer than you'd like to back up everything on your computer to tape, so you use several types of backup. A full backup copies everything on the machine to tape, including a critical Windows data store called the *registry*. A differential backup copies everything since the last full backup. An incremental backup copies everything since the last full or incremental backup. Because differential and incremental backups only copy new or changed files, they do less work and take less time.

Setting up the backup or restore operations can be confusing, so Windows Backup provides wizards, sequences of dialog boxes that help you do the job. You simply start the wizard and answer the questions.

TAKE NOTE

BE READY TO RECOVER YOUR SYSTEM

If you lose your entire system, recovery could be hard. You need Windows running before you can run Windows Backup to reload your tapes. Windows 98 provides System Recovery to solve this problem. All you need is your full system backup, your startup disk, and the Windows 98 CD-ROM. Find all the directions in the file \tools\sysrec\recover.txt on the CD-ROM.

PING PONG YOUR TAPES

If you really understand that computers can foul up at the worst times, you realize that one of the worst times to have a problem is when you're writing a backup tape. If it's your only backup, a worst-case disaster would take out not only your computer, but also your tape. Don't let that happen — have at least two sets of tapes and use them in rotation.

CROSS-REFERENCE

Install Windows Backup using the "Adding and Removing Windows 98 Components" lesson in Chapter 9.

FIND IT ONLINE

The heavy-duty version of Windows 98 Backup is from Seagate. See http://www.seagatesoftware.com/bedesktop98.

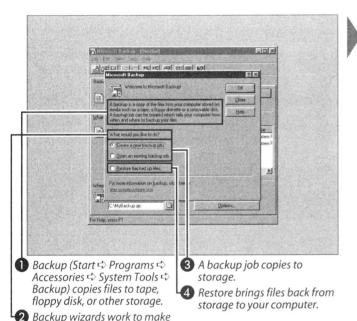

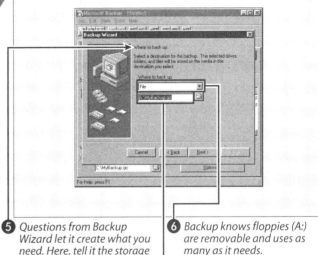

1 Backup (Start ⇨ Programs ⇨ Accessories ⇨ System Tools ⇨ Backup) copies files to tape, floppy disk, or other storage.

2 Backup wizards work to make operation simple.

3 A backup job copies to storage.

4 Restore brings files back from storage to your computer.

5 Questions from Backup Wizard let it create what you need. Here, tell it the storage destination.

6 Backup knows floppies (A:) are removable and uses as many as it needs.

7 Tape drives show up here as another option.

8 The main window shows the files selected for backup or restore.

9 Drives and folders show up in the left pane, folders and files in the right.

10 A gray check says some files are selected.

11 A blue check says all files are selected.

12 This dialog box shows progress as the backup runs.

13 The values in these areas show the total backup (Estimated) and the progress so far (Processed).

14 This dialog box shows backup has filled the current floppy and is waiting for the next.

Personal Workbook

Q&A

1 What can you do if you don't find WordPad or Paint on your system?

_____

_____

_____

2 What is *TrueType*?

_____

_____

_____

3 How do you install new fonts?

_____

_____

_____

4 When should you avoid using tab stops?

_____

_____

_____

5 Why might fonts in documents look funny on another machine?

_____

_____

_____

6 What file types can Paint handle?

_____

_____

_____

7 What can go on a CD-ROM?

_____

_____

_____

8 What track holds the information in a mixed data/video CD-ROM?

_____

_____

_____

ANSWERS: PAGE 339

EXTRA PRACTICE

1 After you've played a few audio CDs, look in the file C:\Windows\cdplayer.ini.

2 Start Paint and maximize the window. Let a young child scribble with the mouse.

3 Type a letter into WordPad and format it with the different fonts you find on your system.

4 Run the command Insert ⇨ Object ⇨ Wave Sound in WordPad. When Sound Recorder starts, insert a file from C:\Windows\Media or record your own.

5 Double-click the icon you created in practice step 5. What happens?

REAL-WORLD APPLICATIONS

✔ Your computer is stolen when thieves break into your apartment, and they take all your data with them. You restore from the backup tapes you made the previous night.

✔ A power failure shuts down your computer unexpectedly, and when the power comes back on you find the computer won't start. You boot the startup disk and run the SCANDISK program. After it repairs problems in your file system, your computer starts and runs normally.

✔ In a dream, you see yourself loading CDs into your computer at work while you explore entertainment Web sites. The Internet Faerie appears in your dream, noting you're violating your company's Internet use policy. Chastened, you leave the CDs at home.

Visual Quiz

What is this dialog box? How do you get to it?

_____

_____

_____

_____

_____

_____

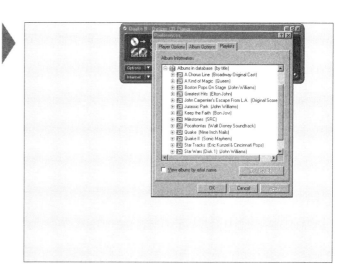

CHAPTER **11**

MASTER
THESE
SKILLS

▶ Using What You Know from WordPad

▶ Using the Hidden Power of Styles

▶ Handling Tables

▶ Importing from Other Applications

Quickstart Word 97

Microsoft Word goes much further than WordPad, adding features not possible on a typewriter. Word adds file formats, different ways to view the text onscreen, stronger abilities to work with other programs, more extensive formatting options, wholesale revision of document formatting, ways to handle data as tables, and a wide variety of tools to help you work with documents. Throughout these lessons, you see that what Word does and how it does it is an expansion of what you've learned in WordPad, not a replacement.

You need Microsoft Word 97 installed on your computer to follow the lessons directly. You can find Word 97 in Microsoft Office 97 or packaged separately. If you have another version of Word, or another word processor altogether, the capabilities and command sequences will differ. Nevertheless, competition in the application software market has been such that there's a lot of feature overlap among different manufacturers' offerings, so you should be able to find the equivalent to what we describe using the help files and manuals.

At one time, the differences among word processors were strictly in what formatting and tools they offered, with the ability to display onscreen what you would print being a major advance. Current generations of word processors go well beyond that, extending back to enhance original document creation and forward to collaboration, review, and publication. Tables, error correction as you type, and continuous speech recognition (using add-on products like Dragon Systems NaturallySpeaking or IBM ViaVoice Gold) make text entry faster and more straightforward. Similarly, annotations, automatic revision marks, and file output ready for Web access make getting your work to other people faster and easier.

With enough computer horsepower, Word is capable of large scale, serious work. We've written business proposals with Word that — in a single file — were hundreds of pages long and had embedded photos, graphics, and drawings. Files for those proposals grew to more than 100MB. We wrote the proposals on a 200 MHz Pentium processor with 64MB of memory, and printed the shippable volumes directly from Word. We write our books with Word too, using one file per chapter.

As good as Word is, you should know it has some warts too. Our personal guidelines are to avoid files bigger than 125MB, keep original files for pictures, and not use what Word calls master documents. Within those limitations, though, Word gets a lot of work done.

Using What You Know from WordPad

S tart Word and take stock of what you see. The window has all the standard elements you're used to, including a title bar, menu bar, toolbars, and a large open area where your documents will show up. Some of the icons in the toolbar are familiar too; you know from WordPad about the ones to create a new document, open a file, save a file, print, and preview the printed page. The second toolbar is somewhat familiar too, with controls to pick the font; set font size; choose bold, italic, or underlined text; set paragraph alignment to left, center, or right; and add bullets to paragraphs.

If you've been working our examples for WordPad on your own computer, open the file in WordPad and then in Word. They look much the same — both WordPad and Word are called *What You See Is What You Get* (or *WYSIWYG*) word processors. The upper-right and lower-left screen shots on the facing page compare the menus you've been using in WordPad (File, View, Insert, and Format) with their equivalents in Word. You see direct correspondence for the File menu (although Word's has some new commands), but things start to look pretty different after that.

Comparing the View menus reveals that Word can show you your document in a variety of ways. View ⇨ Page Layout, for instance, gives you the same ability to see your words the way they'll print as Print Preview does, except that you can edit in the window. Once you're in Page Layout view, Zoom ⇨ Page

Width shifts the display scale so the width of the page, not the length, fills the screen, making the text bigger.

Be sure to compare the Format ⇨ Paragraph commands. Word adds the ability to control line spacing before, in, and after each paragraph, plus an entire tab in the dialog box to control how lines and paragraphs break across pages.

TAKE NOTE

UNDERSTAND THE "FILE IN USE" MESSAGE

If you reversed the WordPad/Word order in the second paragraph of this lesson, opening the file first in Word and then in WordPad, you saw a message saying the file was in use. That's because Word can operate safely on a network where several people might try to work with a file. The message is WordPad's way of telling you Word has reserved, or *locked*, the file. WordPad doesn't lock files, which is why the example in the text works.

LOSE THE EMPTY PARAGRAPHS

Using Word's ability to set line spacing before and after paragraphs is crucial to using formatting styles effectively. Take out the empty paragraphs creating space between text paragraphs by setting the space before each text paragraph to one line.

CROSS-REFERENCE

See how to use styles in the next lesson, "Using the Hidden Power of Styles."

FIND IT ONLINE

Find a higher-power version of WordPad at **http://www.compubridge.net/wordPlus.htm**.

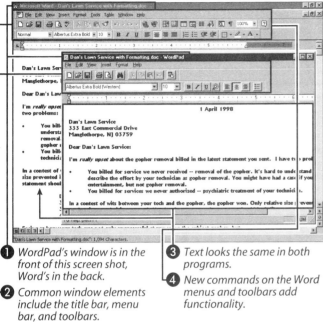

1 *WordPad's window is in the front of this screen shot, Word's in the back.*

2 *Common window elements include the title bar, menu bar, and toolbars.*

3 *Text looks the same in both programs.*

4 *New commands on the Word menus and toolbars add functionality.*

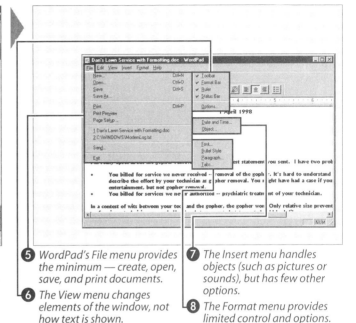

5 *WordPad's File menu provides the minimum — create, open, save, and print documents.*

6 *The View menu changes elements of the window, not how text is shown.*

7 *The Insert menu handles objects (such as pictures or sounds), but has few other options.*

8 *The Format menu provides limited control and options.*

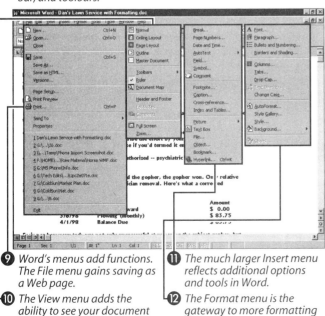

9 *Word's menus add functions. The File menu gains saving as a Web page.*

10 *The View menu adds the ability to see your document in different ways.*

11 *The much larger Insert menu reflects additional options and tools in Word.*

12 *The Format menu is the gateway to more formatting options and to styles.*

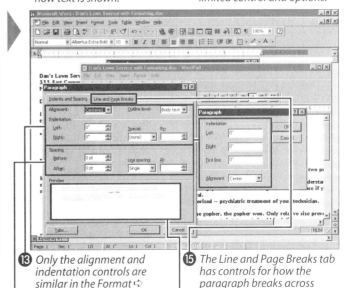

13 *Only the alignment and indentation controls are similar in the Format ⇨ Paragraph menu.*

14 *Set non-zero paragraph before and after spacing.*

15 *The Line and Page Breaks tab has controls for how the paragraph breaks across pages.*

16 *The Preview window shows what your text will look like.*

Using the Hidden Power of Styles

Perhaps no feature of Word is as valuable and generally misunderstood (or ignored) as styles. Styles give you the ability to create a consistent look for your work, to change the look of an entire document instantly, and to separate written content from the look of a particular publication. Although not terribly useful for that quick letter to your old college roommate who won't use e-mail, styles are the right way to work with and manage the formatting for large documents or those that need to follow set format guidelines.

Styles store formatting commands. Word differentiates character formatting — font, bold, superscript, and such — from paragraph formatting (line spacing, justification, and so on). Character styles contain character formatting. Paragraph styles contain paragraph formats plus character formats, page positioning information, and more. Anything you set explicitly on text or a paragraph overrides defaults supplied by styles.

Word looks for formats in this order:

1. Character formatting applied directly to specific characters in the text
2. Character styles applied to specific characters in the text
3. Paragraph formatting applied directly to the paragraph containing the text
4. Paragraph styles applied to the paragraph containing the text
5. Styles upon which the paragraph's style is dependent

You define character and paragraph styles using the Format ⇨ Style command. Once you've defined and named the styles you want, save the file as a Document Template. Attaching the template to a new or existing document makes all the styles in the template available. You can store styles you always use in the Normal template.

TAKE NOTE

▶ MAKE PARAGRAPH MARKS VISIBLE

If you select Tools ⇨ Options ⇨ View, you see Paragraph marks under Nonprinting characters. Turn that on to cause Word to show you the ends of paragraphs onscreen. Think of paragraph formats and styles as being stored in the paragraph mark — if you copy and paste a paragraph mark, its styles come with it. Turn on All in the same place to see every nonprinting character — spaces, tabs, paragraphs, and all.

▶ CLEAR CHARACTER FORMATTING WITH CTRL+SPACE

There's an easy way to clear direct formatting off text so it reverts back to the paragraph text format: Select the text and press Ctrl+space. Word removes all character formats and styles, so the text falls back to the character format in the paragraph or to the style controlling the paragraph.

CROSS-REFERENCE
Go back to Chapter 10's "Formatting in WordPad" for the basics of direct character and paragraph formatting.

FIND IT ONLINE
Get Word enhancements from Microsoft at http://www.microsoft.com/office/enhword.asp.

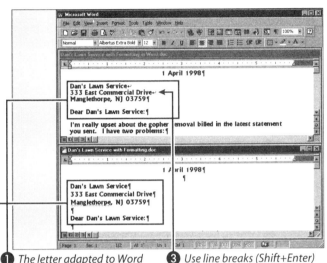

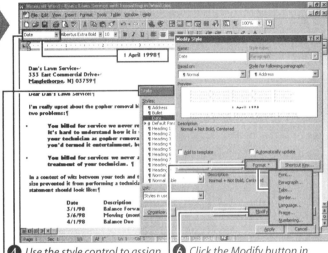

1 The letter adapted to Word uses paragraph formats for spacing between paragraphs.

2 The WordPad version uses empty paragraphs for spacing.

3 Use line breaks (Shift+Enter) to force paragraph text to the next line.

4 Use the style control to assign styles to paragraphs and text.

5 The Format ➪ Style dialog gives you control over all styles in the document.

6 Click the Modify button in Format ➪ Style to change the selected style.

7 Click the Format button in the Modify Style dialog box to change any of these elements.

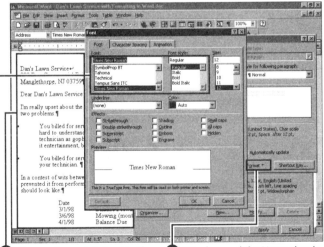

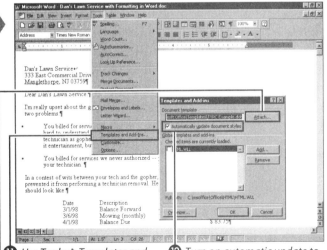

8 Choose Format ➪ Font in the Modify Style dialog to get the usual font dialog box.

9 We chose a lighter font, not bold, in a larger size.

10 We changed the Normal style, the basis for everything, which made the whole document change.

11 Use Tools ➪ Templates and Add-Ins to attach an existing template to a document.

12 Pick from existing templates through the Attach button.

13 Turn on automatic update to force the template to revise the look of the document.

151

Handling Tables

One of the most tedious aspects of a report used to be creating tables of information. On a typewriter (and on early word processors), your only option was to set tab stops and fiddle around with the text until it looked the way you wanted. You'd insert tons of tabs in the process, which you had to move around if you needed to move text from one line to another.

Never again. Word and other word processors inherently know how to handle tables. They give you a grid on the screen showing the rows and columns, resize column widths painlessly, replicate headings on succeeding pages, and more.

Think of each position in a table, called a *cell* in Word, as a tiny page of text. You can have several paragraphs in a cell, add graphics, and change formats. Text wraps to fit the column boundaries. You can force Word to make rows in tables an exact height or let the height float to fit the content. You can allow Word to automatically size columns, or force them the way you want.

The gridlines you see onscreen are guides — they don't print (and can be turned off with Table ⇨ Hide Gridlines). If you want gridlines to print, you have to add *borders* to the table. Word can help you there too, with prepackaged table formats that it applies via the Table ⇨ Table AutoFormat command.

Watch for changes in the shape of the mouse cursor around tables — it's letting you know what you can do. For instance, the cursor changes to a set of vertical bars near a vertical gridline to show you can resize the cell. Select just the cell to resize it; select the column to resize all cells in one column; select the table to resize the column plus adjust the table around it.

TAKE NOTE

▶ SELECT AND NAVIGATE IN TABLES

Word gives you mouse and keyboard tools for tables. Double-click a cell to select it. Hold Alt and left-click (noted from here on as Alt+click) a cell to select the column. Hold Alt and double-click to select the whole table. Click the left edge of a table (when the mouse points to the right) to select a row. Press Tab to go to the next cell (you get a new row at the end of the table).

▶ TAB IN TABLE CELLS

Because the Tab key moves you to the next cell in a table, you have to do something a little different if you want to use a tab stop in a cell (yes, you can set tab stops on paragraphs in tables!). Instead of Tab, press Ctrl+Tab to get what you want.

CROSS-REFERENCE
See Chapter 12, starting with "Working with the Excel Window," for the heavy-duty alternative to tables.

FIND IT ONLINE
See how to fit wide tables on pages at **http://www. microsoft.com/office/word/assistance/wdvarpg1.asp**.

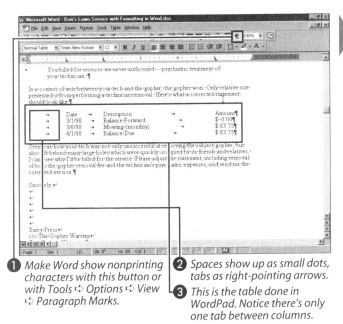

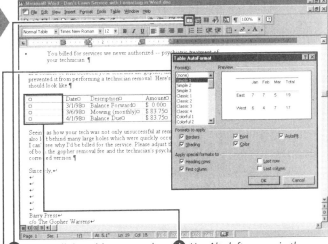

1 *Make Word show nonprinting characters with this button or with Tools ➪ Options ➪ View ➪ Paragraph Marks.*

2 *Spaces show up as small dots, tabs as right-pointing arrows.*

3 *This is the table done in WordPad. Notice there's only one tab between columns.*

4 *Select all the table rows and click this button to convert to a Word table.*

5 *Mouse in the table and use Table ➪ Table AutoFormat to apply the Simple 1 format.*

6 *Use Alt+left mouse in the empty column to select it, and then Table ➪ Delete Columns to remove it.*

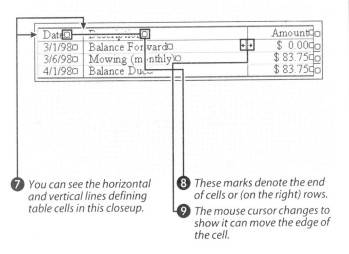

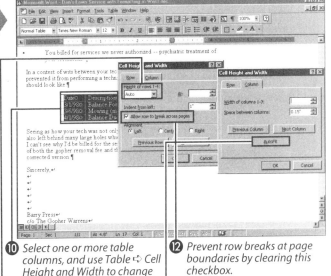

7 *You can see the horizontal and vertical lines defining table cells in this closeup.*

8 *These marks denote the end of cells or (on the right) rows.*

9 *The mouse cursor changes to show it can move the edge of the cell.*

10 *Select one or more table columns, and use Table ➪ Cell Height and Width to change characteristics.*

11 *Force row height to a set amount.*

12 *Prevent row breaks at page boundaries by clearing this checkbox.*

13 *Let Word automatically set column widths with this button.*

Importing from Other Applications

You *could* do much of what you've seen in this book without Windows. Software developers could create graphical interfaces for their programs, and in fact many did before Windows and during its early days. But you'd have to work much harder to set up drivers for all your devices; it used to be that every program had its own display driver, printer driver, and so on.

You'd suffer the most without Windows, though, when you tried to run several programs at the same time (or, at least, programs from more than one manufacturer), and it would be hard to import data from one program into another. Windows inherently runs more than one program at once and provides standard mechanisms for programs to share data. The most important of those mechanisms is the *clipboard*, an information storage and retrieval area. Using the clipboard, you can copy or cut (delete) almost anything you can select using Edit ⇨ Copy and Edit ⇨ Cut. You can paste what's in the clipboard into the same or another program using Edit ⇨ Paste. The clipboard only holds one thing at a time, so when you copy data into it, whatever material was there is lost.

You can *embed* data created by other applications in Word too, either through the clipboard or by using the Insert ⇨ Object command. Embedded objects are nice because they're accessible (you can double-click and edit them). Use the Insert ⇨ Object command to see what kinds of objects your system recognizes. Common uses in Word include embedding pictures and drawings from programs like Adobe Photoshop and Illustrator or Visio's Visio. Once you've embedded an object, you can usually edit it by double-clicking it or by right-clicking and choosing Edit.

TAKE NOTE

► USING EDIT ⇨ PASTE SPECIAL TO GET WHAT YOU WANT

The clipboard can store information in a variety of formats, from complex editable objects to simple raw text. When you paste from the clipboard, you get the data in whatever format the application thinks is best. That may not be what you really want, though. To force what you want, use Edit ⇨ Paste Special and choose the exact format you want.

► SEEING WHAT'S ON THE CLIPBOARD

Under normal circumstances, information stored on the clipboard is invisible — you have to remember what's there. Windows has an accessory to let you see the clipboard: the Clipboard Viewer. You might have to install it (it's a component under System Tools). Select Start ⇨ Programs ⇨ Accessories ⇨ System Tools ⇨ Clipboard Viewer and watch as you copy or cut data into the clipboard.

CROSS-REFERENCE
Take another look at Chapter 10's "Formatting in WordPad" now that you've seen what Insert ⇨ Object really is.

FIND IT ONLINE
Download a converter to let Word 6 and Word 7 read Word 97 files from **http://support.microsoft.com/download/support/mslfiles/Wrd97cnv.exe**.

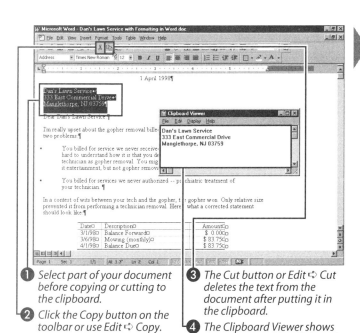

① Select part of your document before copying or cutting to the clipboard.

② Click the Copy button on the toolbar or use Edit ➪ Copy.

③ The Cut button or Edit ➪ Cut deletes the text from the document after putting it in the clipboard.

④ The Clipboard Viewer shows the contents of the clipboard.

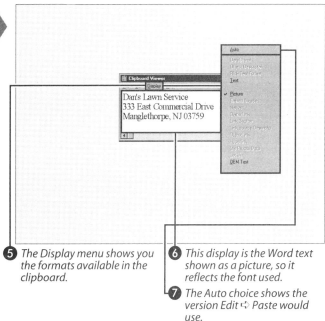

⑤ The Display menu shows you the formats available in the clipboard.

⑥ This display is the Word text shown as a picture, so it reflects the font used.

⑦ The Auto choice shows the version Edit ➪ Paste would use.

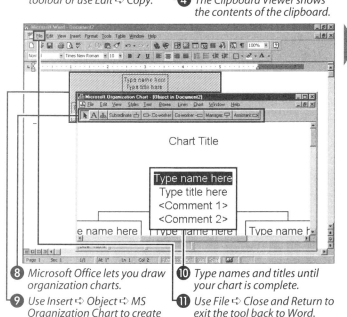

⑧ Microsoft Office lets you draw organization charts.

⑨ Use Insert ➪ Object ➪ MS Organization Chart to create a new org chart in your document.

⑩ Type names and titles until your chart is complete.

⑪ Use File ➪ Close and Return to exit the tool back to Word.

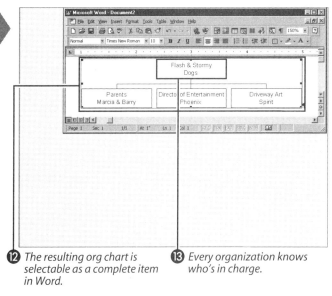

⑫ The resulting org chart is selectable as a complete item in Word.

⑬ Every organization knows who's in charge.

155

Personal Workbook

Q&A

1 List some things a word processor can do that a typewriter can't.

_____

_____

_____

2 What does *WYSIWYG* stand for?

_____

_____

_____

3 What message might you get if two programs (or computers) try to open the same file?

_____

_____

_____

4 What are some examples of character formats? Paragraph formats?

_____

_____

_____

5 What are document templates?

_____

_____

_____

6 How do you make gridlines print in tables?

_____

_____

_____

_____

7 Can you edit graphics in Word?

_____

_____

_____

8 Can you embed MIDI and WAV files in Word documents?

_____

_____

_____

ANSWERS: PAGE 340

EXTRA PRACTICE

① Install the Clipboard Viewer (one of the choices in Windows System Tools). Copy different things to the clipboard and see what happens.

② Copy some text from WordPad or Word to the clipboard and then use the Edit ⇨ Paste Special command. What format choices do you have? What does each one do?

③ Use the different heading styles in a document and turn on View ⇨ Outline. Go back to normal view and turn on View ⇨ Document Map.

④ Open a document and try pressing F7 (or use Tools ⇨ Spelling and Grammar).

REAL-WORLD APPLICATIONS

✔ You write a paper for publication but don't find out what the format guidelines are until after you're done. A quick change to the styles for your paper and it's ready to ship.

✔ You're doing research on the Web for a report. You find a useful quote in a paragraph on a site, so you select the text in your Web browser and copy it to a notes file in Word, adding the Web address so you can properly credit the source.

✔ You're putting together a large document that has been written in sections by a team of people. As they make revisions to the document, you find their sections quickly because you used the heading styles and can go to headings using the document map.

Visual Quiz

We've made no alterations to this screen shot. How did we make Word look like this?

_____

_____

_____

_____

_____

1 April 1998

Dan's Lawn Service
333 East Commercial Drive
Manglethorpe, NJ 03759

Dear Dan's Lawn Service

I'm *really upset* about the gopher removal billed in the latest statement you sent. I have two problems:

• You billed for service we never received -- removal of the gopher. It's hard to understand how it is that you describe the effort by your technician as gopher removal. You might have had a case if you'd termed it entertainment, but not gopher removal.
• You billed for services we never authorized -- psychiatric treatment of your technician.

In a contest of wits between your tech and the gopher, the gopher won. Only relative size prevented it from performing a technician removal. Here's what a corrected statement should look like:

Date	Description	Amount
3/1/98	Balance Forward	$ 0.00
3/6/98	Mowing (monthly)	$ 83.75
4/1/98	Balance Due	$ 83.75

Seeing as how your tech was not only unsuccessful at removing the subject gopher, but also left behind many large holes which were quickly occupied by its friends and relatives, I can't see why I'd be billed for the service. Please adjust the statement, including removal of both the gopher removal fee and the technician's psychiatric expenses, and send me the corrected version.

Sincerely,

Full Screen
Close Full Screen

CHAPTER **12**

MASTER
THESE
SKILLS

▶ **Working with the Excel Window**

▶ **Analyzing with Formulas**

▶ **Graphing the Results**

▶ **Formatting in Excel**

Quickstart Excel 97

The ledger sheet—an array of rows and columns of numbers used for financial analysis—is hundreds of years old. Before computer automation, people used ledgers (now called spreadsheets) to keep company books, analyze financial transactions, track investments and earnings, calculate depreciation schedules, and perform other business and accounting tasks. Working with ledgers was tedious and error-prone, because whenever a number or assumption changed, every calculation dependent on the change required redoing. The formulas that let accountants and business analysts do computations were often assumed and undocumented, leading to confusion when results were shared.

With spreadsheet software, you still see text and numbers onscreen, just like a paper ledger. The difference is that where you traditionally performed a computation with your calculator, you now enter the computational *formula*. Your computer does the calculation and displays the result in the appropriate entry. Your computer automatically—and quickly—recalculates all affected values whenever you make a change to the spreadsheet. It's still possible to enter bad data or bad formulas, but the quality of work goes up because of your computer's error-free calculations.

The rows in a spreadsheet are usually identified with numbers. The first row is 1, the one below it is 2, and so on. Columns are similarly identified, but with letters. The first column is A, the one to the right is B, and so on, from AA to IV. The individual place in a spreadsheet where you can enter text, a number, or a formula is called a *cell*, identified by the row and column that meet there. The top left cell is A1. The cell to the right of A1 is B1. The cell below A1 is A2.

The lessons in this chapter draw on Microsoft Excel for examples, because more people use Excel than other spreadsheets. The concepts are very similar between Excel and programs such as Corel Quattro Pro or Lotus 1-2-3, though. You shouldn't have any problems applying the lessons to those programs.

Electronic spreadsheets have grown to add functionality far beyond what was common with paper ledgers. You can create graphs, format analyses into elegant reports, import from and export to databases, and more.

Working with the Excel Window

The spreadsheet itself covers most of the Excel window. Excel spreadsheets are much bigger than what you'd work with on a paper ledger; a spreadsheet can have 256 columns and 65,536 rows. (You can have 256 sheets in a workbook, but unless you're working on a big or complex project, you probably won't care.) Within a spreadsheet, when you click a cell it becomes *selected*. You can drag the cursor across a group of cells to select a *range*. You can move from one cell to another with the mouse or with the arrow keys on the keyboard. Pressing Ctrl+Home selects and displays cell A1.

Two key features of the Excel window — the *name box* and the *formula bar* — are right below the toolbar and above the spreadsheet. The name box is the smaller control on the left; the formula bar is the larger control on the right. You see the coordinates (called the *address*) of a selected cell or range in the name box. (For example, if you type Ctrl+Home, the name box displays A1.) If you want to go to a specific cell, click in the name box, type the cell address, and press Enter.

Entering data in a cell is simple: just select the cell, type in your data, and press Enter. When you do this, what you type appears in both the cell and the formula bar. If you want to edit the contents of a cell, select the cell, click in the formula bar, and do your editing there. Press Enter when you're done. Editing in the formula bar is almost the same as editing text in WordPad, Word, or dialog boxes; the exception is that under some circumstances the left and right arrow keys insert cell addresses instead of moving the edit point to the left or right. We'll address this in the next lesson, "Analyzing with Formulas."

TAKE NOTE

▶ RIGHT-CLICKING EVERYWHERE

Excel displays a shortcut menu when you right-click the mouse on the screen. The choices in the shortcut menu are designed to be the ones you're most likely to need based on the mouse location, but if what you want isn't there, you can go directly to the commands in the menu bar.

▶ USE WHAT YOU KNOW ABOUT THE TOOLBAR

Although there are a lot of new symbols on the Excel toolbar buttons, much of what's there is familiar — buttons for commands you already know. From left to right, the first buttons are New, Open, Save, Print, Print Preview, Check Spelling, Cut, Copy, and Paste. Much of what you find in the File, Edit, Insert, and Format menus should be equally familiar.

CROSS-REFERENCE

See "Using the Parts of the Window to Type a Letter" in Chapter 2 for window and toolbar basics.

FIND IT ONLINE

Get a free weekly Excel tip by e-mail. Register at http://www.zdtips.com/e97/zdt-f.htm.

QUICKSTART EXCEL 97
Working with the Excel Window

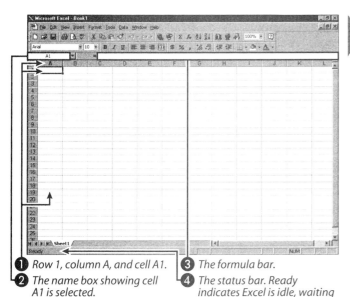

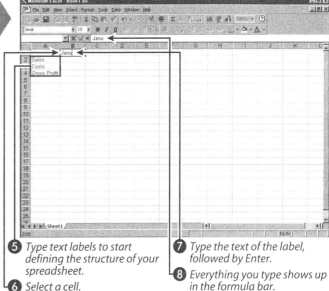

1. *Row 1, column A, and cell A1.*
2. *The name box showing cell A1 is selected.*
3. *The formula bar.*
4. *The status bar. Ready indicates Excel is idle, waiting for your command.*
5. *Type text labels to start defining the structure of your spreadsheet.*
6. *Select a cell.*
7. *Type the text of the label, followed by Enter.*
8. *Everything you type shows up in the formula bar.*

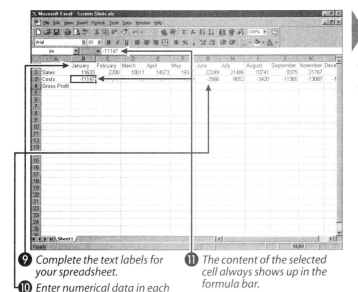

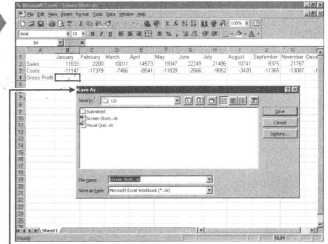

9. *Complete the text labels for your spreadsheet.*
10. *Enter numerical data in each cell.*
11. *The content of the selected cell always shows up in the formula bar.*
12. *Use the same File ⇨ Save and File ⇨ Save As commands you learned with WordPad and Word to save the file.*

Analyzing with Formulas

If all you could do with a spreadsheet was type labels and numbers, it wouldn't be worth the effort — the real power is in your computer's ability to do calculations based on the formulas you enter. Formulas in Excel are similar to what you remember from algebra. You enter an equation that is based on one, or more cells in the spreadsheet. The value of the equation then shows up as the value of the cell containing the formula.

Excel uses a straightforward system to refer to other cells in a formula — you use the cell address. If you're in cell A3 adding the contents of cells A1 and A2, the formula is A1+A2. Formulas require a prefix of an equal sign (to tell Excel that what you're typing isn't a text label), so the complete entry in A3 would be

$$=A1+A2$$

Excel has all the basic arithmetic functions built-in. Formula evaluation follows the usual order: exponentiation first; multiplication and division next; and addition and subtraction last. Equal-precedence operators evaluate from left to right. Use parentheses to force the order of evaluation.

In addition to the basic operators, Excel has a built-in library of hundreds of functions. You write functions as the function name followed by its arguments in parentheses. It's not very interesting, but you could add the first five integers with the formula =SUM(1,2,3,4,5). In practice, you use functions to operate on cells and ranges of cells. For example, you can add the first ten

cells in column A as =SUM(A1:A10), or the first cell in column A, the second cell in column B, and the third cell in column C as =SUM(A1,B2,C3). (You don't have to capitalize the names; we've written them this way to make them easier to read.)

You can mix operators, cells, and functions in Excel formulas as long as you write a well-formed equation. For example, you can subtract the sum of the range B2:B4 from the value of cell B1 with the following formula:

$$=B1-SUM(B2:B4)$$

If you copy a formula from one cell to another, the cell addresses you referenced in the formula move the same way as the destination cell. For example, if you copy the formula =A1+A2 from cell A3 to B3, the formula pasted into the destination is =B1+B2. That automatic adjustment makes it easy to quickly build tables of results.

TAKE NOTE

▶ GET HELP WITH EXCEL'S BUILT-IN FUNCTIONS

It's hard to remember the precise arguments for each of Excel's functions (or even what all the functions are). Press Shift+F3 when you need to enter a function into a formula; Excel gives you a list of all available functions and helps you set up the arguments for the one you choose.

CROSS-REFERENCE

See Chapter 7's lesson "Getting More on the Screen" to learn how to see as much of your spreadsheet as possible

FIND IT ONLINE

Find *PC World*'s e-mail Excel tips (and many more) at **http://www.tipworld.com**.

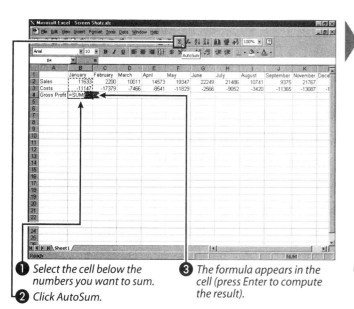

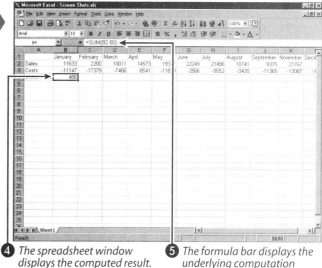

1 Select the cell below the numbers you want to sum.

2 Click AutoSum.

3 The formula appears in the cell (press Enter to compute the result).

4 The spreadsheet window displays the computed result.

5 The formula bar displays the underlying computation formula.

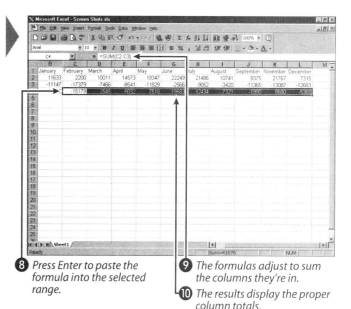

6 Begin copying the formula by selecting the result and pressing Ctrl+C (Edit ➪ Copy).

7 Select the destination range (cells C4 to L4) by dragging the mouse.

8 Press Enter to paste the formula into the selected range.

9 The formulas adjust to sum the columns they're in.

10 The results display the proper column totals.

Graphing the Results

Some people like to read results, and some like to see them pictured. For those who work better with pictures, graphs are often their key to understanding the results shown in a spreadsheet. Excel offers a variety of graphs suitable for almost every application.

Excel calls graphs *charts*, emphasizing that additional information (as depicted in legends and titles, for example) is part of the complete presentation. An Excel wizard makes it easy to create charts. Start by selecting the range of cells you want to chart, including the independent and dependent values. Don't forget to include labels on the rows and columns so Excel can automatically label the chart. Click the Chart Wizard tool and follow its four steps: select the chart type, range of cells to chart, title and legend options, and chart destination. If you highlight the range before starting the wizard, you won't need to do the second step.

You can place a chart directly on the spreadsheet (*embedding* the chart), or you can create a separate worksheet for the chart in the same workbook. If you embed the chart in the spreadsheet itself, it may cover data that you want to remain visible. Move the chart by clicking in it, and then clicking any blank area in it, and then dragging it to the desired location. Resize a chart by moving the mouse pointer to one of the chart handles (the black squares that appear when you click the chart) and dragging. Click outside of the chart to deselect the chart and remove the handles.

You can modify most parts of your chart starting with a double left-click. If the changes you want to make aren't in the resulting dialog box, try a right-click to find the command you need.

TAKE NOTE

▶ FIGURING OUT WHEN TO USE WHICH CHART TYPE

Picking among the basic chart types is relatively straightforward. Use line charts to review patterns and predict trends; bar charts to compare values for different categories of samples; stacked-bar charts to display the total of the values for a series, along with the relationship of each value to the entire series; and XY charts to display values where the independent variable isn't spaced at equal intervals.

▶ AVOID MAKING YOUR CHART A DUCK

Excel offers so many different kinds of graphs that you can easily go astray fiddling with options when you should be focused on your data. The absolute best reference book for lessons on designing graphs and other presentations is Edward Tufte's *The Visual Display of Quantitative Information*. It's both beautiful and essential, and explains why Tufte calls a graph with excessive ornamentation a duck.

CROSS-REFERENCE

Charts are only one part of a complete presentation. Learn how to format your results in the next lesson, "Formatting in Excel."

FIND IT ONLINE

Dr. Edward Tufte is on the faculty at Yale. See **http://www.cs.yale.edu/HTML/YALE/CS/faculty/ tufte.html**.

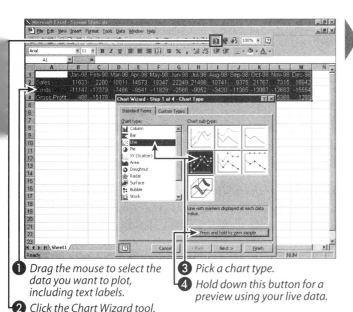

① *Drag the mouse to select the data you want to plot, including text labels.*

② *Click the Chart Wizard tool.*

③ *Pick a chart type.*

④ *Hold down this button for a preview using your live data.*

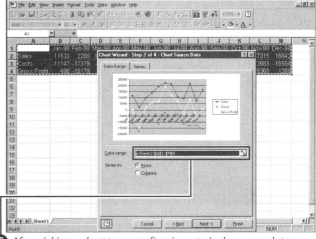

⑤ *After picking a chart type, confirm (or enter) where your data is on the spreadsheet.*

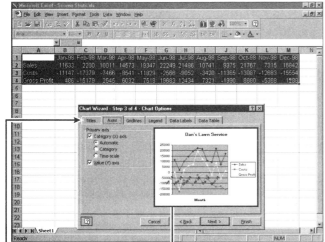

⑥ *Use the tabs in step 3 of the wizard to apply formatting to the chart.*

⑦ *You see a live preview as you change the settings.*

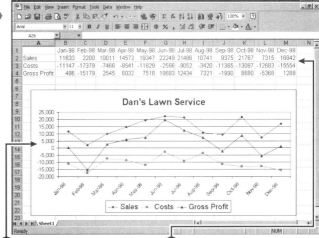

⑧ *Here's the completed chart after formatting the chart area color and scaling the font.*

⑨ *Positioning the embedded chart below the data allows readers to see both the numbers and the graph.*

Formatting in Excel

Formatting tools in Excel let you improve the readability of your spreadsheet and prepare your results for publication. Like Word, Excel lets you format text and numbers with any of the available fonts, font sizes, font styles, and justifications (left, center, and right). Text defaults to left justification; values and formulas default to the right.

As you'd expect from an application emphasizing numbers, Excel gives you total control over numeric display formats. Values and formulas default to display as general numbers (meaning the format changes depending on how big or small the numbers are). You specify the exact number format you want, such as a date, currency, or percent, by selecting the cells you want to format, and then using the Number tab in the dialog box you get with the Format ⇨ Cells command.

It doesn't matter when you apply a format to a cell — you can format before and/or after you enter a value or formula. The format you set applies to all selected cells, so if you want to set a default format for the entire spreadsheet, click the corner between the A and the 1 (which selects the whole spreadsheet), and then choose a format.

Wide text and large numbers work better when you expand the column width to extend the width of the entry. Similarly, you might want to shrink a column width if values contain only a few digits, because the narrower the columns, the more that fit onscreen.

Adjust row height to accommodate a large font that's too tall for the default height. Adjust column width and row height by dragging the right or bottom edge of the corresponding gray border. If you double-click the edge (where the mouse cursor changes shape), Excel will apply a best-fit width or height.

Although Excel prints gridlines by default (unlike Word tables), it's often useful to set off a group of cells by surrounding them with a border. The Border tool is the third button from the right on the formatting toolbar — it looks like a 2 × 2 grid. The tool lets you apply one of twelve border styles; if they don't supply enough choices, you can use Format ⇨ Cells ⇨ Border to get just the style you want. Click the Border tool to apply or remove a border. Click the Border tool arrow to display style options, and then click an option to apply it to a cell.

TAKE NOTE

▶ AUTOFORMAT

Like Word, Excel provides predetermined table formats. Select cells in the table, choose Format ⇨ AutoFormat, and then pick the style you like. To remove an AutoFormat, select None from the styles listing.

CROSS-REFERENCE

Compare Excel with Word tables explained in Chapter 11's lesson "Handling Tables."

FIND IT ONLINE

Get Excel formatting tips from *PC World* at http://www.idg.net/idg_frames/english/content. cgi?vc=docid_9-66592.html

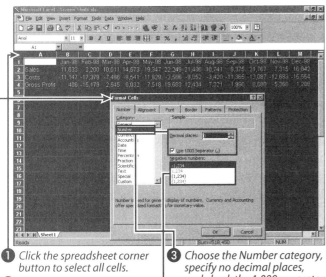

1 Click the spreadsheet corner button to select all cells.

2 Choose Format ⇨ Cells (or press Ctrl+1) to open this dialog box.

3 Choose the Number category, specify no decimal places, and check the 1,000 separator checkbox.

4 Choose your preferred format for negative numbers.

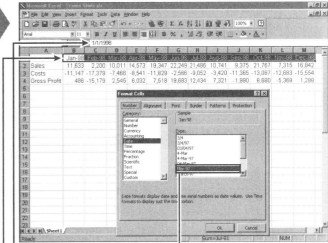

5 Type dates using this format for data entry.

6 Select the range of dates.

7 Pick the date format you want, overriding the sheet-wide format in the last figure.

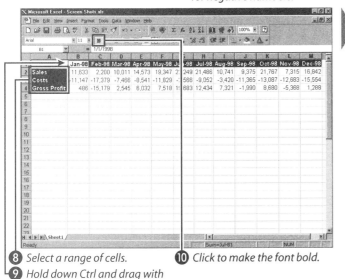

8 Select a range of cells.

9 Hold down Ctrl and drag with the mouse to add a disjoint range of cells to the selection.

10 Click to make the font bold.

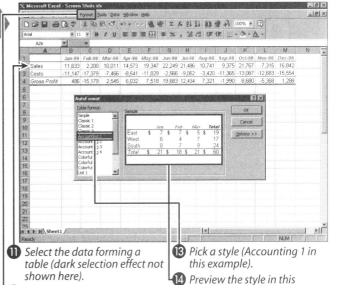

11 Select the data forming a table (dark selection effect not shown here).

12 Choose Format ⇨ AutoFormat.

13 Pick a style (Accounting 1 in this example).

14 Preview the style in this sample.

Personal Workbook

Q&A

1 What keystroke combination can you use to move to cell A1?

_____

_____

_____

2 How do you bring up the shortcut menu?

_____

_____

_____

3 What tool automatically totals a column or row of numbers?

_____

_____

_____

4 What are _functions_ in Excel?

_____

_____

_____

5 What is the term for putting a chart in a spreadsheet?

_____

_____

_____

6 What's the easiest way to build a chart?

_____

_____

_____

7 What command lets you apply preformatted table styles?

_____

_____

_____

8 What two formats make numbers appear with a $?

_____

_____

_____

ANSWERS: PAGE 340

EXTRA PRACTICE

1 Use the Name box to move to cell D23.

2 Total a column of numbers.

3 Copy the total formula to other columns.

4 Find the average, maximum, and minimum of a column of numbers.

5 Create a chart with a chart title and legend from your table. Experiment with different chart formats.

6 Make numbers in your table appear with commas and no decimal places. Make the totals appear as currency with two decimal places. Make all labels bold and italic. Center-align labels in a row. Right-align labels in a column.

REAL-WORLD APPLICATIONS

✔ You need to develop a quarterly sales spreadsheet for the past quarter. You have to input a sheet of paper with the quarterly numbers, so you build a spreadsheet to summarize and analyze the information.

✔ You suspect that the January cost account numbers for your division contain an error, but there are 750 different accounts and you can't find any problems just by looking. You apply the MIN function to the column and discover that one number is 20 times below the normal range.

Visual Quiz

What happens when you click OK?

_____

_____

_____

_____

_____

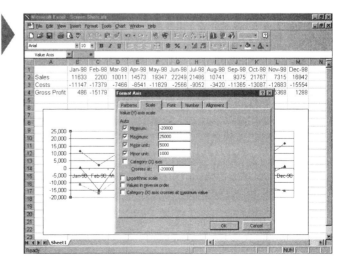

CHAPTER **13**

MASTER
THESE
SKILLS

▶ **Configuring Your Fax System**

▶ **Sending a Fax**

▶ **Receiving a Fax**

▶ **Using Optical Character Recognition**

Running WinFax

It's no accident that fax machines are universal. Regular mail is too slow for much of what business does today — especially international business — while fax is fast. Electronic mail can't substitute for fax (or regular mail) in all cases, because some people don't have e-mail and because fax creates a paper record that's less subject to alteration.

You don't have to abandon your computer just because you need to send or receive a fax. Instead, you can use your computer as an extremely capable fax machine, one with features you find in only the most expensive stand-alone fax units. The reason for this is because a fax machine itself is a computer, but a very specialized one. In addition to the processor and memory a computer has, a fax machine also has a scanner, a printer, and a modem. Your computer does or can have all these items, so it can function like fax machine. Here's how that works:

- ▶ **Scanner** — A fax machine's scanner creates an electronic image of the material you send. You can use a computer's scanner for the same purpose, but you can employ software to generate images from documents already in the computer.

- ▶ Printer — A fax machine's printer outputs copies of documents received from other machines. Your computer's printer can do the same job, or with the right software it can convert the fax image to editable text.

- ▶ Modem — The modem in a fax machine sends data through phone lines in a way that makes it understandable to other fax modems. Most computer modems can transmit and receive to fax modem standards.

A faster processor and more memory, plus a disk and a display, let your computer store much larger programs than a fax machine. Fax programs offer additional functions and information. Using your computer as a fax machine, you can fax directly from your word processor (or any other program that prints), convert received pages to editable text, and (in some cases) send files from one machine to another. Your fax software keeps an index of what you've sent and received, so you can search for faxes sent on a particular day or received from a specific sender.

Configuring Your Fax System

Once you install WinFax, you'll want to tailor the program to get the most out of it. The elements you need are in the Setup menu, and there's a raft of them. The first thing to do is verify that the program is set up to properly identify you and dial the phone the way you'd like it to. (We'll look at sending, receiving, and setting up automatic fax reception later in this chapter. Here we set up the basics that affect everything.)

Fax machines send a *calling station identifier* (CSID) to each other as part of their initial conversation before they transfer data. It's common to include a cover page on faxes too, because often fax machines handle traffic for several people. The cover page simplifies routing to the right person and informs an operator of whom to call if there's a problem. WinFax lets you set up the information it uses for the CSID and cover page in the Program Properties user dialog box (Setup ⇨ Program ⇨ User). The information goes into what WinFax calls *variables*—you choose from program-defined variables if you want to set up a custom cover-page format. The most common entry for the CSID is your fax number.

The other key thing to check is how WinFax will handle your phone line. You have options to require a dial tone, notice when there is a busy signal, and control how WinFax retries a transmission when there's no answer or the line's busy.

Be sure to look at the other tabs in the dialog boxes for Setup ⇨ Program, Setup ⇨ Dialing, and Setup ⇨ Modem—there's a lot more that you can configure.

TAKE NOTE

▶ KEEPING THE CSID SIMPLE
You can enter any characters you want for the CSID in WinFax (but no more than 20). If your CSID has nonnumeric characters, some standalone fax machines will reject the call by failing to connect or disconnecting during transmission. If you're having problems, use the more restrictive numeric CSID and try again.

▶ WAITING FOR THE DIAL TONE IS GOOD MANNERS
Many homes and small offices share a voice phone line with the fax machine, and it's irritating to have a machine dial for a fax transmission when you're having a phone conversation. If you turn on the WinFax option to wait for the dial tone, all you'll hear is a click when the modem picks up the line—the software won't hear a dial tone, so it won't start to dial.

CROSS-REFERENCE
Chapter 9's "Installing a New Program" lesson shows how to do the basic WinFax install.

FIND IT ONLINE
Get a trial version of WinFax at **http://www. symantec.com/winfax/index_downloads.html**.

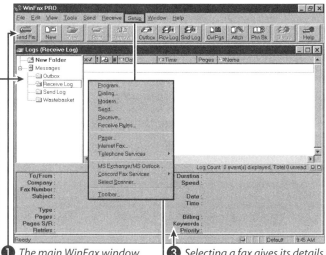

❶ The main WinFax window includes a toolbar with specialized commands for sending and receiving faxes.

❷ The two-pane structure is similar to Windows Explorer.

❸ Selecting a fax gives its details on the bottom.

❹ The Setup menu (shown moved down) lets you configure WinFax.

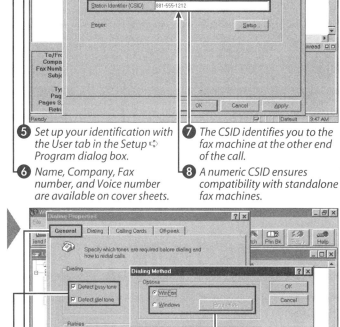

❺ Set up your identification with the User tab in the Setup ➪ Program dialog box.

❻ Name, Company, Fax number, and Voice number are available on cover sheets.

❼ The CSID identifies you to the fax machine at the other end of the call.

❽ A numeric CSID ensures compatibility with standalone fax machines.

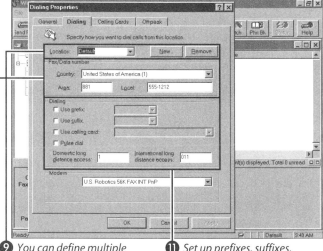

❾ You can define multiple locations, useful for laptop computers.

❿ Specify your dialing location to handle country and area codes properly.

⓫ Set up prefixes, suffixes, and access numbers for local switches (PBX) and competitive long distance carriers.

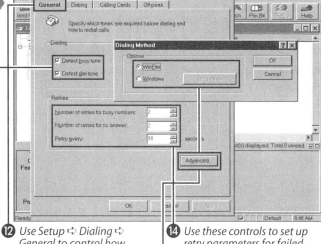

⓬ Use Setup ➪ Dialing ➪ General to control how WinFax handles the phone line.

⓭ Turn on dial tone detection to guard against interruption.

⓮ Use these controls to set up retry parameters for failed connections.

⓯ The Advanced button lets you use the Windows dialer (see the Dialing tab).

Sending a Fax

There's really only one basic thing you need to learn about sending a fax: Your fax software sets up a printer. Because of this, you can print to the fax from any program, using any of a program's capabilities, including fonts, formatting, graphics, embedding, and print preview. When you print, the fax software takes over, asking for addressees, a cover page, and other information it needs. Printing to the fax gives you a wonderful option if you're sending to several people — you can simply send the same fax with multiple addressees, or use the form-letter tools in your word processor (called Mail Merge in Word) to send individually tailored faxes. It shouldn't take more time to send personalized faxes, because WinFax dials for each recipient anyway.

The TrueType fonts in Windows are particularly valuable for faxing, because you're not stuck with limited font sizes. Instead, you can make any True Type font the size you want (and bold, if you choose). The resolution of a fax transmission is inherently not as high as what comes off your printer, so avoid small font sizes. Bold fonts work well too, because you avoid the sections of characters that are only one line wide (think of a lowercase *l*) and likely to vanish.

WinFax adds some convenient tools to the basic print-to-fax capability. As shown in the figures on the next page, you can dash off a quick fax directly in WinFax and not have to wrestle with your word processor. If you have a scanner, WinFax can scan a printed page and fax it, just like a standalone unit. You can maintain a phone book listing the people you frequently fax. You can delay sending a fax to take advantage of lower phone rates. There's a lot of power in the program — discover it by looking through the manual and command menus.

TAKE NOTE

▶ GET THE FORMATTING RIGHT

When preparing a fax in another program, first set the printer to fax. That way, the program's WYSIWYG display gets font information from the fax driver, not your printer. The resulting onscreen displays and print previews more accurately reflect page layout and breaks when you finally send the fax.

▶ FAX FROM ANYWHERE ON YOUR NETWORK

Some fax programs let you fax from any machine on your network that can print to a network-shared printer. Network faxing is nice, because you can work in and send from your office but use a common machine and phone line for faxing. WinFax does network faxing, but only if you buy the network-enabled version.

CROSS-REFERENCE

If you haven't installed a fax modem, look at the "Installing and Testing a Modem" lesson in Chapter 14.

FIND IT ONLINE

Give your faxes that personal handwritten illegibility with a font from http://www.walterware.com.

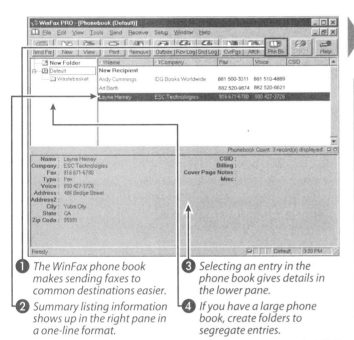

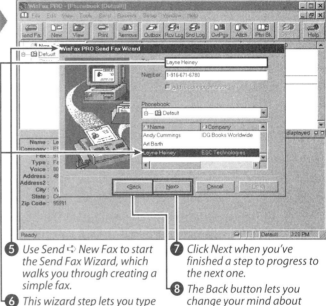

1 The WinFax phone book makes sending faxes to common destinations easier.

2 Summary listing information shows up in the right pane in a one-line format.

3 Selecting an entry in the phone book gives details in the lower pane.

4 If you have a large phone book, create folders to segregate entries.

5 Use Send ⇨ New Fax to start the Send Fax Wizard, which walks you through creating a simple fax.

6 This wizard step lets you type the fax address directly.

7 Click Next when you've finished a step to progress to the next one.

8 The Back button lets you change your mind about what you did.

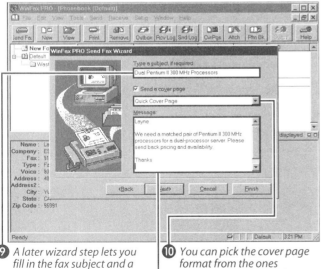

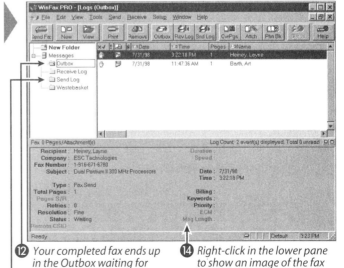

9 A later wizard step lets you fill in the fax subject and a message.

10 You can pick the cover page format from the ones available in this drop-down control.

11 The message you type here goes on the cover page.

12 Your completed fax ends up in the Outbox waiting for transmission.

13 Once WinFax sends the fax, the log entry moves from the Outbox to the Send Log.

14 Right-click in the lower pane to show an image of the fax instead of the details.

Receiving a Fax

Receiving a fax is simple — the phone rings, the modem answers the call, and the pages come down the wire. When it's done, the modem hangs up and the software posts the message so you can read it. The choices you make for fax reception surround these events, controlling when WinFax answers the phone and what it does after it receives a fax.

The Setup ➪ Receive ➪ General dialog box controls when WinFax answers the phone. You can have it answer manually or after a certain number of rings. If you let WinFax answer automatically, you can set its hours of operation. Unless you tell it to, WinFax won't answer outside of those hours.

In Setup ➪ Receive ➪ After Receive, you make choices that specify what happens after a fax arrives. You choose the method of notification (if any), whether you want the fax viewer to open showing the message, if you want automatic optical character recognition (OCR), and if you want an automatic printout. You can turn on some or all of the options — they're independent of each other. If you turn off all the options but the automatic printing, you'll have the equivalent of a standalone fax machine.

Your computer can both reply to a fax sender and forward received faxes to another machine. Because no print/rescan cycle is involved (unlike a standalone fax machine), forwarding loses no image quality. The simplest way to make WinFax reply to or forward a fax is to right-click the corresponding line in the receive log — the pop-up menu has the needed commands. (You can also use Send ➪ Reply to CSID and Send ➪ Forward.) Reply works only if the sender's CSID is the fax number, another good reason to set your CSID to your fax number.

TAKE NOTE

▶ USE THE AUTOMATIC ANSWER SCHEDULE

Suppose you run a small business out of your home and take after-hours fax orders on the same line used for phone orders. During the day, you want WinFax to ignore a call, because if it picks up, you abuse some customer's ear with the modem tones. It's ideal to set the automatic answer schedule for the hours you're closed, because the computer won't forget to do the switch.

▶ GET BILLING DATA

Some standalone fax machines now and then print a transaction log that legal, accounting, and other client service offices use for billing. If you select the Send Log or Receive Log in the left pane, the File ➪ Print List command gives you a summary of all messages in the log.

CROSS-REFERENCE

"Configuring Your Fax System" in this chapter shows how to set the CSID.

FIND IT ONLINE

You can receive faxes as e-mail — see
http://www.faxshield.com.

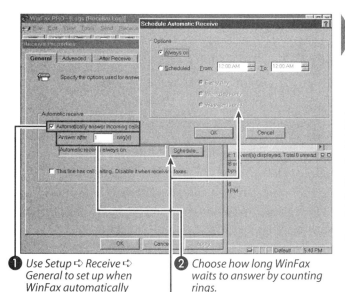

1 Use Setup ➪ Receive ➪ General to set up when WinFax automatically answers the phone.

2 Choose how long WinFax waits to answer by counting rings.

3 Choose if WinFax answers only at certain times by setting a schedule.

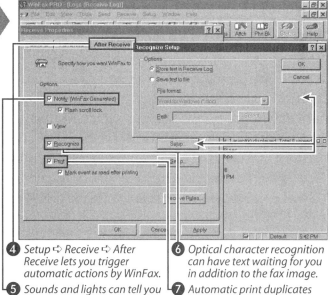

4 Setup ➪ Receive ➪ After Receive lets you trigger automatic actions by WinFax.

5 Sounds and lights can tell you a fax is waiting.

6 Optical character recognition can have text waiting for you in addition to the fax image.

7 Automatic print duplicates the operation of a standalone fax machine.

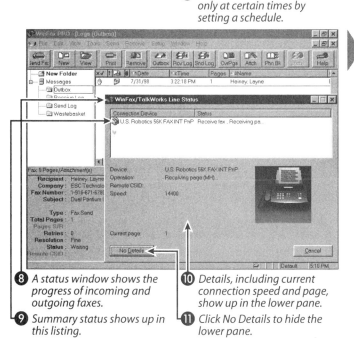

8 A status window shows the progress of incoming and outgoing faxes.

9 Summary status shows up in this listing.

10 Details, including current connection speed and page, show up in the lower pane.

11 Click No Details to hide the lower pane.

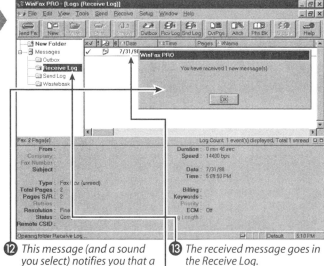

12 This message (and a sound you select) notifies you that a new fax has arrived.

13 The received message goes in the Receive Log.

14 Bold text in the log shows you haven't read the message yet.

Using Optical Character Recognition

Faxes can go almost anywhere, but they have one monumental disadvantage: Despite the format of the original document (paper or computer file), a fax is a picture, not character-based. Sometimes you want editable text but can't get what you need via e-mail.

All is not lost. Programmers found ways to make computers look at a picture of text, decide where and what the characters are, and write the resulting text to a file. This process is called *optical character recognition* (OCR). OCR software is packaged with some fax programs, such as WinFax. If your fax software doesn't do OCR, you can run fax images through separate software. It's clumsier, but not as clumsy as typing pages and pages of text.

As simple as the idea seems, it's hard to write software that does OCR well. Programs must cope with text distortions due to unrecognized fonts, bolding, italics, and page layout (such as two-column formats or embedded graphics). Repeated photocopying of a paper document, low-resolution scanning, or noise during a fax transmission can reduce the image quality for the software. Tell senders to use twelve-point or larger text and to bold the text to reduce the impact of noise or dropouts. What you find easy to read the program finds, too.

The OCR software packaged with fax software is often a limited version of a fully capable package. Check with the fax and OCR software manufacturers for upgrade pricing.

TAKE NOTE

DON'T GET INTERRUPTED BY THE AUTOMATIC PROCESSING

It's quite convenient to have your fax software automatically handle OCR chores after reception. OCR of a multiple-page fax can be time-consuming unless you have a fast computer. Test your automatic OCR setup to make sure it runs to the end without asking for help — it can be really frustrating to find your program stupidly sitting there when you thought it was automatically converting.

CLEAN UP THE SPECKLES BEFORE RUNNING OCR

Fax programs that incorporate OCR often have commands to clean up speckles and other noise in a fax. Try cleaning up faxes that OCR doesn't accurately recognize, but remember that the cleanup process may not be reversible. In WinFax, for instance, there's no Edit ⇨ Undo command to remove the effects of attempting a cleanup. Your only option is to immediately exit the fax viewer without saving changes.

CROSS-REFERENCE

E-mail is more accurate. See Chapter 18's "Sending Files in E-mail."

FIND IT ONLINE

One of the best OCR software programs is Caere's OmniPage Pro. Download the demo at **http://www.caere.com**.

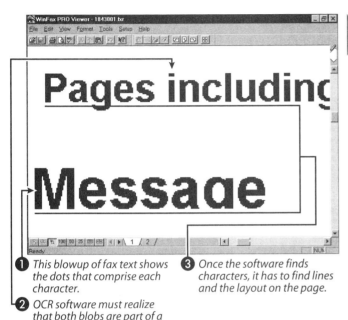

1 This blowup of fax text shows the dots that comprise each character.

2 OCR software must realize that both blobs are part of a single character -- the letter i.

3 Once the software finds characters, it has to find lines and the layout on the page.

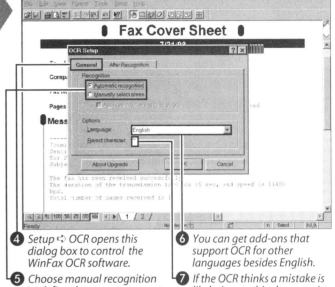

4 Setup ⟹ OCR opens this dialog box to control the WinFax OCR software.

5 Choose manual recognition to define the areas to convert.

6 You can get add-ons that support OCR for other languages besides English.

7 If the OCR thinks a mistake is likely, it puts this character in the text as a marker.

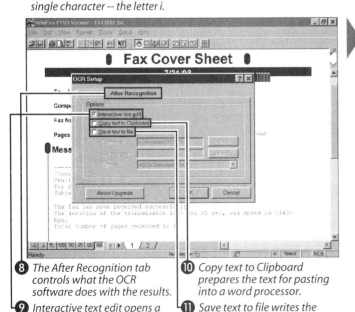

8 The After Recognition tab controls what the OCR software does with the results.

9 Interactive text edit opens a window to let you fix errors and save the file.

10 Copy text to Clipboard prepares the text for pasting into a word processor.

11 Save text to file writes the results on disk for later processing.

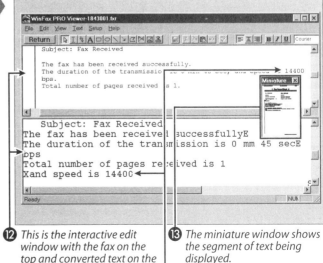

12 This is the interactive edit window with the fax on the top and converted text on the bottom.

13 The miniature window shows the segment of text being displayed.

14 The text ordering difference is from misdetection of page format.

Personal Workbook

Q&A

1 What's the typical maximum transmission speed for a standalone fax machine? For a computer fax?

_____

_____

_____

2 What's a *CSID*?

_____

_____

_____

3 What problems can a nonnumeric CSID cause?

_____

_____

_____

4 How can you send a fax from Word?

_____

_____

_____

5 How should you use fonts for faxes?

_____

_____

_____

6 What does *OCR* stand for? What does it do?

_____

_____

_____

7 How can you check the status of an outgoing fax?

_____

_____

_____

8 How can you delete a fax queued to be sent in WinFax?

_____

_____

_____

ANSWERS: PAGE 341

EXTRA PRACTICE

1 If you don't have fax software (but do have a fax modem), download and install the WinFax trial version from **http://www.symantec.com/winfax/ index_downloads.html.**

2 Look in the help file of your fax software for *variable*.

3 If you have call waiting on your phone line, add *70 as a dialing prefix so calls won't interrupt fax transmissions.

4 Set up a second fax phone line and modem in your computer to increase your fax traffic capacity.

5 Run the tutorial included with your fax software (if there is one — look on the installation CD-ROM).

REAL-WORLD APPLICATIONS

✔ You work for an advertising agency. A client faxes several pages of draft text in the morning, and wants it revised and incorporated into the presentation you're giving tomorrow. You receive the fax on a computer and OCR it to text. You finish the edits and the presentation early in the afternoon, enabling you to go out for an excellent sashimi dinner.

✔ You work in an international trading office. You send and receive faxes with a computer, using its large disk space to make sure you can keep a year's worth of traffic available. You use the search tools in WinFax to find previous traffic to and from specific customers.

Visual Quiz

This is a blowup of a fax in the WinFax viewer. How did we zoom in like this?

_____

_____

_____

_____

PART

IV

Internet

We think Part IV is the most exciting part of this book. It's one thing to use a computer to work in an office, keep a home budget, or play games, but it's quite another to have literally at your fingertips the ability to tap the knowledge stored on hundreds of millions of computers worldwide, and to communicate with any of the users of those computers. Connected to the Internet, your computer is more than a smart appliance, it's your entry into the 21st century.

The best-kept secret about the Internet is how simple it is to use once you get hooked up. In this part you learn what equipment you need to connect and how to install it if you don't have it already. You see how to decide what kind of service you want for your Internet connection, and we show you examples of how to set up the software and what you can expect from the service. You learn about the software that gets you on the World Wide Web — Web browsers — and how to configure your browser to make it do exactly what you want.

Once you're up and running on the Web, you learn about electronic mail — e-mail. You learn how to set up the software, what an e-mail address is, and how to send and receive messages. You finish up this part with lessons on how to access the thousands of programs available on the Internet.

CHAPTER 14

Connecting to the Internet

One of our favorite sayings, attributed to Bob Metcalfe (who invented Ethernet, a networking technology), is: "The value of a network grows as the square of the number of users." We think he's right. And while you may not have a network set up in your home or in a small office, practically everyone can — and should — connect to the Internet. Your computer is far more powerful when when you can access the Internet.

In time, we expect that people will be connected to the Internet whenever their computers are running, and will transfer data at hundreds of thousands of bits per second. For now, unless you're on a company network connected to the Internet, expect to connect with a modem, a device that sends data over a standard phone line. When you want to use the Internet, your computer uses the modem to dial to your Internet service provider (ISP); it disconnects when you're done. Your computer can receive data from the Internet at rates as fast as 56 Kbps; it can transmit at speeds as fast as 33.6 Kbps.

If you're running Windows 95 or 98, you have all the software needed to connect to the Internet. All you have to do is install a modem if you don't already have one, get an ISP account, and tell Windows how to connect. We cover these topics in this chapter's lessons.

Here's something to keep in mind: The Internet has all the virtues and shortcomings of the real world. It encompasses great people and losers, as well as good information, lies, and garbage. No one is going to tell you what's what. You need to be the judge of what you read and do. If you have children and want to shield them from some of the adult world, that's your responsibility. There are tools that can help when you're not around (we'll look at some of them in Chapter 16's lesson "Setting Internet Security and Content Protection Levels"), but the responsibility remains yours. Be aware of what your kids are doing, just as you monitor their other activities. Remember that a smart kid can usually figure out a way to get past a smart tool. Our kids have been on the Internet for as long as they can remember and benefited greatly. So can yours.

Installing and Testing a Modem

A modem is a device that sends and receives data. You connect one side of the modem to your PC and the other side to a phone line. There are internal modems, which you install in your PC, and external modems, which are boxes you wire to your PC with a cable. If you want to add a modem to your PC, decide which type you want. If your PC is no more than a year or two old, an internal modem can be easy to install and costs less than an external modem. If you have an available serial port (a 9- or 25-pin male connector) on the back of the computer, it's simple to connect an external modem. Otherwise, you may want to have a trustworthy computer store or friend do the installation. In older computers or ones with no available ports, the configuration problems can require some expertise.

The most important things to remember when you open up your computer are that you *must* use an anti-static wrist strap, and you *must* carefully document everything as it was before you make changes. You need a wrist strap to prevent damage to the electronics — static electricity can weaken, damage, or destroy computer circuits, leading to expensive repairs. You

need to methodically record what you change because if your changes don't work, you want to be able to get the computer back to running condition. Whatever you do, make sure you follow those rules.

Continued

TAKE NOTE

▶ READ THE MANUAL

Despite what we've said here, read the manual that comes with your modem. We have to generalize to cover different modems — the manual should be specific to your modem. If what the manual says conflicts with something we've said, try to understand the differences. If you're not sure, follow the manual first — fall back on what we've said here if it doesn't work.

▶ RELY ON PLUG-AND-PLAY

The reason we suggest you limit your installs to one- or two-year-old computers is that they're likely to support *Plug-and-Play* installation, which means the computer figures out you've added a modem and does the right thing. This includes work by both the BIOS and Windows. If Plug-and-Play doesn't work, fixing conflicts can be hard. Until you become a computing veteran, we suggest you have a professional do the upgrades on systems that may have installation problems.

CROSS-REFERENCE
More examples of adding a card appear in the Chapter 20 lesson "Adding a Card."

FIND IT ONLINE
See if your phone line supports 56 Kbps at http://www.3com.com/56k/need4_56k/linetest.html.

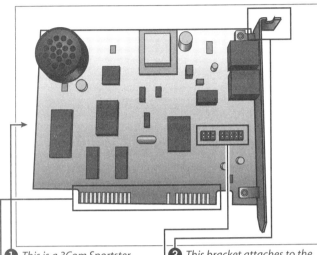

1 This is a 3Com Sportster 56 Kbps internal FAXmodem.

2 These fingers of metal on the bottom plug into the connector in your computer.

3 This bracket attaches to the back of your computer.

4 These are jumpers to configure the modem.

5 The inside of your computer where the modem goes looks like this.

6 These are ISA slots (left) and PCI slots (right). The modem goes in an ISA slot.

7 These are an ISA card (left) and a PCI card (right).

8 These covers unscrew at the top and come out to make an opening for the slot you choose.

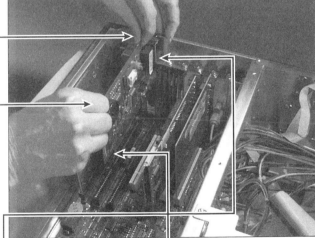

9 Remove the cover bracket for the slot you choose to use.

10 Hold the card by the edges (use a wrist strap!).

11 Position the card straight over the slot and lower it into contact, fitting the bracket into position.

12 Push the card down evenly with your thumbs until it seats. Rock it gently along the length if you must.

13 Fix the card in place with the screw that held the cover bracket.

We've had at least our fair share of problems installing modems, so it was ironic that when we went to take the screen shots of modem software installation for this book, things went so well that there was nothing to shoot. If your installation goes like ours did, here's the sequence of events:

1. Install the modem (as in the previous two pages) and close the computer case.
2. Power up the computer.
3. Windows 98 boots and notices the new modem.
4. If Windows 98 doesn't find a driver, point it to the CD-ROM that came with the modem.
5. The driver loads from the CD-ROM and the Windows 98 boot completes.

You can also install modem drivers from the Modems Control Panel applet, which we show in the pictures to the right.

If Plug-and-Play doesn't work immediately, Windows tries to detect your modem. Automatic detection works much of the time. If automatic detection works but Windows can't find a driver that corresponds to the modem it found, you need a disk from the modem manufacturer, probably the CD-ROM that came with the modem. You might find the driver on the manufacturer's Web site. If Windows can't find a modem, you might need to run a setup routine from the CD-ROM, forcibly install the right driver, or get some help.

TAKE NOTE

▶ DON'T OVERLOOK THE STANDARD MODEM TYPES

You still have options even when Windows doesn't have a driver for your modem and you can't find one on the Internet. Use Settings ⇨ Control Panel ⇨ Modems ⇨ General ⇨ Add and don't let Windows detect the modem. Click Next to find Standard Modem Types at the top of the list of manufacturers. Pick one that's close to what you have. You only get basic features, but it's enough to get to the Internet.

▶ USE THE RIGHT PHONE JACK

Modems have two phone jacks on the back: one to connect to the wall jack, and one for the telephone. They're typically labeled telco (telephone company) and phone, respectively. Some modems don't care if you reverse the connections, but some do and don't work if the connections are backward.

▶ BUY QUALITY MODEMS

A significant percentage of the tech support calls Internet service providers and computer manufacturers get are from people who bought add-on modems based only on rated speed and price, not reliability or the manufacturer's reputation. Buying from established modem makers like 3Com (U.S. Robotics), Cardinal, or Practical Peripherals ensures that you'll get support in Windows, and that you'll get quality help if you do encounter problems.

CROSS-REFERENCE
See "Figuring Out Whom to Call for Help" in Chapter 23 if you have problems with your modem installation.

FIND IT ONLINE
Find modem manufacturers at **http://computers. yahoo.com/computers/modem_zone**.

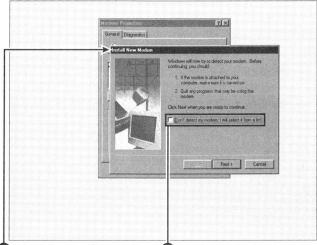

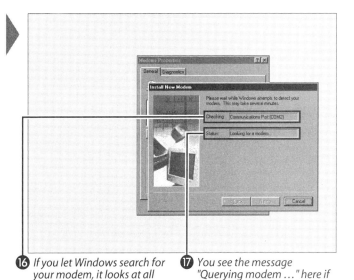

14 *Here's the start of the modem install wizard you see after clicking the Add button in the Modems Properties dialog box.*

15 *Windows tries to find your modem. Check this box to force the choice yourself.*

16 *If you let Windows search for your modem, it looks at all unused ports.*

17 *You see the message "Querying modem ..." here if Windows finds a modem.*

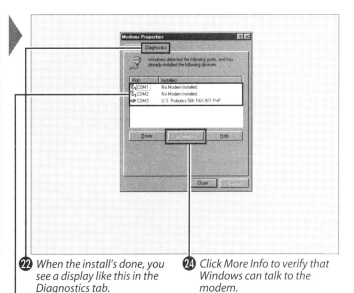

18 *If Windows can't find a modem, or you don't let it try, you choose from this list.*

19 *First pick the manufacturer of your modem.*

20 *Then pick the model from this list.*

21 *Use the Have Disk button to point Windows at a floppy disk or CD-ROM with drivers.*

22 *When the install's done, you see a display like this in the Diagnostics tab.*

23 *Select your modem from the list.*

24 *Click More Info to verify that Windows can talk to the modem.*

Getting Internet Service

Once you have a modem installed, you need someplace to call. Your choices are an Internet service provider (ISP) or a more community-like service such as America Online (AOL). You can get to the Internet from AOL too, so these aren't exclusive choices. The primary difference between direct Internet service and a community-like service is that direct Internet service has few or no filters or censors. You can get at anything on the Internet, but it's your responsibility to locate what you want and deal with what you find.

You can find ISPs with nationwide or worldwide service as well as ISPs local to your area. The giant ISPs offer phone numbers for access from almost anywhere, and consistent service. Local ISPs are more likely to work with you to meet your specific requirements, and in some cases can offer an amazing level of customer support. Finding a good local ISP can be hard; our ISP is local and offers excellent facilities and service. We've seen others that were too incompetent to live. (Satisfyingly, they went out of business.)

Windows 95 and 98 include enough software to get you on the Internet given just an access phone number, a user name, and a password. For most ISPs, all you need to do is set up a new dial-up connection (see the next lesson, "Dialing Up the Internet") and start Internet Explorer. Most ISPs have a software package for you, though, to give you more tools.

The examples in this lesson show software setup for the EarthLink Network, one of the top national ISPs in the United States. EarthLink pricing is typical of many ISPs, offering an unlimited-access, local dial-up account for less than $20 per month (plus a $25 setup fee). An EarthLink account gives you e-mail, a personal Web page, 6MB of storage space, access to more than 25,000 newsgroups, online gaming, and other services. Some accounts use toll-free numbers for access. Unless you have specific Internet tasks, you probably want unlimited access — it's easy to use a few hours at a time, which can multiply to 100 hours or more per month. With a metered rate, your charges can quickly add up.

The EarthLink CD-ROM software installation is one of the nicest setups for a new Internet user that we've seen. Along with a sequenced series of dialog boxes that collect necessary information, each dialog box has a soundtrack that explains on the process. The sensible organization of the dialog boxes and the overall instruction from the soundtrack make setup very straightforward.

Once you hook up with EarthLink, you want to find out what's going on to take advantage of what the Internet has to offer. You see how to set up e-mail in Chapter 17 ("Configuring Outlook Express or Netscape Navigator for Electronic Mail") and operate a Web browser in Chapter 15.

Continued

CROSS-REFERENCE
Find what you want on the Internet using Chapter 15's lesson "Searching the Web."

FIND IT ONLINE
Locate an ISP at **http://thelist.internet.com.**

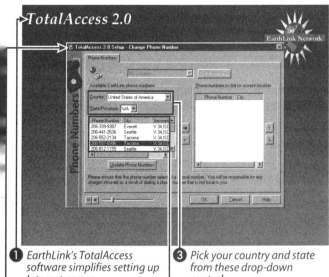

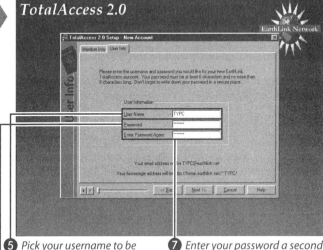

1. EarthLink's TotalAccess software simplifies setting up Internet access.

2. This dialog box lets you configure your computer to use a local access number.

3. Pick your country and state from these drop-down controls.

4. Choose all the numbers in this list that are local phone calls.

5. Pick your username to be something others can remember about you.

6. Choose a password of six to eight characters, including numbers.

7. Enter your password a second time to prevent mistakes. Don't forget your password.

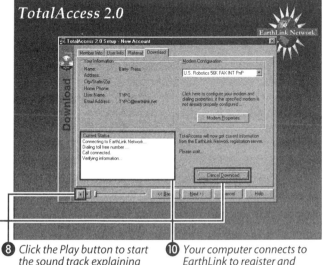

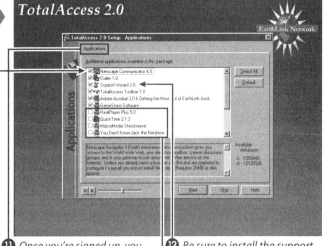

8. Click the Play button to start the sound track explaining what the dialog box does.

9. This button is initially Start Download, and changes during operation.

10. Your computer connects to EarthLink to register and check if the information you've provided is okay.

11. Once you're signed up, you can install additional software from the CD-ROM.

12. Netscape Communicator is included (Internet Explorer comes with Windows).

13. Be sure to install the support tools.

14. You can go back later if you want to add components you didn't pick the first time.

These programs are the most popular Internet applications; the next most popular is real-time chat, by which you can type messages that everyone else connected to the same channel immediately sees.

A great starting point for Internet chat (called Internet Relay Chat, or IRC) is **http://www.newircusers.com**. The site covers ways other than IRC to chat; if you want to learn about IRC directly, take a look at **http://www.newircusers.com/ircintro.html**. There are several programs you can use for IRC — we recommend mIRC at **http://www.mirc.co.uk/index.html**.

The Internet is also host to tens of thousands of non-real-time discussion areas called *newsgroups*. The easiest way to get involved with newsgroups is with the DejaNews service (**http://www.dejanews.com/help/newusers.shtml**). If you want a program to specifically handle newsgroups, there are features in Outlook Express and Netscape Communicator, or you can download the excellent Free Agent (**http://www.forteinc.com/agent/freagent.htm**).

The Internet is a great place to play games. EarthLink has a partnership with The Arena (**http://www.thearena.com**), but once you're connected to the Internet you can play anywhere. Popular game sites include MPlayer (**http://www.mplayer.com** — free access is available), Total Entertainment Network (TEN, **http://www.ten.net**), and the Internet Gaming Zone (**http://www.zone.com** — some free games here too).

CROSS-REFERENCE

Learn how to download software in Chapter 18's lesson "Downloading from the Web."

FIND IT ONLINE

EarthLink is at **http://www.earthlink.com**.

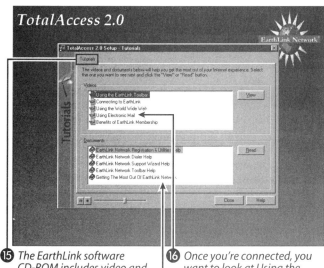

15 *The EarthLink software CD-ROM includes video and written tutorials.*

16 *Once you're connected, you want to look at Using the World Wide Web and Using Electronic Mail.*

17 *Also read Getting the Most Out Of EarthLink Network.*

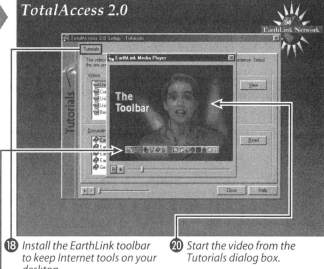

18 *Install the EarthLink toolbar to keep Internet tools on your desktop.*

19 *This tutorial video explains what the toolbar is and how to use it.*

20 *Start the video from the Tutorials dialog box.*

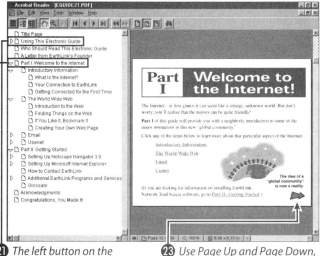

21 *The left button on the EarthLink toolbar opens the electronic Internet guide.*

22 *Pick sections from this table of contents.*

23 *Use Page Up and Page Down, or navigate with onscreen arrows.*

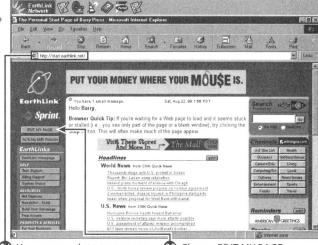

24 *Your personal start page can be **http://start.earthlink.net**. (See "Choosing Your Own Start Page" in Chapter 16 to find out how to set a start page.)*

25 *Choose EDIT MY PAGE to customize what you see.*

Dialing Up the Internet

The hardest part of connccting to the Internet is installing a modem and signing up with an ISP. All that remains is to tell Windows how to call the ISP and connect to the Internet. The setup program for the big ISPs often creates a dial-up connection in Windows; if you're using a local service provider, you might end up creating it yourself. Connection setup is easy to do, though, so don't let that keep you away from a good local provider.

Windows keeps dial-up connection setups in the Dial-Up Networking folder. There's also a special entry in the folder: Make New Connection. Double-click it to start the wizard that helps you set up what you need. You need to know your ISP's phone number,, your account name, and your password. Once your connection setup is done, just double-click to have the modem dial. Almost all ISPs use the Internet-standard dial-up and authorization protocols, which Windows automatically supports, so the connection shouldn't require fiddling.

The password you use when you dial your ISP is your defense against the theft of your account. Ask your ISP how to change the password, then change it soon after you first connect. The next time you dial, Windows won't be able to connect and will ask you to verify the name and password. Type in the new password, make sure to check the box that remembers it (as long as access to your PC is secure), and

click OK. You can expect the same result when you check your e-mail account — the fix is the same.

When you make up a password, include a number or punctuation. Don't use birthdays, names, or other things that someone could easily guess. For example, *neT4You* (note the capitalization) is a good password, but because we've published it here, don't use it! Change your password every one or two months.

TAKE NOTE

▶ **USE MULTIPLE CONNECTIONS FOR MULTIPLE PHONE NUMBERS**

Some ISPs have more than one phone number in an area. If you commonly get busy signals using one number (and don't want to change ISPs!), create a separate connection for each number. Then you can simply choose the one you want and won't have to remember all the numbers.

▶ **PUT A CONNECTION SHORTCUT ON YOUR DESKTOP**

Most programs that use the Web automatically dial the phone when they need to connect. If yours doesn't, or if you need to choose from several numbers, you can create shortcuts on your desktop to the icons in Dial-Up Networking. Just right-click the icon, drag it to the desktop, and choose Create Shortcut.

CROSS-REFERENCE

"Installing and Testing a Modem" earlier in this chapter should get you connected to a phone line.

FIND IT ONLINE

Update Windows 95 Dial-Up Networking at
http://www.microsoft.com/windows/downloads/

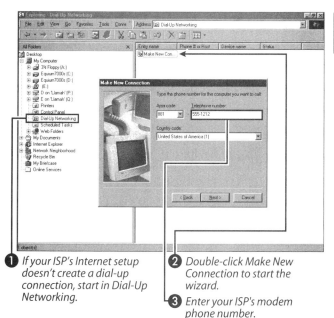

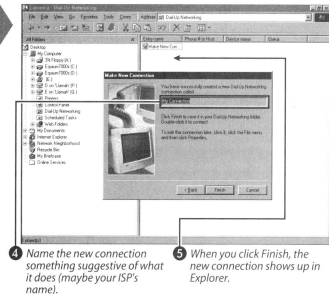

1 If your ISP's Internet setup doesn't create a dial-up connection, start in Dial-Up Networking.

2 Double-click Make New Connection to start the wizard.

3 Enter your ISP's modem phone number.

4 Name the new connection something suggestive of what it does (maybe your ISP's name).

5 When you click Finish, the new connection shows up in Explorer.

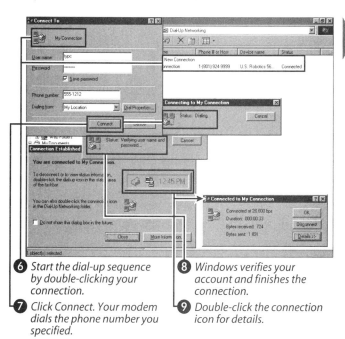

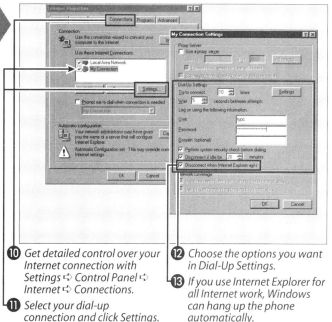

6 Start the dial-up sequence by double-clicking your connection.

7 Click Connect. Your modem dials the phone number you specified.

8 Windows verifies your account and finishes the connection.

9 Double-click the connection icon for details.

10 Get detailed control over your Internet connection with Settings ⇨ Control Panel ⇨ Internet ⇨ Connections.

11 Select your dial-up connection and click Settings.

12 Choose the options you want in Dial-Up Settings.

13 If you use Internet Explorer for all Internet work, Windows can hang up the phone automatically.

195

Signing Up on AOL

A direct connection to the Internet isn't for everyone. If you are a beginner, or simply don't have time to find the different Internet sites, a service that takes out much of the complexity might be the best thing for you.

America Online has become the largest online service in the world using this approach. With AOL you can get e-mail, read the news, find articles and information, have online conversations with people, and get to the Web. A crew of people at AOL develop interesting articles and information for you, and you don't have to find and install additional software (as you do for Internet chat). You can create your own Web page on AOL, as well as do all the things you'd normally do with an Internet connection through an ISP.

The first step to get online with AOL is to get the AOL software. It's included in many computer magazines (look for the CD-ROM), or you can call 1-800-545-9449 to request a copy. Version 4.0 was released in 1998, so if you find a CD-ROM with an older version, plan on upgrading. You can find complete upgrade instructions online.

When you go through the software setup as a new AOL user, you enter the usual information (such as a credit card number or other payment-plan information). Once you tell it your area code, the AOL setup routine calls out through your modem to find you a local phone number. You choose a *screen name*, which is the name you want other AOL and Internet

users to know you by. Your screen name can be your real name or something that identifies you or your interests.

TAKE NOTE

▶ KEEP YOUR PASSWORD SECURE

No one from AOL (or an ISP, for that matter) should ever ask you for your account password. A lot of people make telephone calls or send fraudulent e-mail saying they're from AOL and asking for your password for some realistic-sounding purpose. Don't fall for it.

▶ MAKE NEW FRIENDS AND GET HELP IN THE CHAT ROOMS

At almost any time day or night you can find people in AOL's chat rooms. These are discussion areas that let anyone type a message that everyone in the room can immediately see. Click the People button in the AOL toolbar to find rooms devoted to discussions of almost any topic imaginable. If you don't find one that you're interested in, start your own.

▶ USE THE FIND BUTTON

It's easy to search AOL or the Web. Just use the Find button under the toolbar, and you get a choice of where to search (AOL or the Web). When you search AOL, it returns a list of the service's destinations; when you search the Web it offers you a search engine similar to those outlined in Chapter 15.

CROSS-REFERENCE
If you want just the Internet — unfiltered and unmoderated — see "Getting Internet Service" in this chapter.

FIND IT ONLINE
The Internet version of AOL's chat is Internet Relay Chat. Get software at **http://www.mirc.com**.

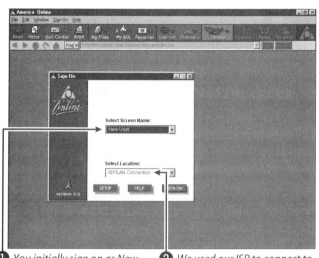

1 You initially sign on as New User; later, you choose a screen name.

2 We used our ISP to connect to AOL; you can do that or connect through your modem.

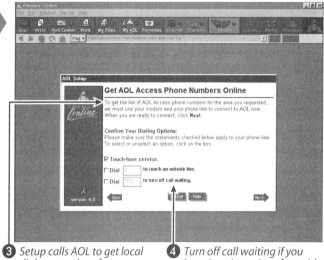

3 Setup calls AOL to get local dial-up numbers for your location.

4 Turn off call waiting if you have it — it can interfere with data transmission.

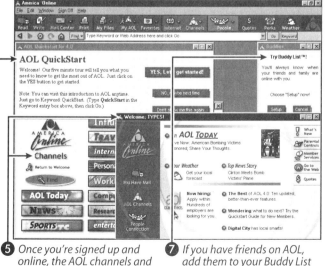

5 Once you're signed up and online, the AOL channels and the Welcome page appear.

6 The first time you connect, you see the QuickStart tutorial.

7 If you have friends on AOL, add them to your Buddy List so you'll know when they're online.

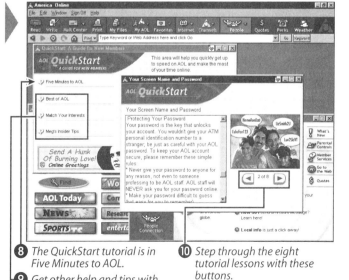

8 The QuickStart tutorial is in Five Minutes to AOL.

9 Get other help and tips with the other QuickStart choices.

10 Step through the eight tutorial lessons with these buttons.

Getting Information on AOL

One of the key advantages of a packaged service such as AOL is that the information you're likely to want is organized and presented in a way that makes it more useful and easier to find. Similar (and maybe equivalent) information is undoubtedly available on the Internet, but if you don't know how to find it, it's no help to you. AOL solves this problem by organizing information you want in ways that make it easier to get.

We've put two examples in this lesson: shopping at the beginning of the school year and finding information when you plan a trip. You can do both directly on the Internet, but AOL puts sources on your screen where you can find them. For example, in the upper left picture on the top of the next page, we start with the *Back to School* keyword phrase and then pick selections that let us shop for books. We then pick SAT Study Guides and end up at the Barnes and Noble online bookstore. Could you do that directly on the Internet? Certainly — you'd simply have to know that you wanted to go to **http://www. barnesandnoble.com, http://www.amazon.com**, or one of the other online bookstores.

The same comparison holds true for travel information, although as in other AOL areas, you find information on AOL that's not on Internet sites. Here's an example: We went searching for great Boston pizza restaurants. That turned out to be easy to do on AOL, but surprisingly difficult on the Internet. We only found one Internet site — **http://www.cuisinenet.com/top_picks/boston/1997/ 00016.html** — with comparative ratings of pizza in Boston. We found many reviews of Boston restaurants at **http://www.fodors.com**, but they weren't organized by specialization or best/worst as they were on AOL.

TAKE NOTE

▶ **SPEND TIME EXPLORING**

Whether you use an online service such as AOL or a direct Web connection through an ISP, you get more out of your network connection by spending time finding out what's there. Neither the tons of keywords on AOL nor the millions of Web sites on the Internet are easy to comprehend in one or a few sittings. The content regularly changes too, just like in a newspaper or magazine, so it's worth going back periodically to see what's new.

▶ **USE GUIDES AND SERVICES**

You don't have to understand everything the Web has to offer all at once: there are companies and services dedicated to explaining what is available. The most immediately useful are the news services (see **http://www.msnbc.com, http://www.nytimes. com, http://www.foxnews.com**, and **http://www. pathfinder.com**). Try the guides from The Mining Company (**http://www.miningcompany.com**) for more general and background information.

CROSS-REFERENCE

See "Searching the Web" in Chapter 15 for more details on how to find information on the Internet.

FIND IT ONLINE

Internet guides are similar to information on AOL. Try **http://home.miningco.com**.

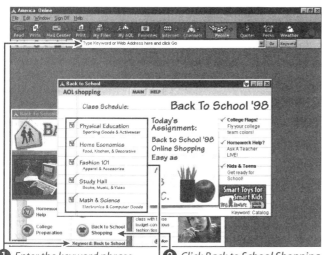

1 Enter the keyword phrase Back to School to reach a guide with homework help, college prep, and more.

2 Click Back to School Shopping to get to the featured online shopping departments.

3 Click a shopping department to get a list of stores in the department.

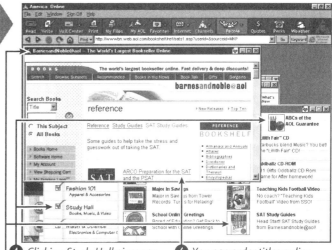

4 Clicking Study Hall gives you this list of stores and products.

5 Clicking SAT Study Guides takes you to the Barnes and Noble store on AOL.

6 You can order titles online and have them shipped to your home or office.

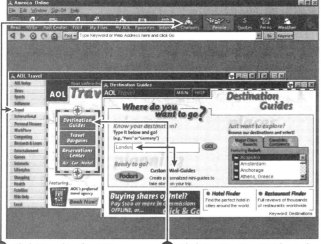

7 Click Travel in the AOL Channels to get this menu.

8 Click Destination Guides to be able to choose by destination or create a miniguide.

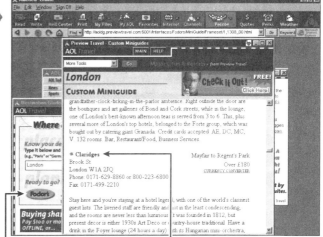

9 We created a miniguide from the Destination Guides option in the figure on the left.

10 After choosing options, including dining, hotels, and entertainment, we found one of our favorite hotels in the resulting miniguide list.

Personal Workbook

Q&A

1 What's a *modem?*

_____

_____

_____

2 Name two critical precautions when opening up your computer.

_____

_____

_____

3 What can you do if Windows Plug-and-Play doesn't detect your modem?

_____

_____

_____

4 Where does Windows keep dial-up network setups?

_____

_____

_____

5 How often should you change your password?

_____

_____

_____

6 What can you do with AOL software?

_____

_____

_____

7 Why would you use AOL instead of a conventional ISP?

_____

_____

_____

8 How does your modem affect playing games over the Internet?

_____

_____

_____

ANSWERS: PAGE 341

EXTRA PRACTICE

1 Open DejaNews (**http://www.dejanews.com**) and search for articles on pork jerk (then make some!). Hint: Use **http://www.dejanews.com/home_ps. shtml** and search the forum **rec.food.cooking** for *pork & jerk*.

2 Visit **http://www.lsf.com**. Decide what you want to have with the fresh tuna you just ordered.

3 You end up on a low-sodium diet, but don't want to give up your favorite foods. Look at **http://www. zeusfoods.com/zeusproducts.html** and **http://www.penzeys.com** for ideas.

4 Go to **http://terraserver.microsoft.com**. What can you do with what's there?

REAL-WORLD APPLICATIONS

✔ You're hosting a party and want to show off your new computer and Internet connection. You set up You Don't Know Jack — the Net Show (**http://www.bezerk.com/netshow**) and discover it's so funny you can't get any of your guests to try the bean dip.

✔ You're going to Denver to meet with a client, but you don't know how to navigate beyond the airport. Before you go, you go to **http://www.mapsonus. com** and get a map of your destination. You then go to **http://www.weather.com** to get a forecast so you know what to pack, and finish by ordering airline tickets through **http://www.expedia.com**.

Visual Quiz

What are we doing here? Why might we do this?

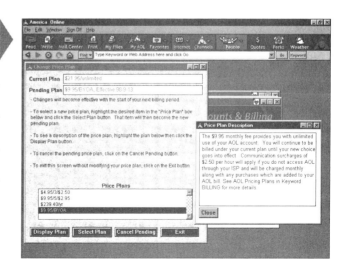

_____

_____

_____

_____

_____

CHAPTER **15**

MASTER
THESE
SKILLS

▶ Visiting Your First Web Site

▶ Linking and Navigating

▶ Using Secure Web Pages and Forms

▶ Buying on the Internet

▶ Searching the Web

Basic Web Browsing

The Internet is an amazing, exciting place. Using the Internet, you can look up people, create a map, go shopping, check today's news, research a topic, retrieve images, download software, hunt for a job, find the perfect chili recipe, find a church, compare car features and prices, get movie listings, win a trip, reserve a hotel, get the best rate on an airline ticket, check your congressperson's voting record, listen to the latest cut from your favorite music group, check your investment portfolio, and more.

All those possibilities work on a single, simple structure: On request from your computer (called a *client*), remote computers providing information (called *servers*) send data back to your computer, which in turn displays the result. The most common (and useful) implementation of clients and servers is what's called the World Wide Web, or the *Web*. You see information on the Web in a combination of text and graphics that connects it all, letting you go from one place to another with a click of the mouse.

Information on the Web is organized into *pages*, which themselves are collected into *Web sites*. Every Web site consists of at least one Web page, although most Web sites have many pages of information. Each page has its own unique address. Specially marked text on pages, called *links*, connect to the addresses of other pages when you click the link with the mouse. It's the linked combination of Web sites all over the world that comprise (big surprise coming here) the World Wide Web.

The client software you need on your computer for the Web is called a *Web browser*. The two most common browsers are Microsoft Internet Explorer and Netscape Navigator (part of Netscape Communicator). Both are free. Given a Web browser and an Internet connection, you have everything you need to open up all the possibilities we listed. Using your Web browser, you point and click your way to anywhere you want to go and can find information on just about any subject.

If you know the exact destination address, your Web browser can take you anywhere you want directly, in one step. If you know what you want to find but don't know where to find it, you can use Web search tools to locate pages covering what you want.

Visiting Your First Web Site

Begin your journey around the Web by starting your Web browser; double-click the icon on the desktop or select the browser from the Start ⇨ Programs menu. Let Windows connect to the Internet when the browser starts so you have live access to the Web.

Once the browser window opens, it shows your *start page*. By default, Internet Explorer opens on the Microsoft Web portal, **http://home.microsoft.com**. Netscape Communicator opens on the Netscape portal, **http://home.netscape.com**. Both of these pages provide links and information you're likely to want to see when you first start the browser, such as news, weather, and search tools.

Web pages link to other pages through *hypertext* items on the page. The mouse cursor changes to a pointing finger over a hypertext-linked item. Links can appear as push buttons, text, or graphics. Linked text is usually underlined. Hold the mouse cursor over the link and both Internet Explorer and Communicator show you the Web address the link ties to in the status bar at the bottom of the window. Click a link and the browser goes to the destination page.

Under the toolbar in the browser window is the address bar. You can type Web addresses into the address bar; when you press Enter, the browser starts trying to open the page at that address. Web addresses have a specific format, explained in the sidebar, "Addresses on the Web," on the facing page.

You must correctly type the address into the address bar. If you err by having the wrong address or mistyping it, you either get a message from the browser indicating the Web site could not be found or end up at a site other than where you intended.

The browser toolbar offers standard Web controls, including ones to go back to the previous page you visited, to stop trying to retrieve a page, to reload the current page from the server, and to go to your start page (Home).

TAKE NOTE

▶ RETRY STALLED WEB-PAGE LOADS

Web pages can be slow to load. The load time is affected by the size and number of the site's graphics, by the performance of the server, and by the load on the Internet between you and the server. Delays also occur when page requests get lost on the Internet, so if a page is taking too long to download, click the Stop button on the toolbar and then click Refresh.

▶ HIDE TOOLBARS YOU DON'T USE

Both Internet Explorer and Communicator let you hide the toolbars and address bar at the top of the screen. The first choices under the View menu enable you to hide the bars or show them if they're hidden.

CROSS-REFERENCE
To specify your own start page, see "Choosing Your Own Web Browser Start Page" in Chapter 16.

FIND IT ONLINE
Another portal site is CNET at **http://www.c-net.com**.

Addresses on the Web

Web addresses have a very specific format, called a *URL* (Uniform Resource Locator). A URL includes (in order) a *protocol identifier*, a *computer name*, and a *page name*. Both the protocol identifier and page name are optional. Your browser fills in the protocol identifier **http://** if you omit it; the prefix **http://** means that the connection should use the HyperText Transfer Protocol, which is the standard language for delivering Web pages across the Internet. If you omit the page name, the computer at the other end (the server) gives you a default page, which is usually what you want when you first go to a site.

Every URL requires a computer name. Most Web server computer names are **www** (as in World Wide Web) followed by the site name (such as **idgbooks.com**). The complete name of the Web server for IDG Books Worldwide is therefore **www.idgbooks.com**, and its complete URL is **http://www.idgbooks.com**.

The dots (periods) in the computer name separate parts of a naming hierarchy in which the last part of the name identifies the location or type of Web site. For example, **.com** indicates a commercial site, **.gov** a U.S. government site, and **.org** an organization's site (typically a nonprofit organization). The country of origin is common in non-U.S. computer names, such as **.uk** for United Kingdom sites, **.ca** for Canadian ones, and **.kr** for Korean ones.

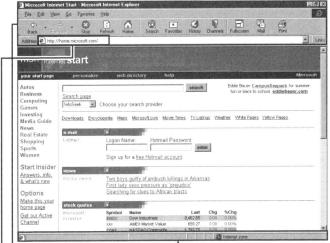

① *The Microsoft Internet Explorer window has a title bar, menu bar, toolbar, and address bar.*

② *The address of the current page is in the address bar.*

③ *Look for progress indicators and other information in the status bar.*

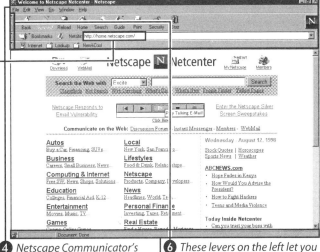

④ *Netscape Communicator's window also includes a title bar, menu bar, toolbar, and address bar.*

⑤ *Netscape calls the address bar the Netsite box.*

⑥ *These levers on the left let you show or hide the onscreen bars.*

⑦ *Find progress and status information in the status line.*

Linking and Navigating

The power of the Web is that it combines massive amounts of information with a Web of connections between pages. When you visit a Web site using just its Web server name, the first thing you see is the site's home page. The Web site may contain hundreds of thousands of pages and may link to hundreds of other Web sites, but everything you can reach on the site should be accessible from that home (or front) page. Command the browser to move to another page on the same site or to a completely different site by clicking a link. (Remember, you're over a link when the mouse cursor becomes a pointing finger.)

If you leave a Web page via a text link and then return (click the Back button on the toolbar), the color of the text link changes on most pages. This is the browser's way of telling you that it believes the link to be live — that you've followed the link and it worked.

Navigating from page to page or site to site leaves a path. Clicking the Back button in the toolbar sends you to the prior page. You can go back as far as you want until you get to the first page you saw when you started the browser. If you've moved backward, you can click the Forward button to move toward the front of the path. If you click a link while you're in the middle of the path, the browser forgets about pages from where you are to the front of the path, setting the page you linked to as the new starting point.

Make note of a site you want to visit again with Favorites ⇨ Add to Favorites in Explorer, or with Communicator ⇨ Bookmarks ⇨ Add Bookmark in Communicator. These commands add the site address to your Favorites list or Bookmark list, respectively. The next time you want to visit the site, pull down the Favorites menu or click the Bookmarks button and click the site entry.

TAKE NOTE

ORGANIZE YOUR FAVORITES AND BOOKMARKS

Both Internet Explorer and Communicator let you create folders and subfolders to organize lists of favorites/bookmarks. Just as you learned to organize files in Chapter 4's lesson on "Understanding Folders," keep these lists organized, too, so you can easily find links you want.

USE THE RIGHT MOUSE BUTTON

Both Internet Explorer and Communicator put command menus on the right mouse button, including Back, Forward, Refresh, and Stop. Another useful command is Copy Shortcut. Put the mouse over a link and use the command to put the destination Web address on the clipboard. You can then paste the URL into an e-mail message to send to a friend.

CROSS-REFERENCE
See "Searching the Web" in this chapter.

FIND IT ONLINE
A good site for finding places to link to on the Web is http://www.linkfinder.com. This site categorizes links.

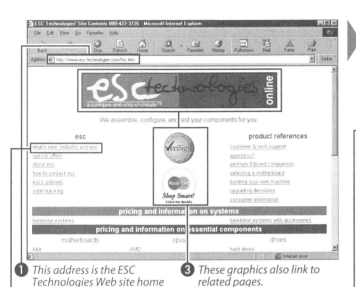

① *This address is the ESC Technologies Web site home page.*

② *Underlined words or phrases link to pages described by the text.*

③ *These graphics also link to related pages.*

④ *Clicking the Computer Books link on the ESC Technologies home page links to this page.*

⑤ *The linked page is still part of the ESC Technologies site.*

⑥ *This link connects to a page at the Amazon.com Web site.*

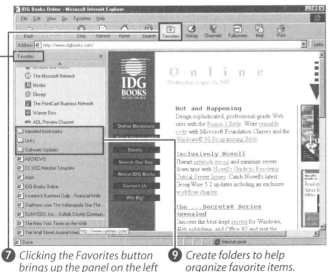

⑦ *Clicking the Favorites button brings up the panel on the left side of the screen.*

⑧ *The Favorites folder lets you go to any of the listed sites by simply clicking the item.*

⑨ *Create folders to help organize favorite items.*

⑩ *This drop-down list shows Web sites you've visited recently.*

⑪ *Click a site URL to return there.*

Using Secure Web Pages and Forms

Internet security is an important issue. As messages transit the Internet, the information they carry can be read by other people without your knowledge. If the information they pick up is a password, phone number, or credit card account, your privacy and security are compromised. You must take these security threats seriously.

Lest you hesitate, though, you have many legitimate reasons to send personal information over the Internet, such as paying for purchases you make. Web sites that need that information can create *secure* pages, places in the site that, when they transfer information to and from your computer, encrypt the data so any eavesdropper sees only gibberish. Transactions you make through a secure site are as safe as orders you place over the phone. As with phone orders, be sure you know whom you're doing business with.

Web pages often use forms to collect information, such as your name, address, card numbers, or messages for the site operator. Forms can contain text entry boxes, checkboxes, buttons, and selection lists in addition to the usual graphics and text. Each of these elements works similarly to its counterpart in dialog boxes. Once you entered the information on the form, click the Send or Submit button. Most forms activate when you press Enter, too.

Forms on Web pages might ask for information that you don't want to provide, such as your address, phone number, income, race, or religion. If the field is optional, you can simply skip the field and continue. If the field is required, you can choose not to send in the form — no information is transmitted until you click the submit button. Don't forget that your privacy is as important when you're filling out a form on the Web as it is when you're filling out one on paper.

TAKE NOTE

EXPERTS CAN AVOID SECURITY REMINDERS

When you attempt to send information to a server through an insecure Web page, both Communicator and Internet Explorer, by default, warn you that the connection is not secure. You can check off the Don't Show This Alert Next Time box to suppress the alert, but you and anyone else using the computer have to remember to check if the page is secure yourself.

HOW DO I KNOW IT'S SECURE?

Both Communicator and Internet Explorer have the ability to create secure connections with certain types of Web servers and can notify you that the connection is secure. Communicator displays an open padlock on the lower-left corner of the screen when the connection is not secure (most of the time) and displays a closed padlock when it is. Internet Explorer displays a lock on the right side of the status bar if the current page is secure.

CROSS-REFERENCE
See "Buying on the Internet" in this chapter for one of the most common uses of forms.

FIND IT ONLINE
Get information on Web privacy at **http://www.anonymizer. com/snoop.cgi**. Find out what kinds of information a site can collect from you automatically.

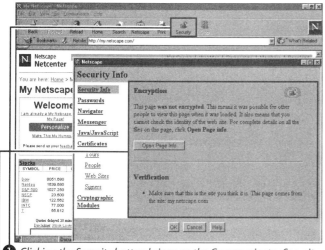

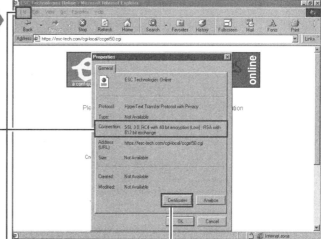

❶ Clicking the Security button brings up the Communicator Security Info dialog box.

❷ This information tells you the security status of this Web page.

❸ Choose File ➪ Properties to bring up this dialog box for the addressed Web page.

❹ SSL (Secure Socket Layer) indicates a secure connection for this page.

❺ Click Certificates to see more about the page's security status (lower-right figure on this page).

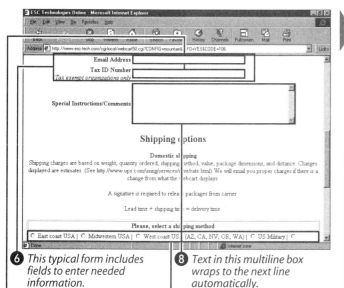

❻ This typical form includes fields to enter needed information.

❼ Type the requested information in these text boxes.

❽ Text in this multiline box wraps to the next line automatically.

❾ These radio buttons let you choose only one of the given options.

❿ Certificates are issued by independent sources to establish security credentials.

⓫ This list tells you what the issuer states the certificate verifies.

⓬ The certificate authenticates security only for the site shown.

⓭ The last two lines tell you who issued the certificate and when it's valid.

Buying on the Internet

Shopping is becoming one of the most popular activities on the Web because it's like having the world's largest mail-order catalog at your keyboard. Because so many stores have an Internet presence, and because you can quickly comparison-shop between stores, shopping online can save time and money. Hotels and airline tickets are easy to buy, as are all sorts of computer products. You can research products before you buy, such as checking the consumer ratings and options for a specific automobile model. You can get one-of-a-kind and hard-to-find items because specialty retailers can broaden their consumer base by selling on the Web. Auctions on the Web work like in-person silent auctions — you can bid, check status, and rebid as much as you want up to the closing time.

Most retail sites give you the ability to purchase items online, although some sites only offer to send a catalog, and some sites simply provide product information. On sites that take orders, you typically have an electronic shopping cart that you use to collect the products you want to purchase. You browse items for sale by using searches or by following links to products in categories. Once you find items you want, you fill in a form stating how many of each product you want to put in your cart. (The button to activate the form is generally marked Order or Buy.)

When you finish filling your shopping cart, you "check out" to complete your order. At this point, you give the store your shipping address and arrange for payment. You want to have your credit card handy — not only do some stores only accept credit or debit cards, but U.S. customers have some protections from fraud, defective products, or other problems when they pay with credit cards. (Circumstances in other countries vary.)

Many popular stores and mail-order outlets now have Web sites. Most have arranged a Web address that incorporates the store name, such as **http://www.llbean.com**, **http://www.landsend.com**, **http://www.wal-mart.com**, **http://www.fredmeyer.com**, and **http://www.macys.com**. If you can't find the address directly, use a search tool such as Yahoo!. (For example, Yahoo! shows that Nordstrom is on the Internet at **http://www.nordstrom-pta.com**.)

TAKE NOTE

▶ FIND AUCTIONS AND GO COMPARISON SHOPPING

You can find Internet auctions at **http://ebay.com**, **http://www.surplusauction.com**, and many places listed under auction on Yahoo!. Services on the Internet make it simple to do price comparisons, too. If you're buying computer equipment, get current pricing at **http://www.pricewatch.com**. Compare book prices at **http://www.mxbf.com**, and get more general comparisons at either **http://www.top10guide.com** and **http://www.bottomdollar.com**. You can find Internet malls too, such as **http://plaza.msn.com/msnlink/index.asp**.

CROSS-REFERENCE

Info in the next lesson, "Searching the Web," can help you find interesting shopping sites.

FIND IT ONLINE

Link to **http://store.yahoo.com/stores** for an enormous list of places to shop.

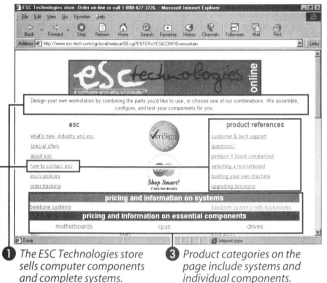

❶ *The ESC Technologies store sells computer components and complete systems.*

❷ *The store provides information to help you make a buying decision.*

❸ *Product categories on the page include systems and individual components.*

❹ *Clicking the barebone systems-with-accessories link on the home page brings up this page. Scroll down to see the specifications for different systems.*

❺ *Click a price to move to the order form.*

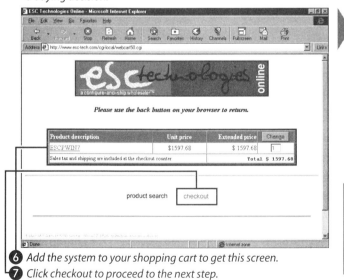

❻ *Add the system to your shopping cart to get this screen.*

❼ *Click checkout to proceed to the next step.*

❽ *Enter the required shipping information in these form fields.*

❾ *Scroll down to choose how your computer gets shipped and to enter payment information.*

Searching the Web

The Web has hundreds of millions of sites worldwide, with new sites being added daily. Finding what you want through random exploration can be hard at best. The Web has tools to help you find the pages you want to see: search engines and directories. Search engines are computer programs that locate sites and index the words they contain, while search directories are site catalogs created by people.

Popular search engines include Digital Equipment Corporation's AltaVista (**http://altavista.digital.com**) and Excite (**http://www.excite.com**). Both engines accept keyword searches and return a Web page that lists the best matches they find. The matches are hyperlinked to the actual pages, so you can click a link to bring up a Web site. Search engine results sometimes include pages that are old and no longer available, but their advantage is that they offer more sites to choose from than directories.

Because the people who compile directories screen Web pages, you can expect their listings to exclude most outdated and less useful sites. Search engines and directories, otherwise, work similarly. You enter keywords for the directory search and get back a hyperlinked list of results. Popular directories include Yahoo! (**http://www.yahoo.com**) and Snap! (**http://www.snap.com**).

Choose keywords that define what you're looking for as closely as possible. Most search services list the sites matching the most keywords first, so you see the best results at the top of the results. Sites can show up in the results list that don't contain all the keywords, so there's no reason not to use as many keywords as you want. You can use phrases as keywords too; for best results, enclose phrases in quotation marks (such as "real estate").

You can get too many results — even though you entered lots of keywords — when some of your keywords are commonly used terms. If a commonly used term must appear in a listing for a match to be useful, however, you can help limit the results by using special symbols in your search query. With AltaVista and Excite, you can prefix a plus sign for required words and a minus sign for words that should be excluded. For example, you might search for Web sites on real estate available in Syracuse, New York, excluding rentals, with the following query: +"Real Estate" +"New York" +Syracuse –rental.

Directories (and some search engines) offer the alternative of a listings hierarchy that you can search. For example, from the home page of the AltaVista search engine, you can find Web pages that advertise houses for sale in New York by selecting Browse Categories ⇨ Shopping & Services ⇨ Home, Garden & Auto ⇨ Real Estate ⇨ Realtors & Listings ⇨ States N ⇨ New York.

Continued

CROSS-REFERENCE
See "Linking and Navigating" in this chapter if you're unclear on how to use hyperlinks.

FIND IT ONLINE
The Mining Company Web search guide is at **http://websearch.miningco.com**.

BASIC WEB BROWSING

Searching the Web

CHAPTER 15

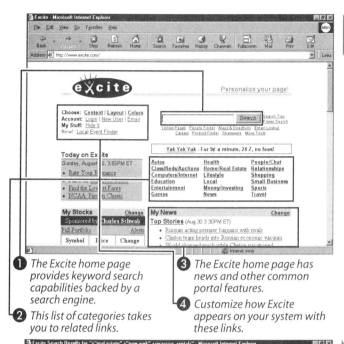

1 The Excite home page provides keyword search capabilities backed by a search engine.

2 This list of categories takes you to related links.

3 The Excite home page has news and other common portal features.

4 Customize how Excite appears on your system with these links.

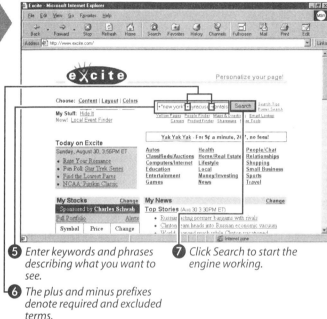

5 Enter keywords and phrases describing what you want to see.

6 The plus and minus prefixes denote required and excluded terms.

7 Click Search to start the engine working.

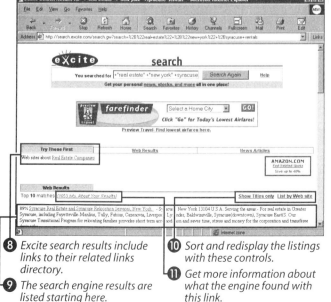

8 Excite search results include links to their related links directory.

9 The search engine results are listed starting here.

10 Sort and redisplay the listings with these controls.

11 Get more information about what the engine found with this link.

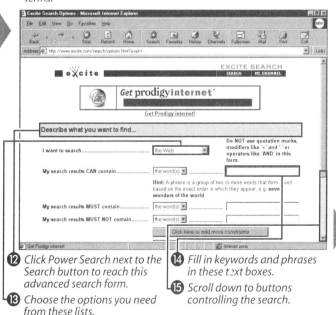

12 Click Power Search next to the Search button to reach this advanced search form.

13 Choose the options you need from these lists.

14 Fill in keywords and phrases in these text boxes.

15 Scroll down to buttons controlling the search.

213

Searching the Web
Continued

Search engines and directories each compile their data banks from a variety of sources. Because so many pages populate the Internet, it's likely that you won't find everything you want using only one service. If you're really going to be thorough, you should use several search tools. The multiple-tool approach is important enough that there are now search pages that combine several popular search tools in a single place.

Search pages take two forms. The simple ones let you choose a search engine or directory from a list and then submit the query to the search tool you specified. The more sophisticated ones run the search on several services at once and then deliver the combined results.

Internet Explorer and Communicator both give you access to a simple search choice page — click the Search button in either browser. Internet Explorer splits the window vertically, with the left side of the screen becoming the search page. You choose the search tool you want and continue with your query. Communicator uses a different approach, linking to a page on the Netscape Web site that provides the search functions. As with Internet Explorer, you choose your search tool and make the appropriate selections.

A more effective way to search the Web than querying one tool at a time is using a multiple search tool such as Dogpile (**http://www.dogpile.com**) or Ask Jeeves (**http://www.askjeeves.com**). Both sites send your query to multiple engines at once, collect the results, and display them through your browser. Dogpile gives you results from Yahoo!, Lycos' A2Z, Excite Guide, GoTo.com, PlanetSearch, Thunderstone, What U Seek, Magellan, Lycos, WebCrawler, InfoSeek, Excite, and AltaVista, so you're likely to find what you're looking for if it's on the Internet. Dogpile can search for weather, business news, and stories on the news wires, too — it's a comprehensive service.

TAKE NOTE

▶ RANKED RESULTS

Search tools rank their results, but the criteria that determine position on the list vary from tool to tool. Some rank based on how well the site text matches what you typed, while others rank based on how many times your search phrase appears. In all cases, refining your query to limit the number of matches is the best strategy.

▶ KEEP DOGPILE READY TO SEARCH

Your Web browser might not include Dogpile in the list of search tools it supports. Internet Explorer version 5 lets you add any search site you want by typing the link, but Netscape Communicator and Internet Explorer version 4 can't do that. Click the Dogpile Remote link in the upper-left corner of the Dogpile home page to fix the problem. A new, small window opens that always has the Dogpile search form ready to go.

CROSS-REFERENCE
You have to have Internet access to use the search engines. Start with Chapter 14's lesson "Getting

FIND IT ONLINE
Find out how to write Dogpile queries at **http://www.dogpile.com/notes.html**.

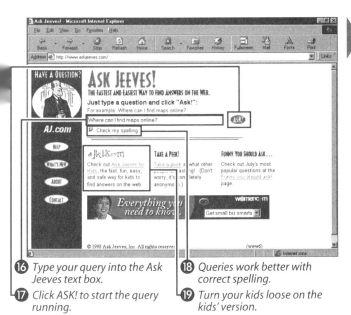

16 Type your query into the Ask Jeeves text box.

17 Click ASK! to start the query running.

18 Queries work better with correct spelling.

19 Turn your kids loose on the kids' version.

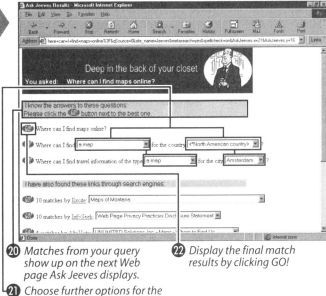

20 Matches from your query show up on the next Web page Ask Jeeves displays.

21 Choose further options for the results with these drop-down lists.

22 Display the final match results by clicking GO!

23 Enter your search terms in the text box.

24 Choose a Web search or one of the other Dogpile searches with this drop-down list.

25 Limit the response time with this drop-down list.

26 Start the search by clicking Fetch.

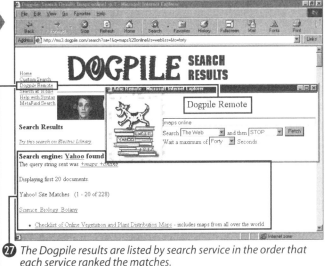

27 The Dogpile results are listed by search service in the order that each service ranked the matches.

28 Click Dogpile Remote to start another browser window that always contains a search form.

Personal Workbook

Q&A

1 What are the two most popular Web browsers?

_____

_____

_____

2 What is a *start page*?

_____

_____

_____

3 What is a collection of Web pages called?

_____

_____

_____

4 Where do you type the Web site address to go to a different Web site?

_____

_____

_____

5 What do Favorites/Bookmarks do?

_____

_____

_____

6 What does *URL* stand for?

_____

_____

_____

7 What are some popular Web search engines or Web search tools?

_____

_____

_____

8 What does it mean when the mouse pointer turns into a pointing finger?

_____

_____

_____

ANSWERS: PAGE 342

216

EXTRA PRACTICE

1 Go to **http://www.cnn.com** by typing in the address.

2 Go to **http://www.excite.com** and search for information on the World Cup.

3 See what Alt+left arrow and Alt+right arrow do after you visit a few sites.

4 Add **http://www.abcnews.com** to your Favorites or Bookmarks list.

5 Visit **http://www.lsf.com** and order a catalog.

6 Use the People Finder on Excite to look up a friend's phone number.

REAL-WORLD APPLICATIONS

✔ You are researching a paper, so you search Dogpile for information on your topic. You find several sites relating to the topic and compile a list of URLs you can use in the bibliography for the paper.

✔ You forgot that your wedding anniversary was coming up, and it's tomorrow! You go online and buy a great watch. The shop guarantees they will deliver it tomorrow.

✔ You are watching the NBA playoffs when the announcers mention nba.com/playoff, a site containing every possible piece of trivia about the playoffs. You realize that the full site address is **http://www.nba.com/playoff**, and visit the site while you watch the game.

Visual Quiz

Go to **http://www.mapsonus.com** and plan a route from Rapid City, South Dakota, to Chicago, Illinois. Does the result look like this? What happens when you click the map?

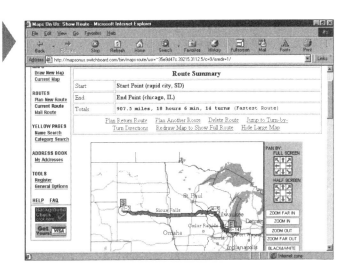

CHAPTER 16

MASTER
THESE
SKILLS

▶ Choosing Your Own Web Browser Start Page

▶ Setting Internet Security and Content
Protection Levels

▶ Installing Plug-ins

▶ Handling Colors, Backgrounds, and Printing

▶ Controlling the Browser Memory and Disk Caches

▶ Setting Key Advanced Browser Options

Customizing Your Internet Browser

Microsoft Internet Explorer and Netscape Communicator are enormously capable all by themselves without any changes or customization — so capable that you can use them just as they come out of the box to see and do much of what the Web has to offer. In the same way that you benefit by customizing Windows, though, you get more out of these Web browsers by tailoring them to work the way you want.

Web browsers are highly adaptable, extensible programs with several built-in programming languages. You've already learned about secure Web pages and forms, which protect sensitive information on its way across the Internet. Now, it's time to look at the security features built into your browser to protect personal information and help safeguard your computer. If you're using Internet Explorer, built-in features can help protect you and your family from viewing Web content that you feel is objectionable or inappropriate.

The pictures, sounds, and other fancy parts of Web pages have to download to your browser.

Sending this information over a slow Internet connection takes time and can make response intolerably slow. You can use browser customizations to choose whether or not you want to download that content, omitting some of the more complex content in exchange for speed.

Yet another way to customize your browser is to add capabilities through *plug-ins*, which are small programs that expand the browser's capabilities so it can handle other kinds of information not designed into the browser program itself. Plug-ins can improve multimedia support, let you play online games, track browsing habits, change the appearance of your browser, follow stocks and current news, and more.

Finally, your browser keeps a historical record of the Web pages you have visited and usually keeps a copy of the Internet files that you download in an area called cache. You can adjust how or even if these records are kept and how much disk space is used for the cache, trading disk space for speed and letting you view Web pages from disk when you're not connected to the Internet.

Choosing Your Own Web Browser Start Page

Web browsers display a *start page* when they first open. If you're using Internet Explorer, that start page is most likely **http://home.microsoft.com**. If you use Netscape Navigator or Communicator, it's likely to be **http://home.netscape.com**. Many users never change the start page, which means that these two addresses are among the busiest sites on the Net.

The number of hits their start pages take make the Microsoft and Netscape (and Yahoo! at **http://www.yahoo.com**) sites among the most valuable real estate on the Net, so all three companies work to make their start pages useful to keep people coming back. But you can choose your own start page. If you use the Internet to search for information, you might want to point directly at your favorite search engine. If you're on a corporate net, you might want to point at the company home page. If you're a game player, you might want to point at a site targeted at your favorite game. Be sure to choose a start page that loads reasonably quickly if you're on a slow modem.

Set your start page by navigating to the page you want on the Web and telling the browser to remember that page. Each browser has its own method; if you're not using Internet Explorer or Netscape Navigator (or Communicator), look for the browser preferences or options.

You can change your start page as often as you like. We tend to use either Microsoft's start page or the initial page for Digital Equipment Corporation's Alta Vista search engine. Don't be swayed by the fact that there's competition between Microsoft and Netscape. You can use Microsoft's start page with Netscape's browser, and can use Netscape's NetCenter start page with Internet Explorer.

TAKE NOTE

► CUSTOMIZE WHAT'S ON YOUR START PAGE

Microsoft and Netscape both let you customize the content of your start page. Using a customization form (look for the link to personalize the page), you can choose to have news, weather, sports, and other timely links current and waiting when your start page comes up.

► DON'T FORGET YOUR OWN LINKS

If you use the Microsoft or Netscape start pages, look in the personalization form for the section that lets you add your own links. You can move the section up to the top of the page, too, making these links quick and easy to find. Use cut and paste through the Windows clipboard to make sure you get the URL for each link right. This way, you don't have to bother typing the clumsy Web syntax and long site path names. If you navigate to just the page you want down inside a site, you can cut and paste its address, enabling you to go there directly.

CROSS-REFERENCE

See "Setting Key Advanced Browser Options" later in this chapter to learn more about using the Internet Options and the Preferences dialog boxes to customize your browser.

FIND IT ONLINE

Consider using **http://www.nando.net** and **http://www.dogpile.com** as start pages. Nando.net is a news site; Dogpile lets you query many search engines at once.

CUSTOMIZING YOUR INTERNET BROWSER
Choosing Your Own Web Browser Start Page

1 *Choose View ➪ Internet Options to begin changing your start page in Microsoft Internet Explorer.*

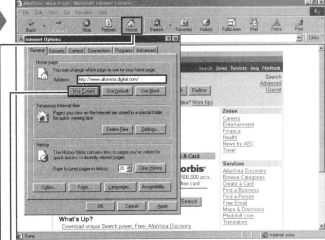

2 *The General tab in the dialog box has a group of settings for Home page. If you've already navigated to the page you want, just click the Use Current button. Otherwise, type the address. Click OK and you're done.*

3 *Test the change by clicking the Home button on the toolbar.*

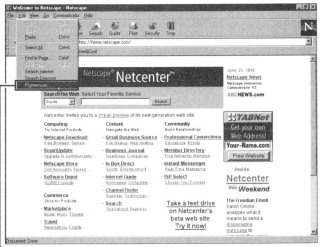

4 *Edit ➪ Preferences is the gateway to browser configuration in Netscape Navigator and Communicator. Choose that menu option and a dialog box comes up.*

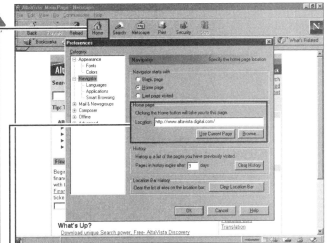

5 *The Home page group in the middle right of the dialog box lets you set your start page. Click the Use Current Page button if you've already navigated to the site or type the address. Click OK to finish.*

6 *Test the change with the Home button on the toolbar.*

Setting Internet Security and Content Protection Levels

Listening to coverage of the Internet in the mainstream press could easily give you the impression the Internet is an electronic Badlands not fit for decent folk to hang their spurs. The truth is, there's plenty of G- and PG-rated material on the Internet, and most people on the Internet are *not* out to get you. Even so, some important security issues are worth considering when you go online. Although most other people on the Internet just want to receive and share information in a harmless manner, a few rabble-rousers out there can cause big problems for you if you're not careful.

One hazard is the possibility that you could unknowingly download a dangerous program to your computer. Many modern Web pages incorporate elements that use the Java, JavaScript, and ActiveX programming languages. When you access one of these Web pages, these special elements run as programs on your computer. Normally this isn't a problem, but it is possible for one of these programs to carry a virus or to otherwise damage files on your computer. Internet Explorer and Netscape Communicator have built-in features to help you avoid computer viruses and other malicious programs. Depending on what security settings you choose, the browser warns you whenever a Web page tries to do something that could present a danger. You must then make a decision to continue or cease the operation altogether. If you know every page you visit is safe (such as on a corporate intranet not connected to the Internet), Netscape and Internet Explorer let you set up the browser so that these elements can run on your computer without further approval.

Another danger is that your personal information — such as credit cards, bank account numbers, home address and phone number — could be compromised. The only safe places to share these kinds of information are on *secure* Web sites with strong and clearly stated privacy policies. Secure Web sites use encryption software to scramble your information in a way that only you and the intended recipient can decode. Security preference options in the browser control the way security and encryption is handled.

Every browser has different options for setting your security preferences. Netscape has a convenient Security button right on the toolbar that opens the Security dialog box. There you set encryption preferences, among other things. Other security settings are available on the Advanced section of the Preferences dialog box.

Internet Explorer makes adjusting security settings a little easier. The Security tab of the Internet Options dialog box lets you set one of three security levels from Low to High or you can customize your security settings to your own needs.

Continued

CROSS-REFERENCE

See "Identifying Viruses and Other Threats" in Chapter 22 to learn more about protecting your computer from viruses, and "Using Secure Web Pages and Forms" in Chapter 15.

FIND IT ONLINE

See VeriSign's Web site at **http://www.verisign.com** to learn more about consumer encryption products.

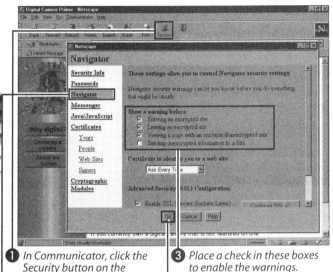

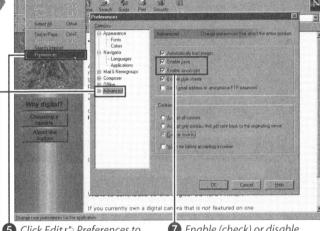

① In Communicator, click the Security button on the toolbar.

② In the Security info dialog, click Navigator to view your Web browser security settings.

③ Place a check in these boxes to enable the warnings.

④ Click OK when you are done.

⑤ Click Edit ⇨ Preferences to open the Preferences dialog box.

⑥ Choose the Advanced category.

⑦ Enable (check) or disable (uncheck) Java and JavaScript. Unless you have specific reasons not to, leave them enabled.

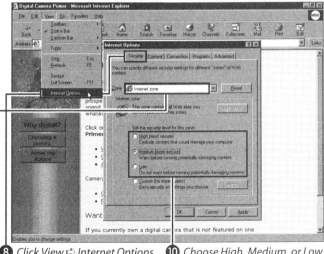

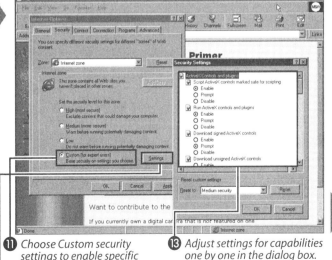

⑧ Click View ⇨ Internet Options ⇨ Security to open Internet Explorer's security preferences.

⑨ Select the Internet zone for changing settings.

⑩ Choose High, Medium, or Low security. Most users should choose Medium or High.

⑪ Choose Custom security settings to enable specific options or restrictions.

⑫ Open the custom settings dialog box with the Settings button.

⑬ Adjust settings for capabilities one by one in the dialog box.

Computer viruses and unintended disclosure of your personal information are not the only dangers lurking on the Internet. The Internet is connected worldwide, and because anyone can have access to the Internet, unedited and uncensored information is available freely all over the world. With hundreds of millions of people on the Internet, it's guaranteed that somewhere someone has posted something on the Internet objectionable or offensive to you, your family, or your community.

Remember, though, that the Internet is worldwide, unedited, and uncensored. What's objectionable or offensive to you may be perfectly acceptable elsewhere. What's acceptable to you may be objectionable or offensive elsewhere. This conflict means it's your responsibility to take control of what you see, not the poster's responsibility to take down content you don't like.

You can help protect yourself or your children from seeing Web sites that don't meet your standards. Internet Explorer and version 4.5 or later of Netscape's products have a built-in Content Advisor that lets you control what kinds of content can be read based on criteria determined by the Recreational Software Advisory Council (RSAC) rating service (see below for its Web address). If you have enabled the Content Advisor, you can adjust what kinds of materials can and can't be viewed and protect those settings with a password.

So far, though, only a few thousand of the millions of Web sites on the Internet are formally rated. You can choose to have the Content Advisor prohibit access to unrated sites. That's good, because it locks out sites that decline ratings because of their content, but it's bad because it locks out unrated sites that are harmless. Many educational sites are unrated, for instance, so you would not be able to view them at all. The answer to this problem is a different style of content filter — one that receives content ratings not from the sites themselves, but from third-party companies. Products include Cyber Patrol, CYBERsitter, Net Nanny, and WizGuard. Some products include filters on outgoing information in addition to incoming content filters, helping solve the problem that young children don't realize the potential dangers in giving out addresses and phone numbers.

TAKE NOTE

► FILTER INTERNET COOKIES

Some Web sites place small files on your computer called *cookies* that hold information the site would like to retrieve the next time you visit. Cookies can hold any kind of information known to the site, such as when you last visited or your passwords for that site. Access to cookies isn't necessarily restricted to the site that left the information, which could disclose information on where you browse. You can use custom settings in your Web browser to disable cookies or to limit access to the site leaving the cookie.

CROSS-REFERENCE

See "Downloading From the Web" in Chapter 18 for help in retrieving content filtering software from **http://www.**

FIND IT ONLINE

Find RSAC at **http://www.rsac.org**.

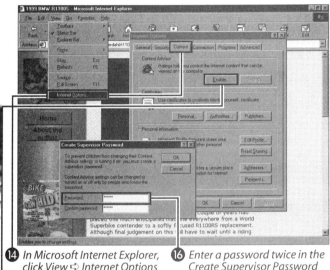

⑭ *In Microsoft Internet Explorer, click View ➪ Internet Options ➪ Content.*

⑮ *Under Content Advisor, click Enable.*

⑯ *Enter a password twice in the Create Supervisor Password dialog box. Don't forget the password!*

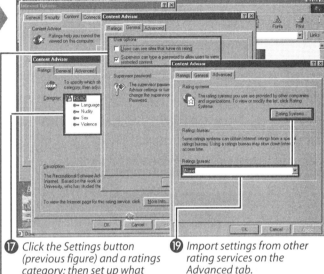

⑰ *Click the Settings button (previous figure) and a ratings category; then set up what viewers are allowed to see.*

⑱ *On the General tab, choose if unrated sites can be viewed.*

⑲ *Import settings from other rating services on the Advanced tab.*

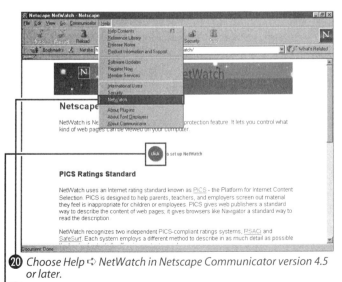

⑳ *Choose Help ➪ NetWatch in Netscape Communicator version 4.5 or later.*

㉑ *Once the page comes up, click the button to set up the NetWatch content filter.*

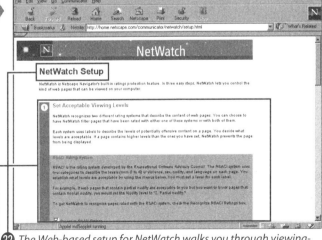

㉒ *The Web-based setup for NetWatch walks you through viewing-level setup.*

㉓ *Scroll down the page to finish setup and submit your choices.*

Installing Plug-ins

Competition between Netscape Communicator and Microsoft Internet Explorer has led each product to include many features in the standard configuration, especially when compared to their predecessors of only a few years ago. The pace of innovation triggered by the resulting *browser wars* between Netscape and Microsoft has led to a dizzying cycle of software upgrades and revisions, resulting in new features constantly being made available for both browsers.

For all of that, both products have the ability to load programs written by other companies as if they were core parts of the browser itself. These additional programs, called *plug-ins*, are software fragments that literally plug into Communicator or Internet Explorer to expand their capabilities. Plug-ins can deliver the ability to watch digital videos on a Web page, listen to music, play interactive games, view complex formatted documents, and more.

Plug-ins help make your browser more efficient, because they let you selectively add capabilities to your browser. You can add capabilities you want specifically and ignore ones you don't care about. Because the browser need not include every possible extension, Netscape and Microsoft can limit their already large programs to manageable size. Were that not true, you'd need far more memory on your computer for the browser to run with reasonable performance.

You almost always get plug-ins by downloading them from the Internet. Installation usually involves merely following a few simple steps, as shown in the figures on the right. Once installed, the plug-in works as part of your Web browser; it launches automatically whenever a Web page contains an element requiring the plug-in or whenever you hyperlink to a file that uses it. You can open some plug-ins (such as the Adobe Acrobat document viewer or the Real Networks RealPlayer) as complete programs in their own right.

TAKE NOTE

▶ FINDING PLUG-INS

Finding plug-ins isn't a problem — they tend to find you. You can download plug-ins from one of the big software Web sites such as Tucows (**http://www.tucows.com/**), but usually a site requiring a plug-in has a link to the manufacturer's Web download site along with a note telling you which plug-ins are needed. For instance, the CDNow Web site (**http://www.cdnow.com**) has a link to download the RealAudio player, a plug-in that lets you hear music on the site.

▶ EXPANDING MULTIMEDIA CAPABILITIES

Multimedia programs are among the most popular browser plug-ins. Programs such as RealPlayer let you listen to live radio broadcasts and watch videos, all from within your Web browser. The *streaming files* used by RealPlayer are sound or video files that can play as their data comes over your Internet connection, eliminating the need to wait for a long file download.

CROSS-REFERENCE

Learn more about installing plug-ins in Chapter 9's "Installing a New Program" lesson.

FIND IT ONLINE

Find RealNetworks' Web site at **http://www.real.com**.

1 Download a plug-in program, such as RealPlayer from RealNetworks. Click the Windows Start button and choose Run to begin installation.

2 Many plug-ins can install for both Netscape and Microsoft browsers.

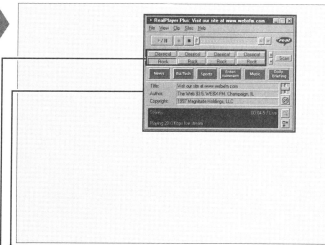

3 The RealPlayer plug-in runs as an application coordinated with the browser.

4 Pick a preset button to hear a radio channel over the Internet.

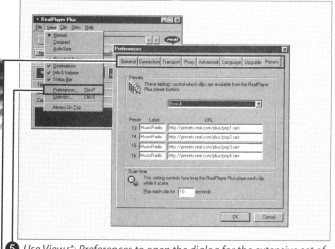

5 Use View ➪ Preferences to open the dialog for the extensive set of customizations.

6 Be sure to explore the dialog tabs. The Presets tab lets you customize the onscreen buttons.

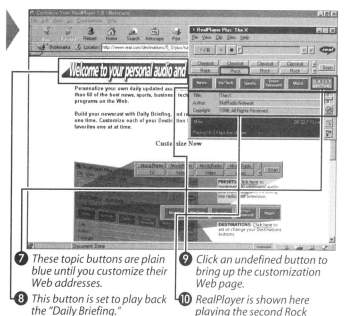

7 These topic buttons are plain blue until you customize their Web addresses.

8 This button is set to play back the "Daily Briefing."

9 Click an undefined button to bring up the customization Web page.

10 RealPlayer is shown here playing the second Rock channel.

Handling Colors, Backgrounds, and Printing

Spend much time on and around the Internet and you begin to see patterns to things, including the one that different colors often mean different things on the Web. For instance, if you are reading a page of text and you come across a word or phrase that is a different color (usually blue) and underlined, that text is probably a hyperlink. Once you follow that link, the text turns to a different color (such as purple).

Web pages can specify the colors the browser uses to display text. Color changes can be a bit confusing until you learn to correlate changes in the appearance of the mouse pointer to appearances on the Web page. If the Web page sets no specific colors, the page displays the default settings from your browser. Both Communicator and Internet Explorer initially set the default color for most text as black, with blue for hyperlinks and purple for visited hyperlinks. You can change the default colors in any browser. In Netscape, look for the Colors section of the Preferences dialog box; in Internet Explorer, use the General tab of the Internet Options dialog box.

Web pages have a background underneath their text and images. The default background in both Netscape and Internet Explorer is a plain gray you can change using the color setting dialog box. Few Web pages actually use the default background, though, so changing the default is not a high-priority job.

Web pages often contain great information you want to print and keep. You print pages the usual way, with the File ➪ Print command, but a few complications may arise. By default, Web browsers omit the background color when they print, but use the text colors specified by the browser. Pages with light colored fonts on a dark background, therefore, don't print well (or at all). You can force the page to display with the colors you specify and then print it, or you can tell the browser to include the background when it prints.

CROSS-REFERENCE

See the lesson called "Printing Your Letter" in Chapter 3 to learn more about printing documents.

FIND IT ONLINE

A good place to test any appearance changes you make is at **http://www-dsed.llnl.gov/documents/WWWtest. html**, the WWW Viewer Test Page.

CUSTOMIZING YOUR INTERNET BROWSER
Handling Colors, Backgrounds, and Printing

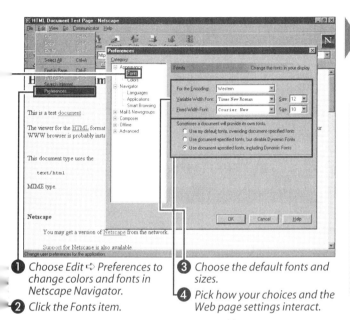

① *Choose Edit ➪ Preferences to change colors and fonts in Netscape Navigator.*

② *Click the Fonts item.*

③ *Choose the default fonts and sizes.*

④ *Pick how your choices and the Web page settings interact.*

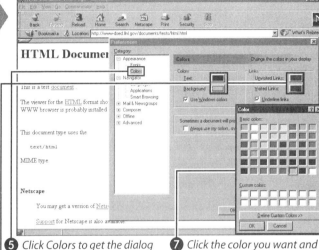

⑤ *Click Colors to get the dialog box for text and link colors.*

⑥ *Click an individual color setting to get the color chooser dialog box.*

⑦ *Click the color you want and then click OK.*

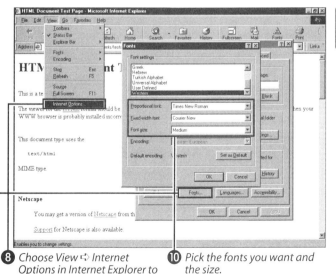

⑧ *Choose View ➪ Internet Options in Internet Explorer to set fonts and colors.*

⑨ *Click the Fonts button to bring up the fonts dialog box.*

⑩ *Pick the fonts you want and the size.*

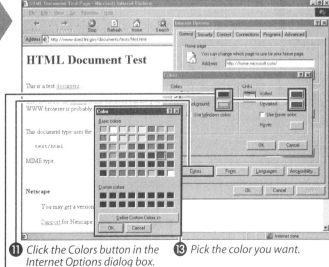

⑪ *Click the Colors button in the Internet Options dialog box.*

⑫ *Click the color option you want.*

⑬ *Pick the color you want.*

Controlling the Browser Memory and Disk Caches

Behind the scenes, viewing a Web page causes your browser to read a specially formatted file over your Internet connection and store the file on the hard drive of your computer. The formatting in the file, written according to the rules of HyperText Markup Language (HTML), describes what the Web pages should look like. Your Web browser uses this information from the file to create the image you see on the screen. Visit a lot of Web pages, and a lot of HTML files will clutter up your hard drive.

Suppose you leave a Web page and then want to go back to it. It takes far less time for the Web browser to reload the page from a file on your disk (or an image of that file in memory) than to retrieve the page again over the Internet, so all Web browsers store recently used HTML files in a special area of your hard drive called the browser *cache* (pronounced like *cash*). The browser checks to make sure that the files have not been updated since the last time you visited them, and if not, it just uses the files from cache.

The browser's cache can also let you view files without actually being connected to the Internet. You can view pages that you downloaded earlier by simply loading the cached copy. This function is useful if you must limit the amount of time you are connected to the Internet, but need to read some long documents. Hyperlinks on the cached pages only work if the link points to another cached Web page. If not, you have to connect to the Internet so the browser can load the missing files.

The browser cache can become quite large, so browsers have provisions to limit cache size. Once the total space occupied by cached files reaches a predetermined point, the browser deletes the oldest cached files. By default, the cache for Internet Explorer is limited to 3 percent of your hard drive, which can be a lot of space on a big drive. Netscape sets a more conservative default limit of 7MB, independent of drive size. You can easily change the limits in either browser and can clear the cache manually to free up space on your hard disk. Once you clear the cache, though, the pages you regularly visit are likely to take longer to retrieve the next time you visit.

Continued

CROSS-REFERENCE
Cached files exist in a folder on your hard drive. Learn more about working with folders in "Understanding Folders" in Chapter 4.

FIND IT ONLINE
Find software to help work with the browser cache at http://www.winfiles.com/apps/98/webtools.html.

CUSTOMIZING YOUR INTERNET BROWSER

Controlling the Browser Memory and Disk Caches

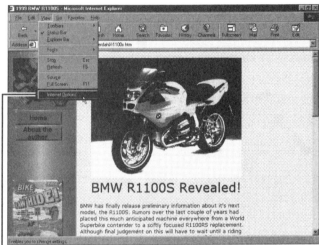

➊ Choose View ➪ Internet Options to adjust your cache settings in Microsoft Internet Explorer.

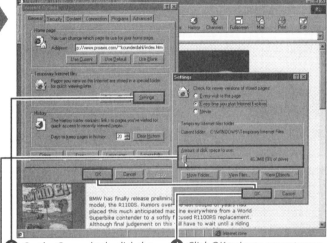

➋ On the General tab, click the Settings button under Temporary Internet Files.

➌ In the Settings dialog box, move this slider to adjust how much disk space is used.

➍ Click OK twice to accept your changes and close the dialog boxes.

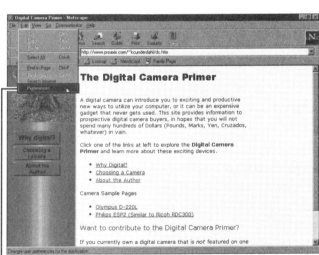

➎ Click Edit ➪ Preferences in Netscape Communicator to open the Preferences dialog box.

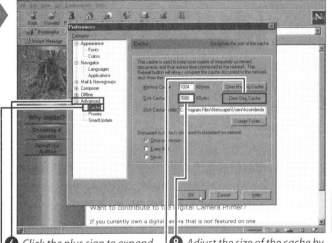

➏ Click the plus sign to expand the Advanced category of the Preferences dialog box.

➐ Click Cache to view cache settings.

➑ Adjust the size of the cache by typing a new number here.

➒ Clear everything out of cache by clicking Clear Disk Cache. Click OK to accept changes and close the dialog box.

Controlling the Browser Memory and Disk Caches *Continued*

If your browser disk cache size limit is small (which helps conserve disk space), files for Web pages you've visited might disappear while you're still interested in them. This limitation means that the cache doesn't work well as a record of places you have been on the Web. Instead, browsers incorporate a history feature to track Web sites you visit. You can use the history feature to revisit previously visited Web sites, track how much time you are spending online, and determine where you are spending it; the history records every Web page you visit, including when you last visited the page and when the site says the item should expire from the cache. (Netscape also tracks when you first visited the page and how many times you've visited; Internet Explorer also tracks the file size and when the cached page was last checked against the site.)

By default, Netscape flushes items in the history after nine days, so a Web page you visited ten days ago will not be listed in the history. Internet Explorer retains history information for 20 days by default. You can adjust these settings with the usual preferences dialog box, or you can clear the history altogether.

Access methods for the history features in Communicator and Internet Explorer differ significantly. To open Communicator's history, choose Communicator ⇨ Tools ⇨ History from the menu bar. The history opens in a separate window, and you can revisit a page by double-clicking its entry. For Internet

Explorer, click the History button on the toolbar to open a History bar along the left side of the browser window. The pane that opens lays out history items in a tree-like structure filed by week, day, Web site, and individual page. As with Communicator, revisit a page by double-clicking an entry.

TAKE NOTE

▶ VISIT WEB PAGES WITH HISTORY

You may find that you want to revisit a Web site you saw recently; however, remembering the site's name — much less the URL — can be difficult unless you use the history to find and revisit those pages. In Netscape, open the history and double-click the page you want to visit. In Internet Explorer, open the history, open the day you visited the page, and click the link for the Web site or page you want.

▶ PROTECT YOUR PRIVACY

The research you do on the Internet can be valuable information to a competitor, revealing the topics you're interested in enough to spend time on. The browser history and disk cache log the Web sites you've visited, so they're a potential security risk. Use the commands in your browser to clear the cache and history to avoid leaving an electronic trail on your hard drive of where you've been.

CROSS-REFERENCE

See the next lesson, "Setting Key Advanced Browser Options," to learn other ways the Internet Options and the Preferences dialog boxes can help customize your browser.

FIND IT ONLINE

CyberClean can clear all browser history and cache files off your disk. Download it from **http://www. thelimitsoft.com/cyberclean.html**

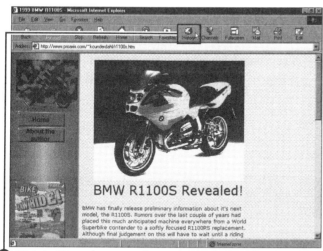

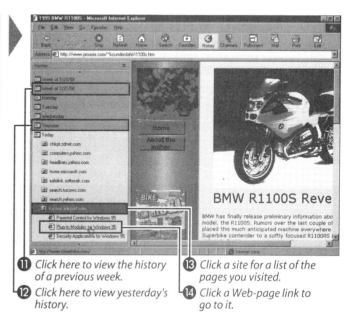

⑩ *Click the History button on the Internet Explorer toolbar to open the history.*

⑪ *Click here to view the history of a previous week.*

⑫ *Click here to view yesterday's history.*

⑬ *Click a site for a list of the pages you visited.*

⑭ *Click a Web-page link to go to it.*

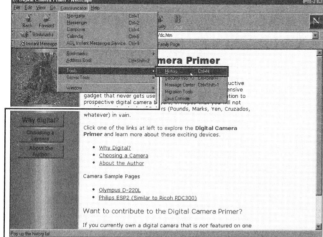

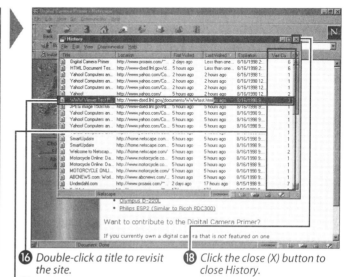

⑮ *In Netscape Communicator, click Communicator ⇨ Tools ⇨ History to open the History window.*

⑯ *Double-click a title to revisit the site.*

⑰ *Review how many times you've visited the page here.*

⑱ *Click the close (X) button to close History.*

Setting Key Advanced Browser Options

Like most other programs on your computer, Web browsers have options you can tailor to your own preferences. You've seen many of the most important options in this chapter's lessons, including how to choose a start page, setting security and content levels, adjusting appearances, and controlling the browser's history and cache.

Each browser has a central area where you can adjust most options. In Netscape Communicator, this area is the Preferences dialog box, reached through Edit ⇨ Preferences on the menu bar. In Microsoft Internet Explorer, you use View ⇨ Internet Options to open the Internet Options dialog box. In other browsers, you can expect to find something similar. It's always a good idea to get familiar with the options that are available to you, even if you don't plan to change any of them.

Which options you adjust is up to you. Many users adjust multimedia options to improve performance by taking into account the limited bandwidth of their modem. A lot of Web pages today are beautiful technological showcases of cutting-edge Web design, but on a slow Internet connection these online parade floats are difficult or impossible to view. You can set options in your browser so that large multimedia elements don't load, eliminating the eons-long wait for the download.

The best way to learn what each option does is to experiment with them a bit. You can discard the changes you selected before you close the options dialog box — just click the Cancel button to close the dialog box without making the changes. The figures on the facing page show you how to change some of the most important options available to you in both Communicator and Internet Explorer. Look through all the options to see what you may want to change.

TAKE NOTE

▶ TURN OFF PICTURES

If you have a modem that is 14.4 Kbps or slower, you probably want to set your browser so it doesn't download image files. If you do this, only the text comes through your modem. If you want to display a picture, right-click the area where it should be and choose Show Picture. If you can, though, replace your modem. We've seen 56 Kbps modems that can double or triple your connection speed for as little as $28.

▶ CHOOSE COMMUNICATOR STARTUP OPTIONS

Netscape Communicator includes several different components. Navigator is the Web browser, Messenger is the e-mail client, Composer is an editor that lets you create your own Web page, and Calendar is a scheduler and day planner. Choose which of these opens first when you click the Netscape icon on your Windows desktop by selecting an option in the Appearance option group of the Preferences dialog box.

CROSS-REFERENCE
Some of the most important options are for security and content. See "Setting Internet Security and Content Protection Levels" earlier in this chapter.

FIND IT ONLINE
Find Internet Explorer 4 updates at **http://www.microsoft.com/ie/download/addon.htm**. Find Netscape Communicator updates at **http://www.netscape.com/download/su1.html**.

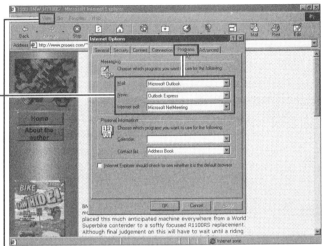

① *Choose View ⇨ Internet Options on the Internet Explorer menu bar.*

② *Click the Programs tab and choose application programs from the drop-down lists.*

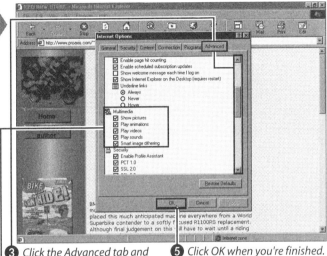

③ *Click the Advanced tab and scroll down the list of options to view them.*

④ *Choose which multimedia elements you want displayed.*

⑤ *Click OK when you're finished.*

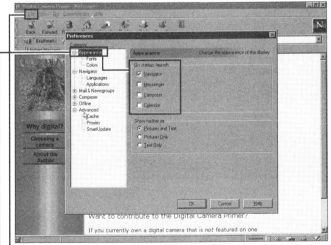

⑥ *Choose Edit ⇨ Preferences in Netscape Communicator.*

⑦ *In the Appearance category, choose which Communicator component you want to open on startup.*

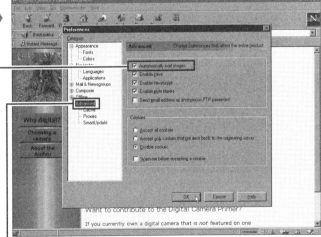

⑧ *Click the Advanced category to display its dialog box.*

⑨ *Click here to remove the checkmark if you don't want pictures to download.*

Personal Workbook

Q&A

1 What is a *start page*?

_____

_____

_____

2 What security hazards do browsers usually protect you from?

_____

_____

_____

3 Does content screening software guarantee that objectionable material cannot be downloaded to your computer?

_____

_____

_____

4 What is a *browser plug-in*?

_____

_____

_____

5 What is the default text color in most Web browsers?

_____

_____

_____

6 Can you print a Web page? How?

_____

_____

_____

7 What is the *browser disk cache*?

_____

_____

_____

8 How do you erase history records in a Web browser?

_____

_____

_____

ANSWERS: PAGE 342

CUSTOMIZING YOUR INTERNET BROWSER

Personal Workbook

EXTRA PRACTICE

➊ Set the IDG Books Worldwide Web page (**http://www.idgbooks.com/**) as your start page.

➋ Disable cookies in your browser.

➌ Go to Tucows (**http://www.tucows.com**). Search for, download, and install a plug-in to play MIDI files called Crescendo.

➍ Change the default color for hyperlinks to the most obnoxious shade of pink you can find.

➎ Clear your browser's history and cache.

➏ Change the settings for your browser so that pictures are *not* automatically downloaded.

REAL-WORLD APPLICATIONS

✔ You are building a music library and have recently discovered the huge selection of music available online at CDNow (**http://www.cdnow.com/**). You install the RealPlayer plug-in so you can listen to sample music tracks from CDs before you buy. You find several disks you want to add to your collection and use the CDNow secure Web site and your own browser's encryption software to make purchases directly over the Internet.

✔ You travel extensively for your job and work on a laptop when you're on the road. You disable pictures on your laptop's browser so that the Web pages download quicker, you spend less time online, and you don't use as much battery power.

Visual Quiz

How do you link to an item that you visited yesterday?

_____

_____

_____

_____

_____

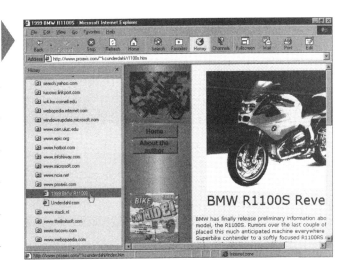

CHAPTER **17**

MASTER THESE SKILLS

▶ Configuring Outlook Express or Netscape Communicator for Electronic Mail

▶ Sending and Receiving Your First E-mail Message

▶ Managing E-mail Addresses

▶ Dealing with Junk E-mail (Spam)

Electronic Mail

Suppose you could send letters to your friends, customers, or suppliers, and have them delivered almost instantly anywhere in the world. This is not a fantasy; it's the reality of electronic mail, or *e-mail*. If you and the people you write to access the Internet, or are on a system such as America Online, you can exchange letters, pictures, documents, sounds, video, and even programs.

E-mail predates the Web and even the Internet. The Arpanet was the network that hosted the early technology developments that became the Internet, and e-mail was the application with the most traffic. Almost all Internet service providers include e-mail in their standard service packages. If yours doesn't, several services on the Internet offer free e-mail accounts.

At one time, e-mail was limited to text messages only. Its capabilities grew to include attached files of any sort. The most recent extensions can send messages that are complete Web pages — you can mix text and graphics anywhere in the message and have a graphical background (to look like stationery).

You need software to send and receive e-mail. Although there are many fine e-mail programs, we will look at the ones that are available for free with the two most popular Web-browser software packages: Outlook Express, which comes with Microsoft Internet Explorer, and Messenger, which is built in to Netscape Communicator. They lack some of the advanced features found in other programs, but both are reasonably capable and are simple to use. Even if you have other software (many service providers give their customers Eudora Lite), the ideas in this chapter translate to most e-mail programs.

E-mail addresses are different than postal addresses, but have the standard form *name@server*. *Name* is your unique ISP account name , and *server* is the name of your ISP's computer that handles e-mail. For example, if your Internet account is named *typc* on the AT&T WorldNet service, your e-mail address would be *typc@worldnet.att.net*. E-mail software knows that your name and account name may differ, so even though you're known only by your e-mail address, the software lets you add your name to the messages you send.

Configuring Outlook Express or Netscape Communicator for Electronic Mail

Windows 98 and Internet Explorer 4 or later versions include the Outlook Express program for reading e-mail. If Internet Explorer is running, use the command Go ⇨ Mail to start Outlook Express.

When Outlook Express starts for the first time, it opens a configuration wizard to help you set it up. Here are the questions it asks you:

1. **Your Name** — This is the name you want people to read. You can type almost anything, although quote-mark and period punctuation can give some e-mail readers fits. Use a name with meaning to the people that will receive your e-mail. If the people you write to know you as ToasterMan (and not A. J. Sunbeam), try that.

2. **Your Internet E-mail Address** — Type your exact e-mail address here. Uppercasing and lowercasing don't matter, but you must get the *name@server* information correct or no one will be able to reply to your messages.

3. **Your E-mail Server Name** — The server name is probably the same as the server given in your e-mail address, although some ISPs are set up differently. Your ISP should tell you what to use.

4. **Your E-mail Account Name and Password** — Your account name is the name from the second step. You chose a password when you set up your ISP account. If you change the ISP password, you have to tell Outlook Express about it.

If you're uncertain about what to do for Steps 2 through 4, call your ISP for help.

It's convenient to have individual e-mail accounts. Businesses usually assign an account to each employee on the network; in the home, personal mailboxes are becoming the Internet version of a private phone line for a teenager. You can get additional accounts from your ISP or one of the free e-mail services. You can use the same computer to access all of your accounts — use the Tools ⇨ Accounts ⇨ Add ⇨ Mail command to let Outlook Express know what you've done. (If you have several computers, you can set up different accounts on different computers.) Outlook Express designates one account to be the default account and periodically checks for mail. You can change the default with Tools ⇨ Accounts. Use the Tools ⇨ Send and Receive command to check for mail on the nondefault accounts.

Continued

CROSS-REFERENCE
See "Getting Internet Service" in Chapter 14 if you need an Internet account.

FIND IT ONLINE
Get free e-mail from Hotmail (http://www.hotmail.com) or Juno (http://www.juno.com).

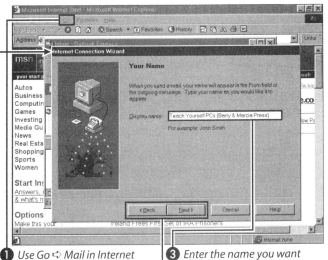

① *Use Go ⇨ Mail in Internet Explorer to start Outlook Express.*

② *When Outlook Express starts the first time, it opens a wizard to help set up.*

③ *Enter the name you want people reading mail from you to see.*

④ *As with most wizards in Windows, click Next to go on or Back to change your mind.*

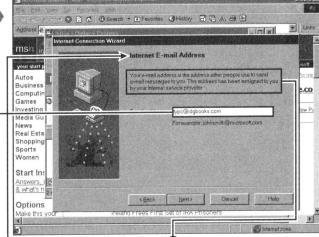

⑤ *The next step in the wizard is to tell it your e-mail address.*

⑥ *Combine your account name and mail server to form a complete e-mail address.*

⑦ *If you enter your e-mail address incorrectly here, people won't be able to reply to you successfully.*

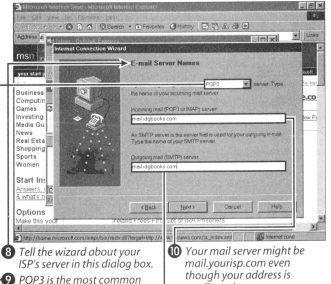

⑧ *Tell the wizard about your ISP's server in this dialog box.*

⑨ *POP3 is the most common server type; the alternative is IMAP. Ask your ISP which it is.*

⑩ *Your mail server might be mail.yourisp.com even though your address is you@yourisp.com.*

⑪ *Some ISPs have different in- and outbound servers.*

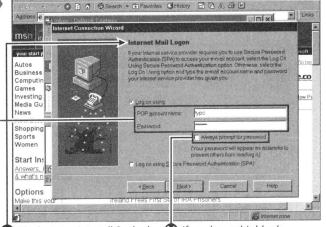

⑫ *The last step is to tell Outlook Express how to log on to your e-mail account.*

⑬ *The essential information is the account name and password.*

⑭ *If you leave this blank, Outlook Express remembers your password and uses it automatically.*

When you download and install Netscape Communicator from the Netscape Web site (**http://www.netscape.com/computing/download**), you get the Messenger e-mail reader. Be sure to get Communicator in addition to Netscape Navigator, because Navigator doesn't include Messenger. The installation program asks you for the same sort of information that Outlook Express wanted. If you don't want to fill in the information at this point, skip to Messenger's Edit ⇨ Preferences dialog box to set up your e-mail account. The headings under Mail & Groups — including Identity, Mail Server, and others — work like dialog tabs to bring you the needed dialog boxes.

Outlook Express and Messenger use the same information for e-mail setup because of standardized Internet e-mail servers — you have little or no choice about how your computer communicates with other computers across the Internet. A group called the Internet Engineering Task Force (IETF) defines the standards for Internet communication. It's because of the IETF's work that all the computers on the Internet work together.

There are two standard languages (called *protocols*) that computers usually speak when handling e-mail: Simple Mail Transfer Protocol (SMTP) and version 3 of Post Office Protocol (POP3). SMTP is the protocol a computer uses to send e-mail across the Internet; POP3 is the protocol a computer uses to retrieve e-mail once it arrives at an ISP's server. Another protocol, Internet Mail Access Protocol (IMAP) is starting to replace POP3, but you're still more likely to run across POP3. Your ISP can tell you which protocol it uses to pick up messages (POP3 or IMAP), as well as the name of the mail server.

TAKE NOTE

▶ AVOID E-MAIL SOFTWARE

Some e-mail services (such as Hotmail) work through your Web browser. This is convenient for getting your e-mail if you don't always know where you'll be or what computer you'll be using. Using a browser, you don't have to configure an e-mail reader and worry about where to leave your messages — everything happens on the server. You simply open the service's Web page, give it your name and password, and connect to your mailbox.

▶ MAKE YOUR E-MAIL UNIVERSALLY READABLE

It's nice to have files, graphics, fonts, and Web pages in your e-mail messages, but keep in mind that not every e-mail reader can handle such technical details. If you send e-mail and people complain about a lot of gibberish in the message, set your e-mail program to send plain text. Some programs let you set this preference by addressee so you don't lose the features for everyone.

CROSS-REFERENCE

Learn how to download programs such as Netscape Communicator in Chapter 18's lesson "Downloading from the Web."

FIND IT ONLINE

Many people like Qualcomm's Eudora Lite e-mail reader. Get it at **http://eudora.qualcomm.com/eudoralight**.

Configuring Outlook Express or Netscape Communicator for Electronic Mail

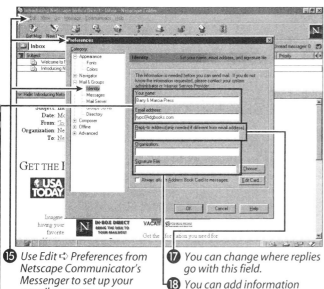

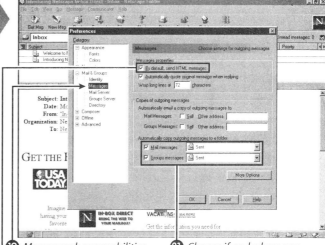

15 Use Edit ➪ Preferences from Netscape Communicator's Messenger to set up your e-mail accounts.

16 These lines want the same information as Outlook.

17 You can change where replies go with this field.

18 You can add information about yourself to your e-mail here.

19 Messenger has capabilities beyond some simpler programs, such as settings for handling outgoing messages.

20 Choose Web-like (checked) or normal text (unchecked) here.

21 Choose if and where you want to file copies of the messages you send.

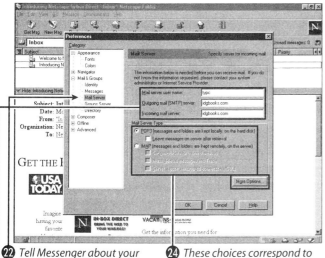

22 Tell Messenger about your ISP's mail server with the Mail Server dialog box.

23 These are the usual account and server name fields.

24 These choices correspond to the POP3 / IMAP choices in Outlook Express, but suboptions are shown directly in the dialog box.

25 Messenger has a powerful feature to search directories on the Internet to find people's e-mail addresses.

26 Set up the directories you want to search in this list box.

27 Set the order of the search with these controls.

Sending and Receiving Your First E-mail Message

Think about sending and receiving e-mail the same way you think about sending and receiving a letter, and you have all the right ideas. Writing a message means you pull out a sheet of paper (*open a window that's a blank message form*), put words on paper (*type into the window*), address an envelope (*enter an address in the To field*), and put the letter in a mailbox (*click Send*). Receiving a message is much the same. A letter shows up in your mailbox (*it's usually automatic, but you can check for mail yourself*), and you open and read it (*double-click the header*). When you're finished reading, you file it (*drag it to a folder*) or throw it away (click *Delete*).

As usual, your computer adds features to this simple model. You can address messages to more than one person, send carbon copies and blind carbon copies, get delivery and read receipts, check spelling before you send, and more.

Typing a message into Outlook Express or Messenger is much like using WordPad—both provide only simple formatting features. If you're sending a message text to someone whose e-mail software doesn't handle even these basic formatting features, you're further limited to blank paragraphs, tabs, and spaces for setting up how your message looks. People sometimes add emphasis to their writing by enclosing words they would make italic or bold in asterisks (like *this*), but your best approach is clear, effective writing.

Remember that you won't be there when your message is read—jokes, sarcasm, and ridicule are quite often misinterpreted. Before sending your message, read it over, top to bottom, from the reader's point of view. You're likely to spot changes you can make that will convey your meaning more clearly. Run the spell checker, too—many people interpret misspellings as a sign of sloppiness or ignorance.

TAKE NOTE

THINK ABOUT WHAT YOU SAY

Normally, the Internet is not secure. Your messages can be intercepted and read as they're routed to their destination. Courts have held that employers can read the e-mail of employees using company e-mail systems. If you're going to send confidential information over the Internet—or a passionate letter to your lover—ask yourself first if you'd mind if someone else read it. The chances of interception may be low, but they're not zero. Double-check the destination address before you click Send, too.

PROTECT YOUR SECRETS

You can help keep your secrets safe. Both Outlook Express and Messenger can encrypt your messages and can sign them to authenticate that they came from you. The security they provide isn't unbreakable for someone who's determined enough and has powerful enough computers, but it should be sufficient to keep most everyone else out.

CROSS-REFERENCE

Trying to remember everyone's e-mail address is a pain. See the next lesson, "Managing E-mail

FIND IT ONLINE

Get a digital ID for encrypted e-mail at the VeriSign Digital ID Center at **http://www.verisign.com/**

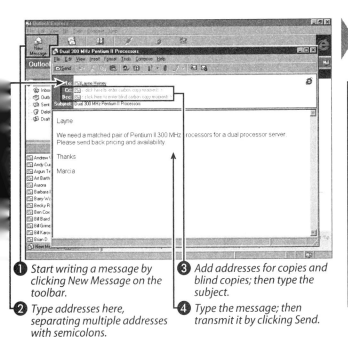

1 Start writing a message by clicking New Message on the toolbar.

2 Type addresses here, separating multiple addresses with semicolons.

3 Add addresses for copies and blind copies; then type the subject.

4 Type the message; then transmit it by clicking Send.

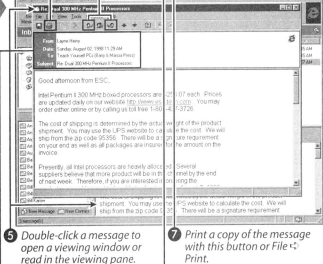

5 Double-click a message to open a viewing window or read in the viewing pane.

6 The upper pane shows the header, with sender, date sent, and subject.

7 Print a copy of the message with this button or File ➪ Print.

8 Reply to the sender or forward the message to someone else with these buttons.

9 Click New Msg to compose a message.

10 Use this formatting toolbar when you're sending text to someone whose reader handles formats.

11 Check spelling before you send.

12 Transmit the message by clicking the Send button.

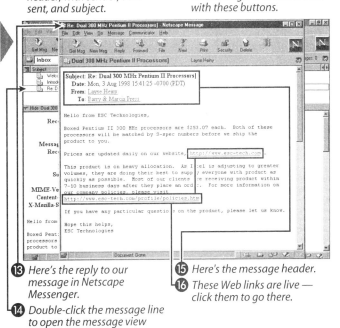

13 Here's the reply to our message in Netscape Messenger.

14 Double-click the message line to open the message view window.

15 Here's the message header.

16 These Web links are live — click them to go there.

Managing E-mail Addresses

People may tell you their e-mail addresses, or you may find addresses on the Web, get them from messages you receive, or look them up in an Internet e-mail directory. Wherever you get an address, though, you need a place to keep it. You can keep addresses anywhere, but the best place is the address book in your e-mail software. That way, you don't have to fish around on your desk to find it, you can pick from a list instead of transcribing from one place to another, and your e-mail software can do lookups for you automatically.

There's a hidden trap in address books, though. Just as with a paper address book, it's awkward to have more than one electronic one. That problem even affects people using only one computer, because many programs on your computer are able to maintain an address book for you. You need to pick one and stick with it. If you change, change completely, and transfer all the data from the old program to the new.

Look at different programs' capabilities before you choose one. For each address book entry, Microsoft's Outlook Express stores name and nickname; several e-mail addresses; home address; phone, fax, cell phone, and personal Web page; business address; title, department, phone, fax, pager, and business Web page; and personal notes. Netscape Messenger's address book stores similar information, but lacks the ability to handle multiple e-mail addresses for one person. If you need to keep track of business and personal addresses, Messenger forces you to have multiple entries for the same person, appending something like (Personal) or (Work) to make them distinct.

TAKE NOTE

KEEP YOUR ADDRESS BOOK ON THE INTERNET

If you use a variety of computers to check your e-mail, you're at a disadvantage — your e-mail address book doesn't travel with you. You can keep your one address book online at several Internet services, including the Four11 directory. Once you register with Four11, you can build an address book that's available on their servers from any computer with a Web browser.

FIND SOMEONE'S E-MAIL ADDRESS

Sometimes you need to send e-mail to someone whose e-mail address you don't have. There are several directories on the Internet you can search. Some of them offer telephone numbers and addresses too. Be careful with the results, though. A lot of the information is outdated, and some of it is simply wrong (see the facing page). Be careful you get the right person, and not someone else with the same name.

CROSS-REFERENCE
Be sure to read Chapter 18's lesson "E-mail Security — Trojans and Hoaxes."

FIND IT ONLINE
Some well-known directories include Four11 (http://www.four11.com) and Bigfoot.com

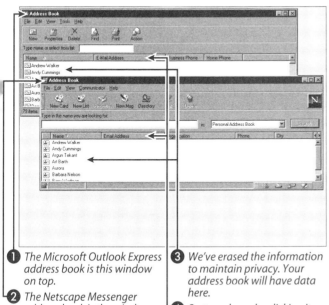

1 The Microsoft Outlook Express address book is this window on top.

2 The Netscape Messenger address book is the window on the bottom.

3 We've erased the information to maintain privacy. Your address book will have data here.

4 Sort a column by clicking its header.

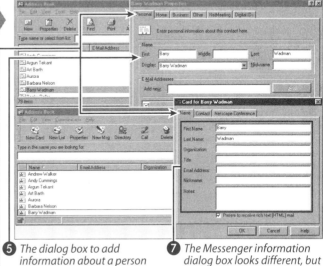

5 The dialog box to add information about a person looks like this in Outlook.

6 Tabs in the dialog box segregate different groups of information.

7 The Messenger information dialog box looks different, but gathers similar information.

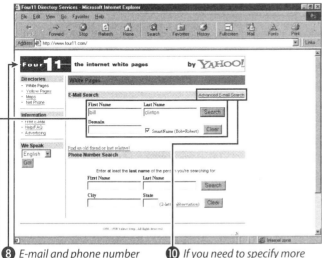

8 E-mail and phone number directories on the Internet help you find addresses.

9 A typical directory lets you specify the person's name.

10 If you need to specify more information to narrow the search, use the Advanced E-mail Search.

11 Here are the actual results of the search. Don't believe everything on the Internet.

Dealing with Junk E-mail (Spam)

Apparently, everything wonderful has its dark side. In the case of e-mail, it's junk e-mail, or *spam* (also called unsolicited commercial e-mail, or UCE). An incredible amount of Internet e-mail traffic is spam (no insult to Hormel Foods Corp. intended), and it wastes both time and Internet resources. So much spam travels over the Internet that eventually you're bound to be targeted no matter how small and unobtrusive you remain. The basis for spamming is that sending out tens of millions of e-mails is very inexpensive, so even a fraction-of-a-percent success rate is a good return.

Spammers reach the Internet through ISPs, who have *terms of service* (TOS) and *acceptable use policies* (AUP). Spammers try to hide themselves, so they forge the standard Internet *mail headers*, the part of the message that tells e-mail software whom the message is for, who sent it, and where it came from. You're almost guaranteed that the return address is fraudulent (unless the spammer is too stupid to lie, of course). Spamming almost always violates the ISP's TOS or AUP, though, so if you can track down the spammer's ISP, you have someone useful to complain to.

The time you waste sifting through useless e-mail isn't the worst part: The content is also a problem. Most spam offers a guaranteed get-rich-quick scheme, secret insider money-cartel data worth a fortune, free access to pornographic Web sites, stock offers made only to the select few, chain letters, multilevel marketing, offers to sell you spamming tools, and more. If you're tempted by any of these offers, ask yourself this: If what you're reading is such a wonderful deal, why is it being sent to you and a few million of your closest friends by someone you've never heard of who has to hide the real return address?

TAKE NOTE

▶ DECODE SPAM HEADERS

You can track down the losers that send spam. Use File ⇨ Properties ⇨ Details in the Outlook Express message window, or View ⇨ Headers ⇨ All in Messenger to see the message headers, and then follow the directions at **http://www.rahul.net/falk/mailtrack.html** to see how to decode the header. Send a complaint (with the headers and full message text) to the sender's ISP.

▶ IGNORE OFFERS TO REMOVE YOU FROM THE SPAMMER'S LIST

More and more, spammers include statements in their messages with directions for how to be removed from their lists. Don't do it — all you do is validate that your e-mail address is a live one that's read, increasing your spam count horribly. Don't send spam complaints back to the spammer either, for the same reason. Complain to the ISP so the account gets canceled.

CROSS-REFERENCE
Be sure to read "Identifying Viruses and Other Threats" in Chapter 22.

FIND IT ONLINE
Find tons of antispam links at **http://www.yahoo.com/Computers_and_Internet/Communications_and_Networking/Electronic_Mail/Junk_Email**.

The FCC released a warning last Wednesday concerning a matter of major importance to any regular user of the InterNet. Apparently, a new computer virus has been engineered by a user of America Online that is unparalleled in its destructive capability. Other, more well-known viruses such as Stoned, Airwolf, and Michaelangelo pale in comparison to the prospects of this newest creation by a warped mentality.

What makes this virus so terrifying, said the FCC, is the fact that no program needs to be exchanged for a new computer to be infected. It can be spread through the existing e-mail systems of the InterNet. Once a computer is infected, one of several things can happen. If the computer contains a hard drive, that will most likely be destroyed. If the program is not stopped, the computer's processor will be placed in an nth-complexity infinite binary loop - which can severely damage the processor if left running that way too long. Unfortunately, most novice computer users will not realize what is happening until it is far too late.

① This is one version of a common hoax, the Good Times e-mail.

② The FCC doesn't release any virus warnings (although other groups do).

③ No text message can corrupt your machine, although programs sent to you can.

④ No program can damage the processor chip.

PLEASE EXCUSE THE INTRUSION. BUT, THIS INFORMATION MAY BE OF GREAT INTEREST TO YOU.

How would you like to BORROW $59,000 and NEVER have to repay the LOAN?

If you answered YES, and who wouldn't, then I would like to invite you to join a very SPECIAL group of people.The FINANCIAL FRIENDS NETWORK.

The FINANCIAL FRIENDS NETWORK is an ever expanding international group of GENEROUS and CARING people who WILL automatically receive $59,000 LOANS, that they NEVER have to repay. All of our members are hard working, family-oriented people, with one common goal that unites us all. We are committed to generating income, to provide the necessities and the comforts for ourselves and our families.

Let us show you exactly how our UNIQUE, HONEST and PROFESSIONALLY MANAGED program, automatically LOANS YOU $59,000.

HERE'S HOW IT WORKS Just LOAN 1 existing member $20 (which is your lifetime membership fee) and THAT'S IT!!! WE DO EVERYTHING ELSE FOR YOU!

ALL YOU HAVE TO DO IS JOIN US TO RECEIVE YOUR $59,000 LOAN!

IT'S REALLY AMAZING HOW EASY THIS IS AND HOW BEAUTIFULLY IT WORKS!

We can assure you that this is a LEGAL and LEGITIMATE offer and complies with US law, title 18, sections 1302 & 1341. After all, who hasn't LOANED a FRIEND money before! And, we don't even expect YOU to repay us.

HERE'S HOW TO JOIN 1) Fill out the membership application at the bottom of this letter.
2) Send us your application along with $20, your lifetime membership fee AND THAT'S IT, WE'LL DO EVERYTHING ELSE FOR YOU!

HOW AND WHEN DO YOU RECEIVE YOUR LOAN.

ONLY the member in the #1 position RECEIVES YOUR LOAN/membership fee (SEE MEMBERSHIP APPLICATION) The FINANCIAL FRIENDS NETWORK will then remove the name of the person in the #1 position and will then add YOUR name and YOUR assigned number to the

⑤ "I'm a lousy spammer. Be nice to me anyway."

⑥ Your too-good-to-be-true alert should be going off by now.

⑦ Here's an attempt at legal confusion. This is an elaborate chain letter, and they're illegal.

⑧ So you send $20, they do all the work, and you get $59K?

This message is sent in compliance of the new e-mail bill: SECTION 301, Paragraph (a)(2)(C) of s. 1618

Sender : ---removed---, Los Angeles, CA 90070-0037
Phone : ---removed---,
E-mail : ---removed---,

To be removed from our mailing list, simply reply with "REMOVE" in the subject.

Will JT's Restaurants, Inc. (OTC BB Symbol: JTSR)

DOUBLE?, TRIPLE? or more?

We can't say, but we can say

NOW IS THE TIME TO GET IN.

JTSR, THE MOVE IS ON!!!

Visit ---removed---, or ---removed---, or call ---removed---, for full details on JT's

⑨ No law or bill requires you to accept spam or excuses spammers from their ISP's terms of service.

⑩ All of these we checked were false.

⑪ Don't do this — it lets them know yours is a live e-mail address.

⑫ Sure to be a winner? Hardly, since it has been sent blindly to millions of people.

INSTANT CASH FINANCING UP TO $10 MILLION

Our network of financial sources has money NOW... for any purpose.

BUSINESS STARTUP / PURCHASE

135 % MORTGAGE FINANCING/REFINANCING AND HOME IMPROVEMENT MONEY

EQUIPMENT AND AUTO LEASING

DEBT CONSOLIDATION

NO INCOME VERIFICATION

CREDIT PROBLEM ? NO PROBLEM ! FAST PROCESSING .

LOW RATES AND GREAT TERMS AVAILABLE NOW SO CALL TODAY.
(NO E-MAIL)

⑬ There isn't anyone standing around with $10 million to give total strangers found on the Internet.

⑭ Let's give you more than your home is worth.

⑮ No income? No credit? $10 million instant cash?

⑯ What's wrong with e-mail? Makes it a little harder to find them, doesn't it?

Personal Workbook

Q&A

1 What can you send via electronic mail?

_____

_____

_____

2 What does an e-mail address look like?

_____

_____

_____

3 If you have the account _zorro_ with AOL, what's your e-mail address? (Hint: the AOL server is aol.com.)

_____

_____

_____

4 What's the password for your zorro account?

_____

_____

_____

5 What are the common e-mail server types? How do you find out which you use?

_____

_____

_____

6 What cautions should you observe when writing e-mail?

_____

_____

_____

7 Who can read the e-mail you send?

_____

_____

_____

8 What do you need to make your e-mail secure?

_____

_____

_____

ANSWERS: PAGE 343

EXTRA PRACTICE

1. Set up an e-mail account on Hotmail, Juno, or another free e-mail service. Set up your e-mail reader to handle both that and your usual e-mail account.

2. Get a digital certificate from VeriSign (**http://www.verisign.com/client**) and distribute the public portion to your e-mail correspondents. Test exchanging secure e-mail.

3. Find your ISP's acceptable use policy and terms of service on the ISP's Web site. What does your ISP do about spammers on its systems?

4. Look at the headers on e-mail your receive. Look at spam headers and see what's different.

5. Search Four11 or one of the other search services for someone you know. If you can verify you found the right address, send the person an e-mail message.

REAL-WORLD APPLICATIONS

✔ You're running a small business. In addition to your personal e-mail account, you set up mailboxes for orders, information, and customer service to help you sort the incoming e-mail.

✔ You decide to take the easy way out and simply reply to a spammer asking that you receive no more junk mail. You discover over the next weeks that your spam traffic goes up wildly after the spammer realizes you have a live e-mail address.

✔ You decide that bulk Internet e-mail (spam) is a great way to build your business. You discover that you've attracted the ire of thousands of people who flood your mailbox with complaints and cause your ISP to terminate your account.

Visual Quiz

What are we doing here? How might you use a signature?

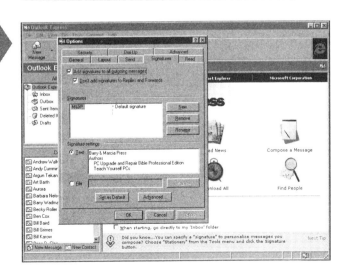

_____

_____

_____

_____

_____

_____

CHAPTER 18

Sending and Receiving Files

Getting the most the Internet has to offer requires that you master another set of skills—learning how to transfer files to and from your computer over the Net. You can transfer programs, pictures, sounds, or any other kind of file, giving you the ability to share information with others.

Possibly the most common Internet file transfers are software downloads from Web pages. Many software developers make their programs available through their Web sites, so you only have to click a hyperlink or two to bring the software to your computer. You can combine the widespread availability of software on the Internet with popular Internet search engines like Yahoo! (**http://www.yahoo.com**) to find a link to a Web site for specific software you're looking for. Software developers both improve customer service and reduce support costs by offering online upgrades, so be sure to check publishers' Web sites periodically for more current versions of your software.

Many other kinds of files are available for download from Web sites, and not all are programs. Many government Web sites, such as the U.S. Internal Revenue Service, offer downloadable versions of their standard forms, which can save you a trip to the IRS office, the library, or the post office. Other Web sites offer multimedia and image files with sound clips, video clips, and pictures. The lessons in this chapter give you the skills to access all of these files and more.

You can also send files to your friends and receive files from them by attaching them to e-mail messages. This chapter teaches you how to work with files in e-mail and explains that it's best to avoid sending really large files—a slow Internet connection causes extremely long file upload and download times. A lesson in this chapter shows you how to help solve that problem by compressing files before you send and explains how to use the common Internet ZIP compression format with the WinZip program.

As with other uses of your computer and of the Internet, you must be careful transferring files—there's always the danger of receiving a file infected with a computer virus. Lessons in this chapter cover key issues about viruses you might receive in e-mail, along with some common hoaxes you're likely to see.

Downloading from the Web

There's no end to the kinds of files you can download over the Web. One of the most common reasons for downloading files over the Internet is to obtain software, such as the low-cost or free software available at sites like Tucows (**http://www.tucows.com**). Many software companies let you download products from their company Web pages.

Downloaded software is sometimes free, sometimes free for a trial period (after which you pay), and sometimes paid up front. If the software is *freeware*, you don't have to pay for it. If it's *shareware*, you're usually allowed to use it at no charge for a short evaluation period. If you decide that you want to keep the shareware, you then pay a registration fee to the developer. Look for registration information and a license agreement to find out if, when, and how much you need to pay.

Don't miss the opportunity for downloading software updates and upgrades via the Internet. Microsoft's Web site (**http://www.microsoft.com/msdownload**), for instance, offers software updates for many of its programs, including Internet Explorer, Windows, and Office applications. Upgrades commonly include bug fixes, improvements for hardware compatibility, or expanded features. Check the company Web sites for all of your software on a regular basis to make sure you have the most up-to-date programs available.

Files you download over the Internet don't have to be programs. Web sites let you download files of music and videos, screen savers, wallpaper for your Windows desktop, and other fun things. Whatever kind of file you are downloading, the procedure is simple. After you click the hyperlink for the file, your browser asks you to choose a location on your hard drive or a floppy drive to save the file. Pick the location and the download starts. A small window opens to show you the status of the download. Some downloads give you a progress meter estimating how much longer they'll take. Depending on the size of the file and the speed of your Internet connection, a download can take anywhere from a few minutes to many hours to complete the transfer. You should figure that you won't get more than 3KB per second on the average dial-up Internet connection and possibly less than that. Downloads almost always work better when Internet traffic is low, such as late at night.

TAKE NOTE

RIGHT-CLICK FOR MORE DOWNLOAD OPTIONS

You can pick from options your browser gives you for downloading files. Instead of left-clicking the download hyperlink, try a right-click to bring up a short command menu. The choice to download the file is there, plus options for copying the hyperlink and other browser functions.

CROSS-REFERENCE

See "Checking for Software Updates" in Chapter 19 to learn more about downloading updates for your programs.

FIND IT ONLINE

Get notified about software updates with a free Versions! account, available at **http://www.versions.com**.

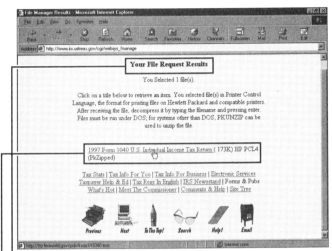

1 Start at **http://www.irs.ustreas.gov/prod/forms_pubs/ index.html** for U.S. income tax forms, eventually reaching an individual form download page.

2 Click this link to download a file with the 1997 Form 1040 in a format you can send directly to an HP laser printer.

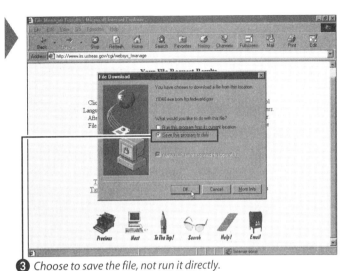

3 Choose to save the file, not run it directly.

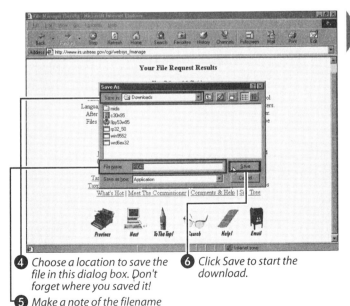

4 Choose a location to save the file in this dialog box. Don't forget where you saved it!

5 Make a note of the filename shown here.

6 Click Save to start the download.

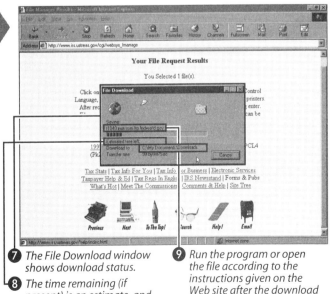

7 The File Download window shows download status.

8 The time remaining (if present) is an estimate, and can be wildly inaccurate.

9 Run the program or open the file according to the instructions given on the Web site after the download completes.

Sending Files in E-mail

eb downloads can't let you send files to others. You need your own Web site for that, and you would have to both create the Web pages and handle security issues. You can share files with friends or coworkers by copying the files to a floppy disk, a simple and effective approach, but if the other person doesn't work in the same building (much less the same state), physically delivering the disk can take a long time. Files you share on floppy disk are limited by the size of the diskette, too — it's hard to share a 3MB Excel workbook using a 1.44MB floppy disk, although you can do it with multiple floppies and WinZip.

Another way to share files is over a *local area network* (LAN). This method is fast, but if the person you need to share the file with is not on your network, it's not going to work. For most purposes, the best way to share files is to send them in e-mail messages. Just as you can download any kind of file over the Web, you can attach any kind of file to an e-mail message. All the popular e-mail software — including Eudora Pro, Netscape Messenger, Microsoft Outlook and Outlook Express, and the AOL software — support file attachments.

You send a file as an *attachment* to an e-mail message. Most e-mail clients give you a toolbar button with a picture of a paperclip for the command to attach a file, because what you are doing is attaching the file with an electronic paperclip. The file goes over the Internet as part of the e-mail message, using the standard e-mail addressing and transport mechanisms. Once the message arrives, the recipient can open and edit the file just as if you had provided it on diskette.

You can attach more than one file to a message. Use the command to attach files as many times as you want.

TAKE NOTE

▶ WATCH THE FILE SIZE

Before you send a large attached file, be aware of the quality of the recipient's Internet connection. A 15MB file that would transmit almost instantaneously over your company's high-speed connection takes hours to receive with a more conventional Internet connection. You should estimate the transmission and reception times for the most common modems as being at least seven minutes per megabyte.

▶ NOT ALL E-MAIL ACCOUNTS ACCEPT ATTACHMENTS

Before you send a file attached to an e-mail message, make sure the recipient can accept the attachment. Some e-mail accounts have limits on the size of attachments, and still others don't allow attached files at all. Many of the free e-mail account services on the Internet today do not allow e-mail attachments.

CROSS-REFERENCE

See the next task, "Saving E-mail Attachments," to learn how to handle receiving attached files.

FIND IT ONLINE

Hotmail is a free e-mail service that allows file attachments. Learn more at **http://www.hotmail.com**.

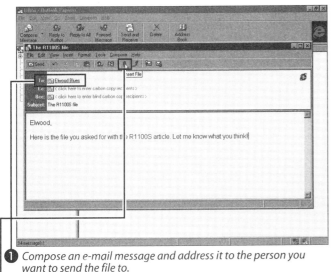

1 Compose an e-mail message and address it to the person you want to send the file to.

2 On the message window toolbar, click the Insert File button. It should look like a paperclip.

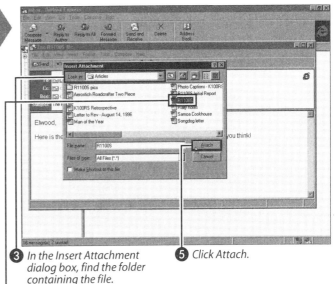

3 In the Insert Attachment dialog box, find the folder containing the file.

4 Click the file you want to send to select it.

5 Click Attach.

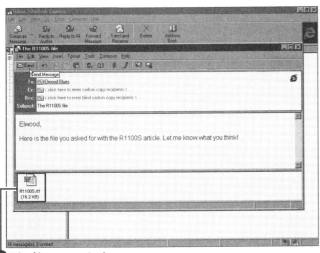

6 The file appears in the message as an icon.

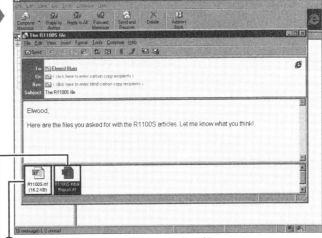

7 Follow the same steps to insert another file, creating separate icons for each one.

8 Remove an attachment by selecting it and pressing Delete on your keyboard.

Saving E-mail Attachments

Just as you can send any kind of file to an associate or coworker by attaching it to an e-mail message, other people can send attached files to you. Attachments in e-mail messages usually appear as icons over the name of the file, and some programs also report the size of the attached file. The icon you see depends on what program your system associates with the file — if the attachment is a Microsoft Word document, for example, the icon is the *W* icon from Word. Programs you receive in e-mail might display with the program's own icon or might use a default icon from Windows. Effective e-mail writers include an indication of what the document is in the message, but that practice isn't universal.

No matter what program is associated with the icon, the safest thing to do when you receive an attached file is to save the file to disk. Once you save to disk, the attachment is safe even if you delete the e-mail, is in a place that fits in with your folder organization scheme on disk, and is subject to screening by your virus scanner. Many e-mail programs let you save attachments by right-clicking the attachment's icon and choosing Save As from the shortcut menu. You then get the usual Windows dialog box letting you choose the folder and filename for the saved file. Navigate to the folder you want, change the filename if you want, and click Save. Make sure that you save the file to a location you can remember. If you plan to scan the file for viruses — always a good idea —

consider saving the file to its own folder or even to a floppy disk.

If you're positive the file can't contain a virus, you can open the file directly into the associated program and then save the file from within the program. You open the attachment in its program by double-clicking the icon for the attachment. Your computer automatically starts the required program and opens the file.

CROSS-REFERENCE

Learn more about saving files in "Saving a File Where You Want It" in Chapter 4.

FIND IT ONLINE

Not sure if it's bad form to send that attachment? Consult the Netiquette guide at **http://www.albion.com/**

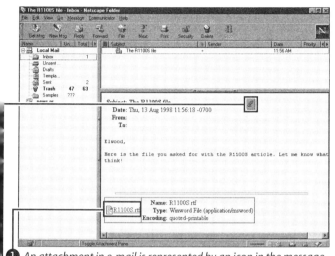

❶ An attachment in e-mail is represented by an icon in the message.

❷ With Netscape Messenger, click the paperclip icon to start saving the file.

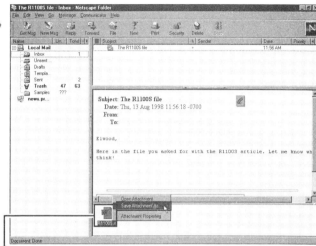

❸ In most any e-mail program, right-click the icon and choose Save As or Save Attachment As.

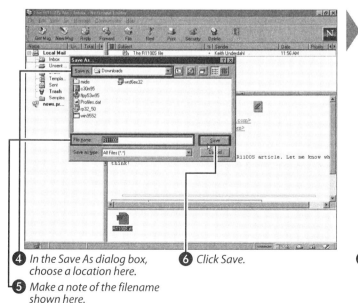

❹ In the Save As dialog box, choose a location here.

❺ Make a note of the filename shown here.

❻ Click Save.

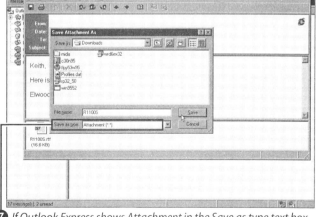

❼ If Outlook Express shows Attachment in the Save as type text box, double-click the attachment icon to open it, and then save from the program.

Running WinZip

Slow Internet connections are a significant problem when you exchange large files over the Internet. Information moves very quickly through the interface for your hard drive — fast EIDE drives can transfer information at up to 16,600 kilobytes per second. The fastest conventional modems, by comparison, transfer information to your computer at a lethargic 53 kilobytes per second, and then only if the phone line is in perfect condition. A file that would take just one second to transfer to your hard drive at 16,600 Kbps would take over five hours to transfer over an ideal modem connection. What's worse, of course, is that most users suffer with connection speeds slower than the maximum.

There is no way to completely solve this problem right now, although faster Internet-connection technology is on the way. Until then, the best way to speed transfer times is to make your file transfers as small as possible. The standard PC file compression format on the Internet is the ZIP file; one of the best programs to handle ZIP files is WinZip from Nico Mak Computing, Inc. WinZip compresses your files into a smaller form and then reconstructs a perfect, bit-for-bit accurate copy of the original file at the receiving end. You can put one or many files in the same ZIP file.

You can use WinZip for much more than Internet file transfers. You can compress seldom-used files so that they take up less space on your hard drive, and you can use it to squeeze relatively large files onto floppy disks. Using WinZip is easy. Drag and drop files into the WinZip window to add files to the ZIP file. You can move and copy ZIP files just like any other file. Double-click existing ZIP files to open WinZip; then drag and drop the files you want into Explorer. There's a complete dialog interface for adding and extracting files, too.

TAKE NOTE

▶ REMEMBER, WINZIP IS NOT FREE

Although you can download WinZip for free from **http://www.winzip.com**, the program is shareware, not freeware. If you keep and use the software beyond the 21-day evaluation period, you must pay a fee and register the software. WinZip sales operate on the honor system, so it's up to you to register the software. Nico Mak regularly updates and improves WinZip, and upgrades are free once you register.

▶ STAY AWARE OF COMPRESSION FACTORS

Some file formats — such as plain text, HTML, and word processing documents — compress significantly, down to as little as one-fourth the original size. But some other formats — such as JPEG, GIF, PCX, and TIF image files — may not compress very much because they're often already compressed themselves.

CROSS-REFERENCE
See "Downloading From the Web" earlier in this chapter to learn more about downloading WinZip from the World Wide Web.

FIND IT ONLINE
Download a trial copy of WinZip or purchase it online at **http://www.winzip.com**.

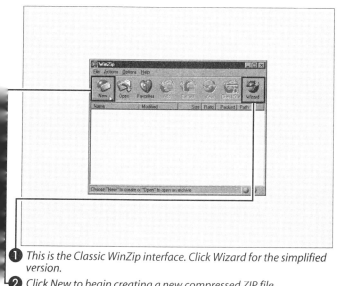

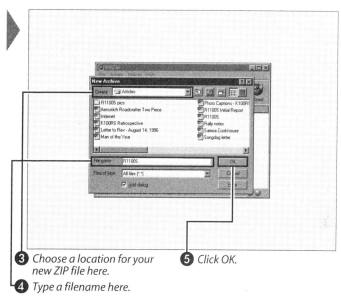

1 This is the Classic WinZip interface. Click Wizard for the simplified version.

2 Click New to begin creating a new compressed ZIP file.

3 Choose a location for your new ZIP file here.

4 Type a filename here.

5 Click OK.

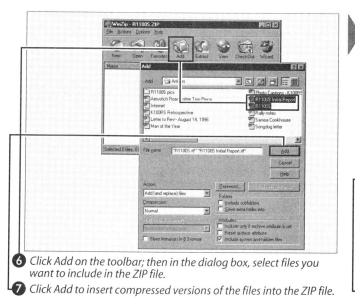

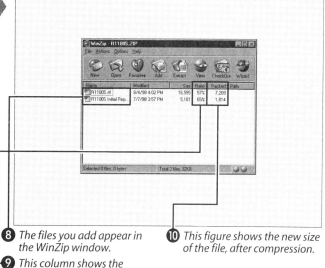

6 Click Add on the toolbar; then in the dialog box, select files you want to include in the ZIP file.

7 Click Add to insert compressed versions of the files into the ZIP file.

8 The files you add appear in the WinZip window.

9 This column shows the compression ratio for each file.

10 This figure shows the new size of the file, after compression.

E-mail Security — Trojans and Hoaxes

Sending files back and forth in e-mail messages is a great way to share information and work with others. It's quick, efficient, and cost-effective, especially when compared to express overnight shipping charges. Unfortunately, it can also be risky. Files you receive via e-mail can infect your computer with viruses that can cause significant damage.

Viruses come in several forms, but your computer cannot be infected by a virus if you simply open a text e-mail document. Read that again: your computer cannot be infected by a virus if you simply open a text e-mail document. Many virus hoaxes claim that opening a message with a certain subject will erase your hard drive and perform other atrocities up to and including causing Bill Gates to hold a garage sale in your front yard. No matter how unlikely, hoaxes persist and flourish.

A virus *can* infect your computer if it is contained in an attachment within an e-mail message. The virus will not infect your computer until you actually open the attachment, so it's a good idea to be cautious when dealing with e-mail attachments from unknown sources. If you have any doubt about the source, don't open the attachment. Not only could the files contain viruses, but they might be *Trojan* programs that make you think they are performing a certain task when in reality they are doing something else entirely. Trojans have been found that expose your passwords to hackers and e-mail documents from your disk to popular Internet sites, all without your knowledge.

Protecting yourself from *real* computer viruses is relatively simple, but it is something you must make a conscious effort to do. Use good virus-scanning software, such as McAfee VirusScan. We've shown you how to scan e-mail attachments using Panda Software's Panda Antivirus program in the figures to the right.

TAKE NOTE

▶ IGNORE THE GOOD TIMES "VIRUS"

The first e-mail virus hoax used the name *Good Times*, because unsuspecting readers were warned not to open an e-mail message containing those words in the subject. Readers of the warning message are advised to forward it to everyone they know to help spread the word. The real virus at work here is that thousands of e-mail accounts are choked with these fake warnings every day.

▶ KEEP UP TO DATE ON VIRUSES AND HOAXES

Computer viruses (and hoaxes for the unwitting) are constantly changing and mutating, just like biological viruses. New strains are constantly popping up and being identified, and it's a good idea to keep yourself abreast of the latest virus news. Knowledge can help you keep your computer healthy and prevent you from becoming unduly paranoid. For more hoax information, visit **http://www.nonprofit.net/hoax/hoax.html**.

CROSS-REFERENCE

See "Identifying Viruses and Other Threats" in Chapter 22 to learn more about protecting yourself from computer viruses.

FIND IT ONLINE

See **http://www.icsa.net/services/consortia/anti-virus/lab.html** to read the latest updates about viruses from the International Computer Security Association.

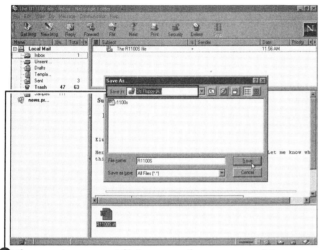

1 *If you receive a suspect file in an e-mail message, save it to a floppy disk if possible; otherwise, save it to the hard disk.*

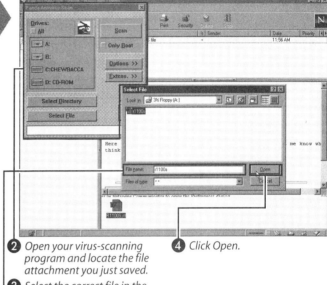

2 *Open your virus-scanning program and locate the file attachment you just saved.*

3 *Select the correct file in the Select File dialog box.*

4 *Click Open.*

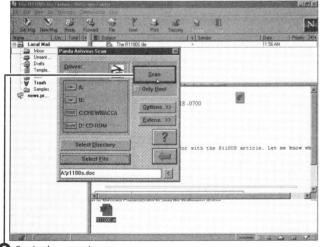

5 *Begin the scanning process.*

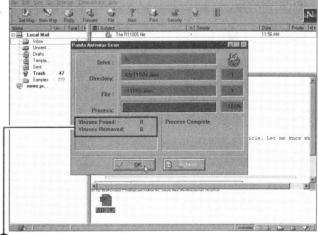

6 *This file was clean.*

Personal Workbook

Q&A

1 What kinds of files can you download from a Web page?

_____

_____

_____

2 What is the best way to send a word-processing document to a distant coworker?

_____

_____

_____

3 How can you deal with limitations on sending files in e-mail?

_____

_____

_____

4 How can you tell if an e-mail message you receive contains an attached file?

_____

_____

5 Can you make a file smaller before you send it? How?

_____

_____

_____

6 Is it a good idea to open attachment files directly within the e-mail message?

_____

_____

_____

7 What is a *Trojan?*

_____

_____

_____

8 Can your computer be infected by simply opening an e-mail message?

_____

_____

ANSWERS: PAGE 344

264

EXTRA PRACTICE

1. Download WinZip from **http://www.winzip.com** and install it on your computer.

2. Locate a word-processing file and compress it with WinZip.

3. Compose an e-mail message and address it to yourself. Attach the compressed file to the message and send it.

4. Receive the message you just sent to yourself and save the attached file to a floppy disk.

5. Scan the file for viruses.

6. Use the Extract feature of WinZip to extract the compressed document from the ZIP file.

REAL-WORLD APPLICATIONS

✔ You're preparing a tax return for the April 15 deadline but just learned that you need a special form. Rather than wait weeks or months for the IRS to mail you one, or go out in the snow to get a copy, you simply download it from the IRS Web site.

✔ You've climbed to the summit of Mount Everest. To commemorate the event, you take a picture of yourself with your digital camera, and then e-mail it via your palmtop computer to your grandmother waiting back in Connecticut.

✔ You receive an e-mail warning telling of an incredible new e-mail virus. Sadly, you follow the instructions in the message that tell you to send the message to everyone you know and end up looking ignorant to many of the people you forward it to.

Visual Quiz

Is the attachment to this message virus-free?

_____

_____

_____

_____

_____

_____

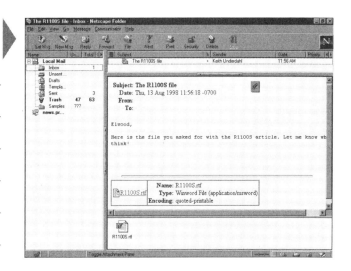

PART

V

Maintenance and Upgrades

As you do for any valuable tool, you want to take care of your computer to make sure it stays in good running order. Part V covers what you need to know, including periodic maintenance upgrades, virus protection, and repair. You learn how to clean the computer, keep its software running smoothly, and how to work with your printer. You also learn how to keep your computer free of malicious viruses and what to do if it gets infected.

One of the best things about PCs is their ability to be upgraded so they can run faster, handle bigger workloads, and communicate with other computers over networks. Chapters in this part show you how to decide if you should upgrade, and how to add memory to your computer, make it faster, and network it with other computers you own.

CHAPTER **19**

**MASTER
THESE
SKILLS**

▶ **Cleaning the Computer**

▶ **Checking for Software Updates**

▶ **Keeping Software Running Smoothly**

▶ **Maintaining Your Printer**

Periodic Maintenance

Your computer needs more maintenance than a VCR or television. It's not that VCRs and televisions are better designed, it's because computers are more complicated. Mechanical maintenance is about the same; what's different is that you have to maintain what's on the disk in your computer.

Keep computer maintenance in perspective. If your computer runs by itself (not on the Internet), if you keep the software you already have (never loading new software), and if your system is running well, your computer needs little maintenance. A lot of computers run perfectly well until well-meaning users louse them up doing maintenance. Why do anything at all? The first reason is to make sure dirt, dust, and spills don't create problems. The second is to solve problems you may encounter or add features you may want.

Dust, dirt, and spills cause a variety of problems. This chapter looks at the different parts of your computer, describes what can happen to them, and shows you what you can do to protect and clean them. (In practice, your printer will probably require more maintenance than your computer.)

Big as they are, disks in computers only store so much information. If they fill up, you can't write any more files until you make some space, which means you have to throw some things away (delete files). Although some new tools in Windows 98 can help, Windows has no way to know what to thrown away. Now and then you need to do a little housekeeping on your own.

Updates can bring you new features, but can bring you trouble, too. If you're careful, there are good reasons to update software. Manufacturers sometimes post fixes for problems (*bugs*) on their Internet sites. If you're affected by the problem, you'll want the update. New software you load may require updates to other software, including Windows. Too many different computer configurations and too many different programs exist for a manufacturer to test them all or even a significant number of them. Updates that are different in some important way from what you have now can cause problems for programs that used to run.

Cleaning the Computer

Heat is the enemy of electronics. Chips that get hot can malfunction; let a chip get too hot and it dies. Heat can cause subtle damage too; chips can fail some time after the overheating is cured. If the processor, memory, or disk electronics malfunction, heat can damage files stored on disk. Personal computers are air cooled—air moving through the case (and monitor) picks up heat from the electronics and exhausts it out the back. The continuous movement of cool air in and warm air out transports heat from inside the case, keeping the chips within acceptable temperature limits.

Dust flies in with the cool air and settles. As it builds up, it blocks airflow and acts as an insulating blanket. Reduced airflow lets the internal temperature build up, and the insulating blanket keeps heat from being carried away by what airflow occurs. Once enough dust builds up, your computer is in danger of overheating. How long that takes, though, depends on where the computer is. The average office has filtered air from air conditioning, so less dust collects. Homes can be dustier (how often do you see dust bunnies in offices?), but not severely so unless the computer is near pets. The worst case of dust and dirt in a computer we've seen, though, was in a veterinarian's office. When we opened the case, it was literally packed with dog and cat hair. It was amazing the computer ran at all.

You can easily remove dust and dirt from your computer. Wipe and vacuum the outside clean, and be sure to vacuum clean the fan on the power supply. Vacuums build up static electricity, though, so it's only safe to vacuum the inside of the computer if you can keep the vacuum tool completely away from the internal components. If not, use a can of compressed air to blow out the dust and dirt, and then vacuum the scattered debris well away from the electronics.

TAKE NOTE

▶ CLEAN UP KEYBOARD GRUNGE

Some keyboards build up a layer of black grunge on the tops of the keycaps. We've seen it on all kinds of keyboards, and have seen identical keyboards used by the same persons that both did and didn't have the problem. The best way we've found to clean up the grunge is to turn the computer off, squirt some Windex or similar cleaner on a paper towel, and rub the key tops clean. Spraying the cleaner on the paper towel should keep it from dripping down into the keyboard.

▶ KEEP DUST OFF YOUR MONITOR

Your monitor attracts dust to the face of the tube. Wipe the monitor clean periodically (we just use a damp paper towel) to remove the dust and keep the image sharp.

CROSS-REFERENCE
Chapter 20's "Adding a Card" lesson shows you how to open your computer if you need to clean it out.

FIND IT ONLINE
Find cleaning supplies at
http://catalog.esselte.com/curtis.

Keep a Clean Mouse

You have to keep your mouse clean. The ball on the bottom sucks up dirt and crud into the body of the mouse, where it accumulates on the ball, rollers, and everything else. You can tell when the mouse needs to be cleaned because the cursor starts to move erratically. It might jump from one point to the next, rather than move smoothly, or might refuse to go further in one direction unless you back off and try moving that way again.

You don't necessarily have to create a schedule for cleaning your mouse at set times — dirt won't cause it any permanent damage. Instead, it's OK to wait until the mouse displays the symptoms above and then clean it.

You'll need a flashlight, clean cloth (an old, clean cloth diaper works well), tweezers, and a can of compressed air. Open the bottom of the mouse and see what's inside using the flashlight. Carefully pick out clumps of dust and dirt with the tweezers. Wipe the ball with the cloth; if that doesn't get the dirt off, wash the ball with soap and water (then set it aside to dry). Use the can of compressed air to blow out the dust, and then take a careful look at the rollers, turning them to look all the way around. You're likely to find dirt caked on them. If you do, you either need to get a mouse cleaning kit or gently scrape them clean with the tweezers. Don't scratch the rollers when you scrape them. Give the insides a final blast of air, then reassemble the dry ball and the cover. Test by moving the cursor around — if all is well, the cursor will once again move smoothly in all directions.

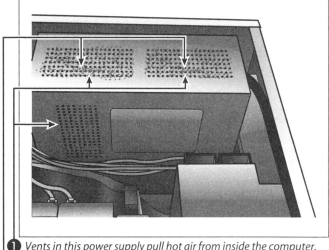

➊ *Vents in this power supply pull hot air from inside the computer.*
➋ *After months of operation, dirt on the vents is blocking airflow.*

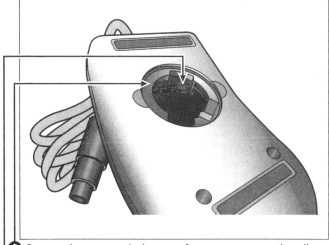

➌ *Remove the cover on the bottom of a mouse to expose the rollers.*
➍ *Dirt on the rollers can cause erratic operation. Clean them gently.*

Checking for Software Updates

Some software updates are worthwhile, including bug fixes and some releases of new features. Others, described as advances, may be little more than public relations campaigns. Some are predictable, such as tax software updates to correspond to final tax laws, while others (such as security fixes) happen when the need arises.

Manufacturers commonly post updates and fixes on the Web, but you could have a lot of places to look for software updates. Because there's no one centralized place that records current versions and updates (although some commercial products try), you end up having to look at each manufacturer's site. If the site is badly organized, this can become tedious, and you're likely to miss things you want.

Manufacturers are slowly recognizing the problem. Microsoft has built "Windows Update" into Windows 98, a Web service that checks the versions of Windows software on your computer against a current version catalog on the Microsoft site and suggests updates you might want to pick up. Some application programs, such as WinFax, can similarly check its manufacturer's Web site through your Internet connection to let you know of updates.

We're going to harp on a point again here. You don't *have* to install updates unless you choose to. Manufacturers can recommend a fix, but you are the one to decide if you should have it. New software comes with new bugs, and an update could well break something you need. A good rule of thumb is that, unless you have a problem you need to fix, don't take updates or new releases when they first come out. A few months of seasoning — letting others get bitten — gives the manufacturer the ability to correct problems.

TAKE NOTE

▶ KNOW YOUR UPDATE SOURCE

Many good software archives exist on the Internet, including **http://www.cdrom.com and http://www.winfiles.com**. You can't assume that everything on these and other sites is screened and tested — some of what you find is excellent, and some is garbage. Your best bet for software updates is the manufacturer's site itself, because it's the manufacturer who has the responsibility for the product.

▶ TEST AFTER YOU INSTALL

Don't just install an update and forget about it — test your different pieces of hardware and your key programs. If you simply stack update on update, you won't have any idea how to track down the cause when something goes wrong. Case in point: we updated a video card driver on one of our computers to fix a problem. The computer then became unstable, crashing at random times. We reverted back to the earlier driver and restored the computer to stability.

CROSS-REFERENCE
Don't overlook "Updating Your Antivirus Software" in Chapter 22.

FIND IT ONLINE
Find Windows Update using Start ➪ Windows Update or at **http://windowsupdate.microsoft.com**.

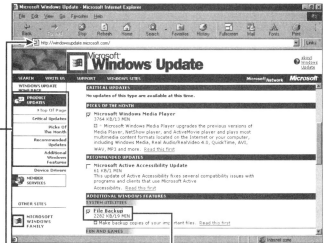

❶ *Microsoft's Windows Update site provides a single point to look for fixes and additions to Windows.*

❷ *Go to Product Updates to find Critical Updates.*

❸ *Check off the items you want; then scroll down the page to the Start Download button.*

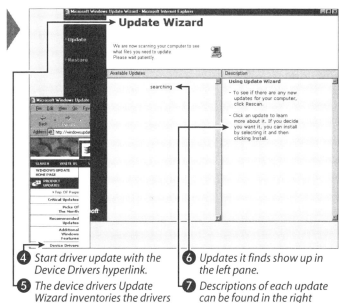

❹ *Start driver update with the Device Drivers hyperlink.*

❺ *The device drivers Update Wizard inventories the drivers installed on your computer.*

❻ *Updates it finds show up in the left pane.*

❼ *Descriptions of each update can be found in the right pane.*

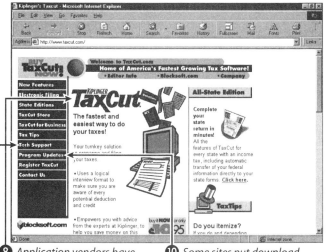

❽ *Application vendors have their own Web sites; this one is for Kiplinger's popular TaxCut software.*

❾ *You usually find updates and patches in Tech Support.*

❿ *Some sites put download links directly on the home page.*

⓫ *Always try to find out what's in an update before you install it.*

⓬ *Make sure you get the version for your software, computer, and version of Windows.*

Keeping Software Running Smoothly

Software maintenance (beyond updates and upgrades) consists of keeping your hard disk and its files healthy. Whether the problem is hardware, Windows, or application software, computers crash now and then. When they do, information held in memory that has not been written to the disk is lost. This can cause problems on the disk including leftover and corrupted files. Even the normal cycle of creating and deleting files scatters the locations where files are stored on disk and slows down access. Programs that don't clean up after themselves properly can leave temporary files and folders on the disk, wasting space.

The most dangerous of these problems is corrupted files on disk. If a key Windows file gets corrupted, your machine might refuse to run. That's why you should always shut down Windows before you turn off the power. Files can be corrupted in several ways, the worst type of corruption is cross-linked files, meaning that the same physical space on the disk is part of two different files. In such a case, it's likely that both files are garbage.

Windows 95 has tools to solve these problems, including ScanDisk to find errors in files and folders and Defrag to clean up scattered files. You have to remember to run the programs now and then, however, and most people don't. The Plus! Pack for Windows 95 introduced System Agent, a tool to run programs such as ScanDisk and Defrag on a schedule.

Windows 98 with its Plus! Pack has a much more comprehensive solution: Scheduled Tasks (replacing System Agent) and the Maintenance Wizard (which helps you set up Scheduled Tasks). The scope of what Windows 98 can do for maintenance in addition to ScanDisk and Defrag is larger too, including a good virus scanner and a temporary and unused file remover.

TAKE NOTE

▶ DON'T BE TOO AGGRESSIVE ABOUT DELETING FILES

Windows has a folder it uses to hold temporary files, called C:\Windows\Temp on most machines. The Maintenance Wizard is willing to clean this out for you periodically; we tend to take a more conservative view and clean it ourselves in case some ill-behaved program happens to put a file there we care about. We can always get the disk space back by removing TMP files from the folder, but we can't resurrect lost files.

▶ THE PLUS! PACK IS GOOD, BUT NOT REQUIRED

Automatic tools are nice to have, but you can do all the most important maintenance tasks yourself. If you simply get in the habit of running ScanDisk from Windows every week and Defrag every month, plus clean up the temporary file folder now and then, you're getting most of the benefit.

CROSS-REFERENCE

Hardware maintenance is covered in "Cleaning the Computer" in this chapter.

FIND IT ONLINE

Find Information on the Windows 98 Plus! Pack at http://www.microsoft.com/products/prodref/719_ov.htm.

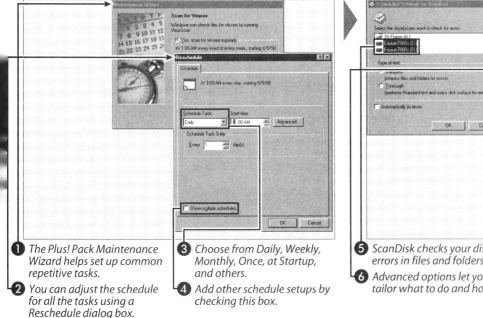

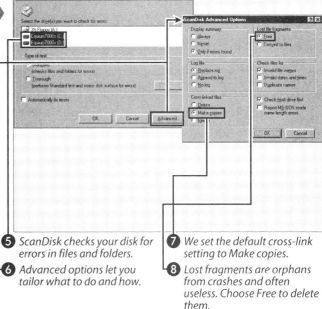

1 *The Plus! Pack Maintenance Wizard helps set up common repetitive tasks.*

2 *You can adjust the schedule for all the tasks using a Reschedule dialog box.*

3 *Choose from Daily, Weekly, Monthly, Once, at Startup, and others.*

4 *Add other schedule setups by checking this box.*

5 *ScanDisk checks your disk for errors in files and folders.*

6 *Advanced options let you tailor what to do and how.*

7 *We set the default cross-link setting to Make copies.*

8 *Lost fragments are orphans from crashes and often useless. Choose Free to delete them.*

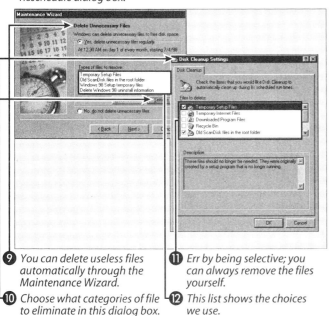

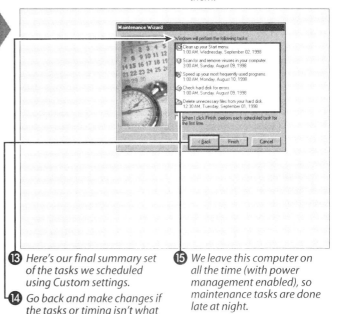

9 *You can delete useless files automatically through the Maintenance Wizard.*

10 *Choose what categories of file to eliminate in this dialog box.*

11 *Err by being selective; you can always remove the files yourself.*

12 *This list shows the choices we use.*

13 *Here's our final summary set of the tasks we scheduled using Custom settings.*

14 *Go back and make changes if the tasks or timing isn't what you expected.*

15 *We leave this computer on all the time (with power management enabled), so maintenance tasks are done late at night.*

Maintaining Your Printer

Printers need a variety of maintenance, none of it complicated but all essential. You have to load paper when it's empty, blow out dust created by paper as it passes through the printer, and replenish ink or toner when it runs out.

Good printer maintenance starts with good paper. The ink jet and laser printers sold today create a decent image on most any copier-quality paper. Ink jet printers can give you sharper, better-defined images using paper surfaces that minimize ink absorption and speed drying. If you have a very high-resolution ink jet printer, such as the 1440 dots per inch (dpi) Epson or PhotoREt HP printers, you can print photographic quality images on photo gloss paper designed specifically for ink jet printers. Laser printers won't (yet) give you photo images; in fact, if you're running a laser printer you should avoid paper with glossy smooth or extremely rough surfaces, including heavily textured or embossed papers.

Good maintenance continues with good quality ink or toner. We recycle toner and ink cartridges rather than refilling them. You should replace some precision components with new, unworn ones every time you change the cartridge, maintaining the fine tolerances the printer needs.

When you do change cartridges, take the time to blow paper dust out of the inside of the printer. Keeping the paper path clean eliminates one of the causes of dropouts in the print and helps ensure that paper moves through the printer reliably. This is more important for laser printers, because you don't change the cartridge as often. A can of compressed air with a tube to direct the blast works well for this operation as long as you keep the can upright (turned over, the can squirts liquid compressed air, not what you want to inject into a printer or other electronics).

CROSS-REFERENCE

Chapter 3's lessons "Unpacking Your Printer" and "Cabling the Printer to the Computer" show you how to hook up your printer.

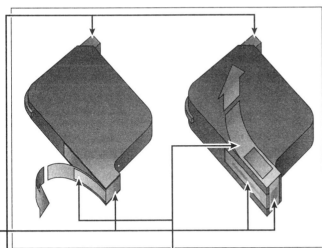

1 Hold ink jet cartridges (such as the typical HP ones in these drawings) at the top.

2 Don't touch the electrical contacts (face) or nozzles (bottom).

3 Remove the protective tape just before installing the cartridge.

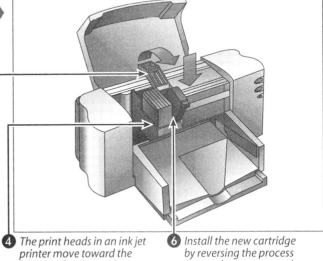

4 The print heads in an ink jet printer move toward the center to load cartridges.

5 Open the latch (if there is one); then rotate the cartridge out of the printer.

6 Install the new cartridge by reversing the process (remember to remove the protective tape).

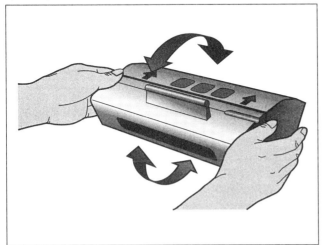

7 Grasp the laser toner cartridge at both ends.

8 Rotate the cartridge to redistribute the toner evenly.

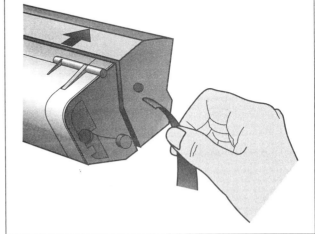

9 Grasp a new cartridge in one hand and the tab of the protective strip in the other.

10 Remove the strip, pulling until the entire strip is out of the printer.

Personal Workbook

Q&A

1 What's the first thing to do when you're upgrading software?

_____

_____

_____

2 What happens to chips that get too hot?

_____

_____

_____

3 What happens when dust accumulates on electronics?

_____

_____

_____

4 Where's the best place to look for software patches and updates?

_____

_____

_____

5 What's the last thing to do when you upgrade software?

_____

_____

_____

6 What Windows tool finds errors in files and folders?

_____

_____

_____

7 What Windows tool cleans up files scattered on the disk?

_____

_____

_____

8 How can you automate periodic maintenance activities?

_____

_____

_____

ANSWERS: PAGE 344

EXTRA PRACTICE

1 Run ScanDisk in thorough mode to check the entire disk surface.

2 Turn on the additional tests in the ScanDisk Advanced dialog box and scan your disk.

3 If your computer has gone a year without cleaning, open it and use compressed air to blow out the dust.

4 Open your mouse and look inside. Clean it if necessary.

5 Reboot and check for files with extension .tmp in your C:\Windows\Temp folder. Delete them.

6 Find out how to recycle your printer cartridges.

REAL-WORLD APPLICATIONS

✔ You're working on a project that has to be shipped tonight, and discover that you've run out of disk space. You look in the C:\Windows\Temp directory and find 347MB of files dating back to 1995 with TMP extensions. You delete all of them, skipping the ones where Windows says the file is in use, and recover 302MB, enough to finish the project.

✔ You install Disney Interactive's *Toy Story Animated Storybook* for your six-year-old, and find the video sequences don't play properly. Reading the manual, you learn that the video uses QuickTime from Apple. You go to the Apple Computer QuickTime Web site at **http://www.apple.com/quicktime**, download the latest version, fix the game, and become a hero.

Visual Quiz

How does this ScanDisk operation differ from the Standard test? Why would you use it?

_____

_____

_____

_____

_____

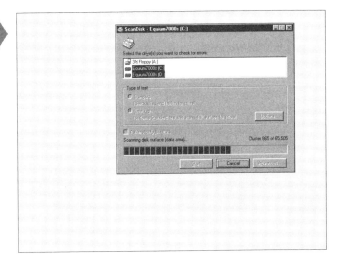

CHAPTER **20**

MASTER
THESE
SKILLS

▶ **Adding Memory**

▶ **Upgrading to a Faster Processor**

▶ **Adding a Card**

▶ **Adding a Disk**

Upgrades

One of the best things about PCs is that, as new products come out or as prices drop, you can change and improve what you have. You might have bought a machine with a 133 MHz Pentium processor and 16MB of memory, but with upgrades you can inexpensively boost it to a 200 or 233 MHz processor, 64MB of memory, and gigabytes of hard disk space.

There are some limits to what you can do. If technology moves past what your machine uses, or if you run out of places to put the upgrades you want, fixing the problem gets much more expensive. At that point, you have to think about a new machine versus upgrading the old one.

Here's an example of a reasonable upgrade. We started with a machine with a 133 MHz Pentium and 16MB of memory that was specified to be capable of running the newer 200 MHz Pentium MMX processor (MMX is a variant of the Intel processors that speeds up some operations). Replacing the processor boosted it to 200 MHz, while adding memory to the two unused memory slots boosted the memory to 32MB. Between the two upgrades, the machine was at least twice as fast as it had been, at a cost of around U.S. $200.

Not all upgrades work out well. We upgraded an old machine with a 66 MHz 486 processor to use the TurboChip 133 from Kingston Technology (roughly equivalent to a 75 MHz Pentium processor). This upgrade was painless and worked as advertised, but when we went to upgrade the memory from 16MB to 32MB we found that no combination of memory modules worked. Depending on what we tried, either the machine wouldn't start at all or Windows wouldn't boot. The machine is stuck at 16MB unless we replace a much more expensive set of electronics.

This chapter teaches you what you need to know in order to decide if a computer you have is upgradable, and if so what upgrades you should consider. The general rule we recommend for computer upgrades and replacements is that if the performance gain is worth more than the cost of the upgrade or replacement, it's time to act. Be sure to comparison shop, including checking prices on the Internet with **http://www.pricewatch.com**.

Adding Memory

Memory is one of the simplest, least expensive, and most effective upgrades possible for many machines. When programs need more memory than the computer has, Windows uses a technique called *swapping* to make slow disk space substitute for fast memory. Every time Windows has to swap between memory and disk, there's a big performance hit. If you're running a word processor, e-mail reader, or Web browser, you're easily going to need 20 to 32MB of memory to hold everything. If you run several of them at once, you want 64MB for the best performance. The many Pentium-class computers running with no more than 8 or 16MB of memory are likely to be running slowly because they're starved for room to run their programs.

It's getting hard to find memory for 486-class computers and will soon be impossible. Pentium computers use what are called 72-pin single in-line memory modules, or *SIMMs*, small circuit cards with memory chips mounted on them. You buy SIMMs of a specific size, speed, and type, and have to install them in matched pairs. Readily available sizes today (per SIMM) are 16, 32, 64, and 128MB. The 32MB modules are presently the least expensive per megabyte. Available speeds are 70, 60, and 50 ns (nanoseconds — one billionth of a second). Types are fast page mode (FPM) and extended data out (EDO). EDO is faster than FPM. SIMMs also come 32 or 36

bits wide, but essentially all Pentium-based computers use 32-bit SIMMs.

Installing memory is as simple as turning off the power, putting on your antistatic wrist strap, opening the computer, and plugging it in. All memory is keyed, so you really have to work to put it in backwards. Pairs of SIMMs go in as a *bank*, usually into adjacent sockets. Memory for video cards and printers is packaged differently, but upgrades the same way.

TAKE NOTE

▶ GET THE MEMORY THAT FITS YOUR COMPUTER

SIMMs aren't the only kind of memory. Newer computers use 168-pin dual in-line memory modules (DIMMs) containing synchronous dynamic random access memory (SDRAM) rather than FPM or EDO. The newest, fastest memory meets the PC100 specification. Rather than try to decipher all the memory types and specifications, you can rely on a dependable vendor to look up what your system needs.

▶ DON'T EXPECT TO MOVE MEMORY TO YOUR NEXT COMPUTER

The change in technology from SIMMs (with Pentium processors) to DIMMs (with many Pentium II processors) makes memory from old computers impossible to move to newer ones. If you're planning to upgrade by buying a new computer, don't assume you can move the memory from your old computer over to the new one. Check first to see if the modules in the two computers are compatible.

CROSS-REFERENCE

See "Isolating the Problem" in Chapter 23 if you have problems after you upgrade.

FIND IT ONLINE

We buy memory (and other components) from ESC Technologies at **http://www.esc-technologies.com**.

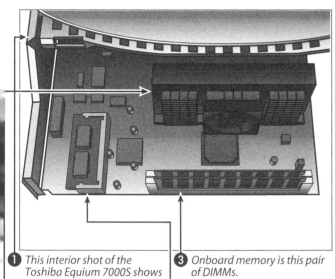

❶ This interior shot of the Toshiba Equium 7000S shows the major electronic components.

❷ The processor is the largest single component.

❸ Onboard memory is this pair of DIMMs.

❹ Video memory upgrades fit into this bracket above the built-in pair of memories.

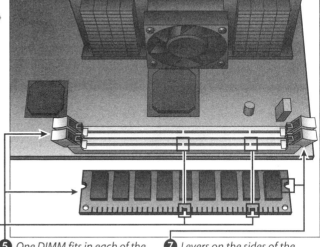

❺ One DIMM fits in each of the two DIMM sockets.

❻ Keyholes in the DIMM match keys in the DIMM socket.

❼ Levers on the sides of the sockets snap into the notches on the side of the DIMM.

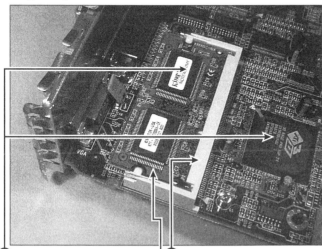

❽ Video memory (module on the left manufactured by Kingston) has to match the requirements of the video system (right).

❾ Push the contacts of the module into the socket.

❿ Snap the memory down into the retaining latches.

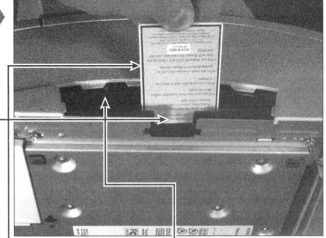

⓫ Printer memory is often packaged as cards rather than SIMMs or DIMMs.

⓬ The memory card for this Hewlett-Packard LaserJet 6L goes in a slot on the side.

⓭ A cover protects the memory and slot after the upgrade is complete.

Upgrading to a Faster Processor

It's time to consider upgrading to a faster processor if giving your computer the memory it needs still results in inadequate performance. Whether or not a processor upgrade will work for you depends on your machine:

▶ **486** — Upgrades to 486 machines are doomed, because the data pathway in the computer (called the *bus*) in most 486 systems is too slow to keep up with a fast chip.

▶ **Pentium** — Pentium systems are good candidates for upgrade, because all Pentium systems have what's called a *PCI* (peripheral component interconnect) bus. PCI is fast enough to support the fastest Pentium processors.

▶ **Pentium II** — Even the slowest Pentium II processors are quite fast. The performance problem could be that you need a faster video display for games. If so, consider upgrading to an accelerated 3D video card. If a processor upgrade is in order, your computer electronics determine how fast a processor you can upgrade to. Some 233 and 266 MHz systems are limited to 300 MHz processors — not enough performance gain to be worth the cost.

Pentium processor upgrades have two problems. First is that Pentium processors are out of production, so you have to find one in stock somewhere.

Second is that the electronics in the computer may limit how fast an upgrade chip you can use. Very early Pentium processors ran at 60 and 66 MHz, later ones for Socket 5 systems ran at speeds up to 133 MHz, and ones in Socket 7 systems could run at up to 233 MHz. Check with your system manufacturer to see if you can replace the chip directly with a faster one or if you need a special upgrade version (Intel calls them OverDrive processors).

TAKE NOTE

▶ CONSIDER HAVING THE UPGRADE DONE FOR YOU

Settings on the motherboard control how fast the chip runs and how much power is fed to it. If the settings are wrong, the best that can happen is that you don't get the benefit of the faster chip. The worst that can happen is that you destroy the chip or another part of your computer. Changing the settings can be difficult, so consider having someone skilled at computer upgrades do the work.

▶ TAKE ADVANTAGE OF MMX UPGRADES

Intel added new instructions, called MMX technology, to the Pentium processors after millions of classic Pentium chips had shipped. Any Pentium processor upgrade you do today is likely to incorporate MMX. If it does, be sure to get any available MMX-upgraded versions of the software you run to get the maximum performance.

CROSS-REFERENCE

Make sure you have enough memory first. See "Adding Memory" in this chapter.

FIND IT ONLINE

Read more about Intel's iCOMP Index 2.0 performance index at **http://www.intel.com/procs/perf/icomp/ icomp_paper/ICOMP.HTM.**

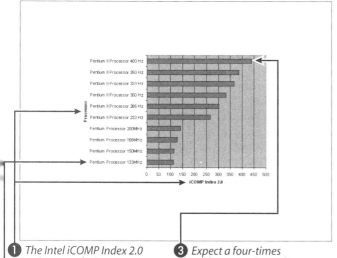

1 The Intel iCOMP Index 2.0 estimates relative processor performance in systems.

2 Systems slower than 133 MHz Pentium processors are excellent upgrade candidates.

3 Expect a four-times performance boost from a Pentium 133 MHz machine to a Pentium II 400 MHz one.

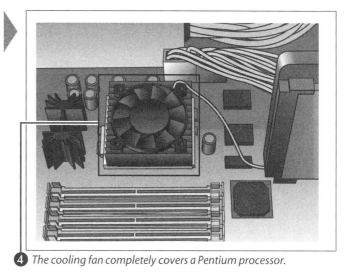

4 The cooling fan completely covers a Pentium processor.

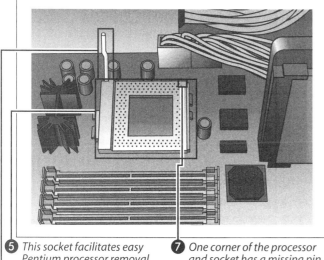

5 This socket facilitates easy Pentium processor removal and replacement.

6 Lift the lever to unlock the processor pins.

7 One corner of the processor and socket has a missing pin — the two must line up.

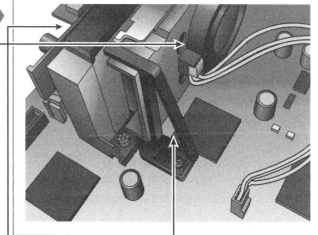

8 The Pentium II processor is a cartridge that mounts vertically on the main board.

9 A vertical fan keeps the processor cool.

10 Some versions use an auxiliary mounting bracket for stability.

Adding a Card

One of the most demanding tasks for your computer is playing 3D action games. Smooth, responsive motion onscreen requires that the game software repaint the screen 15 times a second or more. Some people experience nausea and disorientation when that *frame rate* drops below 20 or 25 updates per second. (For comparison, televisions in North America update the complete screen 30 times per second.)

Every 3D game frame update involves millions of computations by the processor. Most of the work is in rendering objects from three dimensions to the two-dimensional screen while smoothly painting them with *skins* that give them color and texture. Although the processor in your PC can do all the work, the calculations are very specific and specialized. Because of that, dedicated 3D graphics hardware on an add-in card can offload computations from the processor and speed up the frame rate more than a processor upgrade would do and at less cost. Popular 3D accelerators are made by ATI, Canopus, Diamond Multimedia, Matrox, nVIDIA, Permedia, Real3D, and STB. The fastest 3D chipset is presently 3Dfx's Voodoo2, but if your system has an *AGP* (advanced graphics port) slot, boards using the Intel i740 chip offer the best combination of price and performance. Some boards replace your existing video card, while others (such as the one we installed in the photos on the right) coexist with it.

Installing a card into your Pentium or Pentium II, whether a 3D graphics card, modem, or something else, is pretty simple. You have to use an antistatic wrist strap clipped onto a metal part of your computer to protect the electronics, and you should unplug the computer first. Open the case, find an empty slot of the right kind, and follow the steps in the photos at the right. Close the case, install the software, and you're done.

TAKE NOTE

► PICK THE RIGHT KIND OF SLOT

You're likely to find two or three kinds of slots in a Pentium or Pentium II computer. *ISA* (industry standard architecture) slots have larger connectors (usually two in a line, and usually black). *PCI* slots have one smaller connector, usually white. *AGP* slots are similar to PCI, but longer and set back from the edge of the computer. ISA cards are the slowest. PCI cards are usually the best choice unless you're installing a video card — use AGP for video if your computer supports it.

► FOLLOW THE MANUFACTURER'S DIRECTIONS

Although installing cards is a routine operation, it's worth reading and following the manufacturer's directions. You may have to carry out specific steps or follow a specific order to upgrade successfully.

CROSS-REFERENCE

If the installation doesn't work, start troubleshooting with Chapter 23's lesson "Isolating the Problem."

FIND IT ONLINE

Find game news, reviews, and hardware information at the Adrenaline Vault, **http://www.avault.com**.

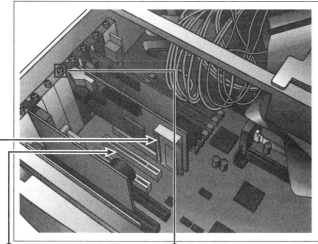

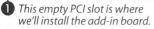

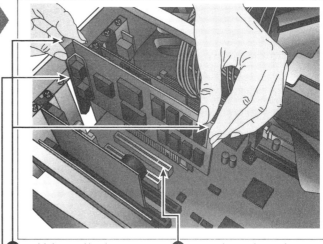

1 This empty PCI slot is where we'll install the add-in board.

2 The memory on this ATI video card is identical to the additional video memory we installed (see "Adding Memory").

3 Remove this screw and bracket to prepare to insert the new card.

4 Hold the card by the corners.

5 Fit the bracket on the card snugly against the back of the chassis.

6 Lower the card, avoiding other cards, until it sits on the slot socket.

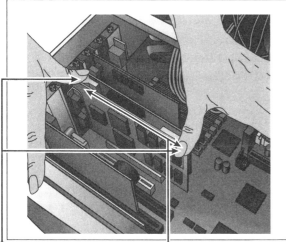

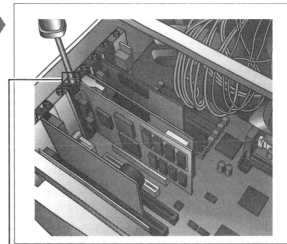

7 Push the board down gently with your thumbs until it seats in the socket.

8 Rock slightly along the length of the card if necessary.

9 Use the screw you removed in the third step, upper-left photo, to hold the new card in place.

Adding a Disk

You'll install a disk in your computer if you want to replace your CD-ROM with a DVD drive or if you need more storage. The installation is less demanding technically than upgrading a processor, but is another upgrade you should consider having done by someone with experience.

The first step in a disk upgrade is configuring the drive and installing it in the computer. Follow the manufacturer's directions for configuration. If you're adding the drive onto the wide, flat *ribbon cable* that already connects to another drive (you can have two on a cable in most computers), set up the new drive as a *slave*. If it's the only one on the cable, set it up as the *master*. If you're replacing an existing drive, set the configuration the same as the old drive, and use the same space in the chassis and the same cable connections.

Once you install a CD-ROM or DVD drive, Windows should see the drive immediately. If not, check the *BIOS* (Basic Input/Output System) to see if it's configured to look for the drive. You may have to call the computer manufacturer's technical support line to find out how to do so for your individual computer. After you install a hard disk drive, you may have to go through a three-step process to set up the information on the drive so the computer and Windows can see it. Again, follow the manufacturer's instructions. The three steps that may be required are to set up the BIOS to see the disk, to *partition* the

disk, which lets the computer know how big the disk is, and to *format* the disk, which lets Windows see it. If you have to do these steps, be extremely careful — if you do them incorrectly, you might wipe out the information on your existing disk.

CROSS-REFERENCE

See "Organizing Your Disk the Way You Work" in Chapter 4 for a lesson on how to lay out folders on your disk.

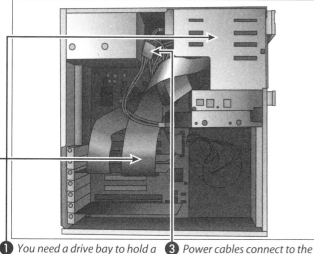

1 *You need a drive bay to hold a CD-ROM, DVD, or hard disk.*

2 *Flat, wide cables from the main electronics board (called a motherboard) bring data to and from the disk.*

3 *Power cables connect to the disk from the power supply.*

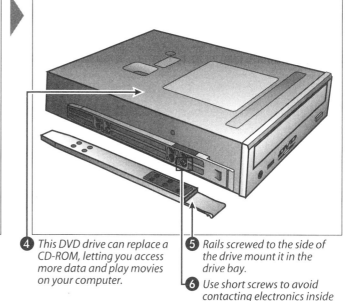

4 *This DVD drive can replace a CD-ROM, letting you access more data and play movies on your computer.*

5 *Rails screwed to the side of the drive mount it in the drive bay.*

6 *Use short screws to avoid contacting electronics inside the drive.*

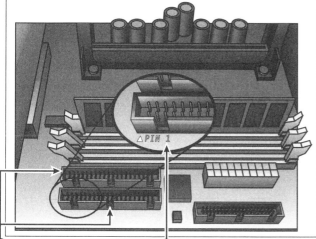

△PIN 1

7 *These connectors hold one end of the ribbon cable going to the disk drive.*

8 *There may be a key on the side of the cable connector to guide cable orientation.*

9 *Look for a pin 1 designation on the board (see inset) to correspond to the stripe on the edge of the cable.*

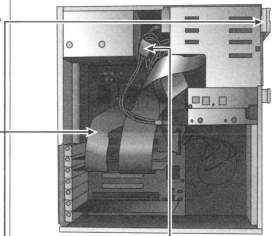

10 *This computer's CD-ROM sits at the top of the case. The hard disk is in the middle.*

11 *Flat ribbon cables connect data to the drives and motherboard.*

12 *Power cables connect from the power supply to drives.*

289

Personal Workbook

Q&A

1 What can limit the upgrades possible for your computer?

_____

_____

_____

2 What's the most effective upgrade for most computers?

_____

_____

_____

3 What is *swapping* (in computer terms, that is)?

_____

_____

_____

4 What upgrades are worthwhile for 486 computers?

_____

_____

_____

5 What's an indication that you might need a faster processor?

_____

_____

_____

6 What makes a processor upgrade challenging?

_____

_____

_____

7 What is *ISA*? *PCI*? *AGP*?

_____

_____

_____

8 What is the *BIOS*?

_____

_____

_____

ANSWERS: PAGE 345

1 Open your computer and identify what each card does. (Hint: look at what the board connects to.)

2 Identify the power and data cables in your computer.

3 Find the disk drive in your computer. Where would you mount another disk drive? (Make sure the cables will reach to the new location.)

4 Trace the ribbon cables to the disk drive and CD-ROM. Are the two on the same cable?

5 Read Intel's paper at **http://www.intel.com/procs/ perf/icomp/icomp_paper/ICOMP.HTM**, and then consider why you can't compare processor speeds accurately by comparing clock rates.

✔ You edit scanned photographs using Adobe Photoshop, but your computer is slow. You upgrade from 32MB to 128MB and find you can edit several photos at once while you keep your e-mail reader and Web browser open.

✔ You look at the cost of replacing most of the insides of your old 486 computer, comparing it to the Pentium-based machines with large disks and 32MB of memory now available for under $800. You decide to upgrade by buying a new machine, keeping the old machine to run the printer on your network.

Visual Quiz

What happens if this fan stops working?

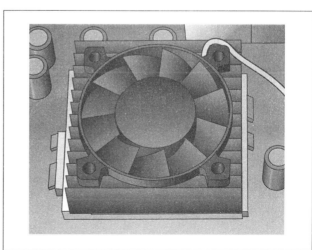

CHAPTER **21**

MASTER
THESE
SKILLS

▶ **Picking Components and Installing Network Cables**

▶ **Installing Networking Software**

▶ **Sharing Drives and Printers**

▶ **Checking Network Security**

Setting Up a Network

The value of the Internet is that it lets people share information. Connecting computers to share information is what all computer networks do, whether they are a local connection of two computers, a campus-wide Local Area Network (LAN), or the Internet itself. The more computers on the network, the more information there is to share.

Computer networks have four components—the wiring between computers, the network interface in the computers, the network communication software, and the network applications that finally make the network visible to you. When you worked through the lessons in Chapter 14 to connect your computer to the Internet, the wiring was your telephone line, the network interface was the modem, the communications software was Dial-Up Networking, and the network application was (usually) your Web browser.

If you connect computers on a LAN, the components are different. The wiring is similar to telephone cable, the network interface is a specialized card in your computer called a network interface card (NIC), the communications software is something called a network protocol stack, and the application software is Windows itself, letting you share disks and printers across the computers on the network. More sophisticated LANs, as we cover in our book *PC Upgrade and Repair Bible, Professional Edition,* let you connect to the Internet, sharing the Internet connection among all the computers on the LAN.

LANs connect computers at speeds far faster than modems. The most common LAN connections run at 10 million bits per second (Mbps), almost 200 times faster than with the latest modems. Higher-performance LAN connections run ten times faster yet.

Once you wire your LAN, you set up Windows to be able to communicate across the network and to specify what disks and printers others are permitted to use. Windows 95 and 98 are quite straightforward to configure for networks. (If you're still running Windows 3.1, a network is the best reason to upgrade; network configuration with Windows 3.1 was difficult and often limited the programs you could run.)

Picking Components and Installing Network Cables

You start picking components for your network by picking the wiring technology to use. If you're connecting two or more computers, 10Base-2 wiring (also called *Thinnet*) is simple and inexpensive. The wires are coaxial cable up to 600 feet long, with connectors at either end that twist a half or quarter turn to lock. You need some other parts (shown in the photo at the bottom-right) at the back of each computer to complete the wiring.

You can also connect two or more computers with what's called 10Base-T (or *twisted pair*) wiring. 10Base-T network cables have fat (8-pin) modular telephone connectors at either end, and can be up to 300 feet long. If you have more than two computers on the LAN, you need a device called a *hub* to join the cables in the middle. Hubs cost as little as $25, and have the advantage that a malfunctioning computer or bad wiring is less likely to take down your network than if you use 10Base-2. By putting the hub in the middle of the site, the 300-foot cable length lets computers be almost 600 feet apart.

The 10Base-T wiring is simpler to put in a building, too, because no matter how many computers you put on the LAN, each computer has one cable going to it, and it's easy to wire the building with RJ-45 modular telephone connectors in the wall so you're ready to plug in a computer wherever there's a wall jack. The 10Base-2 wiring requires all computers except the ones at the ends of the cable to have two cables — one from the computer on the left, and one from the computer on the right. You can't break the loop, either. If you remove a computer from the cable, you still have to keep enough cabling installed to connect the two ends.

You can get a 3Com 10Base-T network starter kit including a four-port hub, cables, and two NICs for around $100. Adding up to two more computers requires only NICs and cables.

TAKE NOTE

▶ MAKE A SMALL 10BASE-T NETWORK WITH A CROSSOVER CABLE

If you're connecting only two computers, you can use a special 10Base-T cable that reverses the signal connections from normal. The crossover cable plugs directly into the NIC on either computer with no intervening hub. You can't use that cable later with a hub if you expand to three or more computers — you'd need to get a new, regular cable for each computer. If both computers have NICs capable of the faster 100Base-T standard as well as 10Base-T, they'll communicate at 100Mbps over the reverser because they won't be limited to 10Mbps by a low-cost hub.

CROSS-REFERENCE

See "Adding a Card" in Chapter 20 for what you need to know to install the NICs.

FIND IT ONLINE

Get a 10Base-T crossover cable at **http://www. cablesnmor.com/10baset.html**.

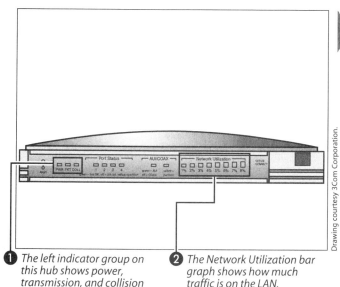

Drawing courtesy 3Com Corporation.

1 The left indicator group on this hub shows power, transmission, and collision (indicating high traffic levels).

2 The Network Utilization bar graph shows how much traffic is on the LAN.

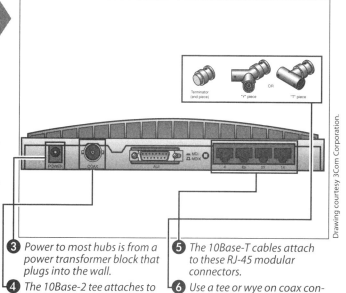

Drawing courtesy 3Com Corporation.

3 Power to most hubs is from a power transformer block that plugs into the wall.

4 The 10Base-2 tee attaches to the COAX connector.

5 The 10Base-T cables attach to these RJ-45 modular connectors.

6 Use a tee or wye on coax connections, with two cables or one cable and a terminator.

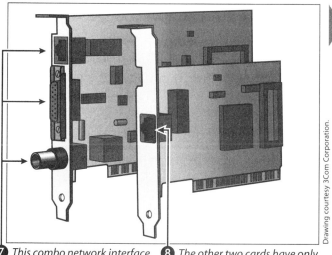

Drawing courtesy 3Com Corporation.

7 This combo network interface card (NIC) has (top to bottom) a 10Base-T connector, an AUI connector (less commonly used), and a 10Base-2 connector.

8 The other two cards have only 10Base-T connectors.

Photo courtesy 3Com Corporation.

9 This 3Com Networking kit includes hub, NICs, cables, and software.

Installing Networking Software

Windows should do most of the work for you once it detects you've installed network interface cards. Windows installs three layers of software: the *NIC driver* that operates the hardware itself, the *protocol* software that sends messages across the network, and the *client* software that enables you to share disks and printers across the network.

Windows 98 lists 71 different NIC manufacturers in the Add New Hardware Control Panel applet. If Windows doesn't have a driver for your NIC, you're dependent on the hardware manufacturer for help. The top NIC manufacturers are 3Com and Intel—you can rely on having Windows drivers for their cards. You can find generic NICs available on the Internet for as little as $10, with similar 3Com units priced at $20. You can't spend very many minutes troubleshooting network problems before you eat up the $10 difference.

You only run two or three of the standard Windows network protocols on top of your NIC driver. Your modem uses the Transmission Control Protocol/Internet Protocol (TCP/IP) to send messages over the Internet, and by default Windows uses the NetBIOS Extended User Interface (NetBEUI) protocol to send messages over your LAN. This combination is enough for many small, simple networks. If you play games over your LAN, you might want to add the Internetwork Packet Exchange/Sequenced Packet Exchange (IPX/SPX) protocol, because most multiplayer games require it or TCP/IP to run.

Windows includes two options for client software usable on small networks—one for Microsoft networks and one for NetWare networks. These two clients correspond to the NetBEUI and IPX/SPX protocols, respectively. Games running on IPX/SPX need only the protocol, not the client, so you can lighten the load on your system by removing the NetWare client. (It often gets loaded automatically when you install the protocol.)

TAKE NOTE

▶ **CONTROL NETWORK SOFTWARE WITH THE NETWORK APPLET**

You install and configure all the network software you see in this lesson through the Network Control Panel applet. The applet is typical in operation; the network software components you have installed are listed at the top of the dialog box. Buttons below let you add, remove, and configure components as you select them.

▶ **USING TCP/IP ON YOUR LAN**

You do have the option of using TCP/IP on your LAN, and in fact must do so if you connect the LAN itself to the Internet. TCP/IP configuration is more complex than that for IPX/SPX (which requires no configuration once it's installed), so if your only objective is to play games, you should stick with IPX/SPX. If you plan on running TCP/IP on your LAN, see your Internet Service Provider for information.

CROSS-REFERENCE

You're not done with your network setup until you work through the next lesson, "Sharing Drives and Printers."

FIND IT ONLINE

To run games requiring IPX over the Internet, see **http://www.kali.net**.

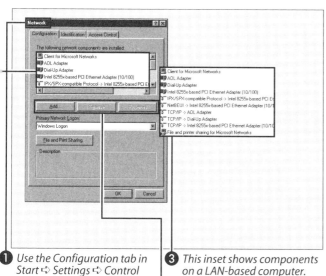

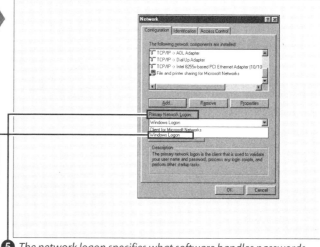

1 Use the Configuration tab in Start ➪ Settings ➪ Control Panel ➪ Network to set up network software.

2 The installed components show up in this list.

3 This inset shows components on a LAN-based computer.

4 Use the Add, Remove, and Properties buttons to work with each component.

5 The network logon specifies what software handles passwords.

6 Choose Windows Logon so Windows handles passwords automatically if possible.

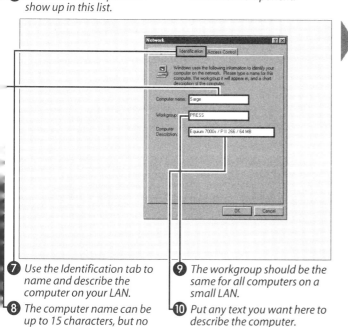

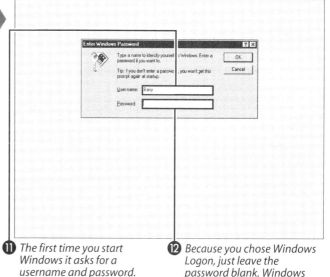

7 Use the Identification tab to name and describe the computer on your LAN.

8 The computer name can be up to 15 characters, but no spaces are allowed.

9 The workgroup should be the same for all computers on a small LAN.

10 Put any text you want here to describe the computer.

11 The first time you start Windows it asks for a username and password.

12 Because you chose Windows Logon, just leave the password blank. Windows won't ask again the next time you start the computer.

Sharing Drives and Printers

Now that you've installed the network hardware and software, you need to tell Windows — on each computer — what disk drive and printers you're willing to let other computers on the LAN see. You have a lot of control over how this works, including the ability to set up sharing for individual folders, to set whether accesses are read-only or read/write, to decide whether passwords are required or not, and to set the names by which shared resources are known.

You set up all drives, folders, and printers to be shared the same way: right-click the resource and choose Sharing. Do this on a drive, and you see the dialog box shown in the upper-left figure on the next page. Choose whether the drive should be shared or not, and then (if it's shared) whether it's to be read-only, read/write, or either depending on the password entered on the other computer.

When you share a drive or folder, every folder it contains becomes shared too. This means that if you want to keep a folder from being shared, every folder containing it (and the drive itself) must not be shared. This hierarchy makes complex security setups difficult, but it's consistent with the operation of Windows 95 and 98, which themselves are not terribly secure.

Once you set up sharing, the computers and their drives or folders are visible in the Network Neighborhood shown in Windows Explorer, while the printers are installable as network printers. You can use Tools ⇨ Map Network Drive to make remote drives and folders locally accessible through drive letters.

CROSS-REFERENCE

Chapter 14's lesson "Getting Internet Service" shows you how to connect to the Internet.

FIND IT ONLINE

Find answers to frequently asked questions on Windows networking at **http://www.orca. bc.ca/win95/faq7.htm**.

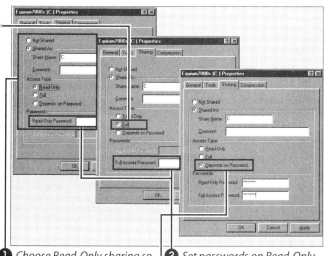

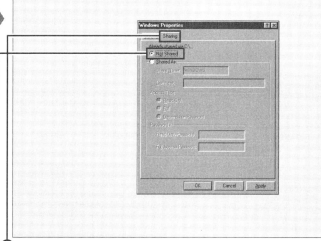

❶ *Choose Read-Only sharing so users at other computers can't modify what's on the drive.*

❷ *Choose Full sharing to let users at other computers read and write files.*

❸ *Set passwords on Read-Only or Full sharing to restrict access.*

❹ *Choose Depends on Password to let other computers use Read-Only or Full access.*

❺ *Set drive C to be shared; then look at the sharing properties for C:\Windows.*

❻ *You can't unshare a folder that's inside a shared drive or folder in Windows 95 or 98.*

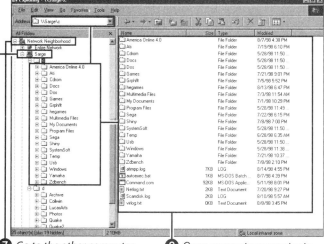

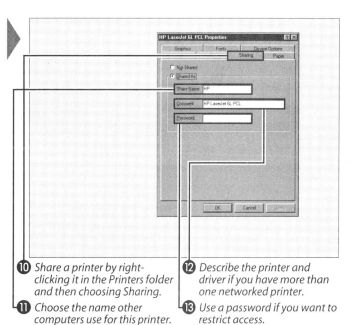

❼ *Go to the other computer, open Windows Explorer, and look at Network Neighborhood.*

❽ *You should see the computers on your LAN listed by name.*

❾ *Open a remote computer to see its shared drives and folders.*

❿ *Share a printer by right-clicking it in the Printers folder and then choosing Sharing.*

⓫ *Choose the name other computers use for this printer.*

⓬ *Describe the printer and driver if you have more than one networked printer.*

⓭ *Use a password if you want to restrict access.*

Checking Network Security

Despite everything an Internet connection can do for you, risks exist in using the Internet — the risk that your children will be exposed to things you'd rather they not see, the risk that you'll be exposed to things your elected officials would rather you weren't, and the risk that you'll confuse opinion with fact (and worse).

You must do two critical things if you use your computer on the Internet. First, you must verify that you have disabled file sharing for your Internet connection. Fail to do that, and your computer could be wide open to attack any time you're connected. Fortunately, it's very simple to check for and fix the problem. Open the Network Control Panel applet and, for every TCP/IP line, click Properties, and look at the Bindings tab. If you find a binding for file and print sharing, clear it and click OK.

Second, if you're running any version of Windows 95, download and install the update to the Windows TCP/IP protocol software from **http://www.microsoft. com/windows95/info/ws2.htm**. This update solves some problems in the software and eliminates some security vulnerabilities. The update is included in Windows 98, so you can also solve the problem by updating from Windows 95 to Windows 98.

Because there are losers on the Internet, many useful tools exist to shield children from inappropriate content. Net Nanny (**http://www.netnanny.com/ allabout/allabout.htm**) is one of many. Under the right circumstances, filtering tools might be worthwhile, but they're no substitute for teaching your values to your children and for knowing what your children are doing.

TAKE NOTE

▶ TAKE SECURITY THREATS SERIOUSLY

Don't underestimate the risk of security threats from the Internet. Hundreds of millions of computers are connected to the Internet, and admittedly, it's not likely you'll be attacked. Nevertheless, as you can see in the examples at **http://www.users. nac.net/splat/winnuke,** serious security threats exist for Windows machines.

▶ GET SECURITY HELP FROM YOUR ISP

Competent ISPs regularly monitor security alerts at **http://www.ciac.org** and **http://www.cert.org**. Ask your ISP if it has a page of security alerts you should know about and what practices it has in place to help prevent attacks on customers' computers. (For example, ask if its network equipment filters out messages to port 139 on your computer, protecting you from attempts to remotely access your file system.)

CROSS-REFERENCE
Finish securing your computer with "Installing Antivirus Software" in Chapter 22.

FIND IT ONLINE
Microsoft maintains a current security alert and patch list at **http://www.microsoft.com/security**.

Be Security Conscious

Just as scams happen everywhere in the real world, scams occur on the Internet. Just as living in a gated community doesn't keep out phone frauds and solicitors, living in an Internet community such as AOL or EarthLink doesn't keep out frauds either. You need to keep your wits about you and apply common sense. Here are a few guidelines:

▶ **Don't give out personal information.** You wouldn't give your bank ATM card and security code to a stranger, and you shouldn't give personal information to people online. Information you should keep *strictly* private includes your account password, your bank account numbers, and your social security number.

▶ **People aren't always who or what they say they are.** The online conversations you can have in AOL chat rooms (and similar places on the Internet) are very popular, but keep in mind that there's no shortage of newspaper accounts of child molesters finding victims in chat rooms. We'll say it again: Know what your children are doing.

▶ **Never send cash.** Make a practice of using credit cards, never sending cash or checks for purchases you make on the Internet (or by phone, for that matter). If the merchant fails to deliver as promised, you can contact the credit card company.

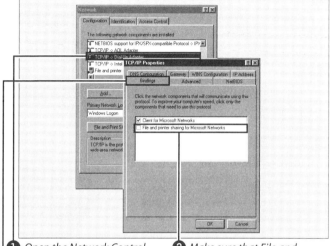

1 Open the Network Control Panel applet and look at each TCP/IP line (NetBEUI sharing is okay).

2 Click Properties and look at the Bindings tab.

3 Make sure that File and printer sharing for Microsoft Networks is disabled.

4 The Microsoft Security Advisor on the Web can keep you up to date on Windows security issues.

5 You can get e-mail when new notices are available — see *http://www.microsoft.com/security/bulletin.htm*.

Personal Workbook

Q&A

1 Name four components of a network.

_____

_____

_____

2 What is a *LAN*?

_____

_____

_____

3 What is the most common LAN speed? What common speed is faster than that?

_____

_____

_____

4 What is *10Base-2*?

_____

_____

_____

5 What is *10Base-T*?

_____

_____

_____

6 Name two advantages of 10Base-T over 10Base-2.

_____

_____

_____

7 What's an inexpensive way to run 10Base-T with two computers?

_____

_____

_____

8 What device is required to connect three or more computers using 10Base-T?

_____

_____

_____

ANSWERS: PAGE 345

EXTRA PRACTICE

① Plot the location of all your computers. Where could you put a hub and still be within the 300-foot 10Base-T cable-length limit?

② Look at the software available from **http://www. sygate.com.** Would you find it useful to share your Internet connection among several computers?

③ Install Web filtering software on your computer (be sure to remember the passwords). Try to circumvent it. How long did it take?

④ Talk to your ISP about security. What precautions do they take? What do they recommend you do?

REAL-WORLD APPLICATIONS

✔ You buy a second computer so your ten-year-old will stop asking you when it's her turn on the computer. After you network the two computers and share the printer, she stops asking when she can use the computer with a printer. After you install SyGate, she stops asking when she can use the computer with the modem.

✔ You set up a LAN for your small office. As individual computers run out of storage, you add an extra computer to the LAN with a lot of disk space in it, making a shared area on the computer's disk for each person in the office.

Visual Quiz

Compare this screen shot to the one on the lower-left in this chapter's "Sharing Drives and Printers" lesson. What's different? How did we do this?

_____

_____

_____

_____

_____

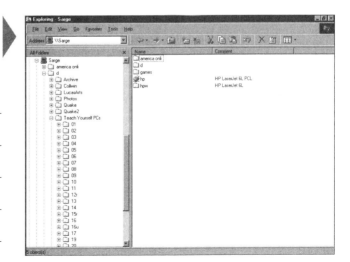

CHAPTER **22**

MASTER
THESE
SKILLS

▶ **Identifying Viruses and Other Threats**

▶ **Installing Antivirus Software**

▶ **Scanning Your Computer for Viruses**

▶ **Updating Your Antivirus Software**

Virus Protection

Early in the history of personal computers, the biggest worry you had about software was that it would be poorly written. But because you couldn't pack much on a floppy disk, you didn't have all that much to lose. Once hard disks became common on PCs, though, enough software and data inhabited a computer that hard disks became a target.

Internet legend has it that the early computer viruses were written in Eastern Europe by programmers trying to build a reputation throughout the world for skill and ingenuity. It would be nice if the legend were true, because if it is they failed miserably; none of the original virus writers is known widely enough to matter. Regardless, the early viruses were written by hand to solve a number of problems: a virus has to stay hidden and undetected until it strikes, yet be able to replicate itself from one machine to another. Morons who tried to write viruses were generally unsuccessful and only a few strains were widespread. Today, the situation is very different (although the morons are still with us). Sophisticated software now exists that creates viruses with the push of a few buttons.

Fortunately, although the threat is always present, viruses are relatively rare in most places. Invest in tools to protect your computers from viruses. Used consistently in combination with a healthy dose of common sense, they can keep your computers clean and virus-free.

The lessons in this chapter tell you what you need to know about what viruses are (including some other bad actors), how they reproduce themselves, and how those threats can reach your system. You learn the approach that virus scanners use to find infections and how to install antivirus software correctly to be sure you're protected. The chapter wraps up with lessons on how to use important features in antivirus software and — don't overlook this — how to make sure the critical data files your virus scanner uses to protect you are always up to date.

Don't think that you can skip these lessons if your computer isn't on the Internet — you could be dangerously wrong.

Identifying Viruses and Other Threats

Computer viruses are much like their biological forerunners, parasites that must reside in a host to live. A virus is different from a *Trojan* (named after the Trojan horse), which is a program that masquerades as another program, often with malicious intent.

All computer viruses are programs, which means they must be run by the processor to have an effect. Three primary types of viruses affect PCs. The earliest forms of viruses infected programs. Later forms infected the low-level startup information on a disk (the *master boot record*, or *MBR*, on a hard disk, and *boot sector* on a floppy). The most recent virus types infect data files. Don't be fooled by this last one — the data files for sophisticated applications such as word processors and spreadsheets can carry their own high-level programs, called macros. Viruses written in the macro language are fully capable viruses that spread their infection to other data files and other computers.

All three forms of virus, plus *multipartite* viruses that use several forms of infection, exist today. Viruses that infect files start running when you start the infected program; they're harmless so long as the file merely sits on the disk. MBR infectors get control as soon as the BIOS starts to launch Windows off the hard disk or another operating system off a floppy disk. Macro viruses run when the application program opens the infected file. Ultimately, your computer catches a virus one of two ways: off an infected floppy disk or from an infected file. Infected floppy disks have to be handed to you, while infected files can come from anywhere (including off the Internet).

TAKE NOTE

▶ TURN OFF FLOPPY-DISK BOOTING IN YOUR BIOS

MBR viruses most often infect your computer when you boot from an infected floppy disk. The most common way to boot an infected disk is to leave it in the drive when you power off the machine, so a good defense is to configure your BIOS so it first tries to boot the hard disk, not the floppy. Talk to your system manufacturer to find out how to do this reconfiguration.

▶ KNOW YOUR SOURCE

A good protection against viruses is to be sure you know who gave you a file before you run it and to be sure they know where it came from. The best practice is to delete files attached to e-mail from people you don't know — without running the attachment. If you must run the program, save it to the disk first and scan it with a good virus scanner using absolutely current virus definition files. Even then, you have no protection against Trojans; virus scanners aren't likely to detect them.

CROSS-REFERENCE

Read the "E-mail Security — Trojans and Hoaxes" lesson in Chapter 18 for more fun with losers.

FIND IT ONLINE

The McAfee Virus Information Library is at **http://www.nai.com/vinfo**.

Keep Your Guard Up

It's possible you will never see a live computer virus. Combine that with having installed a virus scanner and it's predictable that after a while you'll let your guard down. As soon as you do, you're in danger. New viruses are being made and found all the time, so if you don't update your virus definition files regularly, a new one can slip past and strike. Reliable virus prevention requires constant file updates and a strict policy of erasing unknown files you receive. Delete those files, and then empty the Recycle Bin.

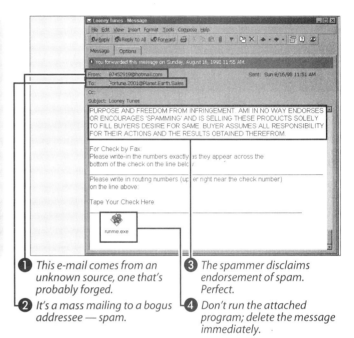

❶ This e-mail comes from an unknown source, one that's probably forged.

❷ It's a mass mailing to a bogus addressee — spam.

❸ The spammer disclaims endorsement of spam. Perfect.

❹ Don't run the attached program; delete the message immediately.

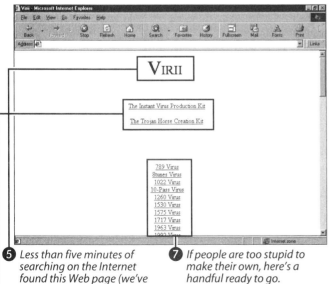

❺ Less than five minutes of searching on the Internet found this Web page (we've removed some things).

❻ Anyone can create Trojans and viruses with these tools.

❼ If people are too stupid to make their own, here's a handful ready to go.

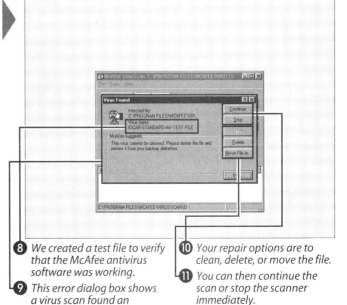

❽ We created a test file to verify that the McAfee antivirus software was working.

❾ This error dialog box shows a virus scan found an infected file.

❿ Your repair options are to clean, delete, or move the file.

⓫ You can then continue the scan or stop the scanner immediately.

Installing Antivirus Software

You have two crucial decisions to make when it's time to install antivirus software: what software you install and how you install it. You want to use software that is comprehensive (so it's likely to pick up any viruses that come by), that is regularly and rapidly updated, and that is reliable. Our preference for years has been VirusScan, by McAfee (now part of Network Associates). A version of VirusScan now ships with the Windows 98 Plus! Pack. The other antivirus software we consider first-rate is F-PROT from Data Fellows (**http://www.datafellows.com**). One of the key services backing up both products is regular posting of update files on the Internet, ensuring you're always protected against the latest viruses.

Choose a Custom setup when you do the installation so you can be sure you get the options you need. VirusScan has five components; we consider three of them mandatory, one advisable, and one optional.

- ▶ **Command Line Scanner (Mandatory)** — The command line scanner protects your computer if you boot to DOS rather than Windows, checks for viruses before Windows starts, and includes a utility to make virus emergency disks.
- ▶ **On-Demand Scanner (Advisable)** — The on-demand scanner lets you select a file or folder in Windows Explorer and direct VirusScan to check it.

- ▶ **Console (Mandatory)** — The console lets you configure VirusScan operation.
- ▶ **On-Access Scanner (Absolutely Mandatory)** — The on-access scanner checks for viruses every time a program opens a file, before the program can touch the file. If the file is found to be infected, you get the chance to abort the operation before your computer is infected.
- ▶ **ScreenScan (Optional)** — ScreenScan checks files on your disk for viruses while your screen saver runs. It's another layer of checking, just in case an infected file slips in.

TAKE NOTE

▶ TAKE ADVANTAGE OF EVALUATION SOFTWARE

You can download evaluation versions of both VirusScan and F-PROT from the companies' Web sites. These are fully functional versions of the software that you register after a period of time if you decide to continue use. Free evaluation is a great way to be sure the software works the way you want on your own system.

▶ MAKE A VIRUS EMERGENCY DISK

Viruses try to hide and make themselves hard to remove. If a virus makes it past your antivirus software, you can only remove the virus reliably if you boot from a floppy disk known to be virus-free. Make a virus emergency disk when you install the software and be sure to write-protect the disk.

CROSS-REFERENCE

Learn how to keep your antivirus software current in "Updating Your Antivirus Software" in this chapter.

FIND IT ONLINE

Download an evaluation version of McAfee VirusScan from **http://www.mcafee.com/download/eval.asp**.

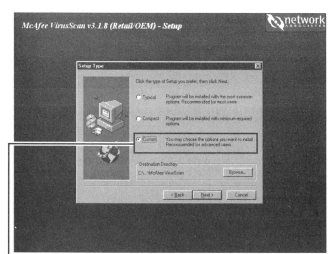

1 Be sure to choose Custom setup for your antivirus software so you're sure what components get installed.

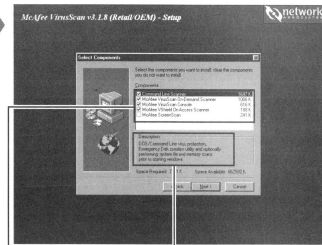

2 Pick components carefully. Consider the Command Line Scanner, Console, and On-Access Scanner to be mandatory.

3 Select a component and read its description if you're unsure whether you want to install it.

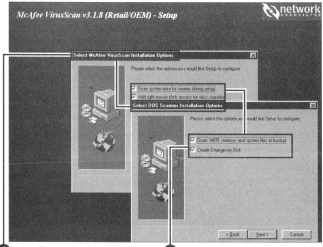

4 Installation options let you choose to scan your system during setup and determine the configuration setup established for the software.

5 We recommend choosing all four options.

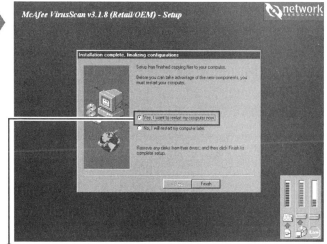

6 Until you restart, you're not protected from viruses. Close any running programs and restart immediately after setup finishes.

Scanning Your Computer for Viruses

We downloaded a live virus from the Internet for the examples in this lesson — one that McAfee VirusScan calls SCREAMIN. STRANGER. The effectiveness of VirusScan made it difficult to create the examples. The On-Access Scanner we recommended you install in the previous lesson looks at files before any other program — including Windows — can get the chance, so any time we tried to do *anything* with the file, VirusScan popped up to ask what we wanted to do.

Because you can acquire files that won't have been scanned (by downloading from the Internet, by saving attachments in e-mail, or through action of a computer on your LAN not protected by antivirus software), and because people give you floppies at times, it's possible to have files you can't be sure are virus-free. The On-Demand Scanner in VirusScan gives you a way to positively check those unknown files.

The easiest way to start the On-Demand Scanner (if you selected the "add right mouse click" option when you installed the software) is through the right mouse button in Windows Explorer. Right-click whatever you want to scan and choose Scan for Viruses. If you declined the right mouse installation option, start the scanner using the shortcut under the Start button.

Your virus emergency floppy disk is a crucial part of your defensive strategy. Because you made the floppy — and write-protected it — when you knew the machine was virus free, you know that the machine is uncontaminated when booted from that disk. Because of that, you can trust what the scanner says. If you think your computer might be infected, *turn the computer off*, wait a minute, and then power it on and boot the emergency floppy.

TAKE NOTE

SCAN WHEN YOU UPDATE YOUR VIRUS DEFINITION FILES

Antivirus scanners can only detect threats known in the virus definition files. When you update the definition files, you're adding knowledge of new viruses not previously checked by your computer. If your computer was infected by one of these new viruses before the update, you won't know about it. If you want to be absolutely sure, boot your virus emergency disk, copy the new definition files onto the disk (replacing the old ones), and rescan.

HAVE THE DISCIPLINE TO SCAN ALL DOWNLOADS

Any time you download a file from the Internet, scan it. Even the most careful sites have problems now and then. Some very popular Internet sites have accidentally posted downloadable files infected with a virus. To make sure you're not the victim of an accident, scan all files after you download them and before you run or install them, and never run files from a source you don't know.

CROSS-REFERENCE

Learn how to keep your virus definition files up to date with the next lesson, "Updating Your Antivirus Software."

FIND IT ONLINE

McAfee/Network Associates provides virus removal instructions at http://www.nai.com/vinfo/0402.asp.

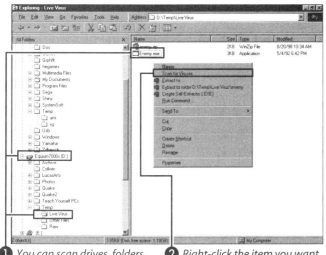

1 You can scan drives, folders, or individual files for viruses using the On-Demand Scanner.

2 Right-click the item you want to scan, and then choose Scan for Viruses.

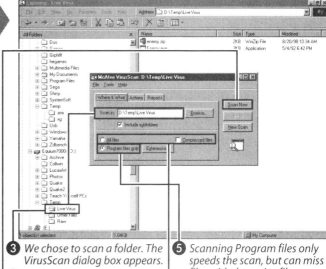

3 We chose to scan a folder. The VirusScan dialog box appears.

4 Click Scan Now to start the scanner.

5 Scanning Program files only speeds the scan, but can miss files with deceptive filenames.

6 Choose to scan all files and to scan encrypted files to know that nothing escapes analysis.

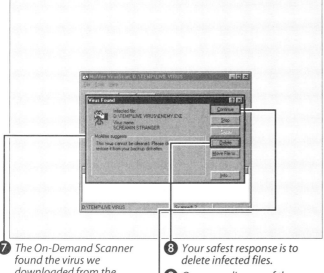

7 The On-Demand Scanner found the virus we downloaded from the Internet.

8 Your safest response is to delete infected files.

9 Once you dispose of the infected file, continue the scan.

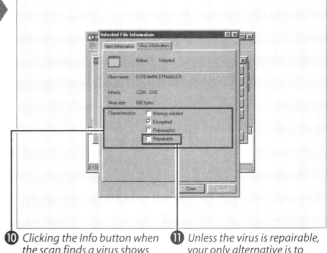

10 Clicking the Info button when the scan finds a virus shows the virus's characteristics.

11 Unless the virus is repairable, your only alternative is to delete the file.

Updating Your Antivirus Software

All commercial antivirus software has two parts: a scanning engine that knows how to look at your computer and its files for infections and data files that tell the engine what to look for. The antivirus software manufacturers distribute updates to cover newly discovered viruses by posting new data files on their Web sites. Keeping your virus definition files up to date is mandatory; you have some choice when to update the engine.

You have two ways to update recent versions of McAfee VirusScan: automatically and manually. Other products may offer automatic update; any worthwhile virus scanner supports manual update. We show automatic update in the top two figures on the opposite page. Close any running programs, start VirusScan, and then choose the File ⇨ Update VirusScan command. A wizard leads you through the update sequence and includes options for updating just the data files or the entire program. Once the download completes, finish the operation to start the update installation. You might be asked to reboot the computer when the update is done; we recommend rebooting — no matter what — to be sure the new data files are in use.

If you have to update manually, as shown in the bottom two figures on the opposite page, you navigate to the manufacturer's Web site and download a new set of data files. McAfee uses the ZIP compressed file format, so once the download is complete you need to open the compressed file with WinZip. Extract the entire contents of the ZIP file to the folder holding the antivirus software (and the old data files); then close the program and reboot.

TAKE NOTE

DON'T GET SCAMMED BY PAID DATA FILE UPDATES

The top antivirus products available today all provide free access to updated virus definition files. An antivirus product manufacturer that charges for those updates is more interested in higher profits than the integrity of the product. Don't buy an antivirus scanner that doesn't get you the data file updates you need (McAfee updates monthly) at a competitive price: free.

GET DATA FILE UPDATES STRAIGHT FROM THE SOURCE

You can't be sure of the integrity of antivirus data files you get from anywhere but the manufacturer's download site. Files that have been out of the direct control of the manufacturer could have been tampered with — however unlikely — to keep them from scanning for all the viruses they should. Always insist on original versions direct from the manufacturer.

CROSS-REFERENCE

See how to use WinZip in Chapter 18's lesson, "Running WinZip."

FIND IT ONLINE

Get updated McAfee VirusScan files at **http://www. mcafee.com/download/dats/3x.asp**.

VIRUS PROTECTION
Updating Your Antivirus Software

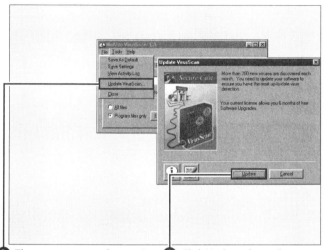

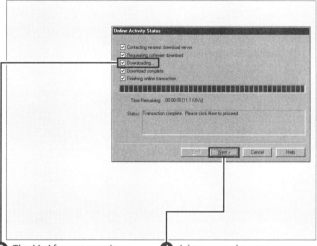

① *The easy way to update antivirus software is to use the built-in automatic update features.*

② *Click Update; then select to update data files or the entire program. Data files are free; only updates to the software are limited.*

③ *The McAfee automatic updater contacts a Network Associates download site and stores the update files on your disk.*

④ *Advance to the next screens to install the update.*

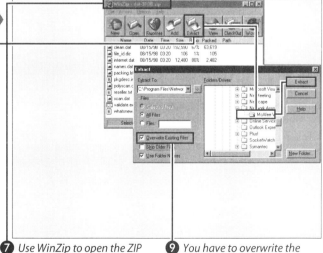

⑤ *If you have to download manually, go to the McAfee Web site.*

⑥ *Choose your download location and save the download file to disk.*

⑦ *Use WinZip to open the ZIP file you downloaded.*

⑧ *Locate the folder holding the antivirus data files and extract.*

⑨ *You have to overwrite the existing data files.*

Personal Workbook

Q&A

1 How are MBR infector viruses spread?

_____

_____

_____

2 How are file infector viruses spread?

_____

_____

_____

3 How are macro viruses spread?

_____

_____

_____

4 What must you do to reliably disinfect a computer?

_____

_____

_____

5 What should you do before booting with your virus emergency disk?

_____

_____

_____

6 How can your disk contain files that haven't been checked for viruses?

_____

_____

_____

7 Why must you update virus definition files?

_____

_____

_____

8 Name two ways to update antivirus software.

_____

_____

_____

ANSWERS: PAGE 346

314

1 If you don't have antivirus software on your computer, install McAfee VirusScan or Data Fellows F-PROT from their Web sites.

2 Update the virus definition files from the Internet.

3 See if your antivirus software includes a test virus (McAfee does). If so, follow the directions to create the file and use it to check your antivirus software for correct operation.

4 Scan all files on all disks on your computer for viruses. Check compressed files too.

5 Make a virus emergency disk with the latest virus definition files.

6 Boot from your virus emergency disk (to make sure it works) and scan your computer.

✔ You receive a file from a coworker that's part of a proposal you're developing for an important customer. You meant to put a virus scanner on your computer, but just haven't had time to do it because this proposal is so urgent. You incorporate the new file, make a few small edits, print, and ship. The next week, the boss calls you in to ask why the customer is finding the word *wazzu* throughout the document.

✔ You receive an e-mail with a program attached. You don't know the sender, so you save the file to disk and scan it with your antivirus software. It comes up clean so you run the program. After realizing your disk is being wiped clean of all files, you belatedly remember that antivirus software won't detect Trojan programs. You call home to report you'll be late.

Visual Quiz

What is this? What's it good for?

_____

_____

_____

_____

_____

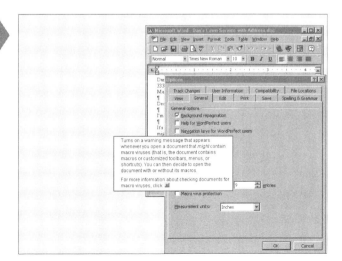

CHAPTER **23**

MASTER
THESE
SKILLS

▶ **Deciding When Something's Wrong with Your Computer**

▶ **Trying the Simple Fixes**

▶ **Making Simple Fixes for Printers**

▶ **Isolating the Problem**

▶ **Figuring Out Whom to Call for Help**

▶ **Calling for Technical Support**

Troubleshooting

Something will eventually go wrong with your computer. We can't predict what or when, but it's as certain that there will be problems as it is that something will eventually break on your car.

The topics for the lessons in this chapter come in the order you want to attack the problem. You first need to decide if something's really wrong; it's possible the hardware or software simply doesn't work the way you expect. If a problem does exist, you can then check to see if some common remedies work. If not, you have to isolate what's wrong, because unless you're working in a large company with an excellent PC support staff, there's no single place to call for help. Once you identify the problem, you need to figure out who can help you. The chapter wraps up with a lesson on getting ready to call for help — assembling the information you're likely to need when you do call.

In a lot of ways, fixing problems with your computer is the same as fixing problems with your car. The more you know about what's wrong, the more likely it is that you can get it fixed. You're going to encounter some support and repair people who are good at what they do and some who are expensive and incompetent. Sadly, there's no reliable way to know the difference up front.

That last point — the difficulty of knowing what's good and what's bad — is what's behind one of the most important principles we try to teach about computers:

Keep track of what works and what doesn't, and of who knows what they're doing and who doesn't. Reward the winners by continuing to buy their products while you punish the losers by avoiding theirs.

We believe this principle to be so important that we sometimes pay more for products we know will work well, and choose products with less than absolute top speed when that benefit comes at the expense of reliability. We have far fewer computer problems than some very knowledgeable people we know, people who always buy the cheapest parts or the fastest components regardless of who made them.

It really comes down to deciding what you want from your computers. We want reliable performance.

Deciding When Something's Wrong with Your Computer

Because computers are complicated machines that perform complex work, they can fail in many different ways. Some are immediately obvious, such as if there's no picture on the screen, while others, such as slow Internet performance, might seem like normal behavior.

The first step when you think something's wrong is to state clearly to yourself what the problem seems to be. It might be that the computer appears to have stopped, that you can't find a file you were working on, that a program won't install, that you can't connect to your ISP, or a million other things. Suppose you state the problem as "I opened Netscape but can't get to the Disney Web page." That's an excellent starting point, because it defines the parts of what you tried to do and the point at which a problem seems to have occurred.

Your next step is to picture the parts of your computer that might be involved. In the Disney example, you know that (at least) your modem, telephone line, ISP, and the Internet have to work to connect your computer to the Disney site. If you reread Chapter 14, you know that some critical software on your computer runs underneath Netscape — the TCP/IP protocol software responsible for transmitting and receiving Internet messages. Knowing about that set of components lets you probe a little deeper to see where the problem might be. For example, you might try to load some other Web page — maybe one for your ISP itself — to see if that works. If it does, chances are that the problem is on the Internet or at the server for the page you want, not at your computer. If so, there's nothing you can do to get the page but wait.

Once you name some of the possible culprits, make sure you're telling the software what it needs to know. For instance, if you try to access the Disney site as **http://www.disnie.com**, the site you get (there is one) has nothing to do with Disney. Computers are very intolerant of incorrect or misspelled commands, but try literally to carry out what you input.

TAKE NOTE

▶ STAY CALM

Don't just throw up your hands when something isn't right with your computer — you won't get anywhere. You can try a number of things and use several tools built into Windows to help you sort out what's wrong. This chapter's lessons show you many of them. More important, stay calm. Your computer is simply a machine, and isn't affected by anger, urgency, or other emotions. You can think much more clearly if you're not spun up.

CROSS-REFERENCE
Start your troubleshooting with the "Trying the Simple Fixes" lesson in this chapter.

FIND IT ONLINE
The Disney Web site is really **http://www.disney.com**.

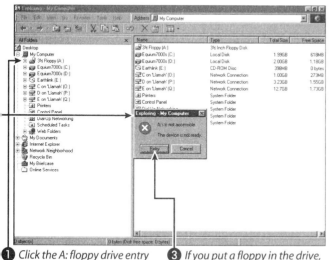

1 Click the A: floppy drive entry in Windows Explorer.

2 The dialog box indicates an access problem — there's no readable floppy in the drive.

3 If you put a floppy in the drive, Retry should read it.

4 Here's a modem problem — no dialtone.

5 The most likely problem is a phone line problem, not a computer problem. Try rebooting if the phone line is okay.

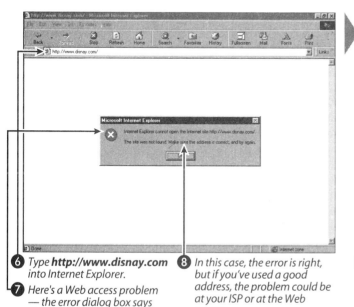

6 Type **http://www.disnay.com** into Internet Explorer.

7 Here's a Web access problem — the error dialog box says the address can't be found.

8 In this case, the error is right, but if you've used a good address, the problem could be at your ISP or at the Web server.

9 Here's a display problem — the left image of the spreadsheet can't display the last computed result. Buggy software?

10 In the right image, we've simply widened column C to make the number in row 7 show up.

Trying the Simple Fixes

If your computer starts to act oddly — programs don't display properly on the screen or normally well-behaved programs crash — try a few simple fixes. The first is to reboot the computer and see what happens. Windows can run out of *resources*, by which we mean some specialized areas in memory that hold key information. If one or another resource area runs low, programs are likely to act strangely or crash.

The next issue to consider is whether you just installed new software. If you did, remove it and see if the problem goes away. If it does, you need to contact the software manufacturer.

If an entire hardware item is dark — the system unit or monitor, for instance — check the power cables and power switch. Check to see if the power is reaching the wall outlet, and verify that the switch on a power strip hasn't been flipped. (That's a lot more common a problem than you might expect!) Check all the data cables to make sure none has been jarred loose, and verify that the air coming from the fan is reasonably cool. Clean the inlets if not.

If Windows won't boot, start your computer with the emergency boot disk and run ScanDisk. If you find cross-linked files in the Windows folder, you're going to want to copy what data you can off the computer, delete the cross-linked files, and reinstall Windows on top of itself. If that recovers the system, count yourself lucky. If not, you have to restore from backups. If ScanDisk finds no problems, boot your emergency virus disk and run that. You can get very erratic behavior from viruses.

Don't be frightened by the recommendation to reinstall Windows on top of itself. With the exception of a few keyboard shortcuts and other settings, the reinstallation should preserve software, data, and settings you already have.

TAKE NOTE

▶ USE THE WINDOWS RESOURCE METER

You can install the Windows Resource Meter with the Add/Remove Programs applet. Put a shortcut to it in C:\Windows\Start Menu\Programs\Startup so it runs every time you boot the computer. The Resource Meter shows up as an icon in the taskbar (you might have to minimize it) that lets you know about available resources. If it gets into the yellow or red area, it's time to reboot.

▶ USE WINDOWS SAFE MODE

If Windows won't start and ScanDisk finds no errors, press F8 when you see Starting Windows and then boot to what's called Safe Mode in the resulting menu. You have a better chance of copying out critical data, and if necessary you can switch to more generic drivers (such as the Standard VGA driver for the display). From Safe Mode, you can also run C:\Windows\Scanregw.exe, a tool to check the Registry for problems.

CROSS-REFERENCE

Install the Resource Meter using the skills in Chapter 9's lesson "Adding and Removing Windows 98 Components."

FIND IT ONLINE

Get more information on Scanreg at **http://support. microsoft.com/support/kb/articles/q183/8/87.asp**.

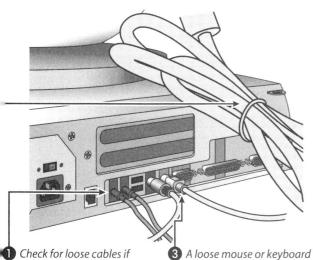

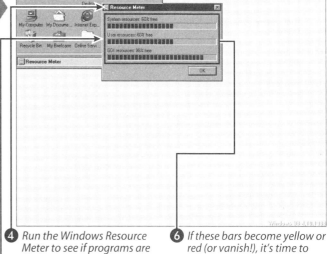

1 Check for loose cables if you're seeing hardware problems.

2 A loose video cable can drop colors from the display or make the image unstable.

3 A loose mouse or keyboard cable can prevent you from controlling the computer.

4 Run the Windows Resource Meter to see if programs are likely to start crashing.

5 System resources is the lesser of the User and GDI resources percentages.

6 If these bars become yellow or red (or vanish!), it's time to reboot.

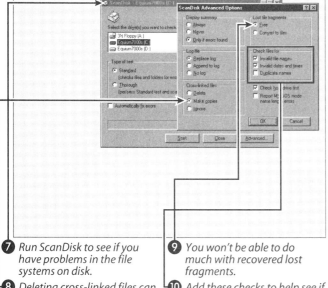

7 Run ScanDisk to see if you have problems in the file systems on disk.

8 Deleting cross-linked files can make a bad problem worse, so make copies.

9 You won't be able to do much with recovered lost fragments.

10 Add these checks to help see if folders have been corrupted.

11 Press F8 when you see Starting Windows while booting; then choose Safe Mode.

12 Safe Mode drops many Windows capabilities so it is more likely to run, letting you troubleshoot problems.

Making Simple Fixes for Printers

The most common problems you can expect to have with printers are also the simplest to fix. Check for power to the printer, that you have paper in the bin, and that the paper isn't damp, curled, or jammed. If garbage is printing, stop all printing (reboot your computer if you must), and cycle power to the printer off and on. Image quality goes bad quickly when printers run out of ink or toner. You must replace empty ink jet cartridges; you can redistribute toner once in a laser printer cartridge (by briskly rotating it) to keep going for awhile. You have to realign the nozzles in some ink jet printers (notably the ones from Hewlett-Packard) when you change cartridges; forget to do so and you'll find that the black print doesn't line up with the colors.

Streaking in ink jet printers can be caused by plugged nozzles, so all ink jet printers have a command to clean the nozzles. A similar operation exists for some laser printers (HP's cleaning utility is at **http://www.hp.com/cposupport/printers/software/ lj123en.exe.html**).

If programs can't print or print incorrectly, you can sometimes solve the problem by deleting and reinstalling the printer driver. Open the Printers folder (choose Start ⇨ Settings ⇨ Printers), select the printer you're having trouble with, and delete it. Then use Add Printer to reinstall the driver. Check the printer manufacturer's Web site for updated drivers if you're still having problems. Check that you have lots of disk space on the drive holding Windows if you're printing large graphics or large documents — printing can use a lot of disk space to hold the output files. If none of these fixes works, see if the problem is isolated to one program or common to all. If it's common to all, the problem is likely in the driver, cable, or printer itself.

TAKE NOTE

▶ **FIX SLOW GRAPHICS PRINTING WITH MORE COMPUTER MEMORY**

If you're printing large graphics files, slow printing can be caused by a lack of memory in the computer. We had a 100-page document printing on an ink jet printer that literally took over 12 hours to print from a machine with 64MB of memory, and it printed in three hours from a machine with 128MB.

▶ **GET ALL THE GRAPHICS RESOLUTION YOUR PRINTER OFFERS**

You can tune drivers for higher-quality graphics output (at the expense of processing time, memory, and disk space) by choosing from coarse, medium, and fine quality. Be sure you're using the highest print resolution the driver offers to improve graphics quality, too. Finer resolution requires more memory for laser printers. If you have only 1 or 2MB, Windows might tell you you're out of printer memory. If so, you have to cut the resolution or upgrade the printer.

CROSS-REFERENCE

See "Maintaining Your Printer" in Chapter 19 for details on keeping your printer purring.

FIND IT ONLINE

HP has a LaserJet print quality troubleshooter at **http://www.hp.com/cpso-support/laserjet/ solutions/prq/home.html**.

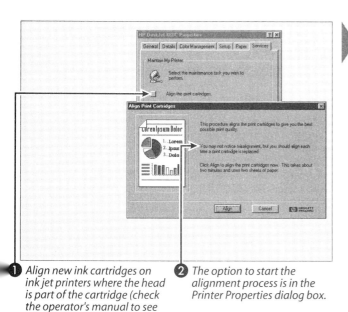

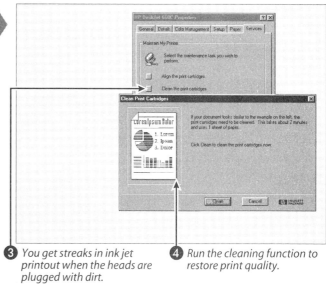

1 *Align new ink cartridges on ink jet printers where the head is part of the cartridge (check the operator's manual to see what type you have).*

2 *The option to start the alignment process is in the Printer Properties dialog box.*

3 *You get streaks in ink jet printout when the heads are plugged with dirt.*

4 *Run the cleaning function to restore print quality.*

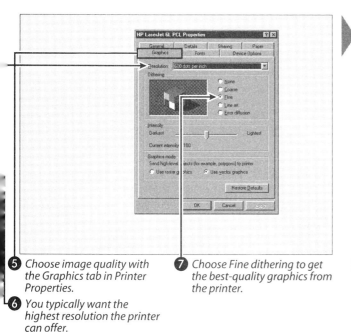

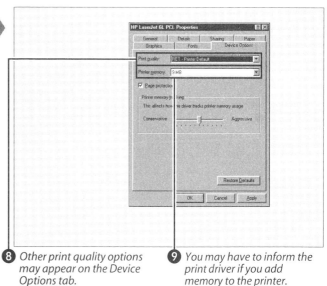

5 *Choose image quality with the Graphics tab in Printer Properties.*

6 *You typically want the highest resolution the printer can offer.*

7 *Choose Fine dithering to get the best-quality graphics from the printer.*

8 *Other print quality options may appear on the Device Options tab.*

9 *You may have to inform the print driver if you add memory to the printer.*

Isolating the Problem

If the simple fixes don't solve your problem, you're probably going to need help from your system or software manufacturer. Some system manufacturers do quite well with support, but if you have a good understanding of what's going, it helps the service technician work with you.

What you want to do is to reproduce the problem reliably with as little else going on as possible. The first step is to reboot the computer and try to discover the shortest sequence of actions you can take that makes the problem happen. Once you do, you want to pin the problem down to one of these categories:

- ▶ **Hardware** — If the system gives you error messages such as "No operating system found" or "Memory parity error" before Windows tries to start, you have a hardware problem. If you're getting read errors from a floppy disk or CD-ROM, try another disk. Use the Device Manager (choose Start ⇨ Settings ⇨ Control Panel ⇨ System ⇨ Device Manager) to look for conflicts. If you see any lines marked with red or yellow icons, the marked device may be involved in your problem.

- ▶ **Software** — If the problem is limited to a specific application, see if a specific sequence of commands and operations causes the problem.

- ▶ **Network** — If your problem is related to the Internet, see if other network operations work or if all network access is failing. Try to pin the problem down to a specific application, Web site, or operation.

You can try cleaning a dirty CD with a soft, lint-free cloth. If the CD is unreadable anyway and just a cloth doesn't work, try a cloth and Windex.

If your computer can't boot into Windows, first try booting into Safe Mode (press F8 at Starting Windows and choose Safe Mode). If this fails, try booting from your emergency boot disk and checking the C: drive with ScanDisk. If the emergency boot disk can't boot, you definitely need hardware help.

Your best tool for isolating Internet problems is *ping*, a program built into Windows you can run from a DOS window. Try pinging your ISP's Web server. If this works, you know the modem and communication software are working. If not, but you can hear the modem connect, you may have an Internet configuration problem your ISP could help solve.

TAKE NOTE

▶ **BACK UP CONFIGURATION FILES FIRST**

If Windows is operational, make a backup of your current system configuration files before you start changing things. Go to the General tab in the System Configuration Utility and click Create Backup. This way, even if you do something disastrous, you can recover using Safe Mode and the Restore Backup button.

CROSS-REFERENCE

Once you isolate the problem, move on to "Figuring Out Whom to Call for Help" later in this chapter.

FIND IT ONLINE

Find the Microsoft troubleshooting wizards at **http://support.microsoft.com/support/tshoot/**

Learn from a Friend

The sheer complexity of what goes into computers makes them extremely hard to troubleshoot from the other end of a phone line. If you have a friend who's good with computers, ask for some help isolating what's wrong. You're likely to get an answer sooner, and gain valuable knowledge in the process. Keep your eyes open, though. There's no shortage of "experts" who start changing things before they really know what's going on. That's not a good idea.

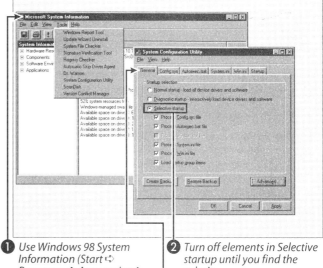

① *Use Windows 98 System Information (Start ➪ Programs ➪ Accessories ➪ System Tools ➪ System Information) to get system details for tech support.*

② *Turn off elements in Selective startup until you find the culprit.*

③ *Adjust specifics of the problem element in the corresponding tab.*

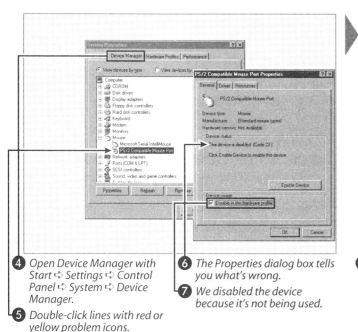

④ *Open Device Manager with Start ➪ Settings ➪ Control Panel ➪ System ➪ Device Manager.*

⑤ *Double-click lines with red or yellow problem icons.*

⑥ *The Properties dialog box tells you what's wrong.*

⑦ *We disabled the device because it's not being used.*

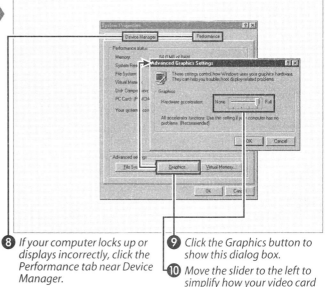

⑧ *If your computer locks up or displays incorrectly, click the Performance tab near Device Manager.*

⑨ *Click the Graphics button to show this dialog box.*

⑩ *Move the slider to the left to simplify how your video card is used.*

Figuring Out Whom to Call for Help

By default, when anything goes wrong you could call the manufacturer who built your system. The manufacturer's support group might help or might walk you through some diagnosis before referring you to some other company. A lot of people use just such an approach.

You can do better. You can check Web sites for such solutions as updates, patches for applications, and drivers — and you can search the same Web sites for information on known problems. You can isolate problems down to the failing component and call that manufacturer directly. You can know when your problem is the Internet, not your computer.

If all else fails and you do need to call for technical support, whom you actually call depends on a lot of factors. Some manufacturers work hard at technical support, while others work hard merely to reduce their support costs. It won't take long for you to sort out which is which. In order, here's who we recommend you call:

1. **The specific product manufacturer or your ISP.** If you can narrow down the fault to a specific application or device (such as a printer or modem), call the manufacturer. If you have an Internet problem, call your ISP.
2. **Your system manufacturer.** Typically, the system manufacturer recognizes the need to support customers no matter what their problem. You might be referred to other manufacturers for hardware or software you've installed, which could lead to a tedious phone chase.
3. **Microsoft.** If you appear to have a problem with Windows itself, and you didn't get your copy of Windows from your system manufacturer, try calling Microsoft using information from the company's Web site.

Finding the tech support phone number for a company isn't always easy. The 80+ page vendor list in our book *PC Upgrade and Repair Bible, Professional Edition* (IDG Books Worldwide) took months of digging to develop — it's surprising the number of companies that don't make their tech support phone numbers easy to locate. If you don't have an organized vendor list available, one of your best resources is a directory such as Yahoo!, or simply trying the company's name to see if the company's Web site has the same name.

TAKE NOTE

▶ HAVE LOTS OF TIME WHEN YOU CALL FOR TECH SUPPORT

Companies spend plenty of money on tech support, so they try to balance staffing against the expected load. Often, you spend a lot of time waiting on hold. If you have to hang up, you go back to the end of the line when you call again. Expect to need a lot of time once you get through, too. You can reduce the time by being well prepared (see the next lesson in this chapter).

CROSS-REFERENCE

See Chapter 15's lesson "Searching the Web" for help with finding manufacturers' Web sites.

FIND IT ONLINE

One of the best resources is Microsoft Support. Search it at **http://support.microsoft.com/support/c.asp**.

System Manufacturers

Acer

http://www.acer.com/

http://www.acer.com/aac/support/index.htm

Acer Aspire: (800) 938-2237

AcerPower or AcerEntra: (800) 445-6495

AST

http://www.ast.com

http://www.ast.com/support

U.S. and Canada (800) 727-1278

Compaq

http://www.compaq.com

http://www.compaq.com/support/index.html

U.S. and Canada: (800) 652-6672

Dell

http://www.dell.com

http://support.dell.com/support/calldell.asp

Tech Support: (888) 560-8324

Gateway

http://www.gateway.com/

(800) 846-2000

Hewlett-Packard

http://www.hp.com/

http://www.hp.com/cposupport/eschome.html

Phone numbers: http://www.hp.com/

cpso-support/guide/psd/cscus.html (800) 322-4772

IBM

http://www.pc.ibm.com/

http://www.pc.ibm.com/support/

IBM Help Center: (800) 772-2227

Micron

http://www.micronpc.com/

http://www.micronpc.com/support/

(800) 209-9686

Packard Bell NEC

http://www.packardbell.com/

http://support.packardbell.com/

In warranty only: (888) 215-6015 or (888) 215-6020

Sony

http://www.ita.sel.sony.com/

http://www.ita.sel.sony.com/support/pc

(888) 476-6972

Toshiba

http://www.toshiba.com/

http://www.csd.toshiba.com/tais/csd/support/Service

Support.html

(800) 400-4172

Calling for Technical Support

The first thing to do, before you pick up the phone, is to gather all the information you can about your computer. This includes the model, version, and serial number of the computer, cards you've installed, and relevant software. Try Help ⇨ About to get support information for software. PCs often have stickers on the back, while cards you install may have a sticker on the card itself. (It's much easier if you record the model and serial numbers when you install a card; nice to think of that now, eh?) Make sure you've worked through the suggestions in "Trying the Simple Fixes" earlier in this chapter, too.

You can print your current system configuration from Device Manager. Take the time to print out this information when the system is working properly because the hardware configuration data it contains may be useful information for tech support when things go wrong. Tech support may want the BIOS manufacturer and date; the most reliable way to get this information is to watch the startup information when the machine boots.

Tech support generally asks for some facts, and then starts asking you to change settings or run sequences of commands. Some of what they ask you to try may not make sense to you. Keep in mind that almost all tech support desks work from a knowledge base similar to what exists on the Microsoft site, and that they have scripts that lead them through different types of problems. Because the scripts are generalized to the variety of problems they see, and because their standard procedure is to follow the scripts, you're likely to be asked to work through tests that aren't directly in line with your problem. Stick with it — it's simply how the industry works, and it will help you in the long run.

Your call is assigned a case number when you call for help, which is an identifier in the tech support database. Ask for the case number before you hang up and write it down, so if you need to call back, you can help the next technician find what the prior one wrote into the database. Having this information available helps keep your issue moving forward without needlessly repeating tests.

TAKE NOTE

▶ BE CALM AND BE PATIENT

Computer tech support is one of the hardest jobs there is. Techs are trying to solve complex problems with limited information and are working with people who are often untrained and under lots of stress. You can get a lot further with calm cooperation than antagonism.

▶ ESCALATE IF YOU NEED TO

Tech support desks operate in levels. Backing up the front-line techs are more skilled, higher-level techs. If you've worked through everything the front-line tech had to try and still don't have a fix, ask to escalate.

CROSS-REFERENCE

The previous lesson, "Figuring Out Whom to Call for Help," showed how to decide whom you need to call.

FIND IT ONLINE

Find an example of what a support database looks like at **http://www.supportsource.com/demos/sampler.htm**.

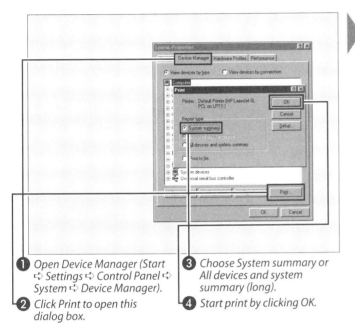

1 Open Device Manager (Start ⇨ Settings ⇨ Control Panel ⇨ System ⇨ Device Manager).

2 Click Print to open this dialog box.

3 Choose System summary or All devices and system summary (long).

4 Start print by clicking OK.

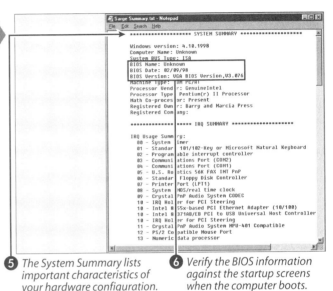

5 The System Summary lists important characteristics of your hardware configuration.

6 Verify the BIOS information against the startup screens when the computer boots.

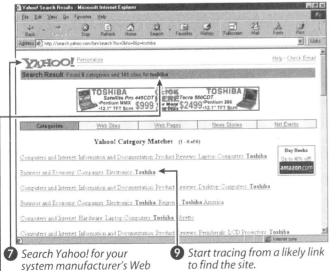

7 Search Yahoo! for your system manufacturer's Web site.

8 We used Toshiba as a search term.

9 Start tracing from a likely link to find the site.

10 The PC support site is often down from the overall company site for large manufacturers.

11 Choose Service & Support first, and then the specific product.

Personal Workbook

Q&A

1 What's the first step you should take when something seems wrong with your computer?

_____

_____

_____

2 What's the second step in troubleshooting?

_____

_____

_____

3 What can you do once you identify the parts that are involved in the problem?

_____

_____

_____

4 What should you check if an entire device won't work?

_____

_____

_____

5 What can you do if Windows won't start?

_____

_____

_____

6 What can you do about cross-linked files?

_____

_____

_____

7 What should you try if your system won't start and the disk checks out okay?

_____

_____

_____

8 How can you try to make Windows start if the disk checks out okay?

_____

_____

_____

EXTRA PRACTICE

1 Install and start the Resource Meter. Look at the levels it reports when you first boot the computer, after you start different applications, and after you close them.

2 Make an emergency boot disk (choose Start ⇨ Settings ⇨ Control Panel ⇨ Add/Remove Programs ⇨ Startup Disk). Boot it to verify that it works, and run ScanDisk to see what happens under normal circumstances.

3 Open an MS-DOS window (choose Start ⇨ Programs ⇨ MS-DOS Prompt) and run **ping www.idgbooks.com**. Then, run **tracert www.idgbooks.com**. What does each program show?

REAL-WORLD APPLICATIONS

✔ You're trying to print a presentation for a new client, but your software refuses to print. You reboot and try again, but it still fails. You delete the printer driver, reboot, and install it again. The presentation prints and you make it to the meeting.

✔ Your computer is running normally, but you run ScanDisk from Windows to see what happens. You find tens of lost file fragments. You recall that there have been power failures recently, and realize that the lost fragments may well have come from those crashes.

✔ You power up your computer and receive a "Memory Parity Error" message. You call the system manufacturer, which sends you replacement memory modules and walks you through the task of replacing the old ones.

Visual Quiz

What have we done here? How might this help you diagnose Internet problems?

_____

_____

_____

_____

_____

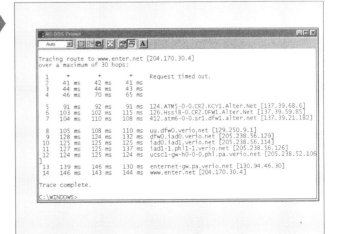

Personal Workbook
Answers

Chapter 1

see page 4

1 **What's the difference between CD-ROM and DVD?**

A: DVD is an advanced CD-ROM technology suitable for movies and other applications requiring over ten times the capacity of a CD-ROM. CD-ROM and DVD equipment and discs look much the same.

2 **Describe the use for each of these connectors: video, monitor power, speakers, microphone, keyboard, and mouse.**

A: The video connector sends the display image from computer to monitor. Monitor power provides power to the monitor electronics. The speaker connector outputs sound from the computer to the speakers. The microphone connector inputs sound from a microphone for recording by the computer. The keyboard connector inputs keystrokes from the keyboard to the computer. The mouse connector inputs mouse movement and button clicks from the mouse to the computer.

3 **What is a *BIOS,* and what does it do?**

A: When power comes on, the BIOS, or Basic Input/Output System, initializes the system and loads the operating system.

4 **What can a surge protector do for you? What about a UPS?**

A: A surge protector can isolate your computer and monitor from out-of-limits voltages due to other electrical equipment or lightning strikes. A UPS does everything that a surge protector does, and also gives you a few minutes of power to save your work if the utility power goes out.

5 **How much video memory do you need to run High Color mode on a display with a 1,280 × 1,024 resolution?**

A: High color is 2 bytes for each dot on the screen. Two bytes multiplied by the screen resolution is $2 \times 1{,}280 \times 1{,}024 = 2{,}621{,}440$ bytes. Because one megabyte is $1{,}024 \times 1{,}024$ bytes, you need 2.5MB of video memory. This is why you can't have that resolution with 2MB video memory.

6 **What happens when you hit the F8 key at the end of the BIOS initialization?**

A: It brings up a menu system that you can use to troubleshoot problems with your PC.

7 **How do you access popup menus to gather information or execute a command in Windows?**

A: Click the right mouse button when the mouse pointer is over an object on which you want to perform an action.

Personal Workbook Answers

⑧ **What happens if the cooling airflow to your computer gets blocked by dust?**

A: Your computer can overheat, which can lead to failure of the processor, memory, or other components, causing you to lose work and requiring expensive repairs.

Visual Quiz

Q: Describe the number of pins and gender of this connector. What signals will go through the connector? Will you find it on the system unit or on a cable?

A: It's a 15-pin female connector used for VGA signals to the monitor. You find it on the back of the system unit.

Chapter 2

see page 18

❶ **Name components of the WordPad window that you're likely to find in other Windows programs and state what they do.**

A: Title bar: shows the running program and contains icons for window control. System icons (in title bar): provide access to the system menu and control of maximize, minimize, and close program functions. Menu bar: provides access to menu commands. Toolbar: provides quick graphical access to commands with the mouse. Windows edges: provides capability to resize the window. Scroll bar: provides capability to reach parts of the file not onscreen.

❷ **Identify the toolbar icons for File ⇨ New and File ⇨ Open.**

A: They are the left and next-to-left icons, respectively.

❸ **Notepad is a simpler text editing program than WordPad. Where is Notepad in the Start button menu?**

A: Start ⇨ Programs ⇨ Accessories ⇨ Notepad.

❹ **What window elements are common between WordPad and Notepad?**

A: Title bar and icons, menu bar, window edges, and scroll bar.

❺ **Notepad has a Search menu on the menu bar. What and where are the equivalent commands in WordPad?**

A: Edit ⇨ Find and Edit ⇨ Find Next.

❻ **What are the WordPad keyboard shortcuts for File ⇨ Save, File ⇨ Open, and Edit ⇨ Find?**

A: For File ⇨ Save: Ctrl+S. For File ⇨ Open: Ctrl+O. For Edit ⇨ Find: Ctrl+F.

❼ **Is the Edit ⇨ Find keyboard shortcut in WordPad the same as Search ⇨ Find in Notepad?**

A: No. Edit ⇨ Find is Ctrl+F, while Search ⇨ Find has no shortcut.

Visual Quiz

Q: This is a shot of a page in WordPad help under Windows 98. Find the equivalent page on your system, either in Windows 95 or 98.

A: We reached this page by choosing Help ⇨ Help Topics, selecting the Index tab, typing tab stops, clicking Display, and choosing "To set or remove tab stops in paragraphs."

Chapter 3

see page 30

❶ **Name the two most common printer technologies in use today.**

A: Ink-jet and laser.

❷ **Name the common printer connection types.**

A: Parallel, serial, network, and infrared.

Personal Workbook Answers

3 How long should a parallel printer cable be?

A: Ten to fifteen feet.

4 Why are four-color ink-jet printers superior to ones using only three?

A: Lower per-page printing costs, because the black cartridge does most of the work and holds more ink.

5 What should you do when a laser printer toner cartridge starts streaking or missing print?

A: Remove it, rotate it briskly forward and back, and place it back into the printer.

6 How can you recycle printer cartridges?

A: Use the shipping label that's often included, or check the manufacturer's Web site.

7 How many pins are on a printer parallel connector (the computer end)? And on a serial connector?

A: On the parallel connector, 25 (36 on the printer end). On the serial connector, 25 or 9.

8 What can happen if you disconnect a parallel printer with the power on?

A: You can damage the computer or printer interface, requiring professional (and possibly expensive) repairs.

Visual Quiz

Q: What happened here? Where would you look if trouble occurs?

A: The printer has gone offline, meaning it's no longer ready to print. Check to see if it needs more paper in the input bin or if it has run out of ink.

Chapter 4

see page 42

1 What are the differences between hard and floppy disks?

A: Hard disks hold far more information, but typically can't be taken out of the computer without disassembling the machine. Floppy disks hold only a few million characters, but are designed to be removed and carried around.

2 What kind of file should you expect to have a .doc extension?

A: Documents written with a word processor, such as Microsoft Word.

3 Suppose the one-pane Windows Explorer is the default when you double-click My Computer. Name two ways to start the two-pane Explorer.

A: Right-click My Computer and choose Explore, or press Windows+E.

4 How big is your Windows folder (including subfolders)?

A: Get the answer with subfolders using the properties dialog box for the Windows folder. Anything in the range of 100MB to 500MB is likely.

5 How big is the file GENERAL.TXT in the Windows folder? How much space does it really occupy?

A: Under Windows 98, our version was 38.9K (kilobytes, thousands of bytes). It used 65,536 bytes (64K) on a 2GB drive. It's also plausible for it to require 40K on a 2GB drive.

PERSONAL WORKBOOK ANSWERS

6 How big is the disk in your computer? Do you have more than one?

A: Typical drive sizes in recently-built computers run from 2 to 4GB. Older machines running Windows may have drives in the 200MB range and higher. It's unusual to see a personal computer with more than 9GB of disk space. If you're running a recent version of Windows, you may only have one drive letter. Older versions might divide large disks up into 2GB partitions.

7 A vertical bar appears to the left of the menu bar and other bars in Windows 98. What happens if you drag the bar?

A: The bar moves to where you drag it. That's how we moved the Address bar in Windows Explorer next to the menu bar in some of the figures in this chapter.

8 Turn off the display of file extensions in Windows Explorer (View ⇨ Folder Options ⇨ View) and look at the files in C:\Windows. How can you tell what kinds of files you're looking at?

A: Use the Details view in Explorer and look at the type column.

Visual Quiz

Q: Find the file ARIAL.TTF on your computer. Do you get this window when you double-click the file?

A: The file should be in C:\Windows\Fonts. You should see this window when you double-click the file. If not, you may have a copy of the file not in the Fonts folder.

Chapter 5

see page 58

1 Name two ports that are used to connect mice to your computer.

A: Serial and PS/2. Extra credit: Infrared or USB.

2 Name the potentially dangerous Control Panel applets.

A: Add/Remove Programs, Display, Internet, Add New Hardware, Network, and System.

3 What's the most common mouse connector style in computers now being made?

A: PS/2, with six pins.

4 Under Windows 98, Internet Explorer and WordPad are different in how they respond to the mouse-wheel scrolling operation. What's the difference, and how can you tell?

A: Internet Explorer only scrolls vertically; WordPad scrolls in all four directions. You can tell by the arrows on the starting point indicator that Windows leaves onscreen.

5 There's a key on a Windows keyboard that looks like a menu with a mouse cursor on it. What happens when you push it? What's it equivalent to?

A: The key does the same thing for the selected item as the right mouse button.

6 What is the most common use for the mouse wheel?

A: Scrolling windows.

7 What commonly happens when you push Ctrl or Shift and roll the mouse wheel?

A: The onscreen image zooms in and out.

8 What are the common problems caused by dirt in the mouse?

A: Jumping of the mouse cursor; refusing to go further in one direction.

PERSONAL WORKBOOK ANSWERS

Visual Quiz

Q: How can you use the mouse to select multiple items on the desktop, as shown here?

A: Left-click the desktop in one corner of the selection rectangle, and then hold the left button down and drag to form a selection rectangle.

Chapter 6

see page 74

❶ **What's the layout on your keyboard? What's an alternative?**

A: Most keyboards use QWERTY, with Dvorak being the most common alternative.

❷ **What are function keys and what are they used for?**

A: Function keys are the keys marked F1 to F12. They commonly trigger specific program operations.

❸ **What's the default drag action for files and folders within one drive? From one drive to another?**

A: The default is to move files on the same drive, and to copy files across drives.

❹ **What's the Start button sequence to open Windows Explorer? The Windows key?**

A: Start ⇨ Programs ⇨ Windows Explorer. Windows+E.

❺ **What's the Windows key to open the Run dialog box?**

A: Windows+R.

❻ **What does Windows+M do?**

A: Minimizes all open windows.

❼ **How do you reverse Windows+M?**

A: Windows+Shift+M.

❽ **In Windows 98, how can you help people with low vision see what's onscreen?**

A: Install the accessibility options and tools, and then run Magnifier.

Visual Quiz

Q: How do you get to this dialog box?

A: Choose Start ⇨ Settings ⇨ Control Panel ⇨ Add/Remove Programs ⇨ Windows Setup ⇨ Accessibility ⇨ Details.

Chapter 7

see page 88

❶ **What is the default Windows screen resolution?**

A: 640 × 480.

❷ **What can you control from the Control Panel Display applet's Appearance tab?**

A: Window and background colors, fonts, and sizes.

❸ **What can you control from the Display applet's Effects tab?**

A: Choice of desktop icons, icon colors and size, font smoothing, and window visibility while dragging.

❹ **How do you control Active Desktop, making your desktop look like a Web page?**

A: Use the Web tab in the Display applet.

❺ **How can you save your desktop appearance, sound scheme, icons, screen saver, and mouse pointers?**

A: Use desktop themes.

❻ **How do you set mouse pointers? Screen savers?**

A: With the Mouse Control Panel applet; with the Display Control Panel applet.

PERSONAL WORKBOOK ANSWERS

7 How can you avoid switching your monitor on and off to reduce power consumption?

A: Use the Power Management Control Panel applet.

8 How can you recover from the loss of your screen saver password?

A: Delete the file with the .pwl extension from C:\Windows.

Visual Quiz

Q: What were we doing here? What went wrong?

A: We clicked Start ➪ Settings ➪ Control Panel ➪ Display ➪ Screen Saver, enabled Password protected, and clicked Settings. Finally, we typed different passwords in the New password and Confirm new password fields.

Chapter 8

1 Name the types of sound your computer can handle.

A: Wave audio, MIDI, audio CD, microphone, and external stereo.

2 Name two types of speaker connections.

A: Analog audio and USB.

3 Why does speaker location matter?

A: Good speaker location gives you good stereo separation and avoids magnetic degradation of your monitor's image.

4 What characterizes a good sound clip for use with a Windows event?

A: A short duration (so it doesn't interrupt your system while it plays) and reminiscent of the meaning of the event.

5 What Windows events should you avoid giving sounds?

A: Open and Close Program.

6 How do you open the sound mixer applet?

A: Double-click the speaker icon in the taskbar, or go through the Multimedia Control Panel applet.

7 How can you quickly mute sounds on your computer?

A: Use the Mute checkbox in the mixer or master volume control, or turn off the speakers.

8 What's the difference between *wave audio* and *MIDI*?

A: Wave audio records the actual sounds; MIDI records the instruments and their notes.

Visual Quiz

Q: What did we do to get this message?

A: We changed the value in the Name control to be None instead of a sound file, which removes all sounds from the event.

Chapter 9

see page 122

1 What's a *Dynamic Link Library*?

A: Programs and data that can be shared among several programs.

2 What's a common source of install and uninstall problems?

A: DLL conflicts.

3 What important step should you take before installing or uninstalling programs?

A: Close all programs running on your computer.

4 **What's the first thing you should do before installing a program?**

A: Look for and read any readme files on the distribution disks.

5 **How are the installed components chosen for a typical installation type?**

A: The software manufacturer decides and builds these choices into the installer.

6 **How are the installed components chosen for a custom installation type?**

A: You choose, based on dialog boxes following the installation type dialog box.

7 **What's the most common top-level folder for program installation?**

A: C:\Program Files.

8 **What's a *startup disk*?**

A: A floppy disk you can boot with if Windows won't start.

Visual Quiz

Q: **What's happening here? How did we get this dialog box?**

A: This is the Add/Remove Programs applet right after we clicked the Install button you see in the figure. It's ready to go look on floppy disks or CD-ROMs for an installation program.

Chapter 10

see page 134

1 **What can you do if you don't find WordPad or Paint on your system?**

A: Use the Add/Remove Programs applet to install them.

2 **What is *TrueType*?**

A: A technology that enables fonts of different sizes to be synthesized as you need them.

3 **How do you install new fonts?**

A: Drag and drop the TTF file into C:\Windows\Fonts.

4 **When should you avoid using tab stops?**

A: For sequences of more than one tab or space character.

5 **Why might fonts in documents look funny on another machine?**

A: The fonts are stored in Windows, and usually not in the document; the other machine might not have them installed.

6 **What file types can Paint handle?**

A: BMP, GIF, and JPG/JPEG.

7 **What can go on a CD-ROM?**

A: Most anything your computer can handle, including data, audio, and video.

8 **What track holds the information in a mixed data/video CD-ROM?**

A: Track 1.

Visual Quiz

Q: **What is this dialog box? How do you get to it?**

A: This is the Playlist dialog box in the Plus! Pack CD Player. Click Options ⇨ Playlist.

Personal Workbook Answers

Chapter 11

see page 146

❶ List some things a word processor can do that a typewriter can't.

A: Different views of your document, formatting, revisions, and spelling checks.

❷ What does *WYSIWYG* stand for?

A: What You See Is What You Get. It's a way of saying that what you see onscreen is exactly the same as what you'll see on the page when you print the document.

❸ What message might you get if two programs (or computers) try to open the same file?

A: You might be told by the second program that the file is in use.

❹ What are some examples of character formats? Paragraph formats?

A: Character formats: bold, italic, underline, font, font size. Paragraph formats: justification, spacing, indents, page breaks.

❺ What are *document templates*?

A: Files that hold styles you can attach to documents.

❻ How do you make gridlines print in tables?

A: Add borders with Table ⇨ Table Autoformat.

❼ Can you edit graphics in Word?

A: Yes, Word has a picture editor. However, we recommend using separate programs such as PowerPoint, Photoshop, or Illustrator.

❽ Can you embed MIDI and WAV files into Word documents?

A: Yes.

Visual Quiz

Q: We've made no alterations to this screen shot. How did we make Word look like this?

A: Maximize the document window within Word and then use View ⇨ Full Screen.

Chapter 12

see page 158

❶ What keystroke combination can you use to move to cell A1?

A: Ctrl+Home.

❷ How do you bring up the shortcut menu?

A: Right-click with the mouse.

❸ What tool automatically totals a column or row of numbers?

A: AutoSum.

❹ What are *functions* in Excel?

A: Computations you can use in formulas that take arguments and return a result.

❺ What is the term for putting a chart in a spreadsheet?

A: Embedding the chart.

❻ What's the easiest way to build a chart?

A: Use the Chart Wizard.

❼ What command lets you apply preformatted table styles?

A: Edit ⇨ AutoFormat.

❽ What two formats make numbers appear with a $?

A: Currency and Accounting.

PERSONAL WORKBOOK ANSWERS

Visual Quiz

Q: What happens when you click OK?

A: The X axis drops down to the −20,000 line.

Chapter 13

see page 170

1 **What's the typical maximum transmission speed for a standalone fax machine? For a computer fax?**

A: 9.6 Kbps and 14.4 Kbps, respectively.

2 **What's a *CSID*?**

A: The Calling Station ID, which tells the remote fax machine your fax number.

3 **What problems can a nonnumeric CSID cause?**

A: Standalone fax machines might reject the call or disconnect.

4 **How can you send a fax from Word?**

A: Choose the fax machine as the printer and then print the document.

5 **How should you use fonts for faxes?**

A: Avoid small sizes, and bold the smaller sizes you do use.

6 **What does *OCR* stand for? What does it do?**

A: Optical character recognition; it converts pictures of text to editable text.

7 **How can you check the status of an outgoing fax?**

A: Look in the Outgoing Log, or if it's not there, look in the Send Log.

8 **How can you delete a fax queued to be sent in WinFax?**

A: Select the fax in the Outbox, and then use Edit ➪ Remove.

Visual Quiz

Q: This is a blowup of a fax in the WinFax viewer. How did we zoom in like this?

A: Use the zoom control in the lower-left part of the window frame.

Chapter 14

see page 184

1 **What's a *modem*?**

A: A device that sends and receives computer data over a phone line.

2 **Name two critical precautions when opening up your computer.**

A: Use an antistatic wrist strap and document everything as it is before you change it.

3 **What can you do if Windows Plug-and-Play doesn't detect your modem?**

A: Let the Modems Control Panel applet search for the modem.

4 **Where does Windows keep dial-up network setups?**

A: In the Dial-Up Networking folder.

5 **How often should you change your password?**

A: Every one or two months, or when you think it might have been compromised.

6 **What can you do with AOL software?**

A: Read e-mail, news, and articles, chat with people, and get to the Web.

7 **Why would you use AOL instead of a conventional ISP?**

A: To get a more packaged, simpler access to the Internet and to services unique to AOL.

Personal Workbook Answers

8 **How does your modem affect playing games over the Internet?**

A: Slower modems, or ones not using the 56 Kbps V.90 standard, slow down response and make play hesitant.

Visual Quiz

Q: **What are we doing here? Why might we do this?**

A: We've set AOL billing (keyword BILLING) for a less expensive rate. We would do that because we have a fast connection via our existing ISP.

Chapter 15

see page 202

1 **What are the two most popular Web browsers?**

A: Microsoft Internet Explorer and Netscape Communicator.

2 **What is a *start page*?**

A: The page that appears when you first open the browser.

3 **What is a collection of Web pages called?**

A: A Web site.

4 **Where do you type the Web site address to go to a different Web site?**

A: In the Address box or Netsite box.

5 **What do Favorites/Bookmarks do?**

A: They enable you to mark a Web site and later go to that Web site quickly by picking it from the Favorites or Bookmarks drop-down list.

6 **What does *URL* stand for?**

A: Uniform Resource Locator.

7 **What are some popular Web search engines or Web search tools?**

A: Yahoo!, AltaVista, Excite, Infoseek, Lycos, Dogpile, and Ask Jeeves.

8 **What does it mean when the mouse pointer turns into a pointing finger?**

A: That the button, text, or graphic you are pointing to is linked to another page or another Web site. You can click the button, text, or graphic and go to that page or Web site.

Visual Quiz

Q: **Go to http://www.mapsonus.com and plan a route from Rapid City, South Dakota, to Chicago, Illinois. Does the result look like this? What happens when you click the map?**

A: It zooms in around the point where you click.

Chapter 16

see page 218

1 **What is a *start page*?**

A: The Web page initially displayed when you open a Web browser.

2 **What security hazards do browsers usually protect you from?**

A: Most browsers warn you when you are in danger of downloading content that might contain a computer virus. They also can encrypt your personal information so it can't be viewed by third parties.

PERSONAL WORKBOOK ANSWERS

3 **Does content screening software guarantee that objectionable material cannot be downloaded to your computer?**

A: No, content screening programs can make mistakes and won't know about new sites coming online after their lists were created. The only guarantee is close supervision.

4 **What is a *browser plug-in*?**

A: An additional software component that adds new features to your existing Web browser.

5 **What is the default text color in most Web browsers?**

A: Default text is black in most browsers, with blue to show hyperlinks and purple to indicate links that you've already visited.

6 **Can you print a Web page? How?**

A: You can print a Web page by clicking the browser's Print button on the toolbar. You might have to adjust colors.

7 **What is the *browser disk cache*?**

A: The disk cache stores downloaded Internet files displayed by your browser.

8 **How do you erase history records in a Web browser?**

A: Open the Preferences or Internet Options dialog box and look for a button marked Clear history.

Visual Quiz

Q: **How do you link to an item that you visited yesterday?**

A: Click the History button and then click the Yesterday item.

Chapter 17

see page 238

1 **What can you send via electronic mail?**

A: You can send practically any file in your computer, including text, voice, video, and other files.

2 **What does an e-mail address look like?**

A: name@server.

3 **If you have the account *zorro* with AOL, what's your e-mail address? (Hint: the AOL server is aol.com.)**

A: zorro@aol.com.

4 **What's the password for your *zorro* account?**

A: We have no idea, and neither should anyone else. No one legitimate will ever ask for your password.

5 **What are the common e-mail server types? How do you find out which you use?**

A: POP3 and IMAP (incoming), and SMTP (outgoing). Ask your ISP.

6 **What cautions should you observe when writing e-mail?**

A: Remember that jokes, sarcasm, and other humor are often misinterpreted.

7 **Who can read the e-mail you send?**

A: Besides the addressee, there's no way to know. Assume that anyone can.

8 **What do you need to make your e-mail secure?**

A: A digital certificate that lets you encrypt messages.

343

Personal Workbook Answers

Visual Quiz

Q: What are we doing here? How might you use a signature?

A: This is the dialog box from Tools ⇨ Options ⇨ Signatures. We're using it to set up an automatic signature to be appended to e-mail we write. It's useful for adding your e-mail and Web address at the end of a message.

Chapter 18

see page 252

1 What kinds of files can you download from a Web page?

A: You can download virtually any kind of file you want from a Web page.

2 What is the best way to send a word processing document to a distant coworker?

A: Attach the file to an e-mail message.

3 How can you deal with limitations on sending files in e-mail?

A: Try to keep the size of files sent in e-mails as small as possible, and make sure that your e-mail account and the recipient's account allow attached files.

4 How can you tell if an e-mail message you receive contains an attached file?

A: File attachments appear as icons in the message.

5 Can you make a file smaller before you send it? How?

A: Yes. The best way to reduce the size of a file is to compress it with a program such as WinZip.

6 Is it a good idea to open attachment files directly from within the e-mail message?

A: Not usually. If possible, scan all incoming files with virus scanning software before you open them.

7 What is a *Trojan*?

A: A Trojan is a program that appears to perform one seemingly harmless task while actually performing another, potentially harmful one.

8 Can your computer be infected by simply opening an e-mail message?

A: No. It is impossible for your computer to get infected with a virus by simply opening an e-mail message.

Visual Quiz

Q: Is the attachment to this message virus-free?

A: You can't tell if it's free of viruses by looking; you have to run a scanner with up-to-date virus definition files.

Chapter 19

see page 268

1 What's the first thing to do when you're upgrading software?

A: Back up your system.

2 What happens to chips that get too hot?

A: They fail.

3 What happens when dust accumulates on electronics?

A: It blocks airflow and acts as an insulator.

4 Where's the best place to look for software patches and updates?

A: On the manufacturer's Web site.

5 **What's the last thing to do when you upgrade software?**

A: Test your system and programs to verify that everything still works.

6 **What Windows tool finds errors in files and folders?**

A: ScanDisk.

7 **What Windows tool cleans up files scattered on the disk?**

A: Defrag.

8 **How can you automate periodic maintenance activities?**

A: Use Scheduled Tasks in Windows 98.

Visual Quiz

Q: How does this ScanDisk operation differ from the Standard test? Why would you use it?

A: This is the Thorough test, which checks the entire surface of the disk for errors in addition to the checks run by the Standard test. You'd use it once a month to get early warning of problems, plus whenever you think the physical disk might be malfunctioning.

Chapter 20

see page 280

1 **What can limit the upgrades possible for your computer?**

A: Changes in technology that make the computer obsolete, and lack of slots or other options to hold upgraded equipment.

2 **What's the most effective upgrade for most computers?**

A: Increasing memory to at least 32MB, or 64MB if you run multiple programs at once.

3 **What is *swapping* (in computer terms, that is)?**

A: Swapping occurs when Windows uses disk storage to substitute for memory you need but don't have.

4 **What upgrades are worthwhile for 486 computers?**

A: Few or none. Most 486 computers have internal limitations that rule out the possibility of getting your money's worth from upgrades.

5 **What's an indication that you might need a faster processor?**

A: You have 32 to 64MB of memory or more, but the computer is too slow.

6 **What makes a processor upgrade challenging?**

A: The need to change settings on the motherboard correctly, with little or no room for error.

7 **What is *ISA*? *PCI*? *AGP*?**

A: Card slots on the motherboard. *ISA* stands for Industry Standard Architecture, *PCI* for Peripheral Component Interconnect, and *AGP* for Advanced Graphics Port.

8 **What is the *BIOS*?**

A: Basic Input/Output System, the program that starts your computer before Windows loads.

Visual Quiz

Q: What happens if this fan stops working?

A: The processor overheats and fails.

Chapter 21

see page 292

1 **Name four components of a network.**

A: Wiring, network interface, network communication software, and network application software.

PERSONAL WORKBOOK ANSWERS

2 What is a *LAN*?

A: Local Area Network.

3 What is the most common LAN speed? What common speed is faster than that?

A: The most common LAN speed is 10Mbps. Faster LANs run at 100Mbps.

4 What is *10Base-2*?

A: LAN wiring based on coaxial cable.

5 What is *10Base-T*?

A: LAN wiring based on twisted pair cable and modular RJ-45 connectors.

6 Name two advantages of 10Base-T over 10Base-2.

A: Only one cable need go to any computer, and failures in a computer or wiring are not likely to take down the entire network.

7 What's an inexpensive way to run 10Base-T with two computers?

A: Use a reverser (or crossover) cable between the two computers.

8 What device is required to connect three or more computers using 10Base-T?

A: A hub.

Visual Quiz

Q: Compare this screen shot to one on the lower-left in this chapter's "Sharing Drives and Printers" lesson. What's different? How did we do this?

A: We turned off sharing on the C drive and then individually shared the America Online 4.0 and Games folders.

Chapter 22

see page 304

1 How are MBR infector viruses spread?

A: Through infected floppy disks or multipartite viruses in files.

2 How are file infector viruses spread?

A: By executing infected program files.

3 How are macro viruses spread?

A: By opening an infected file in the application program.

4 What must you do to reliably disinfect a computer?

A: Boot with a virus emergency disk that you know to be clean, disinfect the computer's boot sequence, and then scan all files on the computer.

5 What should you do before booting with your virus emergency disk?

A: Power off the computer for a minute or so.

6 How can your disk contain files that haven't been checked for viruses?

A: Via downloads from the Internet, attachments in e-mail, other computers sharing disks on your LAN, and floppy disk transfers.

7 Why must you update virus definition files?

A: To protect against new viruses.

8 Name two ways to update antivirus software.

A: Automatic update by the program and manual download from the manufacturer's Internet site.

PERSONAL WORKBOOK ANSWERS

Visual Quiz

Q: What is this? What's it good for?

A: This is the option in Microsoft Word 97 to turn on macro virus protection. It's another line of defense against the most common viruses.

Chapter 23

see page 316

1 What's the first step you should take when something seems wrong with your computer?

A: State clearly and precisely what the problem is.

2 What's the second step in troubleshooting?

A: Picture the parts of the computer that might be involved in the problem (display, disk, modem, and so on).

3 What can you do once you identify the parts that are involved in the problem?

A: Try to rule out problems in each part, such as by trying a Web page different than one that's failing.

4 What should you check if an entire device won't work?

A: See if the device is plugged in and has power.

5 What can you do if Windows won't start?

A: Boot from your emergency boot disk and run ScanDisk.

6 What can you do about cross-linked files?

A: Delete them and then reinstall any software in the folder that held them.

7 What should you try if your system won't start and the disk checks out okay?

A: Scan for viruses with your virus emergency disk.

8 How can you try to make Windows start if the disk checks out okay?

A: Use Safe Mode.

Visual Quiz

Q: What have we done here? How might this help you diagnose Internet problems?

A: We ran the Windows tracer program. If the progression stops before getting to the destination, you know a problem exists out in the Internet.

Glossary

A

acceptable use policy (AUP) A policy that defines allowable conduct using network resources. You usually see an acceptable use policy defined by Internet service providers and other entities providing Internet access. Most companies also have AUPs in place for use of company systems and Internet connectivity.

adapter A board installed in a computer system, usually a PC. Adapters provide a variety of functions, including disk interface, video, sound, and network communications.

ADSL (Asymmetric Digital Subscriber Line) An *x*DSL technology that provides more bandwidth from the network to you than from you to the network.

AGP (accelerated graphics port) A specialized slot on PC motherboards for high-performance graphics and full-motion video.

amplitude The magnitude of a signal. Amplitudes are often compared in decibels (dB).

anonymous FTP The facility that lets you log in to an FTP server without having your own account on that server. You log in with "anonymous" as your user ID and your e-mail address as the password.

ANSI (American National Standards Institute) The nonprofit administrator and coordinator of the United States private-sector voluntary standardization system.

API (Application Programming Interface) Means of interface between programs to give one program access to another. APIs provide a method of enabling programs to work with one another without requiring the programmers to know all the details of all the programs, and provide a means for programs to operate on a standard platform (such as Windows).

ASCII (American Standard Code for Information Interchange) A method of encoding text as binary values. The standard ASCII character set consists of 128 decimal numbers (0–127) for letters of the alphabet, numerals, punctuation marks, and common special characters.

async (Asynchronous) A form of communication in which the absolute timing of the data transmission is variable. Asynchronous data transmission typically frames the bits in each byte with start and stop bits.

ATA (AT Attachment) The standard (IEEE standard X3.221) name for the IDE (Integrated Drive Electronics) disk drive technology found in most desktop PCs.

ATAPI (AT Attachment Packet Interface) Describes a form of ATA (IDE) peripheral devices. Widely used on CD-ROM and tape backup units attached to an ATA bus.

authentication An exchange to ensure that users are who they say they are and are authorized to access remote resources. A common example is the sequence requiring you to enter a username and password to access the Internet through your Internet service provider.

Glossary

B

B channel In ISDN, a full-duplex, 64 Kbps channel for sending data.

backbone A LAN or WAN that interconnects intermediate systems (bridges and/or routers).

back door A preprogrammed hole in an otherwise secure system that compromises its defenses, allowing intruders access.

backup Information copied from a hard disk onto another data storage medium such as minicartridge tapes.

bandwidth Measure of the information capacity of a transmission channel.

binary A method of encoding numbers as a series of bits. The binary number system, also referred to as base 2, uses combinations of only two digits — 1 and 0.

BIOS (Basic Input/Output System) Provides fundamental services required for the operation of a computer.

bit The smallest unit of information a computer processes. A bit can have a value of either 1 or 0.

boot drive The drive from which the operating system loads, usually A or C.

bps Bits per second.

Bps Bytes per second.

bus A pathway for data in a computer system.

bus mastering A high-performance method of data transfer. This is the fastest method of data transfer available for multitasking operating systems.

byte A unit of information made up of 8 bits. The byte is a fundamental unit of computer processing; almost all aspects of a computer's performance and specifications are measured in bytes or multiples thereof, such as kilobytes or megabytes.

C

cache memory High-speed memory located between the CPU and the main memory. Cache memory is designed to supply the processor with the most frequently requested instructions and data. Cache memory can be three to five times faster than main memory. Two levels of cache are typical: Level 1 cache (usually inside the processor), and Level 2 cache, which sits between Level 1 cache and main memory.

CCITT (Comité Consultatif International Téléphonique et Télégraphique) An organization that set international communications standards. The CCITT has been replaced by the ITU-T.

Centronics interface A 36-pin connection that became the standard way to attach printers to a PC parallel data port.

CERT (Computer Emergency Response Team) An organization tasked to facilitate response to Internet computer security events. The CERT security issue archive is at ftp://ftp.cert.org. The e-mail address is cert@cert.org. The 24-hour telephone hotline is (412) 268-7090.

Cheapernet The IEEE 802.3 10Base-2 standard (or cable used in such installations). Thinnet, another term for the standard, specifies a less expensive, thinner version of traditional Ethernet cable.

checksum The result of adding a series of numbers together. Applied to computers, a checksum is the sum of a range of memory locations (or characters in a message).

By recomputing the checksum from stored data and comparing to the checksum supplied with the data, the computer can detect corrupt information.

clock A source of digital timing signals.

coaxial cable Data transmission medium with a single-wire conductor insulated by an outer shield from electro-magnetic and radio frequency interference.

cold boot Starting a computer by applying power.

COM port The DOS and Windows name for a serial port.

compression Reversibly reducing the size of data in order to lower the bandwidth or space required for transmission or storage.

CONFIG.SYS The low-level file on a PC that tells DOS how to configure itself prior to starting the command interpreter.

CPU (Central Processing Unit) The chip in a computer that has primary responsibility for executing program instructions. The basic components of a computer are the processor, memory, display, storage, and input/output devices.

daisy chain A way of connecting multiple devices to one controller in which signals are routed serially from one device to the next.

dialup A widely used method of accessing the Internet. A dialup connection uses regular phone lines to connect one computer to another via modem.

DIMM (dual in-line memory module) A printed circuit board with gold or tin/lead contacts and memory devices. A DIMM is similar to a SIMM, but with a primary

difference: Unlike the metal leads on either side of a SIMM, which are tied together electrically, the leads on either side of a DIMM are electrically independent.

DIN connector A German connector standard. DIN connectors are commonly used for keyboards, PS/2-style mice, and audio/video interfaces.

DIP switch Switch mounted on a PC board for configuration options.

DLL (Dynamic Link Library) A Windows software module typically shared among multiple programs.

DMA (Direct Memory Access) A technology that lets peripheral devices transfer data into and out of the system without loading the CPU, thereby increasing performance.

DNS (Domain Name System) A distributed Internet-wide database used with TCP/IP to associate host names and IP addresses.

DOS partition A section of a disk storage device, created by the DOS FDISK program, in which data and/or software programs are stored.

DRAM (Dynamic Random Access Memory) The most common system memory technology.

DVD (Digital Versatile Disc or Digital Video Disc) A new generation of CD technology combining video, digital audio, and traditional computer data on disc. DVD discs store from 4.7GB to 17GB.

ECC (Error Correction Code) A mathematical extension of the checksum idea. ECC is used to check (and recover) data integrity in memory, on disk, and over communications links.

Glossary

EDO (extended data out) A form of DRAM technology that shortens the read cycle between memory and CPU.

EIDE (Enhanced Integrated Drive Electronics) A set of features (including automatic drive characteristics recognition) added to the basic IDE (or ATA) standard.

EISA (Extended Industry Standard Architecture) A computer bus standard upwards-compatible with ISA and having a 32-bit data path.

e-mail (electronic mail) Messages sent electronically from one user to another over a network. Internet e-mail is based on the SMTP protocol.

encryption Applying a specific algorithm to data so as to alter the data's appearance and prevent other devices from reading the information without the appropriate knowledge. Decryption applies the algorithm in reverse to restore the data to its original form.

Ethernet A physical network technology originally designed by the Xerox Corporation. Ethernet is now an industry standard that specifies protocols for connection and transmission in local area networks. Versions of Ethernet operate at 10 Mbps or 100 Mbps today. A future version will operate at 1 Gbps.

FAQ (Frequently Asked Questions) Files kept on the Internet that address a variety of topics and answer common, widely asked questions.

FAT (File Allocation Table) A DOS data structure, kept on the disk, that shows which clusters are in use for files and which are available for use.

FTP (File Transfer Protocol) The Internet application and protocol used to send complete files over TCP/IP services.

full duplex The ability of a device or line to transmit data simultaneously in both directions.

Gbps (gigabits per second) Approximately 1 billion bits per second.

GBps (gigabytes per second) Approximately 1 billion bytes per second.

general MIDI A table of 128 standard sounds or instruments for MIDI cards and synthesizers.

gigabit Approximately 1 billion bits: 1 bit × $1,024^3$ (that is, 1,073,741,824 bits).

gigabyte Approximately 1 billion bytes: 1 byte × $1,024^3$ (that is, 1,073,741,824 bytes).

H

half duplex Data transmission that can occur in two directions over a single line, but only one direction at a time. Contrast with *full duplex*.

horizontal scan rate The frequency in kHz (kilohertz) at which the monitor is scanned in a horizontal direction; high horizontal scan rates produce higher resolution.

HTML (Hypertext Markup Language) The commands in files for Web pages that describe what the page should look like and what the page should do when you select elements of the page.

HTTP (Hypertext Transfer Protocol) The rules for message exchange between a Web server and a Web browser.

hub A device used to join connections to multiple computers in a 10Base-T network.

IDE (Integrated Drive Electronics) Describes a disk drive built to the ATA drive interface standard. ATA drives are the most common type found in desktop computers.

IEEE (Institute of Electrical and Electronics Engineers) A professional organization that, among other things, defines network standards, such as Ethernet.

Internet The worldwide internetwork, incorporating large backbone nets and an array of regional and local campus networks worldwide. Uses the Internet Protocol suite.

I/O (input/output) Refers to an operation, program, or device whose purpose is to enter data into or to extract data from a computer.

IP (Internet Protocol) A set of communications protocols developed to internetwork dissimilar systems.

IP address The sequence of four numbers that identify your computer on the Internet.

IP address mask A sequence of numbers (such as 255. 255.255.0) that divides your IP address into the network portion (255.255.255) and the host number portion (0).

IRQ (Interrupt Request) A signal generated by a device to request processing time.

ISA (Industry Standard Architecture) A type of computer bus used in most PCs. ISA enables expansion devices such as network cards, video adapters, and modems to send data to and receive data from the PC's CPU and memory 16 bits at a time.

ISDN (Integrated Services Digital Network) A telephone transmission technology that permits up to 128 Kbps access to the Internet.

ISP (Internet service provider) A company that sells dialup (or other) access to the Internet.

ITU (International Telecommunications Union) Charter organization of the United Nations that acts as a formal worldwide telecommunications standards body. The ITU is the parent organization for ITU-T.

ITU-T (International Telecommunications Union Telecommunication Standardization Sector) The part of the ITU specifically dedicated to telecommunications standardization.

Kbps (kilobits per second) Approximately 1,024 bits per second.

KBps (kilobytes per second) Approximately 1,024 bytes per second.

kilobit (Kb) Approximately 1 thousand bits: 1 bit $\times 2^{10}$ (that is, 1,024 bits).

kilobyte (KB) Approximately 1 thousand bytes: 1 byte $\times 2^{10}$ (that is, 1,024 bytes).

L

LAN (local area network) An interconnected set of computers all typically within a several-hundred-meter radius.

line-in A connector on audio equipment to which a device such as a CD player or cassette player may be attached. See also *line-out*.

line-out A connector on audio equipment to which audio components can be attached such as stereo speakers. See also *line-in*.

Glossary

M

Mbps (megabits per second) Approximately 1 million bits per second.

MBps (megabytes per second) Approximately 1 million bytes per second.

megabit (Mb) Approximately 1 million bits: 1 bit × $1,024^2$ (that is, 1,048,576 bits).

megabyte (MB) Approximately 1 million bytes: 1 byte × $1,024^2$ (that is, 1,048,576 bytes).

memory The term commonly used to refer to a computer system's Random Access Memory (see also *RAM*). The term memory is also used to refer to all types of electronic data storage (see also *storage*).

MIDI (Musical Instrument Digital Interface) A standard that enables the exchange of data between two music synthesizers or a synthesizer and a computer.

MIME (Multipurpose Internet Mail Extensions) An Internet standard for converting multiple file formats to ASCII text prior to transmission in e-mail.

motherboard Also known as logic board, main board, or system board; your computer's main electronics board, which in most cases either contains all CPU, memory, and I/O functions, or has expansion slots that support them.

MPEG (Motion Picture Expert Group) A type of data compression for storage and playback of video and audio data that reduces the size of the data in exchange for small distortions in the image and sound.

multitasking The execution of commands in such a way that more than one command is in progress at the same time.

N

nanosecond (ns) One billionth of a second. Memory data access times are measured in nanoseconds. For example, memory access times for typical 30- and 72-pin SIMM modules range from 60 to 100 nanoseconds.

NIC (network interface card) The card that plugs into the computer's main system electronics board to provide the network interface electronics.

P

palette The range of colors from which you can select the actual colors that a video adapter will display simultaneously. Also, the hardware in a video board that stores the available colors.

PCI (peripheral component interconnect) A type of high-speed computer bus.

PCMCIA (Personal Computer Memory Card International Association) Now called PC Card, this standard enables interchangeability of various computing components on the same connector. The PCMCIA standard is designed to support input/output devices, including memory, fax/modem, SCSI, and networking products.

peer-to-peer communications A type of communications and data exchange between peer entities on two or more networks.

peripheral A device (such as a disk drive or modem) installed on a computer system.

ping A program used to test reachability of destinations by sending them an echo request and waiting for a reply. Ping is also used as a verb: "Ping the host to see if it is available."

pixel A single dot on the monitor display. This word is derived from the words *picture* and *element*.

Plug-and-Play A standard to address the problems of adding I/O adapters to a PC computer system. Adapters designed to the Plug-and-Play standard self-configure and automatically resolve system resources such as interrupts (IRQ), DMA, port addresses, and BIOS addresses.

POST (Power-On Self-Test) A set of diagnostic routines that run when a computer is first turned on.

POP (Post Office Protocol) An Internet standard protocol for reading e-mail from a server. The commonly used version is POP3.

POTS (Plain Old Telephone Service) The existing analog telephone lines. POTS is the universal term in the telecommunications industry.

PPP (Point-to-Point Protocol) A protocol to provide router-to-router and host-to-network connections over both synchronous and asynchronous circuits. PPP is the most common protocol for dialup Internet connections.

proprietary memory Memory that is custom-designed for a specific computer.

protocol A standardized set of rules that specifies the format, timing, sequencing, and/or error checking for data transmissions.

Q

QIC (Quarter-Inch Cartridge) A standard for quarter-inch data cartridge drives, cartridges, and interfaces. (Also Quarter-Inch Cartridge Drive Standards, Inc.)

R

R-ADSL (Rate-Adaptive Digital Subscriber Line) An xDSL technology that adjusts speed dynamically to varying lengths and qualities of twisted-pair telephone lines.

RAM (Random Access Memory) A configuration of memory cells that holds data for processing by a computer's Central Processing Unit, or CPU (see also *memory*). The term *random* derives from the fact that the CPU can retrieve data from any individual location, or address, within RAM at any time.

RBOC (Regional Bell Operating Company) The seven regional telephone companies (the Baby Bells) that were spun off as part of the AT&T divestiture in 1984. The seven RBOCs are Ameritech, Bell Atlantic, Bell South, Nynex, Pacific Bell, Southwestern Bell, and US West.

refresh rate Also called *vertical scan rate*, the speed at which the screen is repainted. Typically, color displays must be refreshed at 60 times per second to avoid flicker.

RS-232 The specification for the most common serial data transmission interface. RS-232 defines the electrical and physical characteristics for the 9- and 25-pin male connectors on the back of a PC.

RTFM (Read The [Flipping] Manual) Acronym suggesting a response to (easily answered) questions.

S

sample A measurement of sound taken during a certain duration. In digital recording, sampling means recording voltages that make a sound as a sequence of numerical values representing the sound's amplitude.

GLOSSARY

scan rate The frequency in hertz (Hz) at which the monitor is scanned horizontally. Generally, the higher the scan rate, the higher the resolution.

SCSI (Small Computer Systems Interface) A bus interface standard that defines standard physical and electrical connections for devices.

SDRAM (Synchronous DRAM) Technology that uses a clock to synchronize signal input and output on a memory chip. The clock is coordinated with the CPU clock so the timing of the memory chips and the timing of the CPU are in synch. Synchronous DRAM saves time in executing commands and transmitting data, thereby increasing the overall performance of the computer.

seek time The average time it takes for a hard drive to position its heads on a specific sector.

serial interface Interface that requires serial transmission, or the transfer of information in which the bits composing a character are sent sequentially. Implies only a single transmission channel.

serial port A connection for a serial device such as a mouse or a modem.

server A computer that provides shared resources, such as files and printers, to the network.

SIMM (single in-line memory module) A printed circuit board with gold or tin/lead contacts and memory devices. A SIMM plugs into a computer's memory expansion socket. SIMMs offer two main advantages: ease of installation and minimal consumption of horizontal surface area. See also *DIMM*.

SMTP (Simple Mail Transfer Protocol) Protocol governing mail transmissions across the Internet.

sound file Any file that holds sound data. For example, files with .mid filename extensions are compatible with the MIDI standard; a file with a .wav filename extension contains data in the standard Microsoft file format for storing waveform audio data.

storage A medium designed to hold data, such as a hard disk or CD-ROM.

STP (Shielded Twisted Pair) Common transmission medium that consists of a receive (RX) and a transmit (TX) wire twisted together to reduce crosstalk. The twisted pair is shielded by a braided outer sheath.

synchronous communications A method of transmission in which data bits are sent continuously at the same rate under the control of a fixed-frequency clock signal.

system board See *motherboard*.

T

TCP/IP (Transmission Control Protocol/Internet Protocol) Set of protocols developed by the U.S. Defense Department's Advanced Research Projects Agency (ARPA) during the early 1970s. Its intent was to develop ways to connect different kinds of networks and computers.

Telnet The Internet standard protocol to connect to a computer as a remote terminal.

Thinnet See *Cheapernet*.

timbre How the ear identifies and classifies sound. For example, the timbre of the same note played by two different instruments (flute and tuba) is not the same.

TP (twisted pair) Cable consisting of two 18 to 24 AWG (American Wire Gauge) solid copper strands twisted around each other. The twisting provides a measure of protection from electromagnetic and radio-frequency interference. Twisted-pair cable typically contains multiple sets of paired wires.

Travan A very common, high-capacity minicartridge technology developed by Imation Corporation (formerly a division of 3M Company).

true color Video cards that can show 24-bit color (up to 16.7 million colors).

TWAIN Programming interface for scanners. Used to define the necessary driver interface for applications.

twisted-pair cable A wiring scheme with one or more pairs of 18- to 24-gauge copper strands.

U

URL (Uniform Resource Locator) A form of Internet address used by World Wide Web browsers. Each browser-accessible resource on the Internet has a unique URL (such as http://www.idgbooks.com).

USB (Universal Serial Bus) A high-speed serial interface able to connect the keyboard, mouse, speakers, monitor, and other devices to your computer.

V

V.32bis The CCITT analog modem signaling standard providing up to 14.4 Kbps data rates.

V.42bis The CCITT analog modem data compression standard that increases potential data rate through modems. Provides a theoretical maximum of 4:1 compression (equivalent to 134.4 Kbps through a 33.6 Kbps modem), although a compression ratio of 2:1 or less is more commonly experienced.

V.90 A standard for modems supporting data rates of up to 56 Kbps downstream and 33.6 Kbps upstream. V.90 is backward-compatible with prestandard 56 Kbps technologies including 3Com x2 and Rockwell K56Flex.

VESA (Video Electronics Standards Association) Organization that sponsors efforts to set standards in all areas of graphics and video technology.

VGA (Video Graphics Array) Analog graphics standard introduced with the IBM PS/2 series. Supports a maximum resolution of 640 × 480 pixels in 16 colors out of a palette of 262,144 colors.

W

WAN (wide area network) A network that uses common carrier-provided lines; contrast with *LAN*.

warm boot Rebooting a computer without turning the power off (for example, pressing Ctrl+Alt+Delete).

WAV file A standard Microsoft file format for storing waveform audio data.

WWW (World Wide Web) The Internet-based hypertext system.

GLOSSARY

xDSL (Digital Subscriber Line) Describes one of a number of forms of point-to-point public switched telephone network access technologies that enable data, voice, and video to be carried over twisted-pair copper wire between a network service provider's central office and the customer site. Includes Asymmetric Digital Subscriber Line (ADSL), Rate-Adaptive Digital Subscriber Line (R-ADSL), and other less-common forms.

ZIF socket (Zero Insertion Force socket) A mechanism for a processor socket supporting simple replacement of chips.

Index

INDEX

Index

INDEX

F

F1 (Help) key, 26
F8 key during BIOS startup, 12–13
fair use, 97
fan, 9, 10, 320
FAQs (Frequently Asked
    Questions), 352
fast page mode (FPM) SIMMs, 282
FAT (File Allocation Table), 352
Favorites (Internet Explorer), 206–207
fax(es)
    cleaning up speckles, 178
    configuration for, 172–173
    converting to editable text, 171
    cover pages, 172, 175
    forwarding, 176
    logs, 175–177
    notification, 176–177
    receiving, 176–177
    receiving as e-mail, 176
    replying to, 176
    saving and indexing, 171
    sending, 174–175
    software, 170–181
    viewer, 176
FaxWizard (WinFax), 175
file(s)
    accessing information about, 46
    attaching to e-mail, 239, 242
    backing up, 142–144
    copying, 48, 78–79
    corrupted, 274
    cross-linked, 274
    defined, 14
    deleting, 48, 52
    dragging and dropping, 53, 78–79
    fixing location, 50
    infected, 306
    moving, 48–49, 78–79
    organizing, 42–55
    periodic maintenance, 269,
        274–275
    printing, 38–39

recycling, 48
renaming, 52
saving, 24–25
sending and receiving, 252–265
sharing, 256, 298, 300
file compression, 253, 351
    compression ratio for ZIP files, 261
    file format differences, 260
    programs for, 52, 260–261
file converters (Microsoft Word), 154
filename(s), 24, 44, 52–53
filtering tools, 300
FilterKeys, 85
floppy disk(s)
    backing up with, 142–143
    booting from, 131, 308, 310, 320
    limitations, 256
    read errors, 324
    saving files to, 25
    virus transmission via, 306
floppy drive(s), 7, 319
folder(s)
    accessing information about, 46
    copying, 78, 79
    creating, 48–49, 52–53
    deleting, 52
    desktop themes, 95, 97
    dragging and dropping, 78–79
    inside other folders, 52
    moving, 48–49, 78–79
    naming, 49, 52–53
    organizing disk drives with, 44
    separate data and programs, 50
    shared, 298
font(s)
    downloadable, **174**
    in faxes, 174
    OCR and, 178
    online source, **136**
    overuse, 136
    problems with, 136
    resolution, 104–105
    size, 104–105
    TrueType, 136
    Web browser defaults, 228–229
    in WordPad, 22, 136–137

force-feedback, 68
foreign-language add-ons for
        OCR, 179
forgery, 307
form letters, 174
formatting
    documents, 150–151
    e-mail, 244–245
    in Excel, 166–167
    faxes, 174
forms, online, 208–209, 222
formulas, spreadsheet, 159, 160–163
Forward command (browsers), 206
Four11, 246
Fox network, **198**
FPM (fast page mode) SIMMs, 282
F-PROT (Data Fellows), downloadable
        evaluation version, 308
frame updates, 286
fraud, 210,
    Internet, 301
Fred Meyer, **210**
Free Agent, **192**
freeware, 254
FTP (File Transfer Protocol), 352
full duplex, 352
function keys, 26
functions list (Excel), 162
furniture, computer, 8

G

game(s)
    children's, 104
    controllers. *See* joystick(s)
    digital, 68, 71
    Game Controllers applet, 60–61,
        69–70
    gameport, 59, 70
    index, **192**
    IPX and, 296
    LAN, 296
    latest news, **286**

INDEX

Continued

INDEX

Index

INDEX

trails (mouse), 66
transformers, 111
translation, foreign-language, 82
Travan, 357
travel information online, 198–199
Trojans, 262, 306
troubleshooting, 316–331
   defining problem, 318
   isolating problem, 324–325
   joystick, 70
   printer, 322–323
   at startup, 12
   video problems, 104
True Color display, 102, 357
TrueType fonts, 136, 174
TTF file extension, 136
Tucows (software Web site), **226, 254**
Tufte, Edward, 164
Tunes.com, **140**
tutorial (AOL), 197
TV, 109
TWAIN interface for scanners, 357
Tweak UI, **14,** 66
twisted-pair (TP) wiring, 356–357
typewriters, 75, 82
typical install, 128

U

UL 1283, 13
UL 1363, 13
UL 1449 TVSS, 13
Uniform Resource Locator. *See* URLs
uninstalling programs, 126–127
Uninterruptible Power Supply (UPS),
   13, 100
Universal Serial Bus (USB), 357
   products, **110,** 111
unrated Web sites, 224, 225
Update Wizard, 273

upgrading
   buying new computer vs., 281
   cost of, 281
   hardware, 280–291
   memory, 282–283
   problems, 281
   processor, 281, 284–285
UPS. *See* Uninterruptible Power
   Supply (UPS)
URLs (Uniform Resource Locators),
   205–206, 357
USB (Universal Serial Bus), 357
   products, **110,** 111
username(s), 191, 297

V

V.32bis, 357
V.42bis, 357
V.90 standard (modems), 192, 357
vacuuming, 270
vents, cleaning, 270, 271
VeriSign, **222**
   Digital ID Center, **244**
Versions!, **254**
VESA (Video Electronics Standards
   Association), 357
VGA (Video Graphics Array), 357
ViaVoice Gold (IBM), 84, 147
video, 109. *See also* multimedia
   cable, 9
   card(s), 286–287
   files, 226, 254
   games. *See* games
   memory, 6, 282–283
   problems, 104
View menu 97, 148
ViewSonics, 89
virus(es). *See also* security
   browser protection against, 222
   current information about, 262
   early, 305
   e-mail transmission, 258, 262–263

erratic behavior caused by, 320
infection during software
   installation, 124
Internet transmission, 253
new, 310
scanning for, 310–211
text documents and, 262
virus creation software, 305, 307
virus definition files. *See* virus
   recognition files
virus detection software, 262–263, 305,
   307. *See also security*
virus recognition files, 307–308,
   312–313
virus removal instructions, **310**
VirusScan (McAfee), 262, 307
   components, 308–311
   downloadable evaluation
     version, 308
   live virus test, 310–311
   updating, 312–313
Visio, 154
vision impairments, configuring
   computer for, 84–85
*Visual Display of Quantitative
   Information, The* (Tufte), 164
voltage switch, 9
volume control, 114–115, 117
VooDoo2, 286

W

WACOM Technology
   Corporation, **138**
wallpaper, 90, 95
Wal-Mart, **210**
WAN (wide area network), 357
warm boot, 357
WAV files, 51, 109, 357
wavetable audio, 116
Web. *See* World Wide Web (WWW)
WebCrawler
   Dogpile and, **214**

374

INDEX

World Wide Web (WWW) *(continued)*
    downloading from, 98, 254–255
    failure to load, 318–319
        length of, 228
        printing, 228
        security, 208–209, 222
        slow-loading, 204
    links, 206–207
    pages, 203
    search guides, **212**
    searching, 203–215
    servers, 319
    sites, 232, **326**
    software updates on, 272
wrist straps, antistatic, 186–187
WWW. *See* World Wide Web
WWW ViewerTest Page, **228**
WYSIWYG, 148, 174

*x*DSL (Digital Subscriber Line), 357
XY charts, 164

Yahoo!, **212,** 214
    finding software with, 253
    finding system manufacturer Web
        sites with, 329
    finding vendor phone numbers
        with, 326
Yamaha XG MIDI synthesizers, **114,**
        116, 117
Y-cables, 70

Z

ZIF socket (Zero Insertion Force
        socket), 358
ZIP files, 260–261, 312–313. *See also*
        WinZip
zooming with mouse wheel, 66